EARTHEN VESSELS

Earthen

AMERICAN EVANGELICALS AND

Edited by

WILLIAM B. EERDMANS PUBLISHING COMPANY

Vessels

FOREIGN MISSIONS, 1880–1980

Joel A. Carpenter and Wilbert R. Shenk

GRAND RAPIDS, MICHIGAN

Library of Congress Cataloging-in-Publication Data

Earthen vessels : American Evangelicals and foreign missions,
    1880-1980 / edited by Joel A. Carpenter and Wilbert R. Shenk.
        p.   cm.
    Chiefly revised papers presented at a conference, "A Century of world
evangelization: North American Evangelical missions, 1886-1986,"
sponsored by the Institute for the Study of American Evangelicals and
held at Wheaton College, June 17-19, 1986.
    Includes bibliographical references.
    ISBN 0-8028-0402-0
    1. Protestant churches—United States—Missions—Congresses.
    2. Evangelicalism—United States—History—19th century—Congresses.
    3. Evangelicalism—United States—History—20th century—Congresses.
    4. United States—Church history—19th century—Congresses.
    5. United States—Church history—20th century—Congresses.
    I. Carpenter, Joel A. II. Shenk, Wilbert R. III. Institute for the Study
of American Evangelicals (Wheaton, Ill.)
BV2410.E2   1990
266'.02373'00904—dc20   90-32559
                                                                   CIP

To J. Herbert Kane:
missionary,
teacher,
scholar,
world Christian

Contents

Acknowledgments

This book has its origin in a conference, "A Century of World Evangelization: North American Evangelical Missions, 1886–1986," sponsored by the Institute for the Study of American Evangelicals and held at Wheaton College, June 17-19, 1986. Most of the chapters herein began as conference papers, and we are grateful to the authors for their hard work and patience throughout the process of revising and editing. We must thank all of the conference speakers and registrants as well for the thought-provoking time we had together. The papers, responses, panels, and discussion at that meeting have shaped the authors' and editors' perspectives in ways that the footnotes may not always reflect. We are also grateful for the generous grant from the Lilly Endowment that made this meeting possible. Magnanimous gifts from the Tyndale Foundation and Dr. and Mrs. John G. Stackhouse, Sr., also helped to defray conference expenses. So did a substantial project subsidy from the Billy Graham Center. Its director, James H. Kraakevik, deserves our thanks for his support. Charles Weber, professor of history at Wheaton College, did much to shape this project in its initial stage by sharing his expertise on modern Christianity's encounter with the non-Western world. Two seasoned missions scholars also offered invaluable advice and encouragement; for this we must acknowledge H. Wilbert Norton, dean emeritus of Wheaton College Graduate School, and Gerald H. Anderson, director of the Overseas Ministries Study Center.

One chapter of this book has been published previously. We thank Inter-Varsity Christian Fellowship and Rose Costas for granting permission to use "Evangelical Theology in the Two-Thirds World," by the late Orlando Costas. This important work first appeared in *TSF Bulletin* 9 (September/October 1985): 7-12, and we are happy to give it further exposure here.

Most of the book manuscript's final editing and production took place at the Institute for the Study of American Evangelicals. The Institute's capable secretary, JoAnn Haley, has us much in her debt for her word-processing mastery; but other staff members, past and present, also gave timely and expert assistance at various stages of the project. Our thanks, then, to Brenda Buchweitz, Ron Frank, David Rogers, and Larry Eskridge. Betty Kelsey at the Mennonite Board of Missions also lent her considerable skills to the preparation of the manuscript, for which she deserves our appreciation.

This book owes its existence, to a large extent, to Jon Pott, editor in chief of the William B. Eerdmans Publishing Company. This is the fourth volume generated by an Institute-sponsored conference that Eerdmans has seen fit to publish, and we are grateful to Jon and his editors for their support. Their commitment to Christian scholarship goes far beyond what might be expected of a commercial publisher. May their good work accrue, as Jon put it, to "the greater glory."

Our dedication honors a man whose ministry as a missionary, teacher, author, and missiologist has been exemplary. Ever since he sailed off in 1935 to serve with the China Inland Mission, J. Herbert Kane has experienced and indeed helped to shape many of the changes that have occurred in the past half century of North American evangelical missions. We salute him as one of God's good and faithful servants.

Preface

Contrary to prevailing impressions, the days of the missionary are far from over. While missions historian Kenneth Scott Latourette called the nineteenth century the "great century" of Christianity's expansion, the twentieth century has witnessed an even more astonishing growth of the Christian faith as a world religion. More people are coming to profess Christian faith now than ever before. The geographic center of Christianity's numerical strength has shifted radically since 1900, away from Europe and North America and toward the Southern Hemisphere. Most of this church growth has come from indigenous evangelization, but the ranks of missionaries—notably those who are North American Protestants—continue to grow. In the early 1920s, North American Protestants supported some fourteen thousand foreign missionaries. By the mid-1980s, there were over thirty-nine thousand career Protestant foreign missionaries from this continent, and nearly thirty thousand additional short-term overseas workers. The growth of this North American Protestant missionary force, most of which has occurred in the past forty years, comes from the evangelical sector of American Protestantism. Roughly nine out of ten of today's career missionaries are evangelicals who are not affiliated with the old-line denominational boards.[1]

1. Robert T. Coote, "Taking Aim on 2000 A.D." in *Mission Handbook: North American Protestant Ministries Overseas*, ed. Samuel Wilson and John Siewert, 13th ed. (Monrovia, CA: Missions Advanced Research and Communications Center, 1986), 37-39.

It is surprising to note, then, that very little serious historical attention has been devoted to the distinctly evangelical wing
of the North American missionary enterprise in the twentieth
century. Of the many fine works published during the twenty
years since John King Fairbank challenged American historians
to rescue the missionary from an undeserved oblivion, most
limit their scope to the nineteenth century and the first three decades of the present century. To compound the problem, historians have focused most intently, if not exclusively, on the agencies and personnel of the "mainline" Protestant denominations.

The story now available most often reads, then, as though
the missionary era ended shortly after 1920 and as if the popular
evangelical movements of the past hundred years have been
marginal to the missionary enterprise. To be sure, most evangelicals were alienated from the Protestant mainline by the 1920s;
and their missions efforts, since they were carried forward by independent missionary societies and the boards of younger
evangelical denominations, have been obscured. Furthermore,
American conservative evangelicals made almost no contributions to serious thought about missions until after 1945. Meanwhile, the Protestant missions establishment experienced a crisis
of confidence and began a long decline. It is easy to understand,
given these circumstances, why the story of the conservative
evangelical missions movement has been neglected.

The contemporary configuration of North American Protestant missions, however, suggests that this second story very
much needs to be told. After the fundamentalist-modernist controversies opened up a great divide in American Protestantism,
a very large part of the missionary enterprise lay on the more conservative side of the rift. Indeed, according to data drawn from a
survey of missions during the mid-1930s, conservative evangelical agencies accounted for 40 percent of the 12,000 North
American Protestant missionaries.[2] This contingent grew much
more rapidly than the mainline missions; by the early 1950s,
when the number of North American Protestant missionaries

2. See the appendix to this volume for a discussion of how these figures
were computed. They were drawn from Joseph I. Parker, ed., *Interpretative Statistical Survey of the World Mission of the Christian Church* (New York: International
Missionary Council, 1938), 40-45.

was reported to be over 18,500, the two groups were roughly equal in size.[3] These patterns were but the prelude for the situation since the late 1960s, as the evangelical missionary movement continued to grow and mainline missions shrank at a rapid rate.[4]

Anyone who seeks to understand modern American religion and culture, then, should sense the importance of the questions that this pattern prompts: What fuels evangelicals' missionary dynamism? Why did the conservative evangelicals begin to differentiate their understanding of the church's mission from that of the old-line denominations? How did the rise of popularly supported evangelical movements and the fundamentalist-modernist controversy affect this resurgence of missionary zeal? How have American evangelicals' ideas about missions changed over the decades? What factors, internal and external to this movement, have prompted these changes?

The purposes of this book are to venture some preliminary answers to these questions and to tell the story, in a partial, introductory way, of North American evangelical missions in the twentieth century. In a book of essays, each with a different author, it is easier to accomplish the first task than the second. Nevertheless, the first three sections of the book and most of the chapters throughout follow a chronological progression and are rich with narrative. We hope that they will be of help to seasoned scholars, to students taking courses in history and missions, and to pastors, missionaries, and lay people who wish to know more about missions and American religious history.

The most important operative terms for this book are *American* and *evangelical*. This volume's time frame covers the period when the American contingent among Protestant foreign missions grew from a junior partnership in the British enterprise to the dominant force in virtually every dimension. It also marks the time when a deep and durable polarization developed among American Protestants. Prior to this time, *Protestant* and *evangelical* had been used more or less interchangeably. But the

3. R. Pierce Beaver, "The Protestant Missionary Enterprise of the United States," *Occasional Bulletin of the Missionary Research Library*, 8 May 1953, 1-15.

4. Coote, "Taking Aim," 38-40; Richard G. Hutcheson, Jr., "Crisis in Overseas Mission: Shall We Leave It to the Independents?" *Christian Century*, 18 March 1981, 290-96.

fundamentalist-modernist clash brought about the division, re-inforced over time by ideology and institutions, that has made *evangelical* and *ecumenical* or *mainline* into fairly accurate labels for opposing factions within the Protestant camp. We do recognize that nineteenth-century evangelicalism was the common ancestor of both sides and that the historic traits of evangelicalism—its emphases on the supreme authority of the Bible, salvation by faith alone through grace, conversion as a distinct experience of faith, a pious and morally transformed life, and evangelizing the world—could be found within mainline Protestantism as well as on the other side of the rift. Nevertheless, this book is designed to highlight the more conservative evangelical faction's history.

It will also become clear, from Alvyn Austin's essay if not sooner, that by *American* we mean, in many instances, "North American," including Canadian evangelicals. Canadians have contributed a far higher ratio of missionaries *per capita* than citizens of the United States have; and, as will become clear, Canadians largely led their southern neighbors into the independent "faith" missions that figure so prominently in this book.

When Andrew Walls uses the term *American* in his introductory essay, however, he is speaking largely about the United States and the image, style, and mentality characteristic of its nationality that have become a virtual paradigm for triumphally modern Western culture. Walls, a Scot who has spent many years living in and studying Africa, brings insights about the American-ness of the evangelical missionaries that illuminate much that was distinctive about what they thought and did. It is an important mark of maturity to identify the cultural traits that our ancestors attached to their gospel witness and often sought to impose on other peoples. Yet Walls cautions against further presumption by counseling that one's culture cannot be eradicated; the gospel message will always bear the cultural fingerprints of the messenger. The best lesson to draw from such discoveries, he implies, is to recognize our own cultural traits as the "earthen vessels" in which we carry the gospel treasure. Our local, provisional forms of human expression are no more or less precious in God's sight than those located elsewhere that have been used to create new forms of Christian faith and life.

This book, then, offers an extended treatment of Walls's insights. The authors highlight various aspects of American evangelicals' distinctive traits in foreign missions and point to the ideas, events, and cultural forces that have shaped them.

The first section covers the period of the modern mission movement's great surge in North America between 1880 and 1920. Dana Robert and Alvyn Austin show how some evangelicals' development of premillennial missions theory and nondenominational "faith mission" societies began to divert them from the "mainstream" of North American Protestant missions. Out of the millenarian and pietistic matrix that these chapters describe came three of the most potent movements for twentieth-century missions: fundamentalism, pentecostalism, and holiness Wesleyanism.

Part Two deals with the events and aftermath of one of the great turning points of American religious history, the fundamentalist-modernist controversies. The nature of the Protestant missionary enterprise was one of the major issues in those conflicts, and James Patterson contends that, as a result, the missions movement was irretrievably changed. The broadly evangelical consensus that it had enjoyed was shattered, and both the mainline and evangelical missionary enterprises have suffered as a result. Joel Carpenter's chapter surveys the scope, texture, and thrust of the fundamentalist wing of the larger evangelical missions movement. It shows how, in the wake of the controversies, fundamentalists embraced, greatly expanded, and altered the nondenominational "faith missions" and how in the process fundamentalism was influenced afresh by these missions' distinctive piety. Everett Wilson's chapter takes place in this same time frame, but it moves us outside of North America and away from fundamentalism. It explores the career of the pioneer missionaries and indigenous leaders who laid the foundations for Central American pentecostalism's astonishing recent growth. Wilson's chapter demonstrates the unique character and historic importance of pentecostal missions. We hope that it will incite further work on this sorely neglected subject.

The third section of this book gives an overview of the recent past, when American conservative evangelicals emerged as a missionary world power. Richard Pierard's chapter shows that the surge of American triumphalism generated by World War II rejuvenated evangelicals' dream of global evangelization. This "world vision," as it was called, prompted both the greatest wave of new missionaries in church history and a fresh dose of cultural presumption, for which some American evangelicals have begun to repent. Allen Koop carries this theme out into the trenches, so to speak, as he examines the record of American evangelicals' attempts to secure new "beachheads" of the born-again in postwar France. The great difficulty they experienced and the meager results they garnered point up the danger of assuming that one can simply transfer American evangelicalism into other modern cultures. Charles Van Engen points out, however, that there has been a trend in evangelical missions thought over the past four decades to test older assumptions about the nature of the gospel and its cultural role. Evangelicals have been struggling, he shows, to recover their earlier, full-orbed understanding of the gospel that fell victim to the fundamentalist-modernist controversy.

This theme is given point and a fresh perspective in the fourth and final group of chapters, which focuses on some enduring themes and vital contemporary issues. The lead essay by the late Orlando Costas shows why evangelical theologians from the "Two-Thirds World" have begun to shape North American evangelicals' social thought. Evangelical theology in the Two-Thirds World is preoccupied with a unique set of problems, Costas argues. While evangelical theologians in North Atlantic cultures have aimed their arguments at atheistic intellectuals, in the Two-Thirds World the gospel must confront the alienated and dehumanized masses. The test of good theology, Costas concludes, is that it be not only intellectually sound but also spiritually energizing. Ruth Tucker's survey of evangelical women's role in missions conveys a similar message. Although conservative theologies have often narrowed women's opportunities to minister, the missionary movement has provided women with chances to serve and lead that were denied them at home.

Grant Wacker's chapter brings, as he puts it, a "second opinion." He surveys a half century of liberal Protestants' encounters with the world's great religions and their struggle to reinterpret the missionary enterprise in light of their discoveries. He argues that evangelicals will not earn a full hearing as missiologists until they, too, face the challenges posed by taking other religions seriously.

Although Lamin Sanneh is given the last word among our authors, his chapter will surely provoke rather than close off discussion, since it challenges the operating assumptions of most of current missions history. Sanneh contends that missionaries were fundamentally at odds with the entire colonial enterprise. In the process of translating the Bible into vernacular languages, they helped to promote these languages. Thus they committed themselves to the flourishing of vernacular cultures, which is the opposite of the aims of colonialism. Through the process of translation, Sanneh argues further, Western missionaries became the instruments of the de-Westernization of Christianity. His essay thus transcends yet is richly instructive for the history of American evangelical missionaries in the twentieth century. For all their culture-boundedness, they have been important contributors to the growth of an increasingly universal and de-Westernized Christianity.

A guide to further reading concludes this book. Wilbert Shenk's bibliography is designed especially for those who, after reading about recent developments in evangelical mission thought, will wish to encounter it firsthand. We offer it and all the other chapters as an invitation to learn more about a very important development in recent religious history. These chapters convey the excitement of discovery and the suggestiveness of early interpretations. Most of them are, in fact, preliminary sketches, case and character studies of a much larger and more complex story than can yet be told. We will consider our job to be well done, therefore, if others see the importance of the subjects we have presented and are sufficiently provoked to devote more attention to them. We are all too aware that there are issues and groups that we neglected, nuances that were lost on us, and interpretive opportunities that we missed. Others will, we hope, find our blind spots and presumptions and move the whole discussion forward with fresh research and argumentation. This is a rather unambitious goal, but it is a realistic one. Despite our frequent illusions of omniscience, we historians, like missionaries, carry treasure in earthen vessels.

1 *The American Dimension in the History of the Missionary Movement*

Andrew F. Walls

Can Americans Teach Religion?

Americans themselves know all too well that their genius is not in religion. . . . Americans are great people; there is no doubt about that. They are great in building cities and railroads, as ancient Babylonians were great in building towers and canals. Americans have a wonderful genius for improving the breeds of horses, cattle, sheep and swine; they raise them in multitudes, butcher them, eat them, and send their meat-products to all parts of the world. Americans too are great inventors. They invented or perfected telegraphs, telephones, talking and hearing machines, automobiles . . . poison gases. Americans are great adepts in the art of enjoying life to the utmost. . . . Then, they are great in Democracy. The people is their king and emperor; yea, even their God; the American people *make* laws, as they make farms and farm implements. . . . Needless to say, they are great in money. . . . They first make money before they undertake any serious work. . . . To start and carry on any work without money is in the eyes of the Americans madness. . . . Americans are great in all these things and much else; but *not in Religion,* as they themselves very well know. . . . Americans must *count religion* in order to see or show its value. . . . To them big churches are successful churches. . . . To win the greatest number of converts with the least expense is their constant endeavour. Statistics is their way of showing success or failure in their religion as in their commerce and politics. Numbers, numbers, oh, how they value numbers! . . . Americans are essentially children of this world; that they serve as teachers of religion . . . is an anomaly. . . .

1

> Indeed, religion is the last thing average Americans can teach. . . .
> Americans are the least religious among all civilized peoples. . . .
> Mankind goes down to America to learn how to live the earthly
> life; but to live the heavenly life, they go to some other people. It is
> no special fault of Americans to be this-worldly; it is their national
> characteristic; and they in their self-knowledge ought to serve
> mankind in other fields than in religion.[1]

The year is 1926; the source, the first volume of the *Japan Christian Intelligencer*; the writer, Kanzo Uchimura, one of the outstanding Christian figures of his day in Japan. He was a first-generation Christian, converted through American missionaries, and full of honor and respect for certain Americans. Of "my own teacher in Christian religion," as he called him, Justus H. Seelye, Uchimura wrote, "I could not but bow myself before such a man, place the care of my soul in him, and be led by him into light and truth. The Lord Jesus Christ shone in his face, beat in his heart."[2]

There are reasons for beginning an assessment of twentieth-century American evangelical missions with this view from the outside. Uchimura speaks as a Christian, as a disciple of Christ whose knowledge of Christ has come from American sources. But for him, as for a good part of the world, to hear the words *American missions* is to hear first the word *American*. This opening chapter is concerned with the prehistory of our subject and will say little directly about the evangelical societies of the past hundred years that lie at the heart of it. The flowering of American missions that began a century ago is in full continuity with the American missions of an earlier period. "Evangelical" missions as such belong, as it were, to Volume Two. Volume One of our story is the American-ness of American missions.

And to one highly intelligent and not unsympathetic observer of sixty years ago, one who had drunk deeply of American missions, it seems that the word *American* conveys, first of all, immense energy, resourcefulness, and inventiveness—a

1. Kanzo Uchimura, "Can Americans Teach Japanese in Religion?" *Japan Christian Intelligencer* 1 (1926): 357-61. For other views of Americans see W. R. Hutchinson, "Innocence Abroad: the 'American Religion' in Europe," *Church History* 51 (1982): 71-84.
2. Uchimura, "Americans Teach Japanese," 357.

habit of identifying problems and solving them—and, as a result, first-rate technology. In the second place it reflects an intense attachment to a particular theory of government, one that does not grow naturally in most of the world. Third, it stands for an uninhibited approach to money and a corresponding concern with size and scale. Fourth, it stands for what Uchimura calls "materiality," a somewhat stunted appreciation of certain dimensions of life, notably those relating to the transcendent world. Americans have a tendency to translate those very dimensions into technological terms, problems to be solved, something that can be all worked out—big boots in the Temple, as one might say. Uchimura, a Christian and a convert, not a Buddhist or a Shintoist, senses in the religious culture of his country (traditions that as to their content he has rejected) a recognition of transcendent reality compared to which most of these vigorous, confident American missionaries, in common with most of their countrymen, are on the beginners' slopes.

America as the Ultimate Development of the West

A British commentator can take no comfortable pride in his own position on hearing such an analysis. No doubt much of what Uchimura says would apply to the whole of the Western presence in the East; America looms largest in his consciousness because America has the leading Western presence in Japan and because so many of his own contacts were American. But insofar as America stands for the West, America is the West writ large, Western characteristics exemplified to the fullest extent. Americans themselves have always been aware that they represent the decisive and ultimate development of the West. None other than Rufus Anderson, an American missionary almost a century before Uchimura, has said:

> The Protestant form of association—free, open, responsible, embracing all classes, both sexes, all ages, the masses of the people—is peculiar to modern times, and almost to our age. Like our own form of government, working with perfect freedom over a broad continent, it is among the great results of the progress of Christian

3

civilization in this "fulness of time" for the world's conversion. Such great and extended associations could not possibly have been worked, they could not have been created, or kept in existence, without the present degree of civil and religious liberty and social security, or without the present extended habits of reading and the consequent wide-spread intelligence among the people; nor could they exist on a sufficiently broad scale, nor act with sufficient energy for the conversion of the world, under despotic governments, or without the present amazing facilities for communication on the land, and the world-wide commerce on the seas. Never, till now, did the social condition of mankind render it possible to organize the armies requisite for the world's spiritual conquest.[3]

This passage comes from a sermon of 1837 called "The Time for the World's Conversion Come." It is an attempt to discern the signs of the times. Many contemporary Western European Christians were engaged in a similar exercise; but their energies were usually directed to new schemes of interpretation of Daniel and Revelation, their applications to the conversion of the Jews, or the Eastern Question in European diplomacy.[4] Anderson's identification of the signs of the times is perhaps characteristically and pragmatically American—though to some extent it had been adumbrated half a century earlier by William Carey, himself wide open to the American influences

3. "The Time for the World's Conversion Come" first appeared in the *Religious Magazine*, Boston, in 1837-38. It has been reprinted several times, most recently and accessibly in *To Advance the Gospel: Selections from the Writings of Rufus Anderson*, ed. R. Pierce Beaver (Grand Rapids: Eerdmans, 1967), 59-70, 65-66 (quoted).

4. Cf. the influential preacher John Cumming, minister of the Scots Church in London, whose *Apocalyptic Sketches: Lectures on the Book of Revelation* first appeared in London in 1848. He argues that the drying up of the Euphrates under the sixth vial portends the decline of Turkey: "From 1820 down to the present time, Turkey has been wasting—the crescent waning. . . . Contemporaneous with the wasting of the Turkish power, there should be the rise of an interest in the Jewish race. . . . And such an interest is actually taken in their destiny at the present day" (12th ed., 1850, 494). Cumming was much indebted to E. B. Elliott, *Horae Apocalypticae; or, A Commentary on the Apocalypse, Critical and Historical*, 5 vols. (London, 1844); Elliott began the work in 1837, the same year Anderson's tract appeared. On the changed position of Turkey following the French Revolution, and its wasting from 1820 (see 4th ed., 3:310, 415-17), Elliott is particularly severe on Moses Stuart ("the American professor," as he calls him) for resolving "even what seems more specific into generalizations" (5:522).

of his own day.[5] The signs that Anderson identifies are those of opportunity and capability providentially furnished for direct evangelization of the whole world. It is a practical, activity-directed style of argument of American advocates of mission that runs through A. T. Pierson and John R. Mott to Ralph Winter.[6] What is especially interesting in the passage quoted is that Anderson does not base his judgment that the time for the world's conversion is come solely on what one might call technological criteria—improved communications, ready maritime access, and so on. Equally important are the political, economic, and ecclesiological developments of his day.

Anderson expects the Great Commission to be fulfilled by means of what he calls the Protestant form of association, that is, the voluntary society. And one sign that the time for the world's conversion is come is that social organization has now reached a stage at which voluntary associations can flourish. As Anderson indicates, this cannot happen under despotic governments; one would not expect to find societies for the evangelization of the world arising in the Kingdom of the Two Sicilies. But for voluntary societies to flourish more is necessary than the absence of despotism. One needs a social system that allows for plurality and choice, in which people are not required or prepared to act in the same way as all their neighbors, in which there is a highly developed sense of the individual and of individual autonomy. The voluntary association is part of a wider community but does not act solely by means of that community's recognized channels of activity. Many communities that are by no means despotic do not provide these conditions. In nineteenth-century America they were provided as never before and as nowhere else.

For the voluntary society to operate overseas implies the

5. Cf. William Carey, *An Enquiry into the Obligations of Christians to Use Means for the Conversion of the Heathens* (Leicester, 1791), fascimile ed. with introduction by E. A. Payne (London: Carey Kingsgate, 1961), 67-69.

6. Cf. Pierson's contribution at the Liverpool student conference, *Jesus King!* (London: SVMU, 1896); John R. Mott, *The Evangelization of the World in This Generation* (New York: SVMU, 1900), chap. 6: "The Possibility of Evangelizing the World in This Generation in View of the Opportunities, Facilities and Resources of the Church," and *The Decisive Hour of Christian Missions* (New York: SVMU, 1910), chap. 8: "Possibilities of the Present Situation"; Ralph D. Winter, *The Twenty-Five Unbelievable Years, 1945-1969* (Pasadena: William Carey Library, 1970).

existence of cash surpluses and freedom to move them about. It cannot operate if the surplus of production is marginal or if the movement of surpluses is controlled by the wider community. America provided *par excellence* the economic capability for voluntary societies to operate overseas, just as it had provided a favorable social and political climate for their development.

Explicitly *Christian* voluntary societies imply a conception of the church that does not inhibit their birth and a style of church organization that is not embarrassed by their activity. Anderson recognizes that it is only in his own time that Protestant Christianity had produced an organizational form that was capable of sustaining overseas mission. His description of this new Protestant form of association as "free, open, responsible, embracing all classes, both sexes, all ages, the masses of the people"[7] hardly applies to any of the classical forms of church government, whether Episcopal, Presbyterian, or Independent. In fact, the churches of Christendom were *not* organized for overseas missions in Anderson's time or long afterwards; they were outflanked or subverted for this purpose by the Protestant association, the voluntary society. Voluntary Christian societies flourish through the atomization of the church, the decentralization and dispersal of its organization. Nineteenth-century America produced just those conditions; and by the twentieth century the line between church and association had in America become so fine that the church itself often came to be seen almost in terms of a voluntary society.

Anderson's analysis refers to the whole Protestant world of his day; but note how easily he passes from the whole Protestant Christian world to a statement that could apply only to the United States: "The voluntary society is peculiar to modern times, and almost to our age. Like our own form of government, working with perfect freedom over a broad continent, it is among the great results of the progress of Christian civilization."[8]

There must have been many devout English supporters of missions in 1837 who would have been shaken by the suggestion that American democracy was the finest fruit of Christian

7. Anderson, "Time for the World's Conversion," 65.
8. Ibid.

civilization. It was manifest to them that it owed not a little to demoniacal French atheism. Anderson, however, has no compunction in associating American governmental theory, American continental expansion, and the providential direction of the Holy Spirit. The United States of America represents, under God, a new and higher phase of civilization. And he grasped that the missionary movement in which he was so important a figure at such a formative stage was the product of a particular phase of Western political and economic development, the characteristics of which were to be demonstrated most dramatically in the United States. It was not in his power—or his responsibility—to offer guidance for the period when that phase ended.

When Anderson wrote, Americans were a minority among missionaries. Britain was much the largest source; Germany and other parts of Europe provided others. From the late nineteenth century the American proportion increased, until soon after the First World War North America had become the principal source of missionaries.[9] Since the Second World War that proportion has rapidly increased.[10] As a very general statement it will soon be true that one can assume that a Protestant missionary is North American unless otherwise stated.

In twentieth-century missions, then, North America plays an increasingly dominant role, and in the last section of that century an overwhelming one. That same period has seen an increasing proportion of missionaries from missions not only unmistakably American but insistently claiming the title "evangelical." Here we must return to Uchimura and remind ourselves that among the words *American evangelical missions* the word that most people will hear first and loudest is the word *American*. For the moment we can leave on one side the political associations that must inevitably cling to this word and thus to the words with which it is linked. Perhaps we can restate one

9. W. Richey Hogg, "The Role of American Protestantism in World Mission," in *American Missions in Bicentennial Perspective*, ed. R. Pierce Beaver (South Pasadena: William Carey Library, 1977), 354-402.

10. See the successive editions of *Missions Handbook: North American Protestant Ministries Overseas*, published since 1967 by Missions Advanced Research and Communications (MARC) Center, Monrovia, California.

of Uchimura's observations and put it in less provocative form by saying that Christianity as represented by Americans has been shaped by essentially American cultural influences. American missions are thus both products and purveyors of American culture.

A leading characteristic of historic Christianity is that, though it crosses cultural frontiers, it rapidly acculturates and takes new forms dictated by the culture in which it becomes rooted. It is, then, only to be expected that a specifically North American form of Christianity should arise. It is the inevitable consequence of a genuine rooting of Christian faith in North America. And here we recall a striking fact. Latourette rightly calls the nineteenth century "The Great Century of Missions." But in no part of the world did that century see such a striking outcome as in North America.[11] The main missionary achievement of the nineteenth century was the Christianizing of the United States.

There was nothing inevitable about all of this. After all, modern Australia, New Zealand, and to some extent South Africa were also the products of European emigration, often from the same sources as North America; but their religious history has been quite different. They produced no indigenous "religious tradition." New Zealand, even though large sections of some of its founding communities were shaped by strong Christian influences, soon developed into what one of its own historians has called "a simple materialism."[12] The secular nature of Australian universities of the 1890s was defended with an antireligious verve that shocked John R. Mott, accustomed as he was to the principle of church-state separation and to "secular" state universities in the United States.[13] In the present century,

---

11. Kenneth Scott Latourette, *A History of the Expansion of Christianity;* see esp. vol. 4, *The Great Century in Europe and the United States of America,* A.D. 1800–A.D. 1914 (New York: Harper, 1941). Vols. 5 and 6 deal with the "Great Century" in other parts of the world.

12. K. Sinclair, *A History of New Zealand* (Harmondsworth: Penguin, 1959), 278; but note Sinclair's remarks on the molding of moral attitudes in New Zealand by Puritanism.

13. C. Howard Hopkins, *John R. Mott, 1865–1955: A Biography* (Grand Rapids: Eerdmans, 1979), 161.

although the elements of the church life of Australia, New Zealand, and the English-speaking community of South Africa have been reordered from the European forms, the total religious history has borne much more resemblance to Europe's than to that of North America.

Missions and the Frontier

American overseas missions were a continuation and extension of home missions. The Christianity displayed in twentieth-century American missions was determined by the nineteenth-century Christian movement along the frontier and the evangelization of new cities. The whole climate of American Christian thinking was conditioned by expansion. As early as 1837 Anderson spoke of "working with perfect freedom over a broad continent" and of both religious influences and "our own form of government." Contemporary Europe saw little systematic thought about expansion; newly acquired territories were likely to prove expensive liabilities.[14] Not until the last quarter of the century did imperial acquisition become a major concern. Chronologically, America was the first modern imperial power, or perhaps second after Russia, the former expanding eastward as the latter expanded westward, until the two met.[15]

The specifically Christian aspect of that expansion was vigorous evangelism—primary evangelism, the delivery of the elements of the Christian gospel. The delivery was couched in terms which sought individual commitment yet recognized the family unit and created and strengthened local *communitas*, which both channeled emotion and permitted the development of a popular culture, and which suggested a continuity with old

14. Anderson, "Time for the World's Conversion," 65; Cf. the minutes of James Stephen, Under Secretary for the Colonies, to Lord John Russell in relation to Africa in 1841: "If we could acquire the dominion of that whole continent, it would be but a worthless possession." Quoted in Christopher Fyfe, *A History of Sierra Leone* (London: Oxford Univ. Press, 1962), 217.

15. Sir John Seeley, in *The Expansion of England* (London: Macmillan, 1883), saw America and Russia as the two coming world powers; Britain might take a third, but only if it developed proper relationships with its empire.

traditions while being manifestly free of old institutions. This
concern with primary evangelization differed from most European thinking of the same period. Contemporary Europeans
were aware of a religious crisis, but they generally thought of it
as a *pastoral* crisis. Their concerns were about building churches
large enough and in the right places and getting the right sort of
ministers to staff them, about the place of the church in a
national system of education, and about preventing state coun-
tenance of antichurch or anti-Christian influences. The fundamental desire of European Christians was the preservation of
a Christian society such as Western Europe had been since the
Dark Ages. Its earnest evangelicals, who in Britain reached their
peak of influence toward the middle of the century, were still
thinking of the provision of the gospel for a Christian, if apos-
tasizing, society.

Perhaps this could not be where a new society was
manifestly arising, as on the American frontier. At any rate, the
primary evangelism in such conditions had to be innovative and
adaptive; established East Coast practice offered little guidance
for work under frontier conditions. Europe, despite its unchurched urban working class, was not impressed by the American experience and did not expect to learn much from it; even
English Methodists who bore Wesley's name reacted with hor-
ror to the device of the camp meeting.[16]

As the century proceeded, the focus moved from the expanding frontier to the expanding cities. American Christianity
produced the same concern with expansion, the same basis of

16. The Methodist Conference of 1807 produced the following question and
answer:

Q. What is the judgment of the Conference concerning what are called
Camp Meetings?

A. It is our judgment that, even supposing such meetings be allowable in
America, they are highly improper in England, and likely to be productive
of considerable mischief; and we disclaim all connection with them.

The insistence of some leading working-class Methodists in Midland industrial areas on using this method was a cause of their exclusion and the formation of the Primitive Methodist Connexion. The catalyst seems to have been
the American irregular evangelist Lorenzo Dow. See Holliday Bickerstaffe, *The
History of the Primitive Methodist Church* (London: Joseph Johnson, 1919).

primary evangelism, backed by the same innovation and adaptation. The evangelistic campaign arose from the special conditions of urban America, just as special modes of Christian thinking—adventism, apocalypticism, the holiness movement—were transmitted in its atmosphere. Christianity expanded in urban America; the great new centers of population in Europe saw little comparable response.

American Christianity and the Voluntary Association

One fundamentally different constituent in the experience of Europeans and Americans is space.[17] Nineteenth-century American Christianity developed in a setting of apparently limitless space. In these cicumstances it could be expansive and effective only by being entrepreneurial. Ponderous strategies on a continued wide basis, tight control by hierarchical bodies, were likely to be as self-defeating as the European tendency to think in terms of the parish as "territory." North American Christianity became pluriform and diffuse. There was always room for an inspired individualist; there was even promising scope for the eccentric. Well might Rufus Anderson see America as the natural sphere of the voluntary society. The principle of the voluntary society is: identify the task to be done; find appropriate means of carrying it out; unite and organize a group of like-minded people for the purpose. When this principle was applied to the business of making and sustaining congregations of Christian disciples, the distinction between church and voluntary society, always fundamental in Europe, sometimes all but disappeared in America. A congregation, or a whole denomination, might in principle be no different from a voluntary society. In strife or disagreement, one could always leave and join—or even start—another.

In one respect the United States actually preceded Europe in centralizing missions and relating them to home-church

17. Clyde Curry Smith developed this point in "Some Demographic Considerations in American Religious History," *Bulletin of the Scottish Institute of Missionary Studies* n.s. 3 (1986): 14-21.

structures. In Europe and America alike, effective overseas missions began not with the official machinery of the churches, but with voluntary societies. To a remarkable degree societies continued in Europe (and notably in Britain) to be the principal means of conducting mission, even when the idea of overseas mission had become universally accepted in the churches so that the denominations effectively "adopted" their denominational societies. By the Civil War period in America, however, most denominations had formed their own missions boards (in the process leaving the American Board to the Congregationalists by default).[18] But once more the voluntary principle took over: the apparent ecclesiasticization of American missions was the prelude to the emergence of a surge of new societies outside the major denominational boards. One effect of this vast outlay of energy was to transfer overseas many of the attitudes and values that had produced the evangelization of the frontier.

Missions and Money

Another aspect of American life that was to shape American Christianity and be expressed in American missions was the transformation of the nation's economic base in the course of the nineteenth century and its emergence in the twentieth as the world's greatest industrial nation. Certain differences emerge in any comparison with similar processes in Europe. In the economic and social sphere, the connection between entrepreneurial effort and efficiency on the one hand and financial and social reward on the other was much clearer in America. In Europe there have always been sources of status other than money and sources of wealth other than industrial output. Furthermore, the American industrial transformation took place in the same period as the christianizing of the cities to which we have referred. In Britain and in most of Europe, the industrial process accompanied Christian decline. For whatever reasons, the linking of entrepreneurial activity, efficient organization,

18. Valentin H. Rabe, *The Home Base of American China Missions, 1880–1920* (Cambridge: Harvard Univ. Press, 1978), 15-17.

and conspicuous financing, which was characteristic of American business, became characteristic of American Christianity. The loose structure of American religious organization, essentially societal rather than ecclesiastical, enabled powerful laymen (and what more powerful layman than a substantial businessman?) to play a major part in the shaping of activities. One of Mott's last works has a chapter on "the greatest evangelist of the nineteenth century."[19] One reason Dwight L. Moody was the greatest evangelist was that he produced and mobilized Christian businessmen, who munificently supported missions at home and abroad. Mott himself used a network of wealthy laymen, vigorously and unashamedly solicited funds from the well-to-do as a normal part of student organizational work, and relied for the funding of many special projects on a few exceptionally wealthy people.[20]

In the period in which the new American missions were coming to life it is plain that a whole aspect of American culture—the association of business methods, efficient organization, and financial reward—was unquestioningly accepted not only as a fact of life but as something that could be consecrated to God and employed in Christian activity. One of the officers of the American Board even wrote a book called *The Business of Missions*. In it he wrote:

> . . . of armies, of strategies, of firing lines, of trenches, of conquests, of crusades! We are living in a business age, we believe as never before in business results. It is a working, rather than a fighting church to which we belong.[21]

19. John R. Mott, *The Larger Evangelism* (Nashville: Abingdon-Cokesbury, 1944), chap. 3.

20. For Mott's use of solicitation as part of normal traveling organization, see Hopkins, *John R. Mott*, 172-73. On Mott as fundraiser, see Rabe, *Home Base*, 152-54. For the successive interventions of Mrs. Nettie McCormick to fund posts at Mott's behest, see Hopkins, 205-7, 220, 273, 454. Mott's expensive world tour (*inter alia*, to bring Edinburgh to Asia) of 1912-13 was financed by fifty friends, including Mrs. McCormick and John D. Rockefeller.

21. Cornelius H. Patton, *The Business of Missions* (New York: Macmillan, 1924), Foreword. The dedication states, "If you are a Christian and also a practical man this book is dedicated to you." Chapter headings include "A Going Concern," "The Great Partnership," and "Do We Mean Business?" Patton scornfully rejects a printed appeal suggesting that "Christianity abroad is the best

This is a characteristically American perspective. European missions were always glad enough for wealthy supporters and sometimes relied heavily on them for new projects. And unusual donors such as the eccentric Robert Arthington could facilitate a whole new direction of effort.[22] But the British faith missions of the period that saw the American missionary expansion typically feared lest organization crowd out the Holy Spirit, lamented Mammon as the god of this world, stressed the sacrificial aspect of missionary vocation (often in financial terms), were often hesitant about any form of solicitation, and saw their help rather in the tithes of the (relatively) poor rather than in the abundance of the rich. Extended organization and a "worldly" concern about money were the sort of characteristics they deplored in the older missions.[23] It would need an extended investigation to compare the actual relative importance of solicitation and wealthy donors in mission accounting; but the difference in style is unmistakable. American religious culture had no *inhibitions* about money.

Church and State

If there is one doctrine characteristic of American Christianity as a whole, distinguishing it from the European stream that in

---

business proposition for America" (p. viii) but invites his readers to look forward "to the day when you can support your missionary as your personal representative, your substitute abroad, when you can erect or equip a hospital, build a Church, a school, or a residence, when, possibly, you can endow an institution which will bless mankind in countless ways after you are gone" (p. 264). On Patton, see Rabe, *Home Base*, 136-37.

22. Gustav Warneck, *Urbiss einer Geschichte der protestantischen Missionen* (Berlin, 1901), 222, characterizes Arthington as "a generous but often eccentric [opferwilliger aber oft phantastischer] rich English friend of missions." Arthington's gifts were responsible for persuading the (British) Baptist Missionary Society to begin its operations in Zaire. He left an immense legacy to the B.M.S. and to the London Missionary Society but specified that it be used for new work. The Society had to explain to supporters that it could not use Arthington money to meet its deficits and that the princely bequest would require new income to maintain the work commenced by its agency. (See *114th Annual Report of the Baptist Missionary Society . . . to 31st March [London, 1906]*, 10-11, 71.)

23. Thus J. Hudson Taylor, founder of the China Inland Mission, the prototype of the new societies:

so many respects it continues, it must be that of the separation of church and state. The widespread acceptance of this doctrine was due to a civil rather than a theological proposition, arising from the historic situation of the infant United States. American churches have come to adopt it as an article of faith, and American missions have carried it into a variety of overseas spheres. The effects have been paradoxical. American missions have tended to think of themselves as nonpolitical: how can it be otherwise if church and state live in different spheres? Non-Americans have seen continual political implications in their activities: how can it be otherwise if church and state inhabit the same sphere, or at least overlapping spheres?

Colonial authorities often, with varying degrees of justification, looked askance at American missions as potentially undermining the subjection of subject peoples.[24] In the days of the National movement in India, the British administration was particularly sensitive about Americans working in the country. We have spoken of America as the first of the modern empires; it was also the first colonial independence move-

---

I had determined never to use personal solicitation, or to make collections, or to issue collecting books. . . . We are convinced that if there was *less* solicitation for money and *more* dependence upon the power of the HOLY GHOST and upon the deepening of spiritual life, the experience of Moses [having to call a halt to gifts for the Tabernacle because of the excess] would be more common. . . . Perhaps in many cases what GOD wanted was *not* a money contribution but personal consecration to His service abroad, or the giving up of son or daughter. (*A Retrospect* [London: CIM, n.d.], 110-13)

24. After 1920, North American mission organizations seeking to work in India were required to recognize explicitly that "all due respect should be given to the lawfully constituted Government, and that, while carefully abstaining from political affairs, it is its desire and purpose that its influence, insofar as it may be properly exerted in such matters should be so exerted in loyal co-operation with the Government of the country concerned, and that it will only employ agents who will work in this spirit." Missionaries from continental European countries were required to make still stricter individual pledges. See George Thomas, *Christian Indians and Indian Nationalism 1885–1950: An Interpretation in Historical and Theological Perspective* (Frankfurt: Peter Lang, 1979), 132. On the American missionary Ralph Keitahn, expelled from India in 1930, and the pressure on his mission to disown him, see Thomas, 191-92, and Keitahn's own *Pilgrimage in India* (Madras: Christian Literature Society, 1973).

ment, and one can see how powerfully the American movement appealed to the first generation of nationalist leaders in
both India and Africa. The insistence on the separation of
church and state can give encouragement to deny Caesar what
is not thought to be his; and in such situations Caesar readily
takes offense.

Another side to the separation doctrine as expressed in
American missions was readily allied to premillennial thinking. This was a tendency to posit an entirely "spiritual" concept of the church, which annexed it to a condition distinct
from the world in which political action takes place. The old
European Anabaptists who first formulated the separation of
church and state were at least aware that in itself it is a highly
political doctrine; indeed, when insisting on it could get you
thrown into the Rhine in a sack, the political implications
must have been vividly recognized. By contrast, modern
American missions have sometimes displayed a curious
political naiveté, as though by constantly asserting that
church and state were separate they have somehow stripped
mission activity of political significance. Even the elementary
political implication of their presence, let alone of patriotism,
has not always been recognized.

Theology and Common Sense

We have little space in which to allude to a related and highly
complex matter, the development of specifically North American theologies. In this area we must pay tribute to the work of
Mark Noll, who has explored the influence of Scottish common
sense philosophy in America and especially what he calls the
"methodological common sense" that was rigorously applied to
theology.[25] He points to an eloquent statement by Charles
Hodge at the very beginning of his *Systematic Theology:* "The
Bible is to the theologian what nature is to the man of science. It

25. Mark A. Noll, "Common Sense Traditions and American Evangelical
Thought," *American Quarterly* 37 (1985): 216-38.

is his storehouse of facts, and his method of ascertaining what the Bible teaches is the same as that which the natural philosopher adopts to ascertain what he teaches."[26]

The dispensational schemes of C. I. Scofield (who had the needs of missionaries particularly in mind) and others proceed on the same principle; and their influence has been continued in the present century in a major stream of American religion. Why has this method of using the Bible as a quarry in which the gems are statements of unconditioned fact been so much more characteristic of America than of any other parts of the world? Does it owe something to the new-style Christianity of the frontier, the emergence of new Christian communities that, as it were, started Christianity all over again and saw no need to relate to nineteen centuries of church history?

At any rate, "methodological common sense" led to two features of American Christianity that are particularly relevant to the study of modern evangelical missions. First, it has made a great part of American Christianity immensely conscious of statements of belief, often set out as catalogs of unconditioned fact; and a progressive definition of the Christian faith in these terms has followed until the range of succinctly defined topics runs from the mode of creation to the relation of the Lord's return to the other "last things." Here we see again the characteristically American problem-solving approach at work: identify the problem, apply the right tools, and a solution will appear. Then move on to the next problem. By contrast, European movements born out of the evangelical revival have rarely been creedally creative; when they have wished to define their faith and witness to their distinguishing beliefs, they have generally looked to the ancient creeds and to the sixteenth-century Reformers.

The other, and related, result of the application of methodological common sense to theology has been the American tendency to use the new extended creeds as tests for fellowship and a basis of separation. Perhaps this principle of separation is the converse of the principle of free association that lay be-

26. Charles Hodge, *Systematic Theology*, 2 vols. (New York, 1872), 1:10. Hodge's very first paragraph is headed "Theology a Science."

hind so much of nineteenth-century American Christianity and provided so much of its dynamic. In the peculiar historical circumstances of American church growth, with the church concept often nearly absorbed in the voluntary society, it was easy to identify fellowship with association. The inevitable result was the atomization of the church. This again has been in contrast to the European continuators of the evangelical revival tradition.

Only Uchimura himself could say whether these features have anything to do with the tendency that he thought the least developed of all American excellences, that which we have called wearing big boots in the Temple. Another type of investigation might raise the question whether North America produced a new major branch of the Christian family; whether the separation between evangelicalism-fundamentalism, shaped very much by North American cultural factors, and the older, essentially North European evangelical Protestantism was similar in kind to the latter's breach with Latin Christianity. Such an investigation might also reflect on the special nature of American liberalism (though its direct connection with the mission movement is more problematical), which evidently has been distinct from the European phenomenon.

An American Christianity

Without plunging into such deep waters, we may still recognize a specifically American Christianity, an expression of Christian faith formed within and by American culture. Among the features that mark it out from other such Christian expressions are vigorous expansionism; readiness of invention; a willingness to make the fullest use of contemporary technology, finance, organization, and business methods; a mental separation of the spiritual and the political realms combined with a conviction of the superlative excellence, if not the universal relevance, of the historic constitution and values of the nation; and an approach to theology, evangelism, and church life in terms of addressing problems and finding solutions.

None of these marks, and none of their effects, is nearly as important as the universal Christianity, the gospel of the risen Christ, to which historic American Christianity witnesses. But no one ever meets universal Christianity in itself; we only ever meet Christianity in a local form, and that means a historically, culturally conditioned form. We need not fear this; when God became man, he became historically, culturally conditioned man, in a particular time and place. What he became, we need not fear to be. There is nothing wrong with having local forms of Christianity—provided that we remember that they *are* local.

Sometimes local features can have an important effect, either direct or catalytic, outside the locality. If the evangelization of North America was the most signal success of the great century of missions, its full significance was not evident until North America became the chief source of missionaries in the early part of the twentieth. Within the nineteenth century the sudden emergence of the United States as a Pacific power produced an American missionary consciousness at a period when Britain was still the leading missionary-sending nation. But British perspectives on the Far East were formed by the China trade; Japan seemed just too far away for immediate concern. American innovation beyond the regular church structures was often extremely influential in the quite different church setting of Europe. For instance, the Student Volunteer Missionary Union is very much part of British domestic church history, as well as British mission history, and in many ways a thoroughly "indigenous" institution; but it owed something to the American student movement.[27] The American business sense of John R. Mott produced the international organization of missions, with all that this was to lead to; one has only to reflect that the sole contemporary alternative would have been the British "old boy" network to realize how important was this contribution. Mott's business sense even realized the need to invest in research, and as a result, J. N. Farquhar was seconded for scholarly study of Hinduism—and even in those steamship days he divided his time, for the sake of mission, between India

---

27. Ruth Rouse, *The World's Student Christian Federation: A History of the First Thirty Years* (London: SCM, 1948), chap. 1; and John C. Pollock, *A Cambridge Movement* (London: John Murray, 1953).

and Oxford.[28] And the direct American approach to a particular problem by a specified method has been endlessly demonstrated, for instance, in the emergence of such enterprises as the Wycliffe Bible Translators.

Even markedly local features can be transmitted to another culture and take on a life of their own there. A historian of religion might judge Adventism to be unmistakably a product of the conditions of nineteenth-century America; but it was Adventist teaching that led African communities in Malawi to seek to realize the kingdom of God.[29] Adventist teaching has also given a new form to religious movements in Melanesia;[30] and the special form of Adventism associated with the Jehovah's Witnesses has been potent in millennial movements such as Kitawala[31] in East and Central Africa and the God's Kingdom Society in Nigeria.[32]

In the early 1900s, pentecostalism appeared to be a minor aberrant form of American Protestantism; now it is the natural expression of faith and practice for millions of Latin Americans. John Alexander Dowie was a Scot, but had he stayed in Scotland, no one ever would have heard of him. Only in the United States could he have carried out his great experiment in Zion City.[33] I once spent Easter with the Christian Catholic Apostolic Church in Zion of South Africa (Bantu); as they danced in the Lord's resurrection with the words "We have a Zion which is

28. Eric J. Sharpe, *John Nicol Farquhar. A Memoir* (Calcutta: YMCA Publishing House, 1963), 61-63.

29. George Shepperson and Thomas Price, *Independent African: John Chilembwe and the Origins, Setting and Significance of the Nyasaland Native Rising of 1915* (Edinburgh: Edinburgh Univ. Press, 1958).

30. Gottfried Oosterwal, *Modern Messianic Movements as a Theological and Missionary Challenge* (Elkhart, IN: Institute of Mennonite Studies, 1973). On Adventists in the Pacific, see Charles W. Forman, *The Island Churches of the South Pacific* (Maryknoll, NY: Orbis, 1982), 52-54.

31. H. J. Greschat, *Kitawala: Ursprung, Ausbreitung und Religion der Watch-Tower-Bewegung in Zentralafrika* (Marburg: Elwert, 1967).

32. D. I. Ilega, *Gideon Urhobo and the God's Kingdom Society in Nigeria* (Ph.D. diss., Univ. of Aberdeen, 1983).

33. On Zion City, see Grant Wacker, "Marching to Zion: Religion in a Modern Theocracy," *Church History* 54 (1985): 496-511. On Zionist churches in South Africa, and the connection with Dowie, see Bengt G. M. Sundkler, *Bantu Prophets in South Africa*, 2d ed. (London: Oxford Univ. Press for International African Institute, 1961).

our home," I knew I was watching a thoroughly Zulu Christian development. Yet when the very aged leader showed me his ordination certificate, it bore the signature of J. A. Dowie and the stamp of Zion City, Illinois. And in all of this we have not even mentioned the many side effects of the Christian enterprises of Afro-Americans in Africa. This demands a study in itself. The whole story of Ethiopianism[34] in Africa over several generations, the rise of South African black theology[35] in the present generation, in each of which black American influence has been crucial, are permanent reminders of how relevant and dynamic some local phenomena may be in a quite different locality.

A Changed World

Hitherto our concern has been with origins and prehistory—with the factors that have given American Christianity, and the evangelical missions that are the special subject of our study, a distinctive shape. We can hardly conclude without a glance at the world in which they function today. It goes without saying that it is a world transformed in the course of a century. It is one in which the sea-based empires of western Europe have passed away. It is also one in which the whole center of gravity of the Christian world has been changed. Not only has there been an unprecedented Christian expansion in all of the southern continents and in Africa in particular; there has correspondingly been an almost unprecedented recession in some of the older Christian heartlands, most obviously in western Europe.

Let us consider some of the results.

1. Christendom, the centuries-old concept of certain nations belonging to the Christian society and others lying outside of it,

---

34. See Sundkler, *Bantu Prophets*. For different types of black American influence see Walter R. Johnson, *Worship and Freedom: A Black American Church in Zambia* (New York: Africana Publishing, 1977); Theodore Natsoulas, "Patriarch McGuire and the Spread of the African Orthodox Church to Africa," *Journal of Religion in Africa* 12 (1981): 81-104.

35. See Basil Moore, ed., *Black Theology: The South African Voice* (London: Hurst, 1973), published in the U.S.A. as *The Challenge of Black Theology in South Africa* (Atlanta: John Knox, 1974). The catalytic figure was James H. Cone.

has come to an end. Christians are now much more diffused throughout the world than they have ever been; yet they are also much more diffused *within* societies. Despite burgeoning numbers of new Christians, we are not seeing many new Christian *states*, certainly not in the manner of old Christendom. No longer does the word *Christianity* have a territorial connotation.

But it was the concentration of Christians into certain geographical areas that brought the missionary movement into being. As recently as 1910 the World Missionary Conference could distinguish between "fully missionized" and "not yet fully missionized" lands. The missionary movement was Christendom's last flourish. Today some of what in 1910 appeared to be "fully missionized lands" are most obviously the prime mission fields of the world.

2. In the high days of the missionary movement Christianity was associated with a particular form of civilization and an advanced technology. That technology was offered in all sincerity as undoubtedly beneficial in its effects and was widely accepted in the same conviction. The association is now much less obvious. In the first place, the countries most clearly connected with high technology are not necessarily also connected with Christianity. Second, most Christians now live in areas relatively low in technological capacity and with little hope of ever having access to what the nations of high technology possess. And third, the confident assertions that Christians once made about the gospel-associated blessings of technology have given place to doubts of its efficiency, consciousness of its demonic power for destruction, and desire for its control.

3. But some countries have a special relationship between missions and technology. In some broken-backed nations, those marked out by poverty of resources, technological breakdown, political instability, or economic disaster, the missionary bodies, often working in concert (Missions Incorporated, as one may say), now have the most flexible, powerful, and efficient organization in the country. They can fly people around the country and in and out of it; they can bring in machinery and service ailing plants; they have radio telephones that work; they can arrange currency, get foreign exchange, and send an international message quickly. They can sometimes do things that the government

itself cannot do. And the local church, however independent or indigenous, can do none of these things, except insofar as it can act as a link to an outside mission.[36] In the end, what will be the implications of all this power held by Missions Incorporated?

4. The missionary movement occurred when it did through the co-existence of a certain religious condition with political systems that permitted free association and economic structures allowing movement of capital and export of surpluses. In Europe that co-existence is no more; at present it continues in North America. As a result, the "overseas missionary" will increasingly be North American. But America's position in the world is quite different from that of the missionary movement a century ago, in the high days of the European empires, when Robert E. Speer could rejoice in situations where American missionaries could operate as neutrals without the obloquy attached to Britons.[37] A missionary's effectiveness, or even sincerity, will sometimes be measured by the extent to which the message preached is reflected in the nation from which he or she came; the higher that nation's visibility in the world, the more likely is this measure to be used. We do well to ponder that inasfar as the missionary movement continues *as a separate* identifiable phenomenon, it is bound to be seen, for good or ill, as part of the United States presence overseas.

5. In the older missionary movement, missionary life was represented in terms of the ideal of Christian sacrifice. The missionary was the person who renounced all for Christ, turned his back on nation and family, risked privation and disease. Nowadays Missions Incorporated generally makes it possible to maintain life at a tolerable level. The people who now risk privation are those so-called tent-makers who have taken a position

36. See W. McAllister, "The Heart of Africa Mission and the Unevangelized Fields Mission and the Subsequent Churches" (Ph.D. diss., Univ. of Aberdeen, 1986).

37. See also G. E. Post (of the Syrian Protestant College, Beirut) in *Report of the Centenary Conference on the Protestant Missions of the World*, ed. James Johnston, 2 vols. (New York: Revell, 1889), 1:322: "The English hold the hands—the physical forces; and God has given to the other branch of the Anglo-Saxon race, untrammelled by your political complications, a control of the brains and of the heart."

(perhaps even with similar daily duties to those they might have as missionaries) at a local salary, sharing the housing and frustrations and insecurities of national colleagues and left to their own devices when their contract ends.

6. The Protestant missionary movement developed by means of the voluntary society, and America perfected its application to the purposes of overseas mission. The resultant mission agencies were admirably designed for their task: to direct the resources of Christians in one country to the preaching of the gospel and the establishing of churches in another country. That is, the task in hand was principally giving; the design was essentially for one-way traffic. But with the new shape of the Christian world, there are needs for which the perfect instrument was not designed. Instruments are now needed for *two*-way traffic: for sharing and for receiving.

7. We have argued that Christianity developed in America in a specifically local form. But the rooting of the Christian faith in Africa, Oceania, and in large areas of Asia and its reformulation in Latin America have produced other local forms of Christianity. This means that North American Christianity often will be one of several local forms in juxtaposition. Will we see a competition among local Christianities? The process of encounter will always present difficulties as well as excitements and discoveries. The principal dangers of the encounter come when one party insists that its own local features have universal validity.

Conclusion

The missionary movement is one of the turning points of church history; the whole shape of the Christian faith in the world has been transformed by it. America's contribution to it has been incalculable. But the history of the missionary movement has never been at the center of Christian historical scholarship; like the practice of missions, it has been in the sphere of the enthusiasts, not of the main tradition. Consequently we know curiously little about some of the most crucial events and processes in Christian history. Conferences such as "A Century of World Evangelization: North American Evangelical Missions, 1886–

1986" enable us both to explore what we can know and to prepare for what we cannot yet know. There can be few more rewarding tasks in contemporary scholarship.

The historians of African and Asian Christianity are already seeing the missionary period as an episode, sometimes a rather distant one, in a continuing story. The missionary movement itself will have its own continuity; Christian people of one nation will continue to hear the word from people of another; Christian people will continue to share their faith and life and work. But the movement will change beyond recognition and it will need all that adaptability to situations that was the genius of its American manifestation. Christian expansion hitherto has often involved a period of cross-cultural transmission, followed by the emergence of a new local form of Christianity. But all our local forms are provisional, part of the total Christian process whereby "we all attain to . . . a perfect man, to the measure of the stature of the fullness of Christ (Eph. 4:13).[38]

38. In this chapter I have not considered perhaps the most important of all aspects of the American dimension of missions: that related to the Native American. Properly speaking, it is here that the modern missionary movement starts; it was in North America that Protestant Christians first found themselves in daily contact with a culture uninfluenced by the Judeo-Christian tradition. In another respect, like Australia, it illustrates one of the sadder and more admonitory passages of missionary history. I am conscious also that I have left aside the special features of American Catholic missions and have made only passing reference to the long, and to some degree separate, tradition of Afro-American missions (on which see Walter L. Williams, *Black Americans and the Evangelization of Africa 1877–1900* (Madison: Univ. of Wisconsin Press, 1982). To make adequate reference to any of these important topics would greatly lengthen the paper and broaden its scope.

I TO THE WORLD IN THIS GENERATION, 1880–1920

2 "The Crisis of Missions": Premillennial Mission Theory and the Origins of Independent Evangelical Missions

Dana L. Robert

In the final decades of the nineteenth century, American interest in foreign missions increased dramatically. Student volunteers flooded the denominational sending agencies, and undenominational missions were founded to contain the rising tide. Lay people clamored for mission literature and for access to missionary training schools. By 1915 over three million women had swelled the roll of women's missionary agencies and auxiliaries.[1] The "imperial age" of American foreign policy coincided with a burst of Protestant enthusiasm for "saving" and "civilizing" the world's "heathen."

Little did the average Christian of 1880 realize that the age of foreign missions would irrevocably change the religious landscape at home. By the early twentieth century, American missions had not only influenced the developing world, but a constellation of separatist evangelical missions, often called "faith missions," had emerged from the heady enthusiasm of the mission revival. Such groups as the Africa Inland Mission, the Christian and Missionary Alliance, the Sudan Interior Mission, and the Gospel Missionary Union would eventually attract thousands of evangelical young people into mission service under their banners.

1. Patricia Hill, *The World Their Household: The American Woman's Foreign Mission Movement and Cultural Transformation, 1870–1920* (Ann Arbor: Univ. of Michigan Press, 1985), 3.

After World War II, independent evangelical mission organizations were sending more and more missionaries even as the ecumenically minded denominational missions switched to mission strategies that employed fewer and fewer missionaries. In 1953, missions connected with the National Council of Churches fielded 9,844 missionaries, and explicitly evangelical or independent missions supported 9,296 missionaries. By 1985, however, the number of National Council- or mainline-affiliated missionaries had fallen to 4,349, whereas evangelical or independent agencies were sponsoring 35,386 mission personnel.[2] The founding of late-nineteenth-century separate evangelical missions was only the beginning of what has become the largest sector of American missions today.

It would be easy to read twentieth-century theological controversy between so-called liberals and evangelicals back into the origins of the faith missions of the 1890s. But evangelicals of the late nineteenth century did not join faith missions as a protest against liberalism in the established denominations. In fact, well into the twentieth century, the majority of evangelical American missionaries faithfully served under a denominational mission board, and many evangelical missionaries still find a home in these structures. Why is it, then, that independent evangelical missions began to emerge in the 1890s, when evangelicals were still firmly in control of virtually all denominational mission machinery?

The answer to the question of origins is a complex one. The

2. See Table A, "Overseas Career Personnel Totals," in Robert T. Coote, "Taking Aim on 2000 A.D.," in *Mission Handbook: North American Protestant Ministries Overseas*, ed. Samuel Wilson and John Siewert, 13th ed. (Monrovia, CA: Missions Advanced Research and Communication Center, 1986), 39. Traditionally, separate evangelical missions have been affiliated with either the Interdenominational Foreign Mission Association or the Evangelical Foreign Missions Association. In the last decade, however, most evangelical missionaries have been sent through organiztions affiliated with neither the IFMA nor EFMA. Statistics for 1985 show that approximately 15,481 missionaries were affiliated with either the IFMA or EFMA compared with 19,905 missionaries termed "independent" or "undenominational." However, the figures for unaffiliated missionaries can be misleading because they include those of the Southern Baptist Convention, an unaffiliated yet denominational mission agency that currently has 3,346 full-time missionaries, the largest American mission force (Wilson and Siewert, *Mission Handbook*, 277).

fact that more people wanted to be missionaries than could be funded by denominational structures contributed to the success of independent missions from their beginnings. The personal magnetism of founders of independent mission enterprises often attracted evangelicals who felt neglected by more bureaucratic structures. In many ways, the continued growth of missions independent of denominational control mirrors larger changes in American society, such as a decline in loyalty to umbrella institutions and wide popular access to fund-raising and communications technologies.

Among the many reasons for the rise of independent evangelical missions in the 1890s was the popularization of new mission theories based on premillennialism: belief in the imminence of Christ's Second Coming caused the growth of separate evangelical missions and their supporting institutions in the late nineteenth and early twentieth centuries.[3] Prominent mission leaders such as A. T. Pierson, A. J. Gordon, A. B. Simpson, and others felt that they were living during a "crisis of missions": the Holy Spirit in the late nineteenth century was opening the world to Christianity in preparation for the Second Coming of Jesus Christ.[4] It seemed probable that their generation would be the one to preach the gospel from one end of the world to another in fulfillment of Matthew 24:14, "And this gospel of the king-

3. In his study of American premillennialism, Timothy Weber argues that the combination of beliefs that those who died without Christ would be lost and that Christ's imminent return would "cut short opportunity to save them" provided a "strong drive toward missionary activity" (*Living in the Shadow of the Second Coming: American Premillennialism 1875–1925* [New York: Oxford Univ. Press, 1979], 67). Andrew Porter makes the same point about Anglican missions: premillennial urgency caused an expansion of missionary activity, especially among Anglican students influenced by the student watchword, "the evangelization of the world in this generation" ("Late Nineteenth-Century Anglican Missionary Expansion: A Consideration of Some Non-Anglican Sources of Inspiration," in *Religious Motivation: Biographical and Sociological Problems for the Church Historian,* ed. Derek Baker [Oxford: Basil Blackwell, 1978], 357-58).

4. "The crisis of missions" was a commonly used phrase in late-nineteenth-century mission circles. It indicated that evangelistic missions were at a crossroads. Both unprecedented opposition and unprecedented opportunity for expansion seemed to surface for world mission in the 1880s and 1890s. Arthur T. Pierson popularized the phrase in his book *The Crisis of Missions: or, The Voice Out of the Cloud* (New York: Baker & Taylor, 1886).

dom shall be preached in all the world for a witness unto all nations; and then shall the end come."

Premillennial mission theorists of the late nineteenth century believed that they were living in the last days before Christ's return.[5] The implication for mission theory of their "end-time" hopes was a single-minded emphasis on evangelization. Proclamation of the gospel took precedence over such traditional missionary activity as education and medicine. Premillennialists grew impatient with the educational requirements and the social reform emphasized by denominational missions because they seemed to be delaying the proclamation of the Word and the subsequent gathering in of true believers before time ran out and Jesus returned. Thus, premillennial mission theory led to the development of separate evangelical missions because it argued that world evangelization was immediately urgent. Such premillennial impatience fostered a single-issue mentality and a quick-results pragmatism that was unrealistic for the more wholistic denominational apparatus. Premillennialist visionaries, who were in a hurry to preach to the world and felt they either could not or should not wait for denominational support, began to found independent missions.

The eventual outcome of this independent missions movement was not at all what its founders had intended. The earliest premillennial mission theorists generally felt that their encouragement of separate missions was a way of supplementing the work of denominational boards, not of replacing it. They and their supporters did not foresee that their actions would ultimately encourage the twentieth-century split between denominational and independent mission agencies.

One way of understanding how premillennial mission theory contributed to the rise of separate evangelical missions is to examine its impact in the lives of its earliest proponents. Arthur T. Pierson and Adoniram J. Gordon are today considered

5. For general background on the rise of premillennial dispensationalism in the late nineteenth century, see George Marsden, *Fundamentalism and American Culture: The Shaping of Twentieth-Century Evangelicalism, 1870–1925* (New York: Oxford Univ. Press, 1980); Ernest Sandeen, *The Roots of Fundamentalism: British and American Millenarianism, 1800–1930* (Chicago: Univ. of Chicago Press, 1970); and Weber, *Living in the Shadow.*

to be the fathers of faith missions, yet they were both loyal supporters of denominational missions. In the 1880s, Pierson served as chairman of the missions committee for the Philadelphia Presbytery, and he itinerated as well to raise money and support for Presbyterian missions in the 1890s. Gordon was chairman of the executive committee of the American Baptist Missionary Union from 1888 until his death in 1895. Despite criticism by denominational cohorts, however, both men persisted in supporting nondenominational missions activity.

Arthur Tappan Pierson was the foremost American promoter and theoretician of premillennial missions in the late nineteenth century. A conservative Presbyterian, he served prestigious churches in Detroit, Indianapolis, and Philadelphia. In 1891 he was handpicked to succeed Charles Spurgeon at the Metropolitan Tabernacle in London, then assumed to be the largest Baptist church in the world. Pierson edited the *Missionary Review of the World,* the major interdenominational missions journal of the time. As author of over fifty books, he was in constant demand as a conference speaker on such topics as the unity of Scripture and the miracles of missions.[6]

Pierson's adoption of premillennial theology was typical of many who became involved in the movement. In the 1870s, while a pastor at the Fort Street Presbyterian Church in Detroit, he began to have doubts about his own conversion. He felt keenly his inadequacy to deal with the emerging problems of industrial America—unchurched urban masses and inequalities between rich and poor. His youthful, optimistic faith about progress for God's kingdom on earth seemed empty and unrealistic: the forces of atheism and anarchy were on the rise.

After reconsecrating himself to evangelical doctrine and piety, Pierson remodeled his ministry after that of Charles Finney, "saver of souls," in an effort to reach the urban poor with the gospel. In his attempts to be biblically faithful, Pierson con-

6. For details of A. T. Pierson's life, see Dana L. Robert, "The Legacy of Arthur Tappan Pierson," *International Bulletin of Missionary Research* 8 (July 1984): 120-25; idem., "Arthur Tappan Pierson and Forward Movements of Late-Nineteenth-Century Evangelicalism" (Ph.D. diss., Yale Univ., 1984); and Delavan L. Pierson, *Arthur T. Pierson* (New York: Revell, 1912).

sulted with George Muller, director of orphanages in Bristol, England. Muller, in the United States on a speaking tour, was widely known for advocating "faith" principles in ministry. He ran all his orphanages without ever asking or working for money to support them. Rather, he prayed and proceeded "on faith" that God would provide for the needs of the orphans. By 1870 he was supporting five orphanages of two thousand orphans on the faith method.[7]

In 1879, Pierson and Muller had a series of conversations on the Bible in which Pierson argued for a postmillennial interpretation whereby Jesus would return to earth after the millennium, by which he meant "a thousand year period of prosperity brought in by human effort and benevolent Christian civilization."[8] But Muller silenced Pierson's arguments as to the virtues of postmillennialism with one reply: "My beloved brother . . . not one of them is based upon the word of God."[9]

Muller then convinced Pierson of a premillennial interpretation of Scripture: that the condition of the world would in fact worsen until Jesus returned to usher in the millennium. Late-nineteenth-century premillennialism's view that human effort could not in fact bring in God's kingdom seemed to Pierson to be both more scriptural and more consonant with reality as he experienced it in his own ministry in urban Detroit.

After he became a premillennialist, Pierson began to participate in Niagara Bible conferences, a regular fellowship of church leaders, mostly Presbyterians and Baptists, who had become convinced of a premillennial interpretation of Scripture. Many Niagara participants had been converted to premillennial exegesis by British "missionaries" such as George Muller and John Nelson Darby, who traveled through the United States in the 1870s and 1880s.[10] Niagara participants tended to be prom-

7. A. T. Pierson, *George Muller of Bristol and His Witness to a Prayer-Hearing God*, with an introduction by James Wright (New York: Loizeaux Bros., Bible Truth Depot, 1899), 211.

8. Robert, "Pierson and Forward Movements," 127.

9. Pierson, *George Muller*, 261.

10. On the development of British millenarianism in the nineteenth century and attempts to spread the doctrine in the United States, see Sandeen, *Roots of Fundamentalism*. On Darby, the Plymouth Brethren, and the spread of premillennial dispensationalism in America, see esp. pp. 60-80.

inent urban pastors or evangelists—like Dwight L. Moody of Chicago, A. J. Gordon of Boston, James H. Brookes of St. Louis, and others—who felt a strong commitment to evangelism as a solution to urban social problems. Today scholars consider the Niagara conferences to have been a primary breeding ground for what became fundamentalist biblical exegesis.

In the summer of 1886, evangelist Dwight L. Moody held a Bible school for leaders of the intercollegiate Young Men's Christian Association. College men from throughout the East gathered at Moody's Mt. Hermon School for weeks of Bible study, fellowship, and recreation. In need of another Bible teacher, Moody wired Pierson and asked him to come speak on "The Bible and Prophecy."

A small group of students were praying that enthusiasm for mission would sweep the conference, and they knew of Pierson's leadership in Presbyterian missions. After Pierson arrived at Mt. Hermon, these students convinced him to give a special lecture. On the night of July 16, 1886, Pierson lectured on "God's Providence in Modern Missions." He drew a map of the world and demonstrated how the Holy Spirit was opening the world to Christian penetration. Within the preceding quarter of a century, China, Japan, Korea, and Africa had become open to Christian missions. Pierson argued that all Christians should take upon themselves the task of world evangelization. He believed that with proper planning, the world could be evangelized completely by the year 1900.

Pierson's relentless logic challenged the students to shoulder the task of world evangelization. John R. Mott, future missionary statesman who attended the Mt. Hermon conference, recalled that the keynote that provoked him to think about missions was Pierson's plea that "all should go, and go to all."[11] By the end of

11. John R. Mott, *Five Decades and a Forward View* (New York: Harper and Brothers, 1939), 4; C. Howard Hopkins, *John R. Mott, 1865–1955: A Biography* (Grand Rapids: Eerdmans, 1979), 27. Mott wrote: "On the evening of July 16, a special mass meeting was held at which Rev. Dr. A. T. Pierson gave a thrilling address on missions. He supported, by the most convincing arguments, the proposition that 'all should go and go to all.' This was the key-note which set many men to thinking and praying" ("The Student Missionary Uprising," *Missionary Review of the World* 12 [November 1889]: 824).

Moody's summer conference, one hundred of the student YMCA leaders had volunteered to become foreign missionaries.

The legendary "Mt. Hermon 100" returned to their separate colleges in the fall and began to gather bands of students who were committed to foreign missions. College students from around the country volunteered to become foreign missionaries, and the Student Volunteer Movement for Foreign Missions came into being to conserve and to organize these students.[12] Within the space of a few years, denominational mission boards went from being desperate for missionaries to having more than they could employ. By 1910, five thousand student volunteers had reached the mission field. Missions became one of the most popular Christian causes in America.

The vision that inspired the student volunteers was A. T. Pierson's concept of "the evangelization of the world in this generation."[13] In fact, the Student Volunteer Movement adopted the phrase as its official watchword. In the early 1890s, Pierson was much in demand at student meetings to explain his plan for world evangelization, and he gave addresses on the subject at the first two quadrennial conferences of the Student Volunteer Movement. The idea that their own generation could evangelize the world was tremendously attractive to the idealistic student generations that preceded World War I.

For A. T. Pierson and many of the student volunteers, the secret to the watchword's urgency was its premillennial basis.

12. The Student Volunteer Movement did not sponsor its own missionaries but channeled volunteers through regular mission agencies. For background on this movement and assessments of its impact, see two essays by Clifton Phillips: "Changing Attitudes in the Student Volunteer Movement of Great Britain and North America," in *Missionary Ideologies in the Imperialist Era: 1880–1920*, ed. Torben Christiansen and William R. Hutchison (Aarhus, Denmark: Aros, 1982), 131-45; and "The Student Volunteer Movement and Its Role in China Missions, 1886–1923," in *The Missionary Enterprise in China and America*, ed. John K. Fairbank (Cambridge: Harvard Univ. Press, 1974), 91-109, 388-92 (notes).

13. For a history of the Student Volunteer Movement's watchword, "the evangelization of the world in this generation," see Denton Lotz, "'The Evangelization of the World in this Generation': The Resurgence of a Missionary Idea Among the Conservative Evangelicals" (Ph.D. diss., Univ. of Hamburg, 1970); and Dana L. Robert, "The Origin of the Student Volunteer Watchword: 'The Evangelization of the World in this Generation,'" *International Bulletin of Missionary Research* 10 (October 1986): 146-49.

As a committed premillennialist, Pierson believed that Jesus Christ would not return until the world had been evangelized. Yet the signs of the times were such that it appeared that the Second Coming would be soon. Massive arms buildups, anarchism, and the opening of the world to Christianity indicated the imminence of a world cataclysm. Seemingly the only thing standing in the way of Christ's return was that not every person in the world had heard the Good News and had chosen whether to accept or to reject it.[14]

Pierson further calculated that if one in every hundred Protestants would go as missionaries, then the world could be evangelized within twenty years, or within one generation.[15] By *evangelization*, Pierson did not mean the conversion of the world, but rather the preaching of the Word to the world, regardless of whether people became believers. Though Christians were called to evangelize, Pierson believed that conversions or results should be left to God.[16] If Christians would get to work, Pierson argued, then the world could be evangelized around the year 1900, and Jesus Christ would return to usher in his millennial kingdom. For A. T. Pierson, "the evangelization of the world in this generation" was a call for all Christians to "harvest" or to gather in believers around the world so as to fulfill prophecy in expectation of the Second Coming.

The student volunteer watchword soon took on a life of its own, separate from its premillennial origins. Not all student volunteers were premillennialists, and as the year 1900 approached

14. The fullest single defense of Pierson's premillennial mission convictions was his address to the International Prophetic Conference held in Chicago in November 1886: "Our Lord's Second Coming as a Motive to World-Wide Evangelism," in *Prophetic Studies of the International Prophetic Conference*, ed. George C. Needham (Chicago: Revell, 1886), 27-40.

15. A. T. Pierson, "The Signal Cry of the New Crusade," *Missionary Review of the World* 14 (January 1891): 537 (this magazine will be cited hereinafter as *Missionary Review*).

16. "Our Lord's coming furnishes a motive to world-wide evangelism in emphasizing duty rather than success, and our commission rather than apparent results. . . . Thus, while premillennialism is charged with cutting the nerves and sinew of Foreign Missions, it in fact supplies their perpetual incentive and inspiration in teaching us that duty is ours; results God's" (Pierson, "Our Lord's Second Coming," 41).

with no signs of completed world evangelization at hand, John R. Mott and others reinterpreted the watchword to mean that each generation should evangelize itself.[17] Those Christians alive at any given moment in Christian history should evangelize those persons alive in their own generation. To make the watchword continually relevant to a broad audience, Mott removed its premillennial connotations. He also denied that there was any countdown or timetable by which time the task of world evangelization would be complete.

Though officially stripped of its earlier premillennial connotations, "the evangelization of the world in this generation" continued to carry eschatological urgency for mission volunteers, especially for those who joined independent evangelical missions. Throughout the twentieth century, the phrase has inspired evangelical students to complete the task of world evangelization so that every living person or people group will have heard the gospel. In the 1960s, the Inter-Varsity Christian Fellowship, the Evangelical Foreign Missions Association, and the Interdenominational Foreign Mission Association acknowledged the student-volunteer watchword as a continuing inspiration and goal for evangelical missions.

A. T. Pierson's urgency for world evangelization led him not only to popularize the student-volunteer watchword, but to support faith missions, most of which were founded on a premillennial basis. As a Presbyterian, Pierson wrote articles, raised money, and served as an administrator for many Presbyterian mission causes. His oldest daughter became a lifetime Presbyterian missionary to Japan. Yet Pierson also encouraged what he called "undenominational" missions because they seemed more flexible and economical than the Presbyterian Board. The new faith missions seemed to be unhampered by bureaucratic machinery because missionaries prayed to God for every need instead of depending upon a denominational budget.[18] Pierson was a close friend of

17. See John R. Mott, *The Evangelization of the World in This Generation* (New York: Student Volunteer Movement, 1901), 3-6; Tissington Tatlow, *The Story of the Student Christian Movement in Great Britain and Ireland* (London: SCM, 1933), 80, 98.

18. A. T. Pierson, "Spiritual Movements of the Half Century—Development of Undenominational Missions," *Missionary Review* 21 (June 1898): 405.

J. Hudson Taylor, founder of the China Inland Mission, the first successful faith mission. As already noted, he was also a close friend of George Muller and was strongly attracted by Muller's combination of premillennial theology with faith methods for support of his orphanages. As a missions promoter in the 1890s, Pierson himself lived without a salary, relying on faith that God would meet the needs of his family. In his premillennial zeal for world evangelization Pierson became a prominent supporter of early American faith missions as evangelistic supplements to the work of denominational mission boards.

In 1889, Pierson helped to begin the Kansas-Sudan movement, a group of YMCA members who sought to evangelize the hitherto unexplored Sudan. The Kansas-Sudan movement dissolved in controversy when its original faith missionaries died as a result of their refusal to take quinine for the prevention of malaria. Though Pierson decried the fanaticism of refusing "on faith" to take medicine or to wear protective clothing, he nevertheless urged that the African interior be evangelized.[19]

In 1895, Pierson helped to found the Africa Inland Mission, a faith mission that sought to plant a line of missions through east and central Africa. As in the Kansas-Sudan movement, the earliest missionaries of the Africa Inland Mission died of disease, starvation, or exhaustion. Pierson attributed the setback to satanic opposition and urged the mission to persevere.[20] Pierson's zeal for world evangelization in preparation for Christ's Second Coming meant that even though he was a senior Presbyterian mission theorist, he encouraged early premillennial faith missions against heavy criticism. From these struggling faith missions of the 1890s came today's well-established independent evangelical missions.[21]

19. For the controversy over the Kansas-Sudan movement, see Robert, "Pierson and Forward Movements," 267-71; A. T. Pierson, "The Soudan Pioneers," *Missionary Review* 13 (October 1890): 792; C. Howard Hopkins, *History of the YMCA in North America* (New York: Association, 1951), 350-54.

20. Kenneth Richardson, *Garden of Miracles. A History of the African Inland Mission* (London: Victory, 1968), 26, 40.

21. For a history of the origin of faith missions, see Marybeth Rupert, "The Emergence of the Independent Missionary Agency as an American Institution, 1860–1917" (Ph.D. diss., Yale Univ., 1974).

As an early leader of Niagara and biblical prophecy conferences and as founder of the premillennial journal *The Watchword*,
Adoniram Judson Gordon was one of the most prominent evangelicals of the late nineteenth century. He is best known today
as the founder of the institution that evolved into Gordon College and Gordon-Conwell Theological Seminary. What is less
known about him is that Gordon devoted the last ten years of
his life to world evangelization.[22]

A. J. Gordon was for years the pastor of the Clarendon Street
Baptist Church in Boston, where he conducted an extensive ministry to alcoholics, immigrants, and other needy groups. During
Gordon's ministry, the Clarendon Street church was the chief
fund-raiser in New England for the American Baptist Missionary Union. Gordon himself served as member and then chairman of the Missionary Union executive committee. He was
therefore in charge of Baptist missions during their expansion
into Africa.

Like A. T. Pierson, Gordon was a devoted worker for his own
denominational missions. Yet his premillennial theology set him
apart from most Baptists, and he was frequently called to defend
premillennialism from the charge that it "cut the nerve of all missionary and evangelistic enterprises."[23] In an article entitled "Pre-
Millennialism and Missions," Gordon argued that belief in Jesus'
physical and literal return before the millennium made a person
an even more ardent advocate of missions than one who did not
hold that belief. Of the fifty-four graduates of Princeton Seminary
in 1864, Gordon pointed out, only eight had become foreign missionaries—and all eight were premillennialists.[24]

Gordon believed that the main difference between the premillennialist and the nonmillennialist was that the believer in

22. Dana L. Robert, "The Legacy of Adoniram Judson Gordon," *International Bulletin of Missionary Research* (October 1987): 176-81. For general works
on Gordon, see Ernest B. Gordon, *Adoniram Judson Gordon* (New York: Revell,
1896); George Gerald Houghton, "The Contributions of Adoniram Judson Gordon to American Christianity" (Th.D. diss., Dallas Theological Seminary, 1970);
C. Allyn Russell, "Adoniram Judson Gordon: Nineteenth-Century Fundamentalist," *American Baptist Quarterly* 4 (March 1985): 61-89.

23. A. J. Gordon, "Pre-millennialism and Mission," *The Watchword* 8 (April
1886): 30.

24. Ibid., 32.

the Second Coming put all mission emphasis on preaching the gospel. The purpose of preaching the gospel was to gather out the elect church from all nations so that Jesus would soon return.[25] Gordon explicitly rejected educational, industrial, or other "civilizing" forms of mission work as not only unnecessary forms of mission but as undesirable. For example, not only did higher education not bring the unsaved to Jesus Christ, but Western education prevented them from becoming Christian. "We look in vain," Gordon argued, "in the history of the ancient and the modern mission, for examples of the heathen being slowly prepared, to and through culture, for the acceptance of Christianity; while conversely there is no lack of examples that the systematic way through civilization to evangelization has been not only a circuitous but a wrong way."[26]

In his major statement of mission theory, *The Holy Spirit in Missions*, Gordon argued that the plan for missions outlined in the New Testament was coming to an end—the Christian elect were being gathered out from all nations of the world. After the elect were gathered, the latter days of fulfilled prophecy would occur. Therefore, Christian responsibility consisted of completing the task of world evangelization as quickly as possible.[27] Because of this need for speedy evangelization, Gordon believed in what he called the "decentralization of mission."[28] Each local church should act as its own mission society so that all Christians would be responsible for missions and the work would be accomplished faster. In the interest of efficiency in evangelization, Gordon supported the idea of placing independent evangelical missions alongside denominational agencies.

In his desire to decentralize missions so as to expand the mission force, Gordon realized that the laity needed training in Bible and mission methods. This belief led him to become president of the Boston Missionary Institute in 1889. The school's purpose was to train lay persons in evangelistic methods and

25. Ibid., 30.

26. Gordon, "Education and Missions, Part 1," *Missionary Review* 16 (August 1893): 585.

27. See A. J. Gordon, *The Holy Spirit in Missions* (New York: Revell, 1893).

28. See A. J. Gordon, "Decentralization in Missions," *Missionary Review* 15 (July 1892): 492.

urban rescue work, using only the Bible as a textbook, so that they could go into the "harvest fields" and work as lay missionaries.[29] Seminary training was practical only for men of superior intellectual ability who could expect to be ordained. The Institute was founded not as a substitute for the theological seminary but as an affordable means for less educated laity, especially women, to receive a minimal mission education. Gordon believed that the harvest of souls was plentiful, but the laborers were few. The missionary training school would help fill the need for "11th hour" evangelistic workers.

Despite minimal publicity, a part-time teaching staff, a paltry budget, heavy denominational opposition, and no private buildings, the Boston Training School (as it was also called) attracted lay people who desired to become workers for world evangelization. Women made up a majority of the student body in its earliest years. Gordon believed that the world was in the dispensation of the Holy Spirit prophesied by the prophet Joel: "And it shall be in the last days, saith God, I will pour forth of my spirit upon all flesh: And your sons and your daughters shall prophesy" (Acts 2:17). Since women had spiritual equality in the final days, Gordon argued that women had the right to preach, prophesy, and teach men in the church.[30] He believed not only that women should be enfranchised to vote but also that they should take full responsibility as missionaries. The success of the Boston Training School can partly be attributed to A. J. Gordon's millennial vision for the role of laity in general and of lay women in particular.

By the time A. J. Gordon died in 1895, the Boston Training School had graduated twenty-five missionaries, fifteen ministers, twenty evangelistic workers, and twenty home missionaries. Fifteen graduates had continued into seminary training.[31] Some Boston graduates were accepted by denominational missions, but many others became connected with separate evangelical faith missions. After Gordon's death, the training school

29. Robert, "Legacy of A. J. Gordon," 179.
30. A. J. Gordon, "The Ministry of Women," *Missionary Review* 17 (December 1894): 910-21.
31. F. L. Chappell, "Dr. Gordon and the Training School," *Watchword* 17 (February and March, 1895): 62.

was renamed the Gordon Bible and Missionary Training School, and A. T. Pierson became its second president. Over the years, the school developed into a four-year Christian college and theological seminary.[32]

The evolution of A. J. Gordon's mission institute into a Christian college and theological seminary, both with standard curricula and widely recognized quality, parallels the development of many evangelical missions. Beginning as faith missions, run on a shoestring, and clearly supplemental to denominational work, they later became large, organizationally mature, independent agencies. As in the case of the faith mission, most mission training schools like Moody Bible Institute, Nyack College, and Gordon's Boston Institute were begun on a premillennial basis. The founders of the late-nineteenth-century mission schools believed that the task of world evangelization required the immediate training of thousands of lay workers. Only a thorough mobilization of Christian laity could ensure that the Word would be preached and the elect would be gathered in preparation for Jesus' imminent return. Premillennial mission theory seemed to justify the creation of both the independent mission and the evangelical mission school. It is no coincidence that in the twentieth century, a major source for the recruitment of evangelical missionaries has been Christian colleges, many of which, like Gordon College, were founded as mission institutes.

A. J. Gordon and A. T. Pierson are but two examples of late-nineteenth-century mission advocates whose premillennial zeal led them to develop alternatives to denominational mission institutions. In Pierson's case, he popularized an urgency for "the evangelization of the world in this generation" that remains a primary justification for twentieth-century evangelical missions. Pierson helped to found the Africa Inland Mission as a pioneer evangelistic faith mission. A. G. Gordon justified a decentralization of missions that helped to legitimate separate evangelical missions. His missionary training school was a forerunner of the Bible college or Bible institute, from which many evangelical missionaries have been recruited.

32. For a history of Gordon College, see Nathan R. Wood, *A School of Christ* (Boston: Halliday Lithograph Corp., 1953).

Neither man had any intention of replacing the denominational mission agency with an independent mission. Pierson, in fact, continued to believe that the denominational bureaucracy was the best way to prevent missions from becoming victims of ecclesiastical despotism. He also felt that the denominational mission reflected the will of the church rather than the will of the few.[33] Nevertheless, Pierson's and Gordon's premillennial beliefs caused them to encourage the development of seemingly more spiritual and more efficient, but narrowly evangelistic, missions.

Other late-nineteenth-century premillennialists who contributed to the origin of independent evangelical missions also should be mentioned here. Albert Benjamin Simpson was a Presbyterian premillennialist who founded both the Christian and Missionary Alliance as a faith mission and Nyack College as a missionary training institute.[34] Cyrus Ingerson Scofield was a Congregationalist who founded the Central American Mission, one of the earliest missions to enter Latin America. Scofield is best remembered as the editor of the *Scofield Reference Bible*, an annotated King James Bible that encapsulated the hermeneutical system known as premillennial dispensationalism.[35] What is almost never mentioned about the *Scofield Reference Bible* is that its purpose was not to codify a theological system but to be a one-volume reference work for missionaries who had no access to theological libraries.[36] Scofield was a missions activist whose

33. On denominational mission boards, see *Missionary Review* 22 (August 1899): 620.

34. James H. Hunter, *Beside All Waters; The Story of 75 Years of World Wide Ministry: The Christian and Missionary Alliance*, with an introduction by Nathan Bailey (Harrisburg: Christian Publications, [1964]); Robert L. Niklaus, John S. Sawin, and Samuel J. Stoesz, *All for Jesus: God at Work in the Christian and Missionary Alliance Over One Hundred Years* (Camp Hill, PA: Christian Publications, 1986).

35. For information on the life of C. I. Scofield and the production of the *Scofield Reference Bible*, see Charles G. Trumbull, *The Life Story of C. I. Scofield* (New York: Oxford Univ. Press, 1920); Arno C. Gaebelein, *The History of the Scofield Reference Bible* (New York: Our Hope Publications, 1943); and Frank E. Gaebelein, *The Story of the Scofield Reference Bible* (New York: Oxford Univ. Press, 1959).

36. "[The *Scofield Reference Bible*] is intended as a guide to Bible students who have not time or opportunity to search commentaries and books on the-

premillennial zeal for evangelistic missions helped him to create the best-selling Bible in twentieth-century America.

In examining the development of late-nineteenth-century premillennial mission theology, one is struck at the irony that a theory stressing immediacy, rapid evangelization, and the by-passing of bureaucracy should have generated a veritable establishment of evangelical mission agencies and Bible colleges. Theorists such as Pierson, Gordon, and others had little desire to create permanent institutions, for, like the early church, they believed that Jesus' Second Coming was just around the corner. Rather than hasten the Second Coming, however, the separate evangelical missions they encouraged have contributed to the development of a twentieth-century evangelical subculture.

In a sense, premillennial mission theory was a victim of its own success. It succeeded so well in recruiting enthusiasts who were willing to spend their lives in evangelistic work that what began as a pragmatic, *ad hoc* commitment became systematized. Instead of obtaining liberal-arts-college degrees and seminary training, evangelists and faith missionaries enrolled in courses of practical training that isolated them from dominant religious culture. This isolation contributed, no doubt, to the extreme antagonism and polarization of the later fundamentalist-modernist controversies. On the other hand, one could argue that the greatest success of premillennial mission theory was to involve in mission women, the uneducated, and others who were already alienated from the ecclesial establishment. Nevertheless, the movement's first generation of college and seminary graduates, like Pierson and Gordon, were followed by premillennial leaders who had completed only a practical course of preparation for ministry and mission. Steeped in Bible study that stressed "fundamentalist" exegesis and practical application over such concerns as ecclesiology, pastoral and missionary trainees were by the 1930s likely to follow the commitment to a separatist mission with membership in a separatist church.

---

ology for interpretation and information. . . . No edition of the Bible will probably prove as great a help to missionaries and others cut off from large use of commentaries, by distance from libraries or from lack of time" ("The Scofield Reference Bible," *Missionary Review* 32 [July 1909]: 555).

In recent years the pragmatic separatism of premillennial mission theology has come nearly full circle, however, as this alienated separatist network has become an important force in American religion. The independent evangelical institutions of the late twentieth century are healthy and vigorous with their fully accredited colleges and well-financed, well-organized mission agencies. This prosperity has bred a confidence that often borders on triumphalism. Like the student volunteers of a century ago, many independent evangelical mission leaders of today are asking themselves, "Can the evangelization of the world be far behind?"

3 Blessed Adversity:[1] Henry W. Frost and the China Inland Mission

Alvyn J. Austin

When Dwight L. Moody invited Rev. J. Hudson Taylor to speak at the Northfield and Niagara prophetic conferences in 1888, Taylor emphasized that he would not come to America to establish a branch of the China Inland Mission (CIM, now the Overseas Missionary Fellowship), nor would he solicit either funds or missionaries. Indeed, he stated, he would not even speak directly of China.

Yet, after "the outpouring of the Spirit" at these two meetings led to the spontaneous donation of enough money to support eight missionaries in China for a year, Taylor abruptly changed his mind. The donors had specified they be North American missionaries, and, as Taylor stated in his appeal, "To have missionaries and no money would be no trouble for me, for the Lord is bound to take care of his own. . . . But to have money and no missionaries is very serious indeed." Once he was convinced of the Lord's leading in this new venture, "God's surprises were beyond counting or measuring." By the end of the year, the CIM received sixty applicants for service, fourteen of whom he selected to accompany him immediately to China. The rest became the responsibility of the grandly named temporary International Auxiliary Council. Taylor's visit culminated in a

1. This is the title of a series of meditations on Job by Hudson Taylor, in the British edition of *China's Millions* 15 (January to March, 1890). The phrase was a leitmotif of the mission's history; see *China's Millions* 56 (July 1948): 99.

triumphal torch-lit parade down the main street of Toronto as a thousand well-wishers escorted "the first American party" of the CIM to the train station.[2]

Hudson Taylor was already well-known in America, and his visit had momentous repercussions. At Northfield, he presided over the founding of the Student Volunteer Movement (SVM). At the Believers' Conference, the fifth held at Niagara-on-the-Lake, Ontario, he introduced the CIM as the evangelical "faith mission" model for others to copy. And finally, in Toronto, he was the catalyst for the formation of the Canadian missions to China.

Due to these accomplishments, Taylor has been called "the father of the faith mission movement."[3] Thus the China Inland Mission is perhaps the most important case to study in tracing the transfer of British premillennial mission concepts to North America.

It was no accident that Canada was the intermediary in this transfer. Canadians were, after all, British subjects in the American continent, and religious influences from both directions converged there. Canada has its own distinct missionary history, and, it has been said, in proportion to its size and resources, it sponsored more foreign missionaries than any nation in Christendom. One need only mention three names to indicate the importance of Canadians in specifically evangelical (North) American missions: Albert B. Simpson, founder of the Christian and Missionary Alliance (CMA);[4] Rowland V.

2. The story of "the first American party" has been told many times in the mission histories, in varying detail: see esp. Geraldine Guinness, *The Story of the China Inland Mission*, 2 vols. (London: CIM, 1896), 2:484-87; Dr. and Mrs. Howard Taylor (G. Guinness), *Hudson Taylor and the China Inland Mission: The Growth of a Work of God* (London and Philadelphia: CIM, 1918), 467-72; idem, *"By Faith . . .": Henry W. Frost and the China Inland Mission* (Philadelphia and Toronto: CIM, 1938), 92-97; and Marshall Broomhall, *The Jubilee Story of the China Inland Mission* (London and Philadelphia: CIM, 1938), 183-90.

3. J. Herbert Kane, *A Concise History of the Christian World Mission: A Panoramic View of Missions from Pentecost to the Present* (Grand Rapids: Baker, 1978), 96. Daniel W. Bacon, *From Faith to Faith, The Influence of Hudson Taylor on the Faith Missions Movement* (Robesonia, PA: OMF, 1984), 91-106, lists twenty-three faith missions that were directly influenced by Hudson Taylor, including C. I. Scofield's Central American Mission.

4. Robert B. Ekvall et al., *After Fifty Years: A Record of God's Working through the Christian and Missionary Alliance* (Harrisburg: Christian Publica-

Bingham of the Sudan Interior Mission (SIM);[5] and Jonathan Goforth of the Canadian Presbyterian mission to China.[6]

In the 1890s, there was considerable discussion that Canada should act as a linchpin of the Anglo-American missionary enterprise. Precisely that happened in the CIM: twelve of the fourteen "Americans" in the first party were Canadians, as were fifty-seven of the sixty applications received in 1888. So, when Americans came into the mission, they did so as "junior partners" to Canadians—a most unusual occurrence.

Before Taylor came, there was tremendous missionary enthusiasm in Canada, but no movement. The CIM provided one of the first channels, and denominational missions followed. Canadian churches had been sending missionaries overseas since the 1840s, but by 1888 they had only small missions in Japan, India, and Formosa. A few individuals were stationed elsewhere, mostly under American missions; in fact, the Disciples of Christ and the Christian and Missionary Alliance employed Canadians as pioneers of the China missions in 1886. The Presbyterians had sent Jonathan and Rosalind Goforth as their first representatives barely six months before Taylor's visit and subsequently sent five more by the end of the year. Thus began a major mobilization of China missions from Canada. The Presbyterian mission to Henan was founded in 1888; the Methodist in Sichuan in 1891; and the Anglican in Fujian (later transferred to Henan) in 1897. By the 1920s, about five hundred Canadians were in China, with over a hundred in the CIM; it was thus the second largest Canadian mission,

tions, 1939). Simpson was born on Prince Edward Island and raised in rural Ontario near Chatham. After education at Knox College, Toronto, he held pastorates in Kentucky and New York City. He founded the Missionary Training College in Nyack, the first Bible institute, in 1882, and the CMA in 1887. By the 1920s, the CMA operated four missions in China, including on the Tibetan border, as well as in other countries.

5. James H. Hunter, *A Flame of Fire* (Toronto: SIM Press, 1941). Bingham (1872–1942) was born in Sussex, England, and raised in Toronto. He founded the SIM in Toronto in 1893, although it was not incorporated until 1898. From the beginning, its constitution adopted "the doctrinal principles and methods of the China Inland Mission and similar interdenominational missions"; see Bacon, *From Faith to Faith*, 98.

6. Rosalind Goforth, *Goforth of China* (Grand Rapids: Zondervan, 1938).

and it increased during the 1930s as denominational missions declined.[7]

Goforth had actually been the first person from North America to apply to the CIM, in 1886, but he was too much a Presbyterian to join an interdenominational mission. Nevertheless, the CIM noted on his death that "No missionary not actually a member of the Mission was ever more akin to it in spirit or more closely associated with it in actual service."[8] Two other Presbyterians who applied about the same time did join the mission, and both had influential forty-year careers in its service: Alexander R. Saunders and Henry W. Frost. All three were responding to Hudson Taylor's call for The Hundred new missionaries to join the CIM in 1886-87, in order to capitalize on the enthusiasm generated by the Cambridge Seven. The story of these young English gentlemen giving up everything to live in a Chinese village was published as *The Evangelization of the World* and distributed free to every YMCA in Britain and America. It inspired a whole generation of students on both sides of the Atlantic.[9]

Goforth and Saunders made their mark in China—Goforth by starting the revival that swept China and east Asia in 1907-8, and Saunders as the first North American to sit on the China Council of the CIM.[10] Frost, however, was destined to build the CIM into an institution in North America. He was the father of two works. In 1889, when Hudson Taylor designated him as

7. Alvyn J. Austin, *Saving China: Canadian Missionaries in the Middle Kingdom 1888–1959* (Toronto: Univ. of Toronto Press, 1986), chaps. 1-3.

8. Robert Hall Glover, "Goforth of China," *China's Millions* 46 (March 1938): 43-44.

9. Robert Speer stated that no book except the Bible and William Blaikie's *Personal Life of Livingstone* (Chicago: Student Missionary Campaign Library, 1880) influenced him more than *The Evangelization of the World* (London: CIM, 1894); see Broomhall, *Jubilee Story*, 166.

10. Saunders' career path was remarkably similar to Goforth's. He preached the gospel of poverty in his early years and was forced to flee from the Boxer Rebellion, when two of his daughters were martyred; see A. R. Saunders, *A God of Deliverances* (London: CIM Press, 1901). During the 1910s, he experimented with mass evangelism, including work with the soldiers of "the Christian General," Feng Yu-husiang. He was also influential in North America, by inspiring the mission department of Los Angeles Bible Institute (then under R. A. Torrey) during his furlough of 1918. See Taylor, "By Faith. . . ," 276-78, 308-11.

secretary-treasurer for North America, he founded the Canadian branch of the mission in Toronto; he did this by building a support network of denominational and interdenominational organizations in Canada and the United States. Then in 1901, he moved to Philadelphia to set up the American branch. Because of the incipient modernist controversy, he felt the mission had to preserve its evangelical witness and therefore formed a second, alternate coalition, equally interdenominational but purely evangelical. His tenure as the head of CIM's North American branch thus illustrates the process by which the British-inspired faith missions shaped the network and ethos of conservative evangelical missions in twentieth-century America and were, in turn, grafted into the fundamentalist movement.

Frost was descended from post-Mayflower Puritans and came from Attica in the upstate region of New York, known as a "burned-over district" because of its many revivals. He was converted to premillennial views at the Niagara conference in 1886 by William J. Erdman, who became his lifelong mentor, and to the cause of China missions by the fiery rhetoric of Jonathan Goforth. His application was turned down by the CIM, even though he went to London for an interview; he persisted, however, and became the guiding presence behind Taylor's 1888 North American visit. On his departure, Taylor named Frost as acting secretary, which he confirmed the following year, and asked him to move to Toronto. He was home director in 1893.[11]

Looking back on the mission's first years in Canada, Frost concluded that "God thought our tiny ship needed winds of a strong and even boisterous kind."[12] The winds came from an unexpected direction: the London Council, the main governing body, threatened to resign when they heard of the North American expansion. Until this time, the CIM had been run as "a voluntary association with a family board of directors" under Benjamin Broomhall, Taylor's brother-in-law and secretary in

11. The official biography of Frost is Dr. and Mrs. Howard Taylor, *"By Faith . . .": Henry W. Frost and the China Inland Mission*, which is based on Frost's unpublished memoirs, *The Years That Are Past* (hereinafter cited as *Memoirs;* ms. copy in OMF Archives, Toronto).

12. Frost, *Memoirs*, 221.

London. Some council members thought English people could not work with Americans—there was a lingering anti-American bias until the 1930s—while others were afraid that the American organization would be a drain on the finances.[13]

Broomhall, however, saw internationalization as a diminution of London's power. "When the authority is divided and the responsibility is divided, there is weakness, and there is danger," he said.[14] Taylor himself—whom Frost nicknamed in military terminology "General Forward"—refused to yield to the British opposition and wrote urgent letters to Frost, saying, "If you have any godly men fit for the work, *don't keep them back;* and if you have any suitable women and a suitable escort . . . *don't keep them back.*"[15]

13. The opposite happened: Americans always contributed more than their share of money. By the mid-1930s, they raised some $500,000 annually, half the operating budget of the entire mission, but supplied only one-third of the missionaries. For financial statistics, 1888–1938, see Taylor, "*By Faith . . .,*" 292-93. There has been considerable speculation about the "American" presence of the CIM: Milton T. Stauffer, ed., *The Christian Occupation of China: A General Survey of the Numerical Strengths and Geographical Distribution of the Christian Forces in China* (Shanghai: China Continuation Committee, 1922), in consultation with the mission directors, estimated it at 12 percent (p. 345); M. Searle Bates, "The Theology of American Missionaries in China, 1900–1950," in *The Missionary Enterprise in China and America,* ed. John K. Fairbank (Cambridge: Harvard Univ. Press, 1974), likewise estimates 8 to 12 percent. Since both estimates calculate Canadians as British rather than as North Americans, the actual figures were much higher, especially if one includes the Americans in the Scandinavian Alliance Mission as associates. Here is the actual breakdown of the North American force in CIM:

	NA total	SAM total	CIM total	Associates total	CIM + Assocs.	NA as % of CIM	NA + SAM as % CIM + Assocs.
1900	117	60 (est.)	679	125	804	17%	22%
1921	144	68	782	328	1110	18%	19%
1936	305	43	923	436	1359	33%	25%

Note: these figures do not include non-American spouses of American missionaries, about forty in 1936, nor those who took on Canadian or American citizenship after joining the CIM. Figures from *List of North American C.I.M. Missionaries 1887–1921* (ms. in OMF Archives, Toronto), *CIM Directories.*

14. Robert Caldwell (London Council member) to Frost, 20 February 1899, in Frost, *Memoirs,* 244.

15. "General Forward," in ibid., 554; letter, Taylor to Frost, 5 March 1889, ibid., 254.

Taylor made a special trip to London to convince the brethren and over the next few years pressed forward with the internationalization of the CIM. He had begun this process as early as 1875, but now he empowered the China Council as the supreme governing body; by locating the headquarters in Shanghai, he made the CIM the only major mission to be directed from the field rather than by a board in the homeland. He also set up a branch in Australia in 1890 and accepted ten European missions as associates, independent at home and working under the CIM in China. These represented Lutheran and Free Church groups in Germany, Sweden, Norway, Denmark, and Finland. Frederik Franson brought this revival from Europe to America, where he started the Scandinavian Alliance Mission (now The Evangelical Alliance Mission [TEAM]) among Swedish immigrants; in 1891, they dispatched thirty-five missionaries in one of the largest parties sent under the CIM, followed by another party of fifteen.[16]

Hudson Taylor remained the central authority in the mission as general director, "over all and connecting all,"[17] but from the beginning, he established the North American branch on an equal footing with London. "Being an American," Frost wrote in his memoirs, he had hoped that the "autocratic constitution" could be "Americanized, that is, democratized," but he came to see the value of hierarchical control. CIM was a voluntary association, "not a church, and, hence, not related to the instructions given in the Word in respect to church organization."[18] Moreover, it was different from ordinary mission societies, in which "the donors are the members and the missionaries their agents. . . ." CIM had no society behind it and relied on God for the provisions of their needs.[19] The missionaries of the CIM

16. For the arrival of the SAM missionaries, see *China's Millions*, British ed., 16 (May 1891): 61-64; they were there when Frost visited Shanghai. Many of these missionaries were stationed in Shaanxi, where they were killed during the Boxer uprising; see Marshall Broomhall, *Martyred Missionaries of the China Inland Mission, With a Record of the Perils and Sufferings of Some Who Escaped* (London: CIM, 1901).

17. Frost had a major hand in the reorganization of the CIM structure during his visit to London in 1893; this is from the revised constitution that he wrote on 14 February 1893; see *Memoirs*, 429.

18. Ibid., 894.

19. J. H. Taylor, circular letter, 12 November 1898; in ibid., 551.

were the members, called of God to offer their service, and had signed the *Doctrinal Basis*, which was in effect "a spiritual, moral and even legal contract, between, on the one hand, the Mission Directors, and, on the other, the Mission membership."[20] The distinction was to become crucial when Taylor himself wanted to liberalize the *Principles and Practice*.

Frost's relations with London remained "sympathetic" but distant, and "it became clear," Frost declared, that "we could not look to the Mission in England for advice in the developing of our North American work. . . . Their experience had been insular while our need was continental."[21] Instead, Frost formed a "remarkable friendship" with Hudson Taylor, who once told him that he, Frost, was "the best friend he had ever had. . . . He thought highly of the North American work and somewhat idealized me as the founder of it."[22] Their relationship was bolstered by regular visits, usually of several weeks' duration. Taylor came to America six times after 1888, each time extending the CIM's influence: in 1889, to speak at Northfield and Niagara again and to establish a permanent council; in 1892; in 1894, for the SVM conference in Detroit; in 1897; in 1900, for the Ecumenical Missionary Conference in New York, of which Frost was one of the organizers; and finally as "an aged and broken-down man" in 1905, on his way to China to die. Frost visited China four times, once spending over a year there in 1895-96; he thus became one of the first directors of any mission in North America to have field experience. He also made five trips to London, although collegial meetings were not instituted until the 1920s. Frost enjoyed the same friendship with Taylor's successor, Dixon E. Hoste, one of the Cambridge Seven, though this was more a relationship of contemporaries.

In China, Frost saw how the faith-mission principles of the CIM were translated into practice: the concern for "the regions beyond," the unreached millions of inland China; extended itinerations of unoccupied districts; the use of lay people as mis-

---

20. Frost, *Memoirs*, 700.

21. Ibid., 522.

22. Frost also returned the compliment, describing Taylor as "the ideal man"; ibid., 377.

sionaries, especially the employment of unmarried women; the wearing of Chinese dress in order to get closer to the people, to appear "Chinese to the Chinese"; and the emphasis on direct evangelism over good works. As Frost wrote in 1933 in response to the Laymen's Inquiry report, *Re-Thinking Missions*, "Social reform is good, but it is not the Gospel. Education is good, but it is not the Gospel. Medical work is good, but it is not the Gospel. Indeed these matters, good as they are, may destroy the Gospel."[23]

Frost tried to implement these and other faith-mission concepts, as expressed in the *Principles and Practice*, in his North American setting. The first two precepts immediately set this type of mission apart from more conventional societies.

> First. Its interdenominational character.
> Second. That its workers have no guaranteed salary, but trust in God whom they serve to supply their needs, and are not disappointed in the trust. . . . That no personal solicitation or collection of funds is made, voluntary contributions alone being received.[24]

Rather than denominational unity, the CIM demanded adherence to its *Doctrinal Basis*, which affirmed one's "soundness of the faith on all fundamental truths" but allowed a wide latitude for the accidentals of worship forms and church governance. This gave the mission "a largely homogenous character, both in respect of doctrinal belief and the type of personal piety within it."[25] In China, the mission set aside certain areas for denominational grouping, for example, designating East Sichuan as a Church of England diocese jointly under the CIM and the Church Missionary Society. The mission's denominational makeup was tabulated by *The Christian Occupation of China* in

23. Frost, "What Is Our Commission?" *China's Millions* 41 (February 1933): 20.

24. Hudson Taylor drew up the *Principles and Practice* in 1875, and they continue to form the constitution of the mission. The practices have been revised occasionally (such as the attempt to loosen the restriction against marriage before two years of probationary service) and were incorporated into *Instructions for Probationers and Members of the C.I.M.* (1925, 1978, etc.).

25. D. E. Hoste, "Cooperation in the China Inland Mission," *China's Millions* 33 (April 1925): 52.

1922 on the basis of the number of converts: Anglicans, 3,000; Congregationalists and Presbyterians, 3,000-4,000 each; Methodists, 5,000-6,000; Lutherans, 8,000; and Baptists forming over one-half of the constituency at 25,000.[26]

Frost found Toronto—"Toronto the Good, the city of churches"—fertile ground for the CIM's type of evangelical alliance. Unlike the United States, where denominational headquarters are located in several cities, north and south, in Canada the major Protestant churches had all centralized their operations in Toronto. So, by settling there, one could reach all of English Canada. By the 1920s, there were, within a few blocks of the University of Toronto, some thirty missionary-sending churches and twenty-five mission societies or educational institutions. The CIM was across the street from the (liberal) Canadian School of Missions, down the street from the Sudan Interior Mission, and around the corner from Toronto Bible College. As late as the 1950s, the city environs were home to twenty-five interdenominational evangelical foreign mission societies.[27]

26. *Christian Occupation of China*, p. 333. A somewhat different profile emerges from a tabulation of candidates' application forms for the period 1888–1901 (OMF Archives, Toronto):

	CANADA				U.S.A.			
	Candidates		Missionaries		Candidates		Missionaries	
Presbyterian	74	36%	34	44%	64	21%	22	25%
Baptist	44	22%	20	26%	46	15%	13	15%
Methodist	41	20%	13	17%	57	18%	13	15%
Anglican	15	7%	5	6%	8	3%	2	1%
Congregationalist	16	8%	3	4%	47	15%	14	16%
Other denoms.	11	6%	3	4%	41	13%	12	14%
Moody B.I.*	2	1%	—	—	49	16%	12	14%
Total Known	203		78		312		88	
Unknown	78		1		156		2	
Grand Total	281		79		468		90	

*Note: This includes only those whose sole denominational affiliation is listed as MBI; those who include affiliation with a specific denomination are listed under that group. (This explains, in part, the number of American Congregationalists.)

27. J. W. Grant, in "Asking Questions of the Canadian Past," *Canadian Journal of Theology*, July 1955, characterizes the difference between Canadian and American approaches to denominationalism: "Americans naturally gravitate towards denominational groups and Canadians to interdenominational fellowships." This, he feels, is exemplified by the Canadian tendency to church unions.

Despite their initial suspicion that the CIM would divert funds from connectional channels,[28] the Canadian denominations came to acknowledge the mission's special appeal. The CIM chose its friends judiciously, among spirit-filled lay people; "We were ready," Frost wrote, "to throw in our lot with the socially humble and financially poor, if only we could maintain scriptural and spiritual integrity in our friendships."[29] Its theology was broadly premillennial though not necessarily dispensational, with a strong strand of British amillennialism (especially under the influence of T. T. Shields, leader of the conservative Baptists).[30]

The laymen on the Toronto Council tended to be philanthropists, like the Quaker coal merchant Elias Rogers, or were connected in a growing network of religious enterprises, such as Alfred Sandham of the Christian Institute, under whose auspices the CIM opened in Toronto.[31] One of the most active laymen was Samuel H. Blake, brother of the former premier of Ontario and member of a dozen interdenominational boards; he was also the founder of the Anglican Church's missionary society and its low-church seminary, Wycliffe College. Rowland V. Bingham of the SIM sat on the CIM board, and Frost reciprocated on the SIM board.[32]

The ordained ministers on the Toronto Council showed a

28. Both the Canadian Methodists and Presbyterians were worried about the CIM "stirring up the people"; see Austin, *Saving China*, 37, 59. Many people criticized the denominational missions because they spent twice as much ($500) as the CIM to support a single missionary; to allay this, one Presbyterian missionary, Donald MacGillivray (later of the Christian Literature Society), volunteered to live on the same $250 stipend as the CIM people, but his experiment failed.

29. Frost, *Memoirs*, 433.

30. Interview with W. W. Tyler, August 1988. On Shields, see George M. Marsden, *Fundamentalism and American Culture: The Shaping of Twentieth Century Evangelicalism, 1870–1925* (New York: Oxford Univ. Press, 1980), 182-83.

31. Frost, *Memoirs*, 307. Sandham resigned from the council, and the CIM moved its offices out of the Christian Institute in 1890 because Sandham felt the candidates needed better training. Frost felt the mission home should be used for testing, not for training (p. 310).

32. In 1900, John R. Mott of the SVM stated that "no college in proportion to its size had sent more men to the foreign field than had Wycliffe College" (*Cap and Gown* [April 1921]: 3); see also Austin, *Saving China*, 128.

preponderance of Presbyterians, including the American pre-millennial Bible teacher William J. Erdman and H. M. Parsons of Knox Church, Toronto.[33] Rev. Robert Wallace, director of the Quarrier orphanage in Belleville, had ties to the London Council and even married Benjamin Broomhall's daughter, Alice, who was also Hudson Taylor's niece. After twenty-seven years on the council, Wallace joined the staff of the CIM as treasurer, a post he held for fifteen years.[34] Semiformal relations were established with the Presbyterian Foreign Mission Board from the beginning, when the secretary, Dr. Thomas Wardrope, joined the CIM. He was succeeded in both positions by Rev. R. P. MacKay, a founding member of the Associated Boards of Foreign Mission Societies, who remained an evangelical even as his own church moved toward corporate union with the Methodists into the United Church of Canada.

The Toronto Council never had a Methodist clergyman—reflecting the liberal views of that denomination—but it always had one Anglican. It had strong ties to Wycliffe College, and one of its graduates, H. W. K. Mowll, became bishop of East Sichuan. The principal, T. R. O'Meara, was one of the speakers at the Niagara conference in 1915, even though he was not allowed to share communion with other council members. He was also use-

---

33. William Fitch, *Knox Church, Toronto: Avante-Garde, Evangelical, Advancing* (Toronto: John Deyelle, 1971).

34. There is a significant, as yet unexplored, connection between British orphanages, which were among the first faith missions, and the CIM. This can be traced from George Muller and Thomas Barnardo, who originally applied to the CIM (both sat on early CIM councils), through Grattan Guiness and the East London Missionary Training Home. By the 1880s, these orphanages had become child-immigration societies, which collectively brought some eighty thousand "orphans" from the slums of Britain to Canada; see Kenneth Bagnell, *The Little Immigrants: The Orphans Who Came To Canada* (Toronto: Macmillan, 1980). In addition to Dr. Wallace, two missionaries of the first CIM party were staff members of the Quarrier Home (obituary of Mrs. Wallace, *China's Millions* 34 [September 1926]: 132. Her sister, Gertrude, was married to D. E. Hoste). Wallace's family showed a typical progression from evangelical to liberal missions; his grandson, Edward Wilson Wallace, became a noted Methodist educationalist in China, secretary of the China Educational Association (see Alvyn Austin, *Edward Wilson Wallace and the Modernization of Education in West China, 1906–1928* [Toronto: Univ. of Toronto–York Univ. Joint Centre for Asia Pacific Studies, forthcoming]).

ful to the CIM in identifying suspected high-church candidates; one man, he warned, attended a church "of an advanced ritualistic type.... I cannot myself see how any thoroughgoing Protestant who knows experientially the gladness and liberty of the Gospel of Christ would be comfortable and at home in such surroundings."[35] This comity with the Episcopalians remained characteristic of Britain and Canada but was not transferred to the United States.

Perhaps the most influential of the early council members was Dr. Elmore E. Harris, pastor of Walmer Road Baptist Church and founder of Toronto Bible College (TBC, now Ontario Bible College) in 1893. TBC grew out of training classes Dr. Harris conducted for CIM candidates in the mission home, and there are notations on candidates' records that he rebaptized some who had never been immersed. TBC was supported by the same evangelical network as the CIM; in fact, all the Canadians mentioned above also sat on the board of TBC. Harris's successor as principal, John J. McNicol, continued the missionary emphasis of the college during his forty-year tenure and sat on the CIM council, where he moderated extreme interpretations of scriptural prophecy. The third principal, F. Herbert Rhodes, was born in China of CIM parents and was for many years the mission's Prayer Union secretary. By the mid-1940s, a quarter of the college's 2,000 graduates were serving as overseas missionaries, with over 150 under the CIM or the SIM in Africa.[36]

During its first five years, the CIM received its applicants directly from the churches. In other words, its publicity was spread by word of mouth of people who had been influenced personally by Hudson Taylor. Word traveled from the heartland of southern Ontario and the northeastern United States (especially New York, New Jersey, and Massachusetts) to as far away as Nebraska and Iowa by deputation speakers, mostly British missionaries who tarried for a few months in North America. The founding of TBC in 1893 and Taylor's visit to Moody Bible Insti-

35. T. R. O'Meara to Frost, 4 April 1910, in O'Meara Correspondence, Wycliffe College archives.

36. John G. Stackhouse, Jr., "Proclaiming the Word: Canadian Evangelicalism since World War I" (Ph.D. diss., Univ. of Chicago, 1987), chap. 3: "Toronto Bible College," 20-21.

tute the following year brought the mission to greater prominence, with the result that in 1894 alone, over thirty Moody students applied to the CIM. Frederick A. Steven, the former superintendent of Jiangxi province, where the first parties of Americans were stationed, was responsible for much of the enlargement during the six years (1890–1896) he was seconded to the Toronto office. He traveled widely, for months at a time, throughout the United States and Canada. He also organized the Prayer Union, which eventually numbered over a hundred chapters and several thousand members and was copied in Britain, Australia, and China. He was also first editor of the North American edition of *China's Millions* (1893), the mission's monthly magazine (now published under the title *East Asia's Millions*), which Frost called the CIM's "chief deputation worker."[37]

As a result of the publicity, applications started to pour in at the rate of a hundred a year; in 1895, the Toronto home sent thirty new missionaries to China and housed twice that many candidates. Money, too, started pouring in: in its first year, 1888, the mission had raised $3,400, and by 1895, $30,000. By the end of its first decade, Frost exclaimed that "God's grace rolled over us in billows."[38]

This account makes it seem as though the CIM in North America moved exponentially from victory unto victory—as indeed it did according to its members' spiritual testimonies. But Henry Frost, his family, and the multitude of candidates living in the mission home often suffered times of severe testing. On many occasions the tables were set for dinner, and not a scrap of food was in the house. Miraculously, it seemed, someone would appear at the door with a brace of partridges, a load of coal in the dead of winter, or a check made out in exactly the amount prayed for. So, the CIM family literally prayed without ceasing and blessed God for their adversity. "We lived from hand to mouth in those days," Frost recalled, but it was "God's

---

37. Frost, *Memoirs*, 512. Steven had also worked among the tribes in southwest China, and the concern he showed for them while in Canada led to the designation of an American missionary, Mrs. F. B. Webb, as the first full-time pioneer to these tribes; ibid., 448. See also Taylor, *"By Faith . . . ,"* 213-14.

38. Frost, *Memoirs*, 545.

hand and our mouth; and this is a distinction which makes a great difference. . . . Our episodes of scarcity were intended to be new revealings of God's love and power, if only we could be attentive to the inner meaning of things."[39]

Before he joined the CIM, Henry Frost had pledged himself never to go into debt, even to the fraction of a penny. Consequently, he instituted the mission's policy as literally as the missionaries in the field were expected to do. For example, he refused to permit the mission to sign a mortgage—although he did devise the practice of allowing council members to sign as proxies on its behalf. Frost, like Hudson Taylor, scrupulously avoided making public appeals, not even telling trusted, generous friends of pressing needs. "God was our only confidant in money matters," he wrote. This stringent policy shocked—and deeply impressed—staunch supporters like D. L. Moody.[40]

Moreover, the mission refused to spend funds for the work at home that were designated for the field. So, at a time when Frost was sending thousands of dollars to China—because the donors had noted, however casually, that the money be used to save the Chinese—the Toronto home was passing through continual crises. Frost, however, asked Taylor not to mention these to the London or China Councils. Not until the early 1900s was the home work—candidates' training, literature production and distribution, deputation speakers, as well as Frost's own family needs—placed on the same footing as the field work and all funds put into the general account.[41]

By 1901, the CIM was in an anomalous situation. Although it was located in Canada, about half of its missionaries and three-

39. Ibid., 397.
40. Ibid., 307. In 1899, Frost wrote a "frank" letter to Taylor, criticizing him because he had suggested Frost put a notice in *China's Millions* about the need for money to pay off the mortgage; Frost saw this as an indirect appeal (ibid., 581-83).
41. The thorniest issue was special support, which had been a necessity in the first years when people were encouraged to undertake support for specific missionaries. Having one group with an assured income and the others on a fluctuating one was inconsistent with the faith principles of the CIM, but the issue was not resolved until 1904, after years of discussion; thereafter all monies went into the general fund (*Memoirs*, 529-37, 550-54).

quarters of its general constituency were south of the border. As Frost put it,

> Mr. [Joshua S.] Helmer [treasurer of the Toronto office] and I were Americans, but we were living on British soil. *China's Millions,* our monthly paper, was printed in Toronto, but its chief circulation was in the States. Our Prayer Union was centralized in our Canadian centre, but the larger part of its membership was in America. And, most interestingly, our greatest opportunity for witnessing to the needs of China was in the States, but almost all of our speakers were from Great Britain.[42]

Ever since he had moved to Canada in 1889, Frost "never gave up looking for a new movement of the cloud, this time toward the States,"[43] and in 1901, he gained the support of Hudson Taylor's son, Dr. Howard Taylor, who was touring the eastern states with the SVM. When the mission was offered a spacious house in Norristown, a suburb of Philadelphia, Frost decided to move there with what seemed to the Toronto Council to be precipitous haste. Frost hoped the internationalization of the CIM would mean supranationalization, "keeping the national idea in the background."[44] It came as a surprise that his strongest supporters in Canada thought he was deserting the work and felt "antagonism" toward the superior attitude of Philadelphia. Although technically the two offices were equal and the council members sat on both councils, the Philadelphia office remained the North American headquarters until 1970, when William W. Tyler was named first home director for Canada.[45]

Frost compared his first years in Philadelphia to the death of an ear of corn. He left the mission fellowship in Toronto, where he was in demand as a speaker, for the isolation of a city

42. Ibid., 523; see also *China's Millions* 9 (December 1901): 135.
43. Frost, *Memoirs,* 570.
44. Ibid., 523, 643.
45. The formation of an independent Home Centre in Toronto was not just the result of Canadian nationalism in the mission but was due primarily to the prodding of the Canadian government, which saw the Canadian CIM as a channel for funds going to the United States; a number of other missions in the same situation (including the SIM and CMA) followed suit (interview with W. W. Tyler, Toronto, August 1988).

where few people showed any interest in the mission, and his appointment calendar was blank. The weekly prayer meeting never attracted more than six people. At the downtown office, those who did drop in were often "cranks and had vagaries in faith and prophecy which they desired to set forth in detail." In spite of the "dismal failure," Frost held to his course "by a sort of hard, grim faith."[46]

"Gradually," Frost wrote, "I became aware of the fact that my expositional, devotional and premillennial presentation of God's Word was not particularly welcomed by American Christians." As he explained to J. W. Stevenson, secretary of the China Council:

> The standard of doctrine and life in the States is much lower than that which prevails in Canada, and apostacy has increased so rapidly in these eastern parts that it is impossible to tell what one is going to meet with, even in the most apparently spiritual persons. This is affecting us in two directions: first, it is making it difficult to secure Council members of the right sort; and second, it is becoming increasingly perplexing to solve the question as to what persons and organizations one can or cannot have fellowship with. It is apparent that the great apostacy which the Scripture connects with the last days is advancing upon us, and I feel that we are going to find it more and more difficult to determine just what our course of life should be.[47]

A curious phenomenon occurred during this period: the number of new missionaries dropped by half, but donations doubled. In its first decade, 1888–1897, the North American CIM had dispatched 123 missionaries (71 women, 52 men), more than in the next two decades, 1898–1917: 116 (76 women, 40 men). Meanwhile, the annual income increased from $36,000 in 1897 (ten-year total of $215,000) to $73,000 in 1907 (ten-year total of $509,000) and to $175,000 in 1917 (ten-year total $890,000). This prosperity came from fact that Frost was now in "intimate contact" with wealthy patrons, such as Horace Coleman, who bought the mission home in Norristown, and Miss Charlesanna Huston, who purchased the home in Germantown when the

46. Frost, *Memoirs*, 644, 650-51.
47. Frost to Stevenson, 15 August 1902, in ibid., 699-89.

mission moved there. In 1914, the estate of William Borden, the milk company heir who died on his way to China, gave the mission at least $250,000.[48]

During this bleak period, Frost formulated a new principle: "Right is right, whatever the issue may be; and it is right to do right irrespective of all consequences."[49]

Within a few months of his move, he was called upon to test this resolve. Stanley Smith, one of the Cambridge Seven, had adopted "conditional immortality" views, the theory of "the larger hope, which signifies that all men will come to believe in Christ and so be saved, some in this life, and the others, as a result of adequate punishment and suffering, in the life to come." Smith based this on his interpretation of the New Testament word *alon* ("eon") to mean limited rather than eternal time.

Smith's beliefs had no direct bearing on North America, but Frost felt that each member of the mission "should be required to hold fully and continually to the Constitution of the Mission, including its *Doctrinal Basis*, and, therefore, that Mr. Smith should be asked to retire." The situation was so critical that Frost was asked to go to London, where he found the council—with only one exception—in favor of showing "toleration" and "leniency with an old and esteemed member." Frost used arguments that were repeated extensively by American fundamentalists a decade or two later: allowing Smith to remain in communion would "imperil the spiritual interests of the other members" and would mean "changing the character of the Mission and the losing of its evangelical testimony." Frost convinced the London Council, but this body was only advisory to Hudson Taylor, who favored a policy of toleration, even if that meant allowing a broad interpretation of the *Doctrinal Basis*. Taylor was at this time old and frail and living in Switzerland, and Frost was deputed to take London's resolution to him.

"For the first time in my life, I shrank from meeting Mr. Taylor," Frost wrote. The meeting was bitter. Taylor was like granite. He called Frost "disloyal" and "a disturber of the peace." He

48. Mrs. Howard Taylor, *Borden of Yale*, rev. ed. (London: CIM/OMF, 1952), 176.

49. Frost, *Memoirs*, 668.

said that if Frost continued, he himself would resign. Later, in a letter, he called Frost's position "a temptation of the evil one. . . . Have faith in God, dear brother, and hands off, and He will do well and wisely." Nevertheless Frost felt compelled to speak "frankly" and finally to "sever" the intimate relationship with Taylor.[50]

Taylor reluctantly acceded to London's demand and asked Smith to resign. But Smith refused and continued to publish "almost tomes" on the subject of the larger hope. The controversy dragged on for years, and in 1904, Frost was called to China and traveled there with Howard Taylor. Once again, he found every member of the council (including D. E. Hoste), with only two exceptions (one of whom was Howard Taylor, who thus opposed his own father), set against the North American policy of no toleration. Not only did he convince the council of the need to expel Smith, but also to change the *Principles and Practice.* It had stated that if a missionary changed his views, "he must be prepared to resign"; this was amended to "he will be required to resign." Frost confided in his memoirs that if the council had not taken this step, "our North American part of the Mission, on my return home, would have separated from the work at large and started an independent service."[51]

Frost concluded from the episode that Smith, because of his long contact with "the mystery of the Christless multitudes of heathenism," had made "the unintentional mistake of interpreting the Scriptures by heathenism rather than heathenism by the Scriptures."[52] Barely a few years later, however, he was called upon to deal with another of the Cambridge Seven, Cecil Polhill, whose contact with non-Christians brought him to a very different conclusion, namely, to pentecostal manifestations encouraged by Goforth's revival of 1907-8. Being a Pres-

---

50. Quotations and information in the three preceding paragraphs taken from ibid., 653-61; Taylor's letter to Frost is in the same work, p. 691. In 1891, Frost had traveled with Smith in China, and had found Smith's views "legalistic" because he refused to use the term *Reverend* in addressing a minister, since this was one of the titles of God; *Memoirs*, 379-83.

51. Ibid., 687-709, esp. p. 708. This "major episode" in Frost's life is mentioned anonymously in Taylor, *"By Faith . . . ,"* 262-64.

52. Frost, *Memoirs*, 653.

byterian, Frost had an innate mistrust of "emotionalism" and the performing of miracles. But on his own trips to China he had witnessed events that convinced him of the continuance of apostolic days: he had a physical encounter with Satan, for example, and was cured by divine intervention. These led him to further examination of prophecy. If people—missionaries and Chinese alike—could cast out devils like Pastor Hsi, the opium-den convert,53 or speak in tongues in China, why could they not do the same feats in America? Frost steered the mission on the narrow evangelical path between liberal and pentecostal faith with the result that, a decade later, when the battle started against modernist incursions into missions, the CIM was prepared. It knew what it stood for.

By 1914, the CIM had become well established in the United States, particularly in the Philadelphia-Boston-Chicago triangle. It had an American in the Toronto home, J. S. Helmer, Frost's old associate from Lockport, New York (assisted by his son, Frederic, who later took over as secretary), and a Canadian in Philadelphia, William King of Montreal. Compared to the Canadian Council, the American Council was still modest, with eight members over against fourteen in Toronto. Still concentrated in the Philadelphia area, it included ministers W. J. Erdman and his son Charles, D. M. Stearns of the Church of the Atonement in Germantown, and Reuben A. Torrey, who "came closest to being Moody's successor";54 among the laymen was the benefactor Horace Coleman.

53. Missionaries, evangelicals in particular, were preconditioned to interpret China not as it was, but as though it were the Holy Land in biblical times. As Pastor Hsi's biographer explained, "in lands where Christianity has long held sway, the special manifestations such as demonical possession, and the casting out of evil spirits in answer to prayer . . . are comparatively unknown; the conditions among the heathen being more akin to those prevailing when and where the Gospel was first propagated; it is not surprising that a corresponding energy of the powers of evil should be met with in missionary work to-day" (Mrs. Howard Taylor, *Pastor Hsi: One of China's Christians* [London: CIM, 1903], xix-xxi). As late as 1948, *China's Millions* was regularly carrying stories about missionaries and Chinese casting out devils (e.g., *China's Millions* 46 [July 1948]: 102). For Frost's encounter with Satan, see *Memoirs*, 371; this incident is not mentioned in *"By Faith. . . ."* Frost described Satan as "strikingly handsome and benign . . . [but] his eyes had in their depths the fire and venom of hell," and he warned Frost, "If you do go on, I'll hound you to the day of your death."

54. Marsden, *Fundamentalism and American Culture*, 47. C. I. Scofield was also nearby often; he helped found the Philadelphia School of the Bible in 1913.

Yet, that year, almost inexplicably, Henry Frost took another "leap into the dark." For some years he had been planning to retire to a more contemplative life in Princeton, home of his alma mater, but on the day he was to move, the house he had rented was sold to a third party. Impulsively, he bought a train ticket up to Summit, New Jersey, closer to New York. "This *was* darkness," he recalled, and he reentered the mission work. He explained his return by saying that he was a pioneer, and when helpers came in, he was not able to delegate responsibility. So, after he had laid foundations, he wrote, "my presence in a given center of the Mission was a sort of 'necessary evil.'"[55]

Freed from the day-to-day operations of the CIM, however, Frost turned to a new "somewhat peculiar mission which was quite apart from my work for the Mission." This was "the cure of souls ... to minister to those in need and especially to those in sorrow was my greatest joy."[56] He had long felt that foreign missions had something to teach the North American people, and now, in order to save the American soul from the dangers of modernism, he wrote many expositions on historical prophecy, the spiritual condition of the heathen, and "miraculous healing" (which he carefully differentiated from divine healing because, as he wrote, all healing is divine). Although these books often use material from China, they are not about missions *per se*, for he had last visited China in 1904. In writing them, he worked closely with fundamentalist leaders like R. A. Torrey, C. I. Scofield, and Charles G. Trumbull, editor of *The Sunday School Times* and founder of the American Keswick movement for "the victorious life."[57]

This new direction for the CIM was shown by two interrelated events of 1915, the year after Frost moved to Summit. The first was a disagreement with D. E. Hoste, the mission's general director, over Hoste's appointment of W. B. Sloan, the

---

55. Frost, *Memoirs*, 790.

56. Ibid., 757-58.

57. Several of Frost's books were published by *The Sunday School Times*. The preface to his pamphlet *The Spiritual Condition of the Heathen* (Philadelphia: CIM, n.d.) states that it had been approved by "well-known Evangelists, Teachers in Bible Training Schools and Professors in Theological Seminaries ... [so] the convictions set forth are not only those of the writer but also of persons who are particularly well fitted to form judgement."

assistant director in London, to the continuation committee of the Edinburgh missionary conference of 1910. Frost expressed his doubts concerning "the scripturalness of coordinating evangelical and nonevangelical missionary agencies," and after both Hoste and Sloan came to Summit, Sloan resigned from the committee. This, Frost wrote, "gave us in North America a new sense of spiritual freedom."[58] Over the next few years Frost withdrew the CIM from ecumenical alliances that it had formerly strongly supported. Its membership in the Associated Boards of Foreign Mission Societies was replaced by a new conservative evangelical network of faith missions, the Interdenominational Foreign Mission Association, of which Frost was co-founder, along with R. V. Bingham and others, in 1917.[59] Despite the American movement, the CIM in China did participate in one final ecumenical experiment when it joined the National Christian Council in 1922; it withdrew five years later when the NCC refused to endorse a doctrinal statement for membership. "Separation is forced upon us," the China Council stated.[60]

The second event of 1915 was the resuscitation of the Bible conferences at Niagara-on-the-Lake to commemorate the fiftieth anniversary of the CIM's founding in England. The speakers were "exclusively" officials, council members, and missionaries of the CIM. As Frost explained to Principal O'Meara of Wycliffe, "The testimony will cover three lines: first, the fundamentals of the faith; second, themes which make for the deepening of the spiritual life; and third, missions. The first

---

58. Frost, *Memoirs*, 791-94.

59. Edwin L. Frizen, Jr., "An Historical Study of the Interdenominational Foreign Mission Association in Relation to Evangelical Unity and Cooperation" (D.Miss. project, Trinity Evangelical Divinity School, 1981), 1-13. This withdrawal and reaffiliation was only a half-way separatism, since members of the mission continued their prior denominational affiliations.

60. "Minutes of the China Council meeting held in Shanghai on Friday, March 12, 1926," in Archives of the Billy Graham Center, CN 215, box 2, file 39. Since 1925, every issue of *China's Millions* contained the *Doctrinal Basis*, along with the resolution adopted that year: "In view of the present day ambiguity of thought and language, the Directors and Councils of the Mission have thought it well to reaffirm their agreement with the strictly conservative and evangelical interpretation of the great doctrines of the Christian faith."

subject will naturally include prophesy, and, while the testimony will be premillennial, entire freedom will be granted to each speaker as touching details."[61] The Niagara conference continued for six years, until 1920. "It was a wonderful thing in the life of the country, Canadian and American," Frost recalled, to hold meetings where "Christians could be assured that no heresies, ancient or modern, would be taught."[62]

Rather than diminishing the CIM, this attempt to maintain its exclusive evangelical witness led to its growth from a small, regionally based mission to a continental enterprise. This was accomplished by the opening of subcenters, where a missionary couple resided and carried on deputation tours. These were London, Ontario (1904, under F. A. Steven, which opened southwestern Ontario and the American Midwest); Vancouver (1916); Chicago (1924, under Isaac Page); and Los Angeles (1926). The most important was Vancouver, the terminus of both the transcontinental Canadian Pacific Railway and the CPR "Empress" steamship line. This was crucial during the First World War, when British missionaries were prevented from taking the Atlantic route, and two large parties, each numbering over thirty persons, went via Canada. Charles Thomson, the resident missionary, inaugurated the Vancouver Evangelistic Campaign in 1917 (out of which grew the Vancouver Bible Training School) and spread the mission's influence through monthly prayer meetings in the three western provinces and as far away as Montana. As a result, twenty-eight new missionaries went from the Pacific northwest to China from 1919 to 1929.

The growth of the CIM was also reflected by the number of new missionaries (131 in the decade 1918–1927, larger even than the first decade) and by the increase in the annual income, which reached $300,000 in 1926. Frost's last year as home director was his apotheosis, which climaxed in the call for "The Two Hundred" new missionaries to join the CIM in two years (1929-31). This was a time of upheaval and civil war in China, which had forced the evacuation of missionaries from the interior to the coast, and coincided with the depression in America that devas-

---

61. Frost to T. R. O'Meara, 10 March 1915, in O'Meara correspondence.
62. Frost, *Memoirs*, 831.

tated mission givings.[63] Nevertheless, by the last day of 1931, exactly 203 new missionaries had sailed to China. Of these, 92 were from North America.[64]

Henry Frost retired in 1930, at the age of 73. He was succeeded by his assistant home director, Robert Hall Glover, who had been a missionary in China under the Christian and Missionary Alliance and then professor of missions at Moody Bible Institute.

Looking back on his life, Frost expressed amazement at the mysteries of God's leading, but through it all, he believed, he had kept the CIM true to its first principles. Evangelicals are "a peculiar people" (in the biblical, if not the modern sense), he concluded, a segregated people.

> "We are evangelicals, and hence, liberalists are not attracted to us. We are evangelistic, and hence, educationalists prefer other organizations. We are, in personnel, largely premillennial, and hence, those who hold this view of truth are specially sympathetic to us. And what has been, in these particulars, is likely to be. . . . It is my earnest prayer, whatever separation from others our position may require, that we shall never allow to rise amongst us the critical and censorious spirit. . . . It has been the glory of the China Inland Mission, that, remaining preeminently true to God, it has sought to be to men, the poor as well as the rich, the false as well as the true, the bad as well as the good, their servants for Jesus' sake."[65]

With these words, Frost voiced, albeit in a gracious tone, some of the characteristic ideals of what had become the fundamentalist movement in North America. Under his leadership, the China Inland Mission became a major force in that movement, infusing it by literature and example with a strong dose of the British, faith-missions variety of sacrificial spiritual devotion. And at the same time, Frost had helped to transform this British faith mission—at least in its North American setting—into a fundamentalist institution.

63. North American contributions to the CIM dropped from $502,000 in 1929 (an unusually high amount) to $231,600 in 1930; see Taylor, "By Faith . . . ," 293.

64. There were also six members of the Scandinavian Alliance Mission (Frank Houghton, *The Two Hundred: Why They Were Needed; How They Responded; Who They Are; Where They Are* [London and Philadelphia: CIM, 1932]).

65. Frost, *Memoirs*, 347, 900.

II OUTSIDE THE PROTESTANT MISSIONARY ESTABLISHMENT, 1920–1945

4 The Loss of a Protestant Missionary Consensus: Foreign Missions and the Fundamentalist-Modernist Conflict

James Alan Patterson

Memories of the fundamentalist-modernist conflict during the 1920s and 1930s conjure up images of a sweltering small-town courtroom in Tennessee, colorful and sometimes eccentric pulpiteers sounding alarms against suspected theological subversives (on the left or the right), the partisan broadsides of religious journalists and pamphleteers, the amused and often derisive curiosity of the secular press, contentious denominational gatherings in crowded convention halls, and the traumatic ecclesiastical schisms that realigned the institutional structures of American Protestantism. In several of these dramatic scenes, some of the antagonists vigorously clashed over the character and conduct of Protestant foreign missions. Fundamentalists and liberals alike granted no special exemptions to the missionary enterprise as they waged their storied battles between the two world wars. In fact, their disputes over missions served both to intensify the theological polarization of the period and, more importantly, to transform the nature and direction of the Protestant missionary movement.

In the days "before fundamentalism,"[1] to borrow George Marsden's apt section heading, the Protestant missionary enter-

---

1. George M. Marsden, *Fundamentalism and American Culture: The Shaping of Twentieth-Century Evangelicalism, 1870–1925* (New York: Oxford Univ. Press, 1980), part one.

prise benefited from a widespread and sometimes unappreciated agreement about its essential doctrines, aims, and tasks. This notable consensus was nurtured and articulated by missionary leaders and board administrators who shared the broad evangelical vision of the late nineteenth century. The missionary consensus and its resultant unity of purpose contributed to the dynamism and vibrancy that permeated many mission endeavors between the 1880s and World War I.

The irenic spirit of Protestant missions expressed itself in three conspicuous contexts in the late nineteenth and early twentieth centuries. First, the writings and addresses of prominent missionary promoters and statesmen like James L. Barton, John R. Mott, Arthur T. Pierson, and Robert E. Speer consistently exhorted readers and hearers to seek common goals that cut across denominational lines. Second, the Protestant consensus on missions made possible the cooperative interdenominational agencies like the Foreign Missions Conference of North America, the Laymen's Missionary Movement, and the Student Volunteer Movement. Finally, this basic concurrence about missions was not confined to Protestants in America but also influenced international missionary events such as the famed Edinburgh Conference of 1910.[2]

The American Protestant missionary consensus incorporated four major components, each of which suggested a common rootage in nineteenth-century evangelicalism. First, most Protestant boards would have readily assented to the Presbyterian statement of 1920 that "the supreme and controlling aim of foreign missions is to make Jesus Christ known to all men as their Divine Savior and Lord and to persuade them to become His disciples" and to gather converts into "self-governing, self-supporting, and self-propagating churches."[3] This bedrock con-

---

2. For an exhaustive analysis of the personalities and institutions that buttressed foreign missions in the late nineteenth and early twentieth centuries, see Valentin H. Rabe, "The American Protestant Foreign Mission Movement, 1880–1920" (Ph.D. diss., Harvard Univ., 1964), condensed and published as *The Home Base of American China Missions, 1880–1920* (Cambridge: Harvard Univ. Press, 1978).

3. Quoted in Robert E. Speer, *Are Foreign Missions Done For?* (New York: Board of Foreign Missions of the Presbyterian Church in the U.S.A., 1928), 56, 81. This mirrors the missiology of nineteenth-century Congregationalist Rufus

viction that evangelism and church planting represented the urgent priority of missions did not go completely unchallenged, but it clearly functioned as a working assumption for the great majority of participants in the missionary enterprise.[4]

A second and closely related ingredient in the Protestant consensus was the doctrinal allegiance to the uniquely divine nature of Jesus Christ. Before the 1920s, missionary leaders sometimes took their Christology for granted, even when belief in the deity of Christ was widely recognized as one of the compelling motives for foreign missions. More explicit statements became necessary only after cracks began to appear in the missionary consensus in the 1920s. The Jerusalem Meeting of the International Missionary Council in 1928 set forth what had been broadly accepted in American mission circles for many years:

> Our message is Jesus Christ. He is the revelation of what God is and of what man through Him can become. In Him we come face to face with the Ultimate Reality of the universe; He makes known to us God as our Father, perfect and infinite in love and in righteousness; for in Him we find God incarnate, the final, yet ever-unfolding, revelation of God in whom we live and move and have our being.[5]

It should be added that this Christocentric approach usually implied an affirmation of the superiority of the Christian faith to non-Christian religions.[6]

Anderson. See Anderson, *Foreign Missions: Their Relations and Claims* (New York: Charles Scribner, 1869), 92, 112.

4. Dissent to the prevailing norms was expressed in Joseph E. McAfee, *World Missions from the Home Base* (New York: Revell, 1911), 103-5. See also William R. Hutchison, "Modernism and Missions: The Liberal Search for an Exportable Christianity, 1875–1935," in *The Missionary Enterprise in China and America*, ed. John K. Fairbank (Cambridge: Harvard Univ. Press, 1974), 110-26.

5. "The Council's Statement," in *The Christian Life and Message in Relation to Non-Christian Systems of Thought and Life*, eight-volume published proceedings of the Jerusalem Meeting of the International Missionary Council, March 24–April 8, 1928 (New York: International Missionary Council, 1928), 1:402. One of the important contributors to this statement was Presbyterian missions administrator Robert Speer, who earlier dealt with the issue in a number of contexts. See, e.g., his address at Northfield, Massachusetts, published as *The Deity of Christ* (New York: Revell, 1909).

6. "The Council's Statement," passim. Cf. the earlier comment by the lib-

The third element in the Protestant missionary consensus developed from the willingness of missionaries and board administrators to define and defend the social dimension of their cause. In the late nineteenth century, Presbyterian James Dennis embraced the priority of evangelism but proceeded to justify missions as "a sociological force, with a beneficent trend in the direction of elevating human society, modifying traditional evils, and introducing reformatory ideals."[7] What is remarkable in light of later fundamentalist attacks on the evils of the "social gospel" is that mission promoters before World War I generally saw no dichotomy between evangelism and social involvement. They were content to follow the guidelines of social gospeler Walter Rauschenbusch, who regarded the educational, philanthropical, and medical auxiliaries to foreign missions as "secondary" to "the regeneration of individual souls."[8]

The final integral part of the missionary consensus was the pragmatic ecumenism that undergirded cooperative mission efforts like the Student Volunteer Movement and the Foreign Missions Conference of North America. Most missionary leaders remained cool to an institutional union of diverse church bodies, but they came to regard rigid insistence on denominational distinctives as a hindrance to world evangelization. Robert Speer expressed a commonly held view when he said that

in our cooperative missionary undertakings and associations identity of opinion on the whole body of Christian doctrine is not req-

---

eral William Newton Clarke: "The attitude of the religion that bears the name of Jesus Christ is not one of compromise, but one of conflict and conquest. It proposes to displace the other religions" (*A Study of Christian Missions* [New York: Charles Scribner's Sons, 1900], 107).

7. James S. Dennis, *Christian Missions and Social Progress*, 2 vols. (New York: Revell, 1897), 1:23. Many other missionary supporters echoed Dennis's interest in social concern. See James L. Barton, *Human Progress Through Missions* (New York: Revell, 1912); Edward W. Capen, *Sociological Progress in Mission Lands* (New York: Revell, 1914); William H. P. Faunce, *The Social Aspects of Foreign Missions* (New York: Missionary Movement of the United States and Canada, 1914); and Alva W. Taylor, *The Social Work of Christian Missions* (Cincinnati: Foreign Christian Missionary Society, 1914).

8. Walter Rauschenbusch, "Conceptions of Missions," in *The Social Gospel in America, 1870–1920*, ed. Robert T. Handy (New York: Oxford Univ. Press, 1966), 269, 271.

uisite; . . . but . . . one thing only is essential, and that is that we should hold a fundamentally unitary faith in and about our Lord Jesus Christ as He is set forth in the New Testament.[9]

Fundamentalists later displayed intense hostility toward this ecumenism, viewing it as an essential feature of modernism, but Timothy Smith has shown that nineteenth-century evangelicals were the primary architects for the ecumenical spirit of the missionary movement.[10]

Although this four-part Protestant consensus served the missionary movement well for many years, it gradually unraveled in the 1920s and 1930s. Some of the blame for this can be attributed to financial and cultural issues that plagued not only the mission agencies but also Protestantism in general during this period.[11] However, the missionary consensus probably could have weathered those storms if it had not been for the devastating effects of the fundamentalist-modernist conflict. On the right, fundamentalists worried that crucial theological verities were being compromised—so they initiated divisive searches for modernists among the denominational boards, and some even set up competing missionary organizations. On the left, liberals began to clamor for a radically different approach to foreign missions that sacrificed traditional conceptions of evangelism and the relationship of Christianity to other faiths. Caught in this squeeze, the previously resilient Protestant missionary consensus fell victim by the mid-1930s. While the controversies between fundamentalists and liberals cannot completely explain this development, they contributed heavily to the loss of consensus.

The most visible disputes over missions instigated by fundamentalists occurred in the Northern Baptist Convention and the (northern) Presbyterian Church in the U.S.A. Since conservatives in both ecclesiastical bodies undertook a general investigation of all their respective denominational agencies, it would be

9. Robert E. Speer, "Is Identity of Doctrinal Opinion Necessary to Continued Missionary Co-operation?" *International Review of Missions* 12 (1923): 502.

10. Timothy L. Smith, "The Evangelical Kaleidoscope and the Call to Christian Unity," *Christian Scholar's Review* 15 (1986): 135-36.

11. For an account of the financial and cultural crises, see James Alan Patterson, "Robert E. Speer and the Crisis of the American Protestant Missionary Movement, 1920–1937" (Ph.D. diss., Princeton Theological Seminary, 1980), 66-71.

too much to claim that concerns about foreign missions directly precipitated their combative activities. Nonetheless, fundamentalists quickly established the missionary enterprise as one of their pivotal fronts for stemming the perceived liberal tide.

Baptist and Presbyterian fundamentalists fought separate battles in the context of two very different church polities, yet their campaigns exhibited some remarkable similarities. First, the struggles over foreign missions eventually attracted most of the prominent fundamentalist personalities in both denominations. It is interesting to note that five of the seven "voices" in C. Allyn Russell's collection of fundamentalist biographies took part at some point in the conflicts over missions: Presbyterians Clarence E. Macartney and J. Gresham Machen and Baptists Jasper C. Massee, William Bell Riley, and John Roach Straton.[12] To this list can be added Carl McIntire, a Presbyterian who allied himself with Machen for a time, and W. H. Griffith Thomas, an Episcopalian who was one of the first to raise questions about the doctrinal integrity of Presbyterian missionaries.[13] These men led the assaults on the American Baptist Foreign Mission Society (ABFMS) and the Presbyterian Board of Foreign Missions, even though they had built their reputations in other contexts and were not particularly known or distinguished for their involvement in missionary causes.

A second common thread can be found in the specific issues that surfaced during the Baptist and Presbyterian controversies. Fundamentalists in both groups raised issues that correlated very closely to the various elements of the traditional missionary consensus. They emphasized the priority of evangelism and the centrality of Christ's divine nature, using these items to measure the orthodoxy of missionaries and board officers. At

12. C. Allyn Russell, *Voices of American Fundamentalism: Seven Biographical Studies* (Philadelphia: Westminster, 1976). The exceptions are William Jennings Bryan and J. Frank Norris. Norris, a disruptive presence in Southern Baptist circles, had a very brief association with the Northern Baptist Convention. Within a month of assuming the pastorate of Temple Baptist Church, Detroit, in 1935, he withdrew it from the Northern Convention. See Russell, 40.

13. Patterson, "Speer and the Crisis," 129-31, 161-63. See W. H. Griffith Thomas, "Modernism in China," *Princeton Theological Review* 19 (1921): 630-71, for one of the earliest salvos in the conflicts over missions.

the same time, they challenged the prevailing consensus on the points of social involvement and ecumenism.

In the Northern Baptist Convention, concern over the theological health of missionaries was intimately linked to the fundamentalist push for the adoption of a denominational confession or creedal statement. Their failure in this endeavor in 1922 seemed to heighten their frustration, since it deprived them of a convenient tool to assist in their search for modernist missionaries. They did succeed in persuading the convention to launch an investigation of missions in 1924, and a commission of seven was empowered to review allegations of heresy among Baptist missionaries. After a year of study, the commission found only four missionaries whose doctrinal views justified a recall from the field. Still, fundamentalists were not convinced by this or later affirmations of the Baptist missionary corps for two apparent reasons. First, they remained skeptical of what they termed the ABFMS's "inclusive" policy, which allowed for some theological latitude in the appointment of missionaries. Second, they usually suspected that those active in the social dimensions of missions were surely modernists.

Throughout the 1920s, 1930s, and again in the 1940s, Baptist fundamentalists fought the missionary policies of their denomination, which they felt harbored and encouraged modernism. Chester Tulga, who joined other dissidents in the Conservative Baptist Fellowship, voiced the conclusion that most fundamentalists shared after their failure to change the ABFMS:

> Fundamentalism and modernism are mutually exclusive and all attempts to hold them together in a working fellowship results in loss of integrity for both and eventually to apostasy for the orthodox. To betray the historic faith in the interests of denominational loyalty is to give aid and comfort to the coming world apostasy. . . . Loyalty to a modernistic denomination makes the profession of orthodoxy an empty profession.[14]

14. Chester Earl Tulga, *The Foreign Missions Controversy in the Northern Baptist Convention, 1919–1949: Thirty Years of Stuggle* (Chicago: Conservative Baptist Fellowship, 1950), 201. For an "establishment" account, see Robert G. Torbet, *Venture of Faith: The Story of the American Baptist Foreign Mission Society and the Woman's American Baptist Foreign Mission Society, 1814–1954* (Philadelphia: Judson, 1955), 407-23.

Clearly, polarization was one of the chief products of Baptist struggles over missions.

Similar issues dominated the agenda of Presbyterian fundamentalists, although for a shorter period of time. The Presbyterian Church was a confessional church, so no analogous attempt was made by fundamentalists to commit their denomination to a new creedal statement. However, the Auburn Affirmation of 1924, a call for theological toleration, agitated the Presbyterian right. They utilized that document thereafter to help in their hunt for modernists affiliated with the Presbyterian Board of Foreign Missions. Thomas, Machen, and McIntire, among others, led the charge against liberals and social gospelers, who allegedly had infiltrated the board and undermined its evangelical character. Machen especially scrutinized the mission program of his church, convinced that numerous missionaries were modernists and that board leadership covered this up by being vague, evasive, and doctrinally "indifferentist." The fact that two respected conservatives, Robert Dick Wilson and Donald Grey Barnhouse, gave relatively high marks to the Presbyterian missionary corps in two different decades did not deter Machen's crusade.[15]

Presbyterian fundamentalists raised the issue of ecumenism and cooperative efforts overseas more frequently than their Baptist counterparts, probably because Presbyterians were more inclined toward ecumenical ventures.[16] Reformed precisionists like Machen and John Clover Monsma particularly fretted over the erosion of confessional distinctives in ecumenical contexts. Monsma, the general secretary of the Reformation Fellowship, argued that cooperative projects in the mission field led to the

15. On the positive evaluations by Wilson (1923) and Barnhouse (1935), see Patterson, "Speer and the Crisis," 135, 163. On Machen and the Presbyterian Board, see idem, "Robert E. Speer, J. Gresham Machen, and the Presbyterian Board of Foreign Missions," *American Presbyterians: Journal of Presbyterian History* 64 (1986): 58-68. Cf. J. Gresham Machen, *Modernism and the Board of Foreign Missions of the Presbyterian Church in the U.S.A.* (Philadelphia: by the author, 1933). On the Auburn credo, see Charles E. Quirk, "The 'Auburn' Affirmation: A Critical Narrative of the Document Designed to Safeguard the Unity and Liberty of the Presbyterian Church in the United States of America in 1924" (Ph.D. diss., Univ. of Iowa, 1967).

16. On Baptist resistance to interdenominational cooperation in missions, see Russell, *Voices of Fundamentalism*, 125.

suppression of "our peculiarly Presbyterian, Calvinistic, doctrines."[17] Thus some Presbyterian fundamentalists, particularly
those of the "Old School" tradition, regarded this feature of the
Protestant missionary consensus as disposable and even as a
threat to the elements they affirmed, such as the priority of evangelism and the deity of Christ.[18]

A third similarity in the Baptist and Presbyterian experiences was reflected in the official response to fundamentalist
protests. Beleaguered mission board administrators answered
their more conservative critics by valiantly attempting to
uphold the Protestant missionary consensus in all of its points.
This proved to be a thankless task in both denominations as the
fundamentalists refused to be mollified by a framework that included social action and ecumenism.

The Board of Managers of the ABFMS began their defense
by reaffirming their commitment to the centrality of evangelism. In late 1923, they drafted a statement, later presented in
their report to the heated Milwaukee convention of 1924, in
which evangelism was ranked ahead of social witness in their
priorities:

> We definitely and positively repudiate the idea that social ser-
> vice is the supreme thing, and so far as we are aware, no one con-
> nected with our Society would think of substituting it for salvation.
> At the same time, we believe that we are following in the steps of
> our Master when we establish hospitals for the sick, and support
> other efforts to relieve human poverty and suffering. . . . Far from
> substituting social service for salvation, we teach that salvation of
> the individual and the world must be found in Christ, and we point

17. John C. Monsma, *The Foreign Missionary Situation in the Presbyterian
Church in the U.S.A.* (Philadelphia: Reformation Fellowship, 1933), 11.

18. On the "Old School"/"New School" tensions in Presbyterianism, see
Lefferts A. Loetscher, *The Broadening Church: A Study of the Theological Issues in
the Presbyterian Church Since 1869* (Philadelphia: Univ. of Pennsylvania Press,
1954), 1-8; and George M. Marsden, *The Evangelical Mind and the New School Presbyterian Experience: A Case Study of Thought and Theology in Nineteenth-Century
America* (New Haven: Yale Univ. Press, 1970), 245-49. Presbyterians with "New
School" roots, such as Donald Grey Barnhouse and Charles G. Trumbull, actively
supported non-Presbyterian, independent mission agencies. See Joel A. Carpenter, "Fundamentalist Institutions and the Rise of Evangelical Protestantism,
1929–1942," *Church History* 49 (1980): 72-73.

men to him and his cross as the moving power for every form of service.[19]

In light of fundamentalist pressure, this expression of policy represented a delicate balancing act by maintaining the primacy of evangelism yet refusing to surrender the legitimacy of social involvement in foreign fields. The institutional need of denominational officers to steer a middle course failed to appease the fundamentalists, who pointed out that liberal missionaries tended to fill social-service positions that required minimal evangelistic effort.[20] Board officials and fundamentalist critics now were speaking on very different wavelengths; the mutual trust that once had made consensus possible was gone.

Equal care was demanded when the Board of Managers promised to appoint only evangelical missionaries to overseas posts and, at the same time, to continue an "inclusive" policy that permitted some limited theological liberty. Included in the board's report to the Seattle convention of 1925 was a traditional definition of the gospel drawn up the previous year, which utilized the terminology of good news, eternal life, salvation, regeneration, and sanctification. This statement concluded within the accepted parameters of the Protestant missionary consensus: "The only reason we have for accepting this gospel is our belief in the deity of Christ in whom we see the Father, a faith founded on the trustworthiness of the Scriptures, and the fact that we have experienced this salvation in our own hearts."[21] Fundamentalists cheered this declaration but claimed that it was undermined by excessive theological toleration.

The response by mission board officials to fundamentalist discontent followed a similar pattern in the Presbyterian Church. Much of the burden for answering fundamentalist criti-

---

19. ABFMS, *110th Annual Report*. Presented by the Board of Managers at the Annual Meeting held in Milwaukee, Wisconsin, May 28–June 3, 1924 (New York: Foreign Mission Headquarters, 1924), 69.

20. Tulga, *Foreign Missions Controversy*, 11, 74.

21. ABFMS, *111th Annual Report*. Presented by the Board of Managers at the Annual Meeting held in Seattle, Washington, June 30–July 5, 1925 (New York: Foreign Mission Headquarters, 1925), 56.

cisms fell on Robert Speer, a missionary statesman thoroughly nurtured in the Protestant consensus, who had served the Presbyterian board as a secretary since 1891. Speer was a theological conservative, but he consistently aired his impatience with doctrinal wrangling, especially when it deflected the church from her missionary task. He came to view Presbyterian fundamentalists, and interested outsiders like Griffith Thomas, as a disruptive force, willing to sacrifice the Presbyterian missionary program for the sake of doctrinal precision.

From 1920 until his retirement in 1937, Speer aggressively defended the orthodoxy of Presbyterian missionaries and the integrity of his board as an evangelical agency. In his epic struggle with Machen, he also contended that his own theological perspective was more biblical than that of the Westminster Seminary founder: "You use some words in your statement of essential doctrine which are not found in the Scriptures at all. I can state my convictions wholly in the very words of the Scriptures."[22] As their debate proceeded, it became increasingly apparent that they defined both their doctrinal priorities and their allegiance to the inherited Protestant consensus quite differently.

The final resemblance between the fundamentalist campaigns in the Northern Baptist Convention and the Presbyterian Church is found in their results. In both denominations, the fundamentalists lost their battles and created competing missionary organizations. Northern Baptist fundamentalists embarked on one exodus in 1932 with the formation of the General Association of Regular Baptist Churches (GARBC). This move was not entirely motivated by concerns about foreign missions, but the GARBC promptly endorsed two independent Baptist mission boards formed in the 1920s, Baptist Mid-Missions and the Association of Baptists for the Evangelization of the Orient (later

22. Speer to Machen, 30 April 1929 (the Papers of Robert E. Speer in the Speer Library of Princeton Theological Seminary, Princeton, New Jersey. Hereinafter cited as Speer Papers). See also Patterson, "Speer, Machen, and the Presbyterian Board." In broad terms, this battle reflected "New School" / "Old School" issues. George M. Marsden, "The New School Heritage and Presbyterian Fundamentalism," *Westminster Theological Journal* 32 (1970): 129-47, discusses the relevance of these categories for early twentieth-century controversies.

renamed the Association of Baptists for World Evangelism). In 1943, a group of fundamentalists remaining in the Northern Baptist Convention set up the Conservative Baptist Foreign Mission Society as an alternative to the ABFMS. This group failed to obtain Northern Baptist certification, leading to a separate Conservative Baptist denomination in 1947.[23] Presbyterian separatism was less protracted, precipitated in part by Machen's inability to operate his Independent Board of Foreign Missions, organized in 1933, and still retain his ministerial credentials in the Presbyterian Church. This led to the schism of 1936 and a new denomination eventually known as the Orthodox Presbyterian Church.[24]

The polarizing effect of the confrontations between fundamentalists and denominational mission boards represents one of their unhappy and bitter fruits. For example, Robert Speer discovered that loyalty to his missionaries and his persevering attachment to the missionary consensus cost him friends. Earlier in his career, Speer had written numerous articles for the *Sunday School Times*, and he developed considerable respect for its editor, Henry Clay Trumbull. But beginning in 1933, he experienced a serious falling out with Trumbull's son and successor, Charles. Charles Trumbull went even further than Machen in personal attacks, characterizing Presbyterian board members and secretaries as "unfaithful" and bemoaning "our Modernistic Mission Board."[25] This incident reveals the often tragic personal dimension of the fundamentalist displeasure with mainstream Protestant missions. It also shows that fundamentalists often wounded the moderate upholders of the traditional consensus more deeply than they hurt their more obviously modernist enemies.

Meanwhile, modernists chipped away at the Protestant missionary consensus from the left. As early as 1886, Arthur T. Pier-

---

23. Torbet, *Venture of Faith,* 419-32. Torbet incorrectly dates the GARBC founding in 1933.

24. Patterson, "Speer and the Crisis," 158-59.

25. Charles Trumbull, "Dr. Speer's Position and Teaching," *Sunday School Times,* 25 November 1933, 737-39; and "Foreign Missionary Betrayals of the Faith," *Sunday School Times,* 23 March 1935, 195. Cf. Speer's treatment of the elder Trumbull in *Men Who Were Found Faithful* (New York: Revell, 1912), 156-70.

son expressed alarm that a "new theology" was nurturing indifference in the church toward world evangelization by deny-
ing the lost condition of the "heathen." However, there is little
evidence to suggest that new theological trends ruffled the Protestant consensus to any significant degree before World War I.[26]
By the 1920s, the effects of liberal adjustments in missionary
thinking became much more visible as comparative religion
studies influenced discussion of non-Christian faiths and de-
fused some of the pre–World War I triumphalism of the missionary movement.

Daniel Fleming, professor of missions at Union Theological
Seminary in New York, advocated a "fulfillment" theory as he
urged missionaries "to discover what values have emerged in
the age-long quest of older lands for the Divine."[27] Although he
recognized the risks of a more open approach to other religions,
he consistently defended it in several of his writings.[28]

While Fleming refused to surrender the superiority of Christianity, others looked for an ultimate faith to emerge from the
mingling together of the best of all religions. Clifford Manshardt, a liberal missionary in India, argued that the approach
of Christians toward other faiths should go beyond the tolerance
of the "fulfillment" theory to "mutual respect and co-operation." In his own Indian context, he wanted Hindus and Christians to be "all seekers together, and endeavoring to grow with
our expanding universe." More specifically, he expressed irrita-
tion at missionaries who attempted to convert non-Christians.[29]

---

26. Arthur T. Pierson, *The Crisis in Missions* (New York: Robert Carter and
Brothers, 1886), 274-99. See also the works cited in note 4 above and William R.
Hutchison, *Errand to the World: American Protestant Thought and Foreign Missions*
(Chicago: Univ. of Chicago, 1987), 91-124.

27. Daniel J. Fleming, *Whither Bound in Missions?* (New York: Association,
1925), 85.

28. Daniel J. Fleming, *Attitudes Toward Other Faiths* (New York: Association,
1928[0]; and idem, *Ways of Sharing with Other Faiths* (New York: Association, 1929).
For the broader context, see Sydney E. Ahlstrom, *The American Protestant Encounter with World Religions* (Beloit, WI: Beloit College, 1962); and Grant Wacker's
chapter in this volume, "Second Thoughts on the Great Commission: Liberal
Protestants and Foreign Missions, 1890–1940."

29. Clifford Manshardt, "Converts or Co-operation: A Study in Modern
Missions," *Journal of Religion* 8 (1928): 207-8; and idem, "Some Observations on
Mission Policies in India," *Journal of Religion* 9 (1929): 293-94, 296.

Obviously, this theology posed a direct challenge to the entire Protestant missionary tradition.

In addition, some theologians sharply dissented from the Jerusalem Statement of 1928. Archibald Baker, of the University of Chicago, targeted the Christology of the document as he rejected the view of Christ "as the one supreme revelatory *act* of God" and opted instead for a concept of Jesus "as partly the originator and partly the product of what may be called a creative *process* of God." For Baker, Jesus Christ represented "an idea and ideal in the hearts of his people, an ideal which is incarnated in human lives in the form of virtuous habits and self-sacrificing service."[30] Baker's perspective debated the very basics of classic Christian doctrine, thus reinforcing fundamentalist alarms and anticipating the heated struggles of the early 1930s.

The most salient debate over foreign missions grew out of the publication in 1932 of *Re-Thinking Missions*, the culmination of a two-year project carried out by the Laymen's Foreign Missions Inquiry. John D. Rockefeller, Jr., a major donor to Baptist missionary endeavors, initiated and financed this study. He solicited unofficial representatives from the Congregational Churches, the Methodist Episcopal Church, his own Northern Baptist Convention, the Presbyterian Church in the U.S.A., the Protestant Episcopal Church, the Reformed Church in America, and the United Presbyterian Church to serve as consultants and liaisons to their respective denominations.[31]

Rockefeller's Institute of Social and Religious Research conducted the first phase of study for the Laymen's Inquiry. The *Fact-Finders' Reports* represented the researchers' efforts in the Far East and were eventually published in the Inquiry's *Supplemental Series*.[32] In retrospect, they were probably the least controversial and most objective aspect of the entire project.

---

30. Archibald G. Baker, "Jesus Christ As Interpreted by the Missionary Enterprise," *Journal of Religion* 9 (1929): 8-9.

31. William Ernest Hocking (chairman), *Re-Thinking Missions: A Laymen's Inquiry after One Hundred Years* (New York: Harper and Brothers, 1932), ix-x; and Raymond B. Fosdick, *John D. Rockefeller, Jr., A Portrait* (New York: Harper and Brothers, 1956), 214-15.

32. Orville A. Petty, ed., *Fact-Finders' Reports*, vols. 4-7 of *Supplemental Series*, 7 vols. (New York: Harper and Brothers, 1933).

The phase of the inquiry that held the greatest relevance for the Protestant missionary consensus was assigned fo the fifteen-member Commission of Appraisal. Rockefeller personally selected William Ernest Hocking, a Harvard philosopher, to chair this group. Hocking composed the first four chapters of *Re-Thinking Missions,* the portion of the report that directly challenged the missionary consensus at the points of evangelism and the unique deity of Jesus Christ.[33]

In essence, Hocking called for a radical restructuring of the missionary enterprise's doctrinal base. He preferred that Christians approach people of other religions with a spirit of cooperation rather than conquest, calling for a sympathetic understanding of other faiths and a discovery of "whatever kindred elements there are in them." The task of the missionary then was to be "a co-worker with the forces which are making for righteousness within every religious system." Hocking contended that this mutual sharing had as its ultimate goal "unity in the completest religious truth."[34]

Naturally this obligated Hocking to consider the uniqueness of the Christian faith, a crucial conviction for the missionary consensus. He saw Christianity's distinctiveness primarily in moral terms, particularly in the "simplicity" of the teachings of Jesus.[35] Hocking avoided any definite Christological propositions and even indirectly criticized the Jerusalem Statement of 1928 by questioning the adequacy of saying "Our message is Jesus Christ." Thus Hocking restated the place of Christ in God's redemptive plan by affirming that "through Jesus and through such wills as his, God works throughout human history bringing men toward unity in a love which is universal in its sweep."[36]

Re-Thinking Missions also suggested a substantial reinterpretation of evangelism. The aim of missions, it suggested,

33. Haverford philosopher Rufus Jones assisted Hocking in writing chapter 4. Robert Speer noted the authors of the chapters in the margin of his copy of the Preliminary Report, housed with Rare Books, Speer Library, Princeton Theological Seminary.

34. Hocking, *Re-Thinking Missions,* 33, 40, 44.

35. Ibid., 49-50; see also 56-58.

36. Ibid., 52, 58.

was "to seek with people of other lands a true knowledge and love of God, expressing in life and word what we have learned through Jesus Christ, and endeavoring to give effect to his spirit in the life of the world."[37] The report further challenged the missionary consensus by emphasizing an evangelization "by living and by human service" that would spread "the Christian way of life and its spirit" by "quiet personal contact and by contagion." This view of the scope of missions also implied the sacrifice of at least some missionaries' verbal witness to Christ:

> We believe, then, that the time has come to set the educational and other philanthropic aspects of mission work free from organized responsibility to the work of conscious and direct evangelization. We must be willing to give largely without any preaching.[38]

A further implication for the Protestant consensus was the Hocking Commission's assertion that missionary priority should not be to create institutional churches on the foreign field but rather "to permeate the personal life of the individual and the fabric of human society with creative ideals and energies."[39]

Responses to this evident departure from the missionary tradition ran the entire gamut of the theological spectrum. Among the mission boards, the American Board of Commissioners for Foreign Missions (Congregational Churches) was the most favorably inclined toward the Hocking Report. The American Board sent copies to all its mission stations, accompanied by a very positive interpretive pamphlet.[40] It was one of the few boards to outline seriously the ways in which it was seeking to bring its policies and practices into conformity with the conclusions of *Re-Thinking Missions*. While expressing its desire for a greater emphasis on "our conviction of the uniqueness of the

37. Ibid., 59.
38. Ibid., 65, 70.
39. Ibid., 108-9; see also 327-28.
40. "A Statement of American Board's Attitude to Laymen's Report," *Missionary Herald* 129 (1933): 53. The pamphlet was *Re-Thinking Missions with the American Board* (Boston: ABCFM, n.d.).

revelation of God in Christ," the ABCFM happily acknowledged that "the spirit of the Report is not unlike that which actuates our own denomination."[41]

At the other pole, *Re-Thinking Missions* met with wholesale condemnation. The *Sunday School Times* spoke for many fundamentalists in calling the Laymen's Inquiry "the betrayal commission" and in labeling the report a "strange, sinister, Satanic document."[42] Other conservative journals echoed this fear of a "modernist plot" to undermine foreign missions.[43] Thus the debate over the Laymen's Report very quickly became part of a larger theological conflict. Clarence Macartney, pastor of Pittsburgh's First Presbyterian Church, welcomed the publication of the report as a golden opportunity to resume the long-standing battle with modernism and, at the same time, to force "middle-of-the-roaders" and "peace-at-any-price" men to take a stand.[44]

But most Protestant mission leaders and boards replied to *Re-Thinking Missions* from the framework of the missionary consensus. While they accepted some of the report's practical suggestions, they made it clear that they were in no hurry to surrender traditional, evangelical conceptions of missions. They expressed particular consternation over Hocking's positions on Christology, the relation of Christianity to other religions, and the primary aim of foreign missions. In addition, many negative criticisms were aired at special meetings sponsored by the For-

41. "A Statement of American Board's Attitude," 49; *The American Board and the Laymen's Report* (Boston: ABCFM, 1933), 1.

42. "The Betrayal Commission: Reports on the Laymen's Foreign Missions Inquiry," *Sunday School Times*, 7 January 1933, 7.

43. See, e.g., "Foreign Missions Called to Account," *Presbyterian*, 8 December 1932, 4. Historian Charles E. Harvey lends some plausibility to the fundamentalist fear that John D. Rockefeller, Jr., the leading instigator of the Laymen's Inquiry, was plotting to unite American Protestants under liberal auspices. See Harvey's several articles, notably "John D. Rockefeller, Jr., and the Interchurch World Movement of 1919–1920: A Different Angle on the Ecumenical Movement," *Church History* 51 (1982): 198-209; "Religion and Industrial Relations: John D. Rockefeller, Jr., and the Interchurch World Movement of 1919–1920," *Research in Political Economy* 4 (1981): 199-227; and "Speer Versus Rockefeller and Mott, 1910–1935," *Journal of Presbyterian History* 60 (1982): 283-99.

44. Clarence E. Macartney, "'Renouncing Missions' or 'Modernism Unmasked,'" *Presbyterian*, 26 January 1933, 6.

eign Missions Conference of North America.[45] The debate between liberals, fundamentalists, and the upholders of the Protestant consensus eventually settled down, but not before it helped
to polarize positions on the nature and aim of foreign missions.

One would think that the moderate champions of the missions consensus and their fundamentalist antagonists would
find a common cause in opposing the Laymen's Report, but they
no longer trusted each other. Militants such as Machen accused
moderates such as Speer of soft-pedaling their critiques and thus
trying to accommodate the liberals. The fight over *Re-Thinking
Missions* was in fact a fatal blow to the missions consensus.[46] In
its wake was a greater polarization than had ever existed in the
long history of American Protestant missions. As the old pragmatic unity of an earlier generation disappeared, the missionary movement was seriously weakened.

The most enduring legacy of the battles of the 1920s and
1930s, then, is to be found in the evangelical/conciliar and evan-
gelism/social-action polarities that continue to divide Protestant missions half a century later. There has been some evident
convergence in discussions of missions' cultural context and the
cultural integrity and independence of non-Western churches,
as well as some preliminary attempts to synthesize the evangelical and ecumenical traditions.[47] Further, recent historical schol-

45. On the theological issues, see Kenneth Scott Latourette, "The Laymen's
Foreign Missions Inquiry: The Report of Its Commission of Appraisal," *International Review of Missions* 22 (1933): 153-73; John A. Mackay, "The Theology of
the Laymen's Foreign Missions Inquiry," *International Review of Missions* 22
(1933): 174-88; and Robert E. Speer, *"Re-Thinking Missions" Examined* (New York:
Revell, 1933). On the FMCNA conferences, see Robert E. Speer to Margaret Speer
(daughter), 1 November 1933, Speer Papers.

46. Hutchison, *Errand to the World*, 158-75; Patterson, "Speer, Machen, and
the Presbyterian Board."

47. On these more recent mission trends, see Charles Van Engen's chapter
in this volume, "A Broadening Vision: Forty Years of Evangelical Theology of
Mission, 1846-1986." Other informative studies are Rodger C. Bassham, *Mission
Theology: 1948-1975; Ecumenical, Evangelical and Roman Catholic* (Pasadena: William Carey Library, 1980); Emilio Castro, "Evangelical and Ecumenical," *Reformed Journal* 37 (January 1987): 17-22; Donald A. McGavran, ed., *The Conciliar-
Evangelical Debate: The Crucial Documents, 1964-1976* (Pasadena: William Carey
Library, 1977); and D. A. McGavran, "Mission and Evangelism—An Ecumeni-
cal Affirmation," *TSF Bulletin* 7 (September-October 1983): 21.

arship demonstrates that liberals and conservatives in the late nineteenth and early twentieth centuries were not as theologically disparate as is often assumed and that some transcended their differences in cooperative efforts like the Men and Religion Forward Movement.[48] Even so, the ruptures caused by fundamentalists and modernists in the 1920s and 1930s have not healed, and the prospects for a full restoration of the Protestant consensus any time soon do not appear very promising.

48. See Grant Wacker, "The Holy Spirit and the Spirit of the Age in American Protestantism, 1880–1910," *Journal of American History* 72 (1985): 45-62; and Gary Scott Smith, "The Men and Religion Forward Movement of 1911–1912," *Westminster Theological Journal* 49 (1987): 91-118.

5 Propagating the Faith Once Delivered: The Fundamentalist Missionary Enterprise, 1920–1945

Joel A. Carpenter

Throughout its history, American fundamentalism has been a missionary movement. This fact might seem so obvious to those who know fundamentalism well that they would consider it to be a truism, not an arguable thesis. But its implications, if not its simple truth, have yet to make an impact on the writing of American religious history. It is well known, thanks to the work of George Marsden and others, that fundamentalism's roots are thoroughly embedded in the same North American revivalist matrix from which sprang a new surge of missionary commitment from 1880 to 1920; and Dana Robert has shown that premillennialist, "proto-fundamentalist" pastors and evangelists were important leaders in this movement.[1] Indeed, fundamentalists' fervent commitment to conversionist missionizing clashed with liberal Protestants' attempts to move the missionary enterprise away from aggressive proselytism.

1. George M. Marsden, *Fundamentalism and American Culture: The Shaping of Twentieth-Century Evangelicalism, 1870–1925* (New York: Oxford Univ. Press, 1980); and several articles by Dana Robert: "The Legacy of Arthur Tappan Pierson," *International Bulletin of Missionary Research* (hereinafter, *IBMR*) 8 (July 1984): 120-25; "The Origins of the Student Volunteer Watchword: 'The Evangelization of the World in This Generation,'" *IBMR* 10 (October 1986): 146-49; and "The Legacy of Adoniram Judson Gordon," *IBMR* 11 (October 1987): 176-81. See also Robert's chapter in this book, "'The Crisis of Missions': Premillennial Mission Theory and the Origins of Independent Evangelical Missions."

This missions debate became one of the most explosive issues in the fundamentalist-modernist controversies.[2]

It seems to have been forgotten, however, that in the wake of these controversies, a very large part—about 40 percent—of the twelve thousand North American Protestant missionaries came from the more conservative and evangelical side of the rift. The fundamentalists in particular contributed about one out of every seven North American Protestant missionaries in the mid-1930s, and by the early 1950s, the fundamentalists' portion had doubled.[3] Their dynamic missionary movement was an important factor, along with other evangelical missions efforts, in the survival and growth of the foreign missions enterprise in the twentieth century. Our gap in knowledge about fundamentalists' foreign missions, then, is more than an esoteric corner of American (and global) religious history. It is a critical missing piece. This chapter will start to fill in the gap by assessing the scope, texture, thrust, and legacy of the fundamentalist missionary enterprise. We need to find out what gave the fundamentalist missions their force for another reason as well. Be-

2. See the editor's introduction to *Modernism and Foreign Missions: Two Fundamentalist Protests*, ed. Joel A. Carpenter (New York: Garland, 1988); Robert Moats Miller, *Harry Emerson Fosdick: Preacher, Pastor, Prophet* (New York: Oxford Univ. Press), 105-9; James A. Patterson, "Robert E. Speer, J. Gresham Machen, and the Presbyterian Board of Foreign Missions," *American Presbyterians: Journal of Presbyterian History* 64 (Spring 1986): 58-68; and Patterson's chapter in this book, "The Loss of a Protestant Missionary Consensus: Foreign Missions and the Fundamentalist-Modernist Conflict."

3. Missionaries representing the denominational boards or independent societies supported by conservative evangelicals totaled 4,784, or 40.2 percent of the 11,899 North American Protestant missionaries that I have located in Joseph I. Parker, ed., *Interpretative Statistical Survey of the World Mission of the Christian Church* (New York: International Missionary Council, 1938), 40-45. Fundamentalist boards and societies totaled 1,721 missionaries, or 14.5 percent.

According to figures provided in R. Pierce Beaver, "The Protestant Missionary Enterprise of the United States," *Occasional Bulletin of the Missionary Research Library*, 8 May 1953, 1-15, the total North American Protestant missionary force in 1952 was 18,500; evangelical agencies accounted for about half of this total, and 5,565 missionaries (30.1 percent of the total) were from fundamentalist-related agencies.

For an explanation of how I arrived at these figures and a discussion of the problems involved in counting nondenominational missionaries, see the Appendix of this book.

cause the missionary impulse stirred the movement so powerfully, any research of it becomes a character study of fundamentalism itself.

"Missions That Stand for the 'Faith Once Delivered'"

Why has the record of fundamentalist missions since 1920 been
neglected? The best answer may well be that historians tend to
write about the most influential sectors of the culture first, and
fundamentalists, like the other inhabitants of North America's
vast and varied mosaic of evangelicals, became alienated from
the centers of cultural influence. By the 1920s, these heirs of a
once-dominant religious tradition found that their ideas and actions were considered quaintly passé or worse, bizarre. As religiously liberal points of view came to dominate the Protestant
denominational "main line," fundamentalists (along with other
evangelicals) felt marginalized.[4] This held as true in the field of
foreign missions as in religious life more generally.

Few incidents illustrate fundamentalists' growing estrange-
ment in missions more dramatically than what transpired at the
quadrennial convention of the Student Volunteer Movement
held in Detroit from December 28, 1928, to January 1, 1929. The
theme of the convention was "world christianization," and
Sherwood Eddy, a veteran leader of the SVM, led a rhetorical
barrage against the wickedness of the present social order and
the need for a new one. Conspicuous by their absence, however,
were SVM platform stalwarts Robert Wilder and Samuel
Zwemer, both ardently evangelical promoters of world evangelization. John R. Mott and Robert E. Speer made appearances,
but in rather secondary roles.[5]

Eddy seemed to have shocked many of the delegates when
he publicly repudiated the SVM's watchword, "The evange-

4. Marsden, *Fundamentalism and American Culture*, 6-8, 21-32. See also
R. Laurence Moore, *Religious Outsiders and the Making of Americans* (New York:
Oxford Univ. Press, 1986), chap. 6: "The Protestant Majority as a Lost Genera-
tion—A Look at Fundamentalism," 150-72.

5. Editorial, "Youth and Missions," *Christian Century*, 12 January 1928,
39-40.

lization of the world in this generation," likening it to "taking a Paul Revere's ride across the world." His substitute slogan, "world christianization," explained one observer, meant a "comprehensive gospel" in all the "social, economic and political implications that the most advanced prophets . . . have been preaching since the days of Rauschenbusch."[6]

While the editor of the *Christian Century* remarked that this "magnificent program" showed that "the missionaries are rapidly readjusting their thinking; [and] that the social gospel finds its highest expression and greatest power in the missionary enterprise," he also noted with great dismay that "a clear majority" of the students present seemed, in their questions and discussion, to be very critical of the perspectives presented from the platform. They were giving vent to what the *Century* called "an aggressive, uncritical, and astonishingly naive fundamentalism."[7] As one might imagine, given this polarized climate, the number of students volunteering for foreign missions diminished greatly; already in decline after a high of 2,700 in 1920, by 1928 only 252 answered the summons.[8] In a brief aside that spoke volumes, a report in the *Moody Bible Institute Monthly* mentioned that "the Moody Bible Institute did not send any delegates to the convention." Apparently, the old watchword

6. Ibid., 40. See also, in the same issue of the *Century*, Ernest Thomas, "Student Volunteers Hold Quadrennial Convention in Detroit," 54-55. Sherwood Eddy, "Can We Still Believe in Foreign Missions?" in *Students and the Future of Christian Missions*, Report of the Tenth Quadrennial Convention of the Student Volunteer Movement for Foreign Missions, Detroit, Michigan, December 28, 1927, to January 1, 1928 (New York: Student Volunteer Movement, 1928), 75-93, is an edited version of Eddy's speech. The explicit repudiation of the watchword reported by several witnesses and the "Paul Revere's ride" characterization of it evidently were expunged from the text.

7. "Youth and Missions," 40.

8. Robert T. Handy, *A Christian America: Protestant Hopes and Historical Realities* (New York: Oxford Univ. Press, 1971), 201. Doubtless other important reasons contributed to the rapid decline of student volunteers, but the disenchantment of conservative evangelical students with the new emphases of the SVM's leadership should be taken into consideration. Cf. Clifton J. Philips, "Changing Attitudes in the Student Volunteer Movement of Great Britain and North America, 1886–1928," in *Missionary Ideologies in the Imperialist Era, 1880–1920*, ed. Torben Christiansen and William R. Hutchison (Aarhus, Denmark: Aros, 1982), 131-45.

was still good enough for them, and if the SVM no longer was going to uphold it, they would find other fellowship.[9]

This episode—and other favorites of historians, such as J. Gresham Machen's epic battle against the Presbyterian Board of Foreign Missions, which resulted in his establishing a separatist Presbyterian missions society and denomination—can be misleading, however. We should not interpret them to suggest that the fundamentalist movement in particular (as part of the wider mosaic of pentecostal, Southern Baptist, Wesleyan holiness, restorationist, adventist, anabaptist, and other evangelicals) contributed very little to the Protestant missionary enterprise after the controversies. It might have appeared that way, because once having drawn away from the missions establishment, fundamentalists' and other evangelicals' activities became hard to locate. It is also true that these groups contributed little or nothing positive to discussions in the theology of missions or to the formation of ecumenical Christian councils. And yet the collective size and scope of this conservative evangelical force shows that the mainline boards' domination was more a matter of prestige, wealth, and intellectual sophistication than of numerical superiority.

Another misleading interpretation of fundamentalists' departure from the missions establishment is to suggest, as did some of their opponents, that a "rule or ruin" mentality led fundamentalists to attack the mainline mission boards.[10] Fundamentalists were not, for the most part, attacking the denominational boards out of sheer dogmatic zeal or desire for denominational control. They were intensely committed missionizers, and they wanted to get on with the task of world evangelization as it had been defined a generation earlier. The dynamism of their missions movement speaks of alienation being converted into positive action.

If fundamentalists were not giving up on foreign mission,

9. T. J. Bach, "Convention of the Student Volunteer Movement," *Moody Bible Institute Monthly* 28 (March 1928): 314-15. See also John Horsch, "The Modern View of Missions in the Light of the Student Volunteer Convention," *Moody Bible Institute Monthly* 28 (April 1928): 367-68.

10. E.g., Robert E. Speer once accused J. Gresham Machen of this (Patterson, "Speer, Machen, and the Presbyterian Board," 62).

where was their support going, if not (for the most part) to the denominational boards?[11] A very good answer comes from the *Sunday School Times,* a nondenominational weekly magazine published in Philadelphia. Its editor, Charles G. Trumbull, was a Presbyterian and one of the organizers of the World's Christian Fundamentals Association in 1919. With some eighty thousand subscribers regularly considering its point of view, the *Times* made Trumbull an important power broker. He had been a watchdog on the missionary front from the very beginning of the controversies.[12]

In 1931, after over a decade of antimodernist agitation, Trumbull published what would become a regular feature, a list of "sound interdenominational missions." While admitting that there were still some worthy denominational enterprises, Trumbull encouraged his readers to support a group of independent "faith" missionary societies. They were, he stated, worthy of "full confidence" because they stood for "'the faith once delivered.'"[13] His first list contained forty-nine agencies, ranging from the China Inland Mission, the largest mission in China with well over a thousand missionaries, to the tiny Woman's Union Missionary Society, which sent out some two dozen missionaries.

Some of these agencies were famous; others were obscure. Over half would not even appear in the International Missionary Council's *Interpretative Statistical Survey of the World Mission of the Christian Church* conducted in 1935-36, and another ten would not appear on the survey's list of North American sending agencies. Some were based in Europe, as was the Liebenzeller Mission; or on the mission sites, as were the Latin American Evangelization Campaign in Costa Rica and the Ramabai Mukti Mission in India; or with so many branch offices, as had

11. A few mainline denominational missions allowed supporters to designate the use of their gifts to the mission boards. By this means, fundamentalists could selectively support work within the mainline agencies that squared with their convictions. See Robert G. Torbet, *Venture of Faith: The Story of the American Baptist Foreign Mission Society and the Woman's American Baptist Foreign Mission Society, 1814-1954* (Philadelphia: Judson, 1955), 174-75, which explains the American Baptist Foreign Mission Society's policy of allowing gifts to be designated to particular mission stations but not to individual missionaries.

12. Introduction to *Modernism and Foreign Missions.*

13. *Sunday School Times,* 26 December 1931, 737.

the China Inland Mission, that they were cataloged as "inter-national" societies. Tiny and unfamiliar or very large and world-renowned, these nondenominational missions were becoming the major focus of fundamentalists' missionary commitment, constituting two-thirds of the total fundamentalist missions force.[14]

Faith Missions and American Fundamentalism

By 1930, faith missions were a familiar and fully accepted part of the fundamentalist institutional network. At least since the first North American candidates left from Toronto to serve with the China Inland Mission in 1888, these independent societies had become increasingly integrated into the millenarian and revivalist movement that formed the core of later fundamentalism.

Like so many other features of this "proto-fundamentalist" movement, the faith-missions concept had been borrowed from the British. The "father" of faith missions was James Hudson Taylor, who in 1865 was a discouraged young English missionary returned from China. He had become convinced, after seven years of conventional missionary work, that God was calling him to evangelize the interior of China. Taylor could get no mission board to support him in such a venture, so in 1865 he founded the China Inland Mission "with ten pounds and a prayer."[15]

The China Inland Mission proved to be the first of a growing number of independent missions. Prodded by images of hundreds of millions of lost souls and by the premillennial belief

14. From the mission agencies reported in Parker, *Interpretative Statistics*, I have found twenty nondenominational societies that are easily identified as fundamentalist in a North American context of affiliation and constituency. These had a total of 1,231 North American missionaries, constituting 71.5 percent of the fundamentalist total of 1,721.

15. Alvyn J. Austin, *Saving China: Canadian Missionaries in the Middle Kingdom, 1888–1959* (Toronto: Univ. of Toronto Press, 1986), 4. On Taylor's role in directly influencing a number of early faith missions, see Daniel W. Bacon, "The Influence of Hudson Taylor on the Faith Missions Movement" (D.Miss. project, Trinity Evangelical Divinity School, 1983), chap. 9, "Father of the Faith Missions Movement," 87-108.

that time was short before Christ's return, the founders of independent missions decided that direct and widespread evangelization was the highest priority and that all else that missions customarily did should come second. In order to avoid the criticism that they would compete for funds with the older boards and to exercise their trust in God's provision, the independent missions practiced a "faith principle" of not directly soliciting funds. Furthermore, the faith missions characteristically required candidates to subscribe to a doctrinally conservative and evangelical statement of faith.[16]

These characteristics made independent missions a very good fit with the American evangelistic and premillennialist movement centered about evangelist Dwight L. Moody. Like the faith-missions pioneers, the urban revivalists had a "reform" agenda; they sought to narrow and intensify their churches' focus on evangelism.[17] Missions became the "foreign policy" wing of their movement, and they began to found independent societies of their own on the faith-mission model. Important early agencies were the International Missionary Alliance, founded by A. B. Simpson of New York City in 1887; the Scandinavian Alliance Mission, founded in 1890 by Swedish immigrant Fredrik Franson; premillennialist Bible teacher C. I. Scofield's Central American Mission, founded in 1890; the Sudan Interior Mission, founded by the young Canadian evangelist Rowland V. Bingham and two associates in 1893; and the Africa Inland Mission, founded in Philadelphia in 1895 by Peter Cameron Scott with the help of the eminent missions advocate A. T. Pierson.[18]

16. Marybeth Rupert, "The Emergence of the Independent Missionary Agency as an American Institution" (Ph.D. diss., Yale Univ., 1974), 112-18; Kenneth G. Grubb, "The Work of Undenominational Missions," *International Review of Missions* 27 (1938): 497-99; Robert Hall Glover, "What Is a Faith Mission?" *Missionary Review of the World* 58 (September 1935): 409-11.

17. Virginia Lieson Brereton, "Bible Schools and Conservative Evangelical Higher Education, 1880–1940," in *Making Higher Education Christian: The History and Mission of Evangelical Colleges in America*, ed. Joel A. Carpenter and Kenneth W. Shipps (Grand Rapids: Eerdmans, 1987), 111-12. For a more extended discussion of this point, see Brereton's *Protestant Fundamentalist Bible Schools* (Bloomington: Indiana Univ. Press, forthcoming).

18. Rupert, "Emergence of the Independent Missionary Agency," 111-23.

While late-nineteenth-century premillennial evangelical leaders like A. J. Gordon of Boston eagerly supported faith missions, they did not abandon denominational missions. At a time when the missions force was expanding rapidly and denominational boards were exuding the crusading spirit of evangelical revivalism, faith missions functioned like auxiliaries, taking up the surplus volunteers who couldn't fit into the denominational programs.[19] By about 1915, however, faith missions were beginning to take on a new role. In addition to being exercises in faith, they were being looked upon as trustworthy conservators of the "faith once delivered to the saints."[20] Perhaps the most important indication of this trend was the formation in 1917 of the Interdenominational Foreign Mission Association of North America by seven faith missions. Among its purposes were holding conferences on world evangelization and "the fundamentals of the faith" and providing conservatives with an alternative fellowship to the theologically inclusive Foreign Missions Conference of North America.[21]

When the World's Christian Fundamentals Association was launched in Philadelphia in 1919, seven of the principal speakers and committee members were officers of IFMA missions; and the conference committee reporting on missions was simply composed of IFMA representatives.[22] Leaders of these independent missions thus had become part of the inner circle of interdenominational fundamentalism. Although faith missions had played a relatively minor role in the missionary commitment of

19. Robert, "Legacy of Adoniram Judson Gordon," 179.

20. CIM's North American director, Henry W. Frost, as Alvyn Austin points out, was becoming increasingly fundamentalistic and separatistic in his outlook in these years. See Austin's chapter in this book, " 'Blessed Adversity': Henry W. Frost and the China Inland Mission."

21. The seven faith missions that chartered the IFMA were the Africa Inland Mission, Central American Mission, China Inland Mission, Inland South America Missionary Union, South Africa General Mission, Sudan Interior Mission, and the Woman's Union Missionary Society. See Edwin L. Frizen, Jr., "An Historical Study of the Interdenominational Foreign Mission Association in Relation to Evangelical Unity and Cooperation" (D.Miss. project, Trinity Evangelical Divinity School, 1981), 3, 7, 23-24, 28.

22. *God Hath Spoken* (Philadelphia: Bible Conference Committee, 1919), 5-6, 17, 23-26.

conservative evangelicals up to this point, by the early 1920s they were becoming integral to fundamentalism.

Missions and the Fundamentalist Network

At the same time that the fundamentalist-modernist controversies were raging during the 1920s and early 1930s, fundamentalists were busily consolidating an institutional network. Although fundamentalists found their very identity in protecting a "testimony to the truth" in "days of apostasy," as they would put it, their commitment to the more traditional evangelical pursuits of evangelism, Christian nurture, and, of course, foreign missions drove them to establish a base of operations. So, like Nehemiah's band, they used both the sword and the trowel. Since the denominational agencies were the focus of much of their discontent, fundamentalists depended upon the institutions of the older "Bible school" movement and created new organizations to meet their needs.

It is striking how thoroughly fundamentalist institutions served the missionary enterprise. Certainly this was true of the most primary of fundamentalists' institutions—their homes, Sunday schools, congregations, and local leaders. Missionary recruits commonly referred to the influence of missionary biographies given them by friends and relatives, their parents' dedication of them as babies to "full-time Christian service," Sunday-school missionary stories, weekend missions conferences or Sunday night missionary slide lectures, and encouraging pastors and pastors' wives who recommended going to a Bible school for evangelistic training. Fundamentalist young people grew up in a subculture that saw evangelism as the all-consuming priority for the church and its people and vocational religious careers as the highest calling. Missionaries were the noblest models of all for the life of heroic Christian service; they comprised the elite advance troops of spiritual warfare.[23]

23. Interview of Jeannette Louise Martig Thiessen, Collection #260, Archives of the Billy Graham Center, Wheaton College, Wheaton, Illinois (hereinafter, BGC Archives); interview of Paul Kenneth Gieser, Collection #88, BGC

Larger institutions also furthered the missionary movement. Bible conferences were major means of missionary promotion and recruitment. Established conference centers, such as those at Winona Lake, Indiana, might have week-long missionary conferences, as well as at least one missionary address during the more general conferences.[24] Annual week-long missionary conferences in the leading regional "cathedrals" of fundamentalism, such as the People's Church in Toronto, also attracted many hundreds. The IFMA itself sponsored "Bible and missionary conferences" across North America during the 1920s, 1930s, and 1940s. These featured such leading fundamentalist pulpiteers as Harry Ironside, the revered Bible teacher and pastor of the Moody Church in Chicago.[25]

Fundamentalist magazines were important missions promoters also. Charles Trumbull's *Sunday School Times*, in addition to its editorials and features on missions topics and lists of endorsed missions, had a regular column by Ernest B. Gordon, the son of A. J. Gordon, entitled "A Survey of Religious Life and Thought" that favored missions topics. Perhaps the second most influential fundamentalist magazine, *The Moody Bible Institute Monthly,* featured a regular "Missions Department," edited from the late 1920s into the mid-1940s by William H. Hockman, formerly of the China Inland Mission, who directed the Institute's missions program. *The Evangelical Christian,* founded in Toronto in 1904 as a missionary's journal and edited by R. V. Bingham, never lost its missions emphasis as it broadened its coverage in subsequent years.

No other institutions worked more closely with the mission societies than did the Bible institutes. By the 1920s, faith missions had become dependent on schools such as Toronto Bible College; Gordon College of Theology and Missions, in Boston; Nyack Institute of the Christian and Missionary Alliance, just

Archives; interview of Susan Schultz Bartel, Collection #57, BGC Archives; interview of Elizabeth Stair Small, Collection #164, BGC Archives; interview of Zoe Anne Alford, Collection #177, BGC Archives; interview of Jennie Elizabeth Kingston Fitzwilliam, Collection #272, BGC Archives.

24. See *Winona Echoes,* the annual volumes of addresses published by the Winona Lake Bible Conference.

25. Frizen, "Historical Study of the IFMA," 2-3, 74-75, 78, 80-81.

north of New York City; the Philadelphia School of the Bible; the Bible Institute of Los Angeles; and the Moody Bible Institute for the recruitment and training of their foreign staff. In addition, new schools, such as Columbia Bible College in South Carolina and the Prairie Bible Institute in rural Alberta soon became important sources of missionaries.

Bible institutes were somewhat like business colleges or normal schools in the sense that they offered practical training to their vocationally focused students. Instead of an accounting or teaching certificate, the Bible schools credentialed their students in some kind of "full-time Christian work," such as evangelism, Sunday school administration, the pastorate, or foreign missions. Courses provided them with the Bible knowledge and practical skills thought to be demanded by those callings, and students usually had some "practical work assignment" to get on-the-job experience. The institutes' relatively brief, one- to three-year courses and pragmatic thrust were well tailored for the narrowly evangelistic contours of the faith missions.[26]

For some students, however, the gritty daily routine of Bible school life was their most valued preparation. Street preaching, singing at the rescue mission, or door-to-door calling in a tough ethnic neighborhood could teach humility, compassion, courage, and cross-cultural sensitivity. The exhausting weeks that combined studies with bouts of spiritual struggle, Sunday service assignments, and waitressing or busing dishes to earn room and board could teach endurance and perseverance. And learning to wear old clothes and worn-out shoes while trusting God for their replacements was an authentic foretaste of the life of a faith missionary.[27]

At least as influential as curriculum and practical experience was the atmosphere. These schools were tightly knit, familial, and religiously and emotionally intense places designed to foster spirituality and evangelistic zeal. Prayer, hymn singing,

26. Brereton, "Bible Schools and Conservative Evangelical Higher Education," 114-22.

27. Ibid., 121-22; Isobel Kuhn, *By Searching* (London: CIM, 1957), 65-70, 79-93; E. Schuyler English, *By Life or By Death: Excerpts and Lessons from the Diary of John C. Stam* (Grand Rapids: Zondervan, 1930), 20, 27, 34; Mrs. Howard Taylor, *The Triumph of John and Betty Stam* (Philadelphia: CIM, 1935), 17-23.

and devotional meetings were the way of life, and outbreaks of revival were fairly frequent. Student publications were filled with the exalted language of service and heroic spiritual aspirations, and it was simply assumed that each student had a call to some field of service.

The enthusiasm for missions was palpable in these schools. Student-organized missionary prayer bands, each of which focused on a different country, met regularly to discuss news of their fields and to pray for specific missionaries. Returned missionaries commonly joined the faculty or staff of Bible schools and offered students valuable advice, encouragement, and personal models. Missionary speakers—often alumni—were regular fare in daily chapels and week-long missions conferences. Students testified to their call to a specific field or their appointment to a mission or announced their departure date. Missionary maps and Bible verses on missions themes frequently decorated the walls; and some schools had display cases filled with such "trophies of grace" as cast-off idols and fetishes, and photographs of smiling, born-again Africans.[28] As an observer of daily life at the Prairie Bible Institute remarked, "They ate, drank, studied, slept, and sang missions morning, noon, and night."[29]

Bible schools were contributing significant numbers of missionaries during the 1920s, 1930s, and early 1940s. Two institutes in Philadelphia, the Philadelphia School of the Bible and the Bible Institute of Pennsylvania, both founded in 1913, had produced a combined total of some 150 missionaries by their twentieth anniversaries. Under the leadership of Robert McQuilkin, a young associate of Charles Trumbull whose plans to sail with Africa Inland Mission were frustrated, Columbia Bible College

28. Kuhn, *By Searching*, 60-70; interview of Elizabeth Stair Small; interview of Zoe Anne Alford; interview of Helen Nowack Frame, Collection #255, BGC Archives; interview of Ruth Sundquist, Collection #266, BGC Archives; interview of Jennie Elizabeth Kingston Fitzwilliam; Brereton, "Bible Schools," 122-28. Bible school life receives sensitive, carefully detailed treatment in Shirley Nelson, *The Last Year of the War* (New York: Harper & Row, 1978), a novel situated at the Moody Bible Institute in the mid-1940s.

29. W. Phillip Keller, quoted in John Kayser, "How a Bible Institute Imparts Missionary Vision," *Evangelical Missions Quarterly* 21 (October 1985): 406-7.

in Columbia, South Carolina, was intensely missions focused. By its twenty-first year in 1944, 135 of its alumni had become missionaries. William Bell Riley's Northwestern Bible and Missionary Training School in Minneapolis had produced 110 missionaries by 1936, while by 1938 the Bible Institute of Los Angeles had produced 426, over 120 of those in the preceding decade.[30]

The most productive training ground for foreign missionaries was that self-proclaimed "West Point of Christian Service," the Moody Bible Institute in Chicago. "Moody" was first in size, reputation, and scope of its programs. Between 1932 and 1942, some 500 Institute alumni sailed to the mission fields, bringing the school's total contribution since its founding to 2,416. In 1936, 142 students were enrolled in Moody's missions course, and 1,410 Moody alumni were active missionaries. These constituted nearly 12 percent of the reported total North American Protestant force for that year.[31] The faith missions seemed to be Moody's major clients. The 21 Moody alumni who sailed in 1933 listed among them thirteen sponsoring agencies, nine of which were faith missions.[32]

30. John B. Cole, "What Hath God Wrought," *Alumni News* 8 (June 1934): n.p. (Bible Institute of Pennsylvania); J. Davis Adams, "Facing Our Twentieth School Year," *Serving and Waiting* 23 (November 1933): 150 (Philadelphia School of Bible); R. Arthur Mathews, *Towers Pointing Upward* (Columbia, SC: Columbia Bible College, 1973), 143; Marguerite C. McQuilkin, *Always in Triumph: The Life of Robert C. McQuilkin* (Columbia, SC: Columbia Bible College Bookstore, 1956), 88-91, 102-15; notices in *Northwestern Pilot* 7 (December 1926): 2; and *The Pilot* 17 (October 1936): 16; "Twentieth Anniversary," *The King's Business* 18 (March 1927): inside back cover; "Giving to BIOLA Means Giving to Missions," *The King's Business* 29 (February 1938): 62.

31. Moody was much larger than the other Bible schools mentioned, which ranged from about one hundred to seven hundred day students in the mid-1930s, compared to Moody's one thousand or more. Figures for new and total Moody alumni missionaries were reported each year in a winter or spring issue of the *Moody Bible Institute Bulletin*. For 1936 figures, see "The World-Wide Ministry of Moody Students," *Moody Bible Institute Bulletin* 15 (March 1936): 18; and "Fields of Service," *Moody Bible Institute Bulletin* 16 (September 1936): 9 (Parker, *Interpretative Statistics*, 43).

32. James M. Gray, "Report of the President of the Moody Bible Institute of Chicago," *Moody Bible Institute Bulletin* 14 (November 1934): 4. The missions listed were Africa Inland Mission, Sudan Interior Mission, China Inland Mission, the Mennonite foreign mission board, Inland South America Mission, Cey-

Indeed, faith missions were building many interlocking connections with the Bible schools. A. R. Saunders, a Canadian with the China Inland Mission, who had become blind and returned from China with his wife in 1917, took up residence in the hotel of the Bible Institute of Los Angeles. Before long, the Saunderses' apartments became a West Coast center for CIM, and a dozen BIOLA students were accepted as CIM missionaries. The Philadelphia School of the Bible had an interlocking directorate through its board and administrators with four different faith missions at one time or another in the 1920s and 1930s: Africa Inland Mission, China Inland Mission, the Inland South America Missionary Union, and the Central American Mission. The missionary connections of the Toronto Bible College were equally strong, if not stronger. Its president, John McNichol, served the home councils of both the China Inland Mission and the Sudan Interior Mission. It is no surprise, then, that five hundred of the school's total of two thousand graduates by 1946 were missionaries, and a third of those were with CIM or SIM.[33]

Faith missions also did a great deal to promote their work. Although direct requests for funds were not in keeping with Hudson Taylor's maxim that "God's work, done in God's way, will never lack God's supplies,"[34] letting people know about a mission's work was permitted; and these missions certainly knew how to generate publicity.[35] Their speakers were familiar

---

lon and India General Mission, Philippine-Borneo Mission, the boards of foreign missions of the northern Presbyterian, southern Presbyterian, and United Presbyterian denominations, the Evangelical Union of South America, Association of Baptists for the Evangelization of the Orient, and the Plymouth Brethren (who sent out faith missionaries).

33. Dr. and Mrs. Howard Taylor, "By Faith...": Henry W. Frost and the China Inland Mission (Philadelphia: CIM, 1938), 308-12; Frizen, "Historical Study of the IFMA," passim; Ronald E. Showers, "A History of Philadelphia College of Bible" (M.Th. thesis, Dallas Theological Seminary, 1962), passim; John G. Stackhouse, Jr., "Proclaiming the Word: Canadian Evangelicalism since World War I" (Ph.D. diss., Univ. of Chicago, 1987), chap. 3, "Toronto Bible College," 20-21.

34. J. Hudson Taylor, quoted in Dr. and Mrs. Howard Taylor, Hudson Taylor's Spiritual Secret (London: CIM, 1932), 86.

35. Mona J. McKay, "Faith and Facts in the History of the China Inland Mission, 1832-1905" (M.Litt. thesis, Univ. of Aberdeen, 1981), provides a careful examination of the CIM's principles and actual methods in its early years. She concludes that the mission acted honorably in light of its principles, but the sources

to the audiences at congregationally sponsored missionary conferences, Bible school chapels, and especially at summer conferences such as McQuilkin's "Ben Lippen" in North Carolina (a frequent haunt of AIM and Latin America Mission representatives) or "The Firs" in Bellingham, Washington (near a CIM outpost in Vancouver). Missionary magazines, such as the Scandinavian Alliance Mission's *Missionary Broadcaster,* AIM's *Inland Africa,* and the Central American Mission's *Central American Bulletin* reported mission news to international constituencies.

In the mind of one critic, and probably many others, such publicity was disingenuous as an expression of a "no solicitation" policy, for the mere statement of the mission's current affairs could in fact become a compelling argument for additional support. No doubt there was a "pump-priming" effect when readers browsed through the stories, reports, and contributions lists (always anonymous) in each issue of their favorite mission's magazine. And the same potential, whether calculated or not, was present in missionary devotional books.[36]

No agency was more energetic about publicity than the largest and most adamantly faith-principled of them all, the China Inland Mission. In addition to *China's Millions,* the mission's magazine, CIM published a mountain of books. One prolific CIM author was Marshall Broomhall, the mission's home secretary in England, who published a popular life of Hudson Taylor in 1929 and some thirty other books. The chief publicist, however, was Mary Geraldine Guinness (Mrs. Howard) Taylor, Hudson Taylor's daughter-in-law. Perhaps her highest achievement among the more than twenty books she wrote was a two-volume, exhaustively researched biography of Hudson Taylor, co-authored with her husband. Devotional in thrust but richly detailed as well, *Hudson Taylor in Early Years: The Growth of a Soul*

---

of its support were much less mysterious than they are often portrayed. Networks of support followed lines of personal contact and publicity.

36. Grubb, "Work of Undenominational Missions," 503. For examples of the implicit financial appeal of missionary literature, see Amy Carmichael's books about God's miraculous provision for her ministry to children in Dohnavur, India, such as *Meal in a Barrel* (Madras: Christian Literature Society's Press, 1929).

(1911) and *Hudson Taylor and the China Inland Mission: The Growth of a Work of God* (1918) sold fifty thousand volumes by 1929 and became an oft-reprinted evangelical classic.[37]

All told, by 1952 the mission's authors had published nearly three hundred titles. The impact of these works (beyond their accrual to the mission's revenues) is incalculable. But certainly they helped to build and sustain a broad constituency, which by the late 1930s included 1,459 prayer circles in North America.[38] Mrs. Howard Taylor, Marshall Broomhall, Isobel Kuhn, and others saturated American fundamentalism with faith-missions piety, raised CIM's status to legendary levels, inspired fundamentalist young people to become missionaries, and very often prompted them to select China Inland Mission as the agency most worthy of their life's investment.[39]

Students and Missions: Wheaton, Moody, and the China Connection, 1925–1933

Having described the institutional network that produced fundamentalist missionaries, we need to look more closely at the movement's recruits. Before we begin, however, we must recall the prior record of North American missions recruitment. According to two recent histories of turn-of-the-century American missions to China, American volunteers for major Protestant mission boards in that era were predominantly rural and small-

---

37. Bacon, "Influence of Hudson Taylor," 130-40. Mrs. Howard Taylor's *Borden of Yale, '09: The Life That Counts* (1926) is still in print, as is *Hudson Taylor's Spiritual Secret* (1932), co-authored with her husband. Mrs. Taylor's *The Triumph of John and Betty Stam* (1936), about two young CIM missionaries who were murdered by communist bandits, had a first printing of sixty thousand.

38. Ernest B. Gordon, "A Survey of Religious Life and Thought," *Sunday School Times*, 24 June 1934, 430.

39. Bacon, "Influence of Hudson Taylor," 139. For examples of CIM books' influence, see English, *By Life and By Death*, 14; J. Herbert Kane, "My Pilgrimage in Mission," *IBMR* 11 (July 1987): 129; interview of Helen Torrey Renich, Collection #124, BGC Archives; interview of Jeannette Louise Martig Thiessen. Many accounts of the impact of Geraldine Guinness Taylor's book on the life of Hudson Taylor appear in the testimonies of outgoing missionaries published in *China's Millions*.

town midwestern people of lower-middle-class, well-churched Protestant backgrounds. The dominant source of these missionaries was the network of midwestern, coeducational church-related colleges. The Student Volunteer Movement made its deepest inroads in these schools; their tradition of service was strong, and in them the revival-inspired missions meeting was still the vehicle for the call.[40] For the fundamentalist missionary of the 1920s and 1930s, some of these conditions would continue, but there were important changes as well.

When D. E. Hoste, director of the China Inland Mission, issued a summons in 1929 for two hundred new missionaries in two years, ninety-one of the two hundred who sailed by 1931 came from North America. Who were these people whose serious portraits and glowing testimonies filled the pages of *China's Millions*? Seventy were from the United States, and 70 percent were women (all but four of whom were single). Four of the CIM recruits were nurses, one was a physician, and seven were seminary trained. Twenty-two gave no clues about their education, but eighteen of the other sixty-nine reported having attended college. Of these collegians, six had attended Wheaton College, a fundamentalist liberal arts institution west of Chicago. Of all the educational experiences reported, however, Bible-institute training dominated; fifty-five mentioned having received some. The two Bible schools reported most often were the Bible Institute of Los Angeles, mentioned by thirteen, and the Moody Bible Institute, referred to by eighteen. In sum, what was true about fundamentalist leadership in general seemed to hold for their missionaries; they were less educated than their mainline denominational counterparts.[41]

40. Valentin H. Rabe, *The Home Base of American China Missions, 1880–1920* (Cambridge: Harvard Univ. Press, 1978), 77-107; Jane Hunter, *The Gospel of Gentility: American Women Missionaries in Turn-of-the-Century China* (New Haven: Yale Univ. Press, 1984), 28-51.

41. If one could get a representative sample of all fundamentalist missionaries, including those serving with denominational boards, the average level of education might look higher, for one of the original purposes of the faith missions had been to open a way to the mission field for zealous but less-educated volunteers. In the early days, recruits might go out with only a few weeks of training in the rudiments of missionary work. Among the faith missions most favored by fundamentalists, Bible-institute training became the norm by the

These faith missionaries were also decidedly less countrified than their turn-of-the-century mainline missionary predecessors had been. Fully half of the CIM recruits were from urban areas. More came from the West Coast region than any other, including twenty-three from the U.S. Pacific states and another six from British Columbia. The northeastern and Great Lakes regions of the United States added eighteen and nineteen respectively, and the next largest group was the ten whose parents were China missionaries.[42]

Not many more clues can be drawn from the names, portraits, and the brief accompanying statements for each new missionary. Fortunately, oral histories exist for eight students from Wheaton College and the Moody Bible Institute who sailed with CIM between 1926 and 1933, and for five others from Wheaton who in those years became missionaries with other boards. These interviews afford us a glimpse into the experiences of fundamentalist missionaries-in-the-making in the late 1920s and early 1930s.

These Moody and Wheaton recruits came from an educational environment that differed a great deal from that of the surrounding schools. By the late 1920s and early 1930s, the coeducational church-related colleges of the midwest that had been the seedbed of missionary commitment were rapidly secularizing. The earnest calls to love and duty that had characterized the Student Volunteer Movement sounded increasingly out of place

---

1920s, although college-educated missionaries were prized. Fundamentalists with a college or seminary degree, however, also met the qualifications of the more traditional denominational missions, either conservative evangelical or mainline Protestant. They seemed to self-select away from the faith missions. It is interesting to note, nevertheless, that quite a few college-educated people went to Bible institutes to train for foreign missions or other religious work. Seven of these CIM recruits reported having attended both college and Bible school. Records show that this was not uncommon. E.g., of the 1,354 enrolled in Moody Bible Institute's day school in 1940-41, 266 had already received some college education, and 93 were college or university graduates (Will H. Houghton, "A New Spiritual Victory," *Moody Bible Institute Bulletin* 20 [February 1941]: 3).

42. D. E. Hoste, "For the Evangelization of Unreached Areas," *China's Millions* 37 (May 1929): 67-68; background information on the new recruits was gleaned from their testimonies, which appeared in *China's Millions*, vols. 37-40 (1929-1932), passim. For a list of the North American recruits, see "North America's Contribution to the Two Hundred," *China's Millions* 40 (February 1932): 30.

on these campuses.[43] Nevertheless, there were still a number of northern liberal arts colleges, most of them operated by small denominations of holiness Wesleyan, "peace church," or conservative Calvinist heritage, where religiosity was still the norm and the call to missions continued to compel students.[44]

The fundamentalists had only one college, however, that was not either just half-evolved from a Bible-school origin or still waiting for the ink to dry on its charter. That was Wheaton College. Wheaton's history to about 1900 was unexceptional for a small midwestern college. But, probably because of its leaders' ties to Dwight L. Moody and his network, Wheaton had not become a theologically liberal or an academically and socially secularizing institution like most of its sister colleges. Indeed, the Wheaton of the 1920s and 1930s was something of a throwback to an earlier era.[45]

It is not surprising, then, to find six Wheaton graduates among CIM's "Two Hundred" of 1929–1931. At Wheaton, the SVM chapter was still strong, and the faith-missions kind of spirituality and doctrinal proclivities were welcome. Furthermore, the ties between Wheaton and the Chicago-area fundamentalist network, including that missions-training giant, the Moody Bible Institute, were old and well established. An addi-

43. Philips, "Changing Attitudes in the Student Volunteer Movement"; Paul A. Varg, *Missionaries, Chinese, and Diplomats: The American Protestant Missionary Movement in China, 1890–1952* (Princeton: Princeton Univ. Press, 1958), chap. 9, "The Crusade Runs into Stumbling Blocks at Home Base, 1919–1931," 147-66; William C. Ringenberg, *The Christian College: A History of Protestant Higher Education in America* (Grand Rapids: Eerdmans, 1984), 121-54. See also Timothy L. Smith, *Uncommon Schools: Christian Colleges and Social Idealism in Midwestern America, 1820–1950* (Indianapolis: Indiana Historical Society, 1978).

44. For a survey of such colleges as they exist today, which is at least suggestive of the evangelical college network of sixty years ago, see Timothy L. Smith, "Introduction: Christian Colleges and American Culture," in *Making Higher Education Christian*, 1-15.

45. A college spokesman quoted a liberal Protestant educator's nostalgic recollection of an old-time college and announced proudly that, if written in the present tense, this passage would make "an admirable description of Wheaton" (William J. Jones, "A Study in Contrasts," *Bulletin of Wheaton College* 8 [October 1931]: 7). See also Thomas A. Askew, Jr., "The Liberal Arts College Encounters Intellectual Change: A Comparative Study of Education at Knox and Wheaton Colleges, 1837–1925" (Ph.D. diss., Northwestern Univ., 1969).

tional source of missionary connections came from the college's 50 percent discount on tuition for missionaries' children.

Certainly these features helped make Wheaton attractive to Katherine Dodd, a daughter of Presbyterian missionaries to China; to Helen Nowack, whose parents served with CIM; and to Ruth Elliott, whose parents had been American Bible Society agents in China. These young women entered the college in the fall of 1926, where they joined Ruth's sisters Margaret and Frances, who had enrolled the year before.[46]

Others coming in 1926 and 1927 were from less exotic circumstances but were nevertheless drawn to Wheaton by its connections throughout the fundamentalist network. For Ken Gieser of suburban Highland Park and Ruth DeVelde of Irving Park in Chicago, Wheaton was close by and a natural choice. In fact, DeVelde's father, a high school teacher in the city, had moved his family to Wheaton four years earlier to enroll his teenagers in the college's secondary academy. For Lyndon Hess of Buffalo, Ruth Mellis of St. Louis, and Vincent Crossett of Grand Island, Nebraska, the choice to attend Wheaton was shaped by recommendations of relatives, friends, or pastors who were alumni. These students, like the China recruits of the prior generation, were all from actively Protestant homes, and most had experienced conversion.[47]

Life at Wheaton included the round of academics, daily chapel, athletics, part-time work, and social activities common to a small midwestern college. But woven through it all was a pervasive evangelical emphasis, including prayer before each class and social event, Tuesday evening all-campus prayer meetings, Sunday evening Christian Endeavor, weekly dorm-floor prayer meetings, annual evangelistic services, missionary-band

46. Interview of Katherine Hasting Dodd Schoerner, Collection #51, BGC Archives; interview of Helen Nowack Frame; interview of Eleanor Ruth Elliott, Collection #187, BGC Archives; interview of Margaret Rice Elliott Crossett, Collection #287, BGC Archives.

47. Interview of Paul Kenneth Gieser; interview of Ruth Edna DeVelde Hess, Collection #242, BGC Archives; interview of Lyndon Roth Hess, Collection #228, BGC Archives; interview of Ruth Margaret Mellis, Collection #363, BGC Archives; interview of Rev. Vincent Leroy Crossett, Collection #288, BGC Archives.

prayer meetings, Bible-study groups, and Student Volunteers meetings. All of the extracurricular religious activities (except chapel) were voluntary, and most were student organized. So were the various "gospel teams" and musical groups, such as a vocal trio formed by the Elliott sisters, and the S.D.S. (Scripture Distribution Society) chapter. These groups went out to area churches, rescue missions, youth homes, hospitals, campuses, and jails. In sum, Wheaton College offered religious activities that were virtually identical to those featured at the Bible schools.[48]

In the 1920s and early 1930s, Wheaton College had a strong, if not overpowering, missions emphasis. The Student Volunteers had twenty to thirty people at its meeting each week, and it sponsored campus visits from missions leaders such as Robert Hall Glover of the China Inland Mission. The various missions prayer bands hosted speakers from their respective fields of interest, and missionaries frequently spoke in chapel. There were also people like Mrs. Shapleigh, the dean of women, who personally encouraged her charges to consider becoming missionaries.[49]

Unlike Bible school students, Wheaton students did not all enroll with a prior commitment to "full-time Christian service." Those who were missionaries' children, however, had been constantly confronted with the option, if not the expectation, of returning to the field. Katherine Dodd made a decision to be a missionary as a young child. She remembered what had prompted it: her father used to haul out his watch and tell her that every time it ticked, a Chinese person went to "a Christless grave."[50]

Helen Nowack had no such clear-cut decision; she seemed to let others' expectations lead her. She had always thought that she might become a missionary, but she was apparently not very active in mission groups at Wheaton. After graduating, she spent two terms at Moody with her sister Esther. Another sister,

48. Detailed descriptions of campus life at Wheaton in the 1920s and early 1930s are contained in the interviews of Paul Kenneth Gieser, Eleanor Ruth Elliott, Margaret Rice Elliott Crossett, Ruth Margaret Mellis, Katherine Hasting Dodd Schoerner, and Helen Nowack Frame—all from BGC Archives. See also interview of Elizabeth Howard Warner, Collection #75, BGC Archives.
49. Interviews of Elizabeth Howard Warner and Ruth Margaret Mellis.
50. Interview of Katherine Hasting Dodd Schoerner.

Ruth, had already joined CIM. When Esther answered CIM's call for the Two Hundred, Helen hedged. Perhaps what she really wanted was to be a secretary. But she was a stranded missionary kid with no money and nowhere to go. With some encouragement, she applied to CIM "just as a matter of course; I thought that it was the thing to do. . . ." After all, China was more home than America, the CIM was family, and missionary life was virtually all that she had known. "They have taken good care of me," she mused, some fifty years later.[51]

For the others, of course, the "mission field" was not home. Yet for Ruth DeVelde and Lyndon Hess, who became engaged at Wheaton, it was familiar nonetheless. Both of them were raised among the intensely missionary-minded Plymouth Brethren. Their decision to go to Northern Rhodesia to teach in a mission school was shaped not only by a missionary speaker on campus, but by Ruth's extended correspondence with an old missionary friend.[52] Neither Vincent Crossett nor Ken Gieser had thought much about being a missionary before coming to college, but that vocation was high on the list of options for "full-time Christian service" that they had learned from their home churches and young people's fellowships. Their promptings toward foreign service came especially when they encountered missionary speakers in Wheaton's chapel services.[53]

Margaret Elliott became a candidate with the China Inland Mission almost immediately after her graduation from Wheaton in 1929, as did her sister Ruth in 1930. Both had attended BIOLA before coming to Wheaton, and they felt fully schooled for their vocation. Some of their friends, however, saw the need for some practical missions training and had some time on their hands while they were applying to the missions. So Helen Nowack, Katherine Dodd, and apparently some others from Wheaton enrolled in the Moody Bible Institute after their graduation in 1930. According to Ruth Elliott, these Wheaton students had been drawn into the Moody orbit by the monthly

51. Interview of Helen Nowack Frame.
52. Interview of Lyndon Roth Hess; interview of Ruth Edna DeVelde Hess.
53. Interview of Rev. Vincent Leroy Crossett; interview of Paul Kenneth Gieser.

CIM prayer meetings in Chicago hosted by Mr. and Mrs. Isaac Page.[54]

The Pages, like the Saunderses at BIOLA, were Canadians who had served in China. After returning for health-related reasons, they were reassigned to Chicago as the CIM's midwest area representatives. Soon the jolly, lovable "Daddy" Page had a regular contingent of Moody students coming to his home on Monday nights. Jennie Kingston, a Moody student who eventually sailed with CIM, told how important the Pages had been to Moody's China Prayer Band in the mid-1920s. The Pages radiated spirituality and good cheer; they often entertained the group socially after the meetings. Mr. Page loved to tell stories and read passages from his favorite books.[55]

These times were as important to Mr. Page and the mission as to the students. Page could get to know potential candidates and begin an informal orientation and screening process. He encouraged his protégés but gave them frank advice as well. He stressed the importance of their call to China and urged them to allow nothing to distract them, especially the prospect of marriage. Page watched the students very carefully in this regard, but as one said, "he was so nice about it that no one resented it." Nevertheless, romances regularly grew out of the group, and according to Jennie Kingston, the Pages' Monday night meetings in the mid-1920s developed into something of a "China Clique," to which the young men were sure to follow the young ladies who frequently attended.[56]

When Katherine Dodd, Helen Nowack, and three or four other Wheaton graduates arrived at Moody in 1930, the China prayer meetings with the Pages were still going strong, with thirty or forty in attendance, and they included such earnest young China volunteers as Betty Scott, the daughter of Presbyterian missionaries in China; John Stam, her future husband, who

54. Interviews of Margaret Rice Elliott Crossett, Rev. Vincent Leroy Crossett, Eleanor Ruth Elliott, Helen Nowack Frame, and Kenneth Paul Gieser.
55. Interview of Jennie Elizabeth Kingston Fitzwilliam; see also interview of Elizabeth Stair Small.
56. Interview of Jennie Elizabeth Kingston Fitzwilliam. Among the regulars were John Kuhn and his future wife, Isobel Miller, the latter a young university graduate from Vancouver who would eventually become a famous CIM author.

was the son of a rescue-mission superintendent in Paterson, New Jersey; and Otto Schoerner, a young businessman from Butler, Pennsylvania, who would marry Katherine Dodd in China.[57]

By entering into this fellowship with the Pages, these young people were nearing the inner circle of what is probably best described as a Protestant religious order. Some had been on or near the inside already, having been the children of CIM missionaries. For others, the relationship had been that of admiring supporters who had befriended CIM workers, faithfully read *China's Millions*, and upheld the mission's staff with friendship, prayer, and money. Others had been introduced to the CIM by biographies of Hudson Taylor and were impressed by his principle of living by faith. Said Otto Schoerner, "it was the inspiration of my life." Jennie Kingston was awestruck by the prospects of joining the agency of such legendary spiritual giants. She mused, "I don't know how they ever let me in."[58]

It wasn't easy to get in. The first point of personal contact might be a conversation with Mr. Page, or perhaps with Mr. Hockman of the Institute, or with the North American director, Robert H. Glover, during one of his frequent speaking trips to the area. If the inquirer was encouraged to apply, he or she would fill out an application that asked for a spiritual autobiography, a doctrinal statement, a sense of one's calling to a particular area of work, and the like. One was asked to provide three references, and each of them was also asked to provide three references; so the mission could investigate one's background and character very deeply if any question arose. It was a daunting screening process, recalled Vincent Crossett.[59]

If an application was approved, the candidate would be invited to spend some time at one of the mission homes—in

57. Stam and Scott were married on the field and were slain by communist bandits in 1934; see the editor's introduction to *Sacrificial Lives: Young Martyrs and Fundamentalist Idealism*, ed. Joel A. Carpenter (New York: Garland, 1988); and Mrs. Howard Taylor, *The Triumph of John and Betty Stam* (Philadelphia: CIM, 1925), reprinted in *Sacrificial Lives*. On Schoerner and Dodd, see interview of Otto Frederick Schoerner, Collection #55, BGC Archives, and interview of Katherine Hasting Dodd Schoerner, Collection #51, BGC Archives.

58. Interview of Otto Frederick Shoerner; interview of Jennie Elizabeth Kingston Fitzwilliam.

59. Interview of Rev. Vincent Leroy Crossett.

Toronto or Philadelphia. There the novices underwent a month to six weeks of study, prayer, and scrutiny under the direction of returned missionaries and the mission officials. The candidates were introduced to the history, principles, and work of the CIM, taught the rudiments of the Chinese language, and given time to "get acquainted." It was crucial for the mission to see whether the candidates would fit into the tight-knit community they were seeking to enter. At the end of this period, if the candidates still felt the call, got along with the others, and showed promise of being able to learn Chinese, they were each interviewed by the North American Council, which voted whether or not to accept them. As soon as their support was in place, the new missionaries assembled their outfits and were put on a train for Vancouver and then a steamer to Shanghai.[60]

Thus began a life of trust, self-denial, and obedience, not only in relation to God, but also to the hierarchy within the mission. No doubt the faith missionaries serving with smaller or more recently organized societies experienced less procedural formality, but the principles were largely the same. These were paternally led religious orders, which had a camaraderie and ethos all their own.

The Surrendered Life: Keswick Holiness and Faith Missions

This faith-missions ethos permeated North American fundamentalism in the 1920s, 1930s, and 1940s. The religious language commonly used by fundamentalist students, Bible teachers, and missionaries in these decades reflected this influence. The terms *surrender* or *consecration* and expressions such as *the life of faith,* the *Christ life, the fullness of the Holy Spirit's power, proving God,* or *being willing to be made willing* that crop up repeatedly were not simply generically evangelical expressions,

60. The interviews of Margaret Rice Elliott Crossett, Rev. Vincent Leroy Crossett, Elizabeth Stair Small, Jennie Elizabeth Kingston Fitzwilliam, Eleanor Ruth Elliott, and Otto Frederick Schoerner contain detailed accounts of the process and experience of being a candidate with the China Inland Mission. So does Isobel Kuhn, *By Searching,* 96-128.

but in fact the code words of a particular school of thought and style of piety. Commonly called the "Victorious Christian Life" or the "Higher Christian Life" or simply the "Keswick" movement, it was a particular branch of the larger holiness movement that was especially attractive to the Baptist, Congregationalist, and Presbyterian evangelicals who laid the foundations for fundamentalism.[61]

This movement took its cue from the teaching featured at a summer Bible conference begun in 1875 at Keswick, England. Keswick teaching, like that of its parent, the holiness movement emanating from American Methodism and revivalism, emphasized that the key to a more holy and efficacious Christian life was an experience subsequent to conversion in which one fully yielded to God. While in most holiness teaching this act of consecration would result in a "baptism of the Holy Ghost" and lead to the eradication of one's propensity to sin, Keswick teachers stressed that a fresh infilling of the Holy Spirit would occur, bringing communion with God, power to do his will, and the active suppression (but not the annihilation) of the proclivity to sin. The Victorious Life, then, came to those who surrendered any claims to their own lives and entrusted them totally to God.[62]

While these beliefs were adopted and widely disseminated by most of Moody's associates in the late nineteenth century, the movement had influential promoters in the twentieth century as well. Foremost, perhaps, was Charles G. Trumbull. He was converted to the doctrine in 1910 and then helped to found the

61. George M. Marsden, "Fundamentalism," in *Encyclopedia of the American Religious Experience: Studies of Traditions and Movements*, 3 vols. (New York: Scribner's, 1988), 2:952. See also Marsden's extended treatment of the Victorious Life holiness teaching in *Fundamentalism and American Culture*, 72-101.

62. Helpful historical backgrounds and explications of the Keswick movement are Steven Barabas, *So Great Salvation: The History and Message of the Keswick Convention* (London: Marshall, Morgan and Scott, 1957); and John Pollock, *The Keswick Story: The Authorized History of the Keswick Convention* (London: Hodder & Stoughton, 1964). For a treatment of the movement's development in North America, see C. Melvin Loucks, "The Theological Foundations of the Victorious Life: An Evaluation of the Theology of the Victorious Christian Life in the Light of the Present and Future Aspects of Biblical Sanctification" (Ph.D. diss., Fuller Theological Seminary, 1984).

"America's Keswick" conference center in southern New Jersey in 1913. Trumbull also established the Victorious Life Council to sponsor speakers and conferences, and he promoted the movement in the *Sunday School Times*. Other leading speakers on the Higher Life circuit were Trumbull's protégé, Robert McQuilkin; W. H. Griffith Thomas; and Rowland V. Bingham, who founded the "Canadian Keswick" in northern Ontario in 1924. By the time of the fundamentalist-modernist controversies, Keswick holiness teaching was thoroughly integrated into the fundamentalist network of Bible schools, summer conferences, and faith missions.

This is all fairly well known to historians of fundamentalism, but its impact has been largely taken for granted. It is important to stress, then, what the Keswick holiness movement meant to the faith-missions network, and to fundamentalism more generally.

The first thing to notice is that the "life of faith" taught at Keswick was at the very heart of the faith-missions movement. Hudson Taylor, who seems to have arrived at his conclusions about living the "exchanged life," as he called it ("I live; yet not I, but Christ liveth in me. . ."; Gal. 2:20), prior to the Keswick movement, was a regular on the Keswick and other Higher Life platforms in the 1880s and 1890s, as were in later years other faith-missions leaders, such as C. T. Studd, founder of the Heart of Africa Mission, Rowland V. Bingham of the Sudan Interior Mission, and Charles Hurlbut of the Africa Inland Mission. The "total surrender" of one's life to God that formed the heart of the Keswick teaching offered faith missionaries the courage they needed for dangerous "inland" missions[63] and the humility, trust, and unselfishness they required to serve with agencies that directed their lives but did not guarantee their salaries.

The Victorious Life principle of surrender, or "consecration," or "yielding" of one's will and all claims to one's life became a major theme in faith-missions recruiting. Charles Hurl-

63. Andrew Porter, "Late Nineteenth-Century Anglican Missionary Expansion: A Consideration of Some Non-Anglican Sources of Inspiration," in *Religious Motivation: Biographical and Sociological Problems for the Church Historian*, ed. Derek Baker (Oxford: Basil Blackwell, 1978), 358-59.

but, general director of the AIM, freely added the task of "seeking additional workers" to his ministry of teaching "the secret of the Victorious Christian Life" on the Bible-conference circuit. So when he and the other founders of the IFMA were planning cooperative missionary conferences, Hurlbut called for a combined presentation of the cause of worldwide evangelization "together with such teachings of the victorious life and complete surrender as might be needful to secure desirable candidates for the mission field."[64]

The summons to the mission field followed the call to full surrender in at least two ways. First, it was a logical outcome of a life fully yielded to God. Running through the Higher Life movement was the idea that yielding oneself brought not only victory over sin and closer communion with God, but also the power to serve him effectively. The fifth and final day of the English Keswick Convention was customarily given over to the topic of service; and high, if not highest, on the agenda for Christian service was the mission field.[65]

Second, responding to the call to missions could be an important sign and seal of a person's full surrender. More than any other, the missionary vocation was considered to demand the most radical self-denial and devotion to the evangelical cause. So volunteering for missionary service seemed a sure indication that one was a fully consecrated, Spirit-filled Christian. After "giving [her] life to Jesus" at the Keswick, New Jersey, summer conference in 1925 and entering into the "victorious life," collegian Betty Scott wrote her parents that she was "willing to be an old-maid missionary, ... all my life, if God wants me to...."[66]

Ruth Sundquist, a Moody Bible Institute student in the early 1940s, encountered the missionary call in terms that virtually equated it with being a serious Christian. While attending a conference at the nearby Moody Church, she heard the missionary speaker ask the young people to come forward and offer themselves to go to the field, even if they did not yet have a call. Up

64. Quoting Frizen, "An Historical Study of the IFMA," 2; and Hurlbut in ibid., 3.

65. Barabas, *So Great Salvation*, 148-55.

66. Porter, "Late Nineteenth-Century Missionary Expansion," 358; Mrs. Howard Taylor, *Triumph of John and Betty Stam*, 39.

to then, Ruth recalled, "I thought I was a committed Christian." But now she had her doubts because she didn't feel "willing to go forward." The speaker persisted, in what was by then a time-honored tactic: "'If you aren't willing to go, ask the Lord to make you willing to go'"; and then, "'if you aren't willing to do that, ask him to make you willing to be willing to pray that prayer.'" Said Ruth, "that's about where I had to start!" The sincerity of one's commitment to Christ became tied to at least an acquiescence to the possibility of accepting a missionary call.[67]

In addition, therefore, to the classic missionary motivations of the past century—responding to God's saving love by proclaiming it to all humanity, obeying Christ's command to do this, or seeing in missionary service the ultimate opportunity to make one's life count to the fullest[68]—the Higher Life movement added the matter of personal consecration. Did one trust fully in God? Was one fully surrendered to his will? Was the life that one was now living in fact being lived through the indwelling Christ? Then one would be willing to go anywhere, do anything. And what most needed doing? As the modern American missionary martyr William Borden put it, "If ten men are carrying a log, nine of them on the little end and one at the heavy end, and you want to help, which end will you lift . . . ?"[69] Thus the Keswick holiness ideal of "my utmost for His highest"[70] worked

---

67. Interview of Ruth Sundquist, Collection #266, BGC Archives. On the vintage character of the "being willing to be made willing" appeal, see William Borden's use of it some thirty years earlier on the Student Volunteers circuit in Mrs. Howard Taylor, *Borden of Yale, '09: The Life that Counts* (Philadelphia: CIM, 1926), 216-18; and see the interview of Eleanor Ruth Elliott for her encounter with this appeal at a Christian Endeavor conference circa 1920.

68. These respective themes are discussed in R. Pierce Beaver, "Missionary Motivation through Three Centuries," in *Reinterpretation in American Church History*, ed. Jerald C. Brauer (Chicago: Univ. of Chicago Press, 1968), 113-51; and Hunter, *Gospel of Gentility*, 42-51. See also Rabe, *Home Base of American China Missions*, 97-107; and Stuart Piggin, "Assessing Nineteenth-Century Missionary Motivation: Some Considerations of Theory and Method," in *Religious Motivation*, ed. Derek Baker, 327-37.

69. Mrs. Howard Taylor, *Borden of Yale*, 218; for a contemporary example of this argument see David M. Howard, "The Road to Urbana and Beyond," *Evangelical Missions Quarterly* 21 (January 1985): 17.

70. This is, of course, the title of one of the devotional favorites of the fundamentalist movement: Oswald Chambers, *The Golden Book of Oswald Chambers:*

in tandem with the faith-missions' drive to penetrate the "regions beyond." This potent combination helped make North American fundamentalism a leading recruiter of twentieth-century missionaries.

Faith Missions and the Character of American Fundamentalism

Fundamentalists' embrace of the faith-missions movement and its distinctive piety had some important effects. The first, it seems, was that at a time when the movement might have become preoccupied with more "domestic" issues, fundamentalism kept alive and intensified its commitment to being a missionary movement. The growing fundamentalist missionary enterprise rode upon a new wave of perfectionist piety, now coming more directly from the international faith missions and Keswick network than from the older American holiness sources, as the growing popularity of the works of Geraldine Guinness (Mrs. Howard) Taylor, Oswald Chambers, Amy Carmichael, and others seems to indicate.

The faith-missions ethos certainly triumphed at Wheaton College. According to several observers, Wheaton under its third president, J. Oliver Buswell, Jr. (1926–1940), was supportive of missions, but during the 1930s Buswell became involved in the disputes and splintering of fundamentalist Presbyterianism, and missions took a backseat to these squabbles at home.[71] But the atmosphere changed considerably after V. Raymond Edman, a former missionary to Ecuador with the Christian and Missionary Alliance, assumed the school's presidency in 1940. An avid promoter of missions and missionary spiritu-

---

My Utmost for His Highest: Selections for the Year (London: Simpkin, Marshall, 1927), and many reprintings. Chambers was a young Bible teacher who worked for the Y.M.C.A. during World War I, and in that capacity served the British troops in Egypt. He died there in 1917. His devotional works, published posthumously from his lectures and addresses, express a fairly radical (some might say morbid) version of the Keswick movement's stress on self-denial.

71. Interview of Helen Torrey Renich; interview of Torrey Maynard Johnson, Collection #285, BGC Archives.

ality, Edman frequently used episodes from the life of Hudson Taylor in his chapel talks, and he personally counseled students in their pursuit of the surrendered life.[72]

As a result, Wheaton was fairly pulsating with missionary piety and enthusiasm by the mid-1940s. The Wheaton chapter of the Student Foreign Missions Fellowship, a conservative evangelical replacement for the SVM founded by Wheaton and Columbia Bible College students in 1936, had one hundred students attending.[73] Some of its leaders, notably David Howard, his sister Elisabeth, and her future husband, Jim Elliot, would become evangelical missionary legends.[74] Fortified by the missions commitment of returning veterans and a campus revival, one-fourth of the Wheaton class of 1950 found its way to the mission field.[75] This rapid rise of new recruits, as Richard Pierard points out, was a movement-wide phenomenon;[76] and the faith-missions ethos, if the situation at Wheaton is typical, gave it shape and thrust.

Another feature of fundamentalism that needs to be understood in light of the Keswick faith-missions influence is the apparent contradiction between fundamentalism's militancy and its pietism. It is difficult to understand how fundamentalist con-

72. Interview of Donald Cook, Collection #259, BGC Archives; interview of Jeannette Martig Thiessen; interview of Helen Torrey Renich.

73. On the formation of the Student Foreign Missions Fellowship and its eventual incorporation into the emerging Inter-Varsity Christian Fellowship, see H. Wilbert Norton, *To Stir the Church: A Brief History of the Student Foreign Missions Fellowships, 1936–1986* (Madison, WI: Student Foreign Missions Fellowship, 1986).

74. Jim Elliot became a celebrated missionary martyr when he, fellow Wheaton alumnus Ed McCully, and three other young missionaries died at the hands of Auca Indians in the jungles of Ecuador. *Time, Reader's Digest,* and *Life* carried stories, and Elisabeth Howard Elliot immortalized her husband and the others with her account, *Through Gates of Splendor* (New York: Harper and Brothers, 1957). David Howard served for fifteen years as a missionary to Colombia, then was missions director for Inter-Varsity Christian Fellowship, and is currently general director of the World Evangelical Fellowship. See his reflections on the enthusiasm for missions growing among fundamentalist students in the 1930s and 1940s in his article "The Road to Urbana and Beyond," 7-21.

75. Paul Bechtel, *Wheaton College: A Heritage Remembered, 1860–1984* (Wheaton: Harold Shaw, 1984), 194.

76. See Pierard's chapter in this volume, "*Pax Americana* and the Evangelical Missionary Advance."

tentiousness could be supported by the sweetly pious, rather quiescent style of the Higher Life movement. British historian Andrew Porter points to an answer, though, in his studies of British evangelical missionaries to Africa. He found that the Keswick-fired faith-missions movements' spiritual intensity and evangelistic zeal often penetrated the older British mission societies in the late nineteenth century, most frequently in the hands of young university recruits. Once on the field, Porter discovered, these evangelicals sometimes wreaked havoc among the veteran missionaries and their native evangelists. Not only were they hard on themselves in their quest for holiness; they could be extremely judgmental toward other more "ordinary" Christians.[77]

This insight helps to explain the seeming paradox of Charles G. Trumbull, who was at once the leading American apostle of the Victorious Life and one of the foremost power brokers of American fundamentalism. Trumbull taught, on the one hand, that God could give those who were fully surrendered to his will a life that is "brand new, fresh from the hands of God," and marked by love for one's enemy ("a positive outgoing of love, so that you would do anything for him"), patience ("taking 'all that is coming to you' with a smile"), and self-control—all by means of the Holy Spirit's power.

On the other hand, few equaled Trumbull's ability to stir up trouble as a watchdog for the fundamentalist faith. Trumbull was not the meanest of fundamentalists by any stretch of the imagination, but his testimony to having gained victory over all known sin loses credibility in the face of his actions. He labeled the Presbyterian Board of Foreign Missions "apostate"; he relentlessly attacked fellow evangelical and holiness advocate E. Stanley Jones for his alleged modernism; and Trumbull's assault on John MacInnis, a fellow fundamentalist, resulted in MacInnis's being hounded from the presidency of BIOLA. As-

---

77. Andrew Porter, "Evangelical Enthusiasm, Missionary Motivation and West Africa in the Late Nineteenth Century: The Career of G. W. Brooke," *Journal of Imperial and Commonwealth History* 6 (October 1977): 25-29; and idem, "Cambridge, Keswick, and Late-Nineteenth-Century Attitudes to Africa," *Journal of Imperial and Commonwealth History* 5 (October 1976): 5-34.

surance of his personal spiritual victory apparently gave Trumbull a similar assurance of his doctrinal and ethical rectitude and sanctioned his merciless attacks on those whose views differed from his own.[78] In an American context, at least, Keswick's promise of spiritual power for effective service and the faith-missions example of establishing new (and, in effect, separated) agencies seemed to enhance fundamentalists' proclivity for judgmental attitudes.

To be fair, we should add that the faith-missions movement probably helped many fundamentalists to avoid the most extreme alienation of which the movement was capable. Faith-missions leaders were generally moderate to "progressive" along the spectrum of attitudes within fundamentalism toward other Christians. They implemented, within a conservative evangelical doctrinal consensus, interdenominational cooperation and fellowship on their own staffs, and they were among the organizers of the National Association of Evangelicals and the rejuvenated World Evangelical Fellowship in the 1940s. These two organizations reflected the capacity—and the limits—inherent in fundamentalism for ecumenicity. The faith-missions ethos, it seems, helped to shape both.[79]

The faith-missions impulse had at least one further effect on fundamentalism. It reinforced the movement's tendency, already well underway since Moody's day, to narrow the church's mission to direct evangelization. As we have seen, faith missions focused intently on evangelization and on pioneering mis-

78. For an extended discussion (and critique) of Charles G. Trumbull's teaching on the Victorious Christian life, see Douglas W. Frank, *Less than Conquerors: How Evangelicals Entered the Twentieth Century* (Grand Rapids: Eerdmans, 1986), 109-23, 145-54, 119-20 (quotes).

79. Rowland V. Bingham explained the nonsectarian principles for the Sudan Interior Mission in *Seven Sevens of Years and a Jubilee!* (Toronto: Evangelical Publishers, 1943), 101-8. Both Ralph Davis of the Africa Inland Mission and T. J. Bach of the Scandinavian Alliance Mission were involved in the early planning for the National Association of Evangelicals. For fundamentalists' role in organizing the N.A.E., see Joel A. Carpenter, "The Fundamentalist Leaven and the Rise of an Evangelical United Front," in *The Evangelical Tradition in America*, ed. Leonard I. Sweet (Macon, GA: Mercer Univ. Press, 1984), 257-88. On the renewal of the W.E.F., which tended to follow evangelical missions networks, see David M. Howard, *The Dream That Would Not Die: The Birth and Growth of the World Evangelical Fellowship, 1846–1986* (Exeter: Paternoster, 1986).

sions—taking the gospel to hitherto unevangelized regions. Embracing this mission strategy allowed fundamentalists to pursue missions work much as Hudson Taylor had in the 1880s and, in the process, largely to ignore the theological, cultural, and ethical issues that the denominational-ecumenical mission establishment had been encountering since the late nineteenth century.

Robert Hall Glover's widely used text, *The Progress of World-Wide Missions* (1924), which one of his students at Moody Bible Institute appropriately called "*the* book" on missions, is a case in point. It was largely an inspirational survey of the modern missionary enterprise. Only a few pages in the last chapter, "The Present Missionary Outlook," acknowledged that there was any sort of discussion occurring over the theology and ethics of missions. Glover treated these subjects as mere by-products of theological liberalism, which he blamed for the current malaise of missionary commitment. What was needed was an old-fashioned revival. His only theological response to the current debates was a brief, simple, biblically reinforced reiteration of the lostness of the heathen. A revised version of this work appeared in 1939, but this last chapter stood unchanged.[80]

William Hutchison's assertion that fundamentalists were so far removed from the missionary establishment by the mid-1930s as to be no longer a party to its central debates is right on the mark.[81] Their defeat in the controversies of the 1920s and early 1930s was not the only reason for this isolation, however. Through their embrace of faith missions and a narrowly evangelistic agenda, fundamentalists were able to ignore the ethical and theological issues about which other Protestants earnestly contended. Left to their own nonreflective, activist proclivities, fundamentalist missions and their leaders exhibited the epitome

80. Only an entry in the revised edition's bibliography for the conservative Dutch theologian Hendrik Kraemer's defense of Christianity's uniqueness and fundamental separation from other world religions indicated a recognition that an important discussion was afoot (Glover, *The Progress of World-Wide Missions* [New York: George H. Doran, 1924], 360-71; rev. ed. [New York: Harper and Brothers, 1939], 374).

81. William R. Hutchison, *Errand to the World: American Protestant Thought and Foreign Missions* (Chicago: Univ. of Chicago Press, 1987), 174-75.

of what European missions leaders thought was the great fault of the American missionary enterprise: its anti-intellectual, impatient, pragmatic, and technique-oriented outlook.[82]

This last point suggests some ways in which the faith-missions movement itself was being transformed. Andrew Walls's description of the distinctive features of *American* Christianity—especially its "vigorous expansionism, readiness of invention, [and] a willingness to make the fullest use of contemporary technology, finance, organization, and business methods"[83]—began to show up dramatically among the North American faith missions by the late 1930s and early 1940s.

A good example of this trend comes from the Sudan Interior Mission. Expansion, if not expansionism, was its hallmark during the 1920s, 1930s, and early 1940s. SIM had increased in size from 44 missionaries in 1920 to 494 missionaries by 1945. The mission's finances underwent a parallel growth over the same period, as its income increased from $29,000 in 1917 to $388,000 in 1941.[84] In the process of promoting this expansion, SIM's speakers and circular letters were beginning to annoy some of the mission's colleagues in the IFMA. SIM's "high-pressure salesmanship," it was alleged, amounted to a breach of the IFMA's nonsolicitation policy. Such behavior may have struck other faith-mission leaders as unbecoming of a faith mission. Yet it was characteristically American.[85]

---

82. See ibid., 125-38, for a discussion of Americans' activism and pragmatism and European critiques of these traits. There is a certain irony, of course, in their embrace of faith missions allowing fundamentalists to avoid engaging in critical missiology, for, as Andrew Porter pointed out, the faith missions first came into being as efforts to reform the missionary enterprise of the 1860s and 1870s. See Porter, "Evangelical Enthusiasm, Missionary Motivation, and West Africa," 25-29.

83. See Andrew F. Walls, "The American Dimension in the History of the Missionary Movement," the first chapter of this volume.

84. Gary Corwin, "Evangelical Separatism and the Growth of Independent Mission Boards, 1920–1945: Some Preliminary Observations from the History of the Sudan Interior Mission," paper presented at the conference "A Century of World Evangelization," June 16-19, 1986, at Wheaton College, Wheaton, Illinois; Bingham, *Seven Sevens of Years*, 62.

85. Robert Hall Glover to Arthur J. Bowen, 11 June 1942; Arthur J. Bowen to Rowland V. Bingham, 17 June 1942; Rowland V. Bingham to Arthur J. Bowen, 20 June 1942; Arthur J. Bowen to Rowland V. Bingham, 30 June 1942; and Robert

The founder of SIM, Rowland V. Bingham, an English immigrant to Canada, seemed to have imbibed some American triumphalism and entrepreneurship by the end of his years. In the last chapter of his missions memoir, *Seven Sevens of Years and a Jubilee!*, Bingham cast British reserve to the winds. He interpreted the apostle Peter's admonition to "[give] all diligence" (2 Pet. 1:5) to mean "speed up!" the missionary enterprise. "Speed up!" was the "characteristic of the age," he noted, whether in business, travel, or in manufacturing war materials for the present conflict. Bingham took this to mean that "God is giving us the facilities for speeding up [missions] work in our day as never before." With airplanes and radio broadcasting at their disposal, missionaries could, given just a tithe of the money being devoted to the war effort, "finish the task" of world evangelization in five years and "bring in the great consummation of the age. . . ."[86] Perhaps such views were not formally incompatible with Hudson Taylor's determination to see "God's work done in God's way," but they betrayed a typically American departure from the prayerful reticence about ways and means that people had come to expect from faith missions.

The organizational model of the faith mission also underwent several "American" mutations during the 1930s and 1940s. With increasing frequency, the more generalized, self-sufficient missionary-society model, which resembled a Catholic religious order, was being converted into a highly specialized agency. Perhaps the epitome of this trend was the founding in 1931 of radio station HCJB near Quito, Ecuador, by two Americans, Clarence Jones, a young associate in Paul Rader's innovative Chicago Gospel Tabernacle, and Reuben Larson, a Christian and Missionary Alliance worker in Ecuador. "Gospel Radio" was new enough in the United States, but its use in South America, where few as yet even owned radio sets, seemed unthinkable. But Jones and Larson were well versed in what Jones called "spiritual lo-

---

Hall Glover to Arthur J. Bowen, 14 July 1942 discuss these charges. Rowland V. Bingham, circular letter, "Dear Prayer Helper," 15 July 1942, shows some of the tactics that got him into trouble. These documents are all from Records of the Interdenominational Foreign Mission Association, Collection #352, box 1, folder 14, BGC Archives.

86. Bingham, *Seven Sevens of Years*, 112, 114, 116.

gistics," as well as American "hustle." As a result, the station grew by the mid-1940s to include five transmitters and a broadcast schedule of six hundred gospel programs in fourteen languages. By that time, Jones, like Bingham, envisioned radio and aviation leading a postwar missionary advance. He urged fundamentalist mission leaders to borrow techniques from business, government, and the military and to raise a "spiritual expeditionary force" of new agencies to accomplish the task.[87]

Another product of American fundamentalists' tinkering with the faith-missions model was the Wycliffe Bible Translators. In 1933, L. L. Legters, a frequent Keswick speaker and pioneer missions promoter, and W. Cameron Townsend, a veteran evangelist and colporteur in southern Mexico, encountered an obstacle in getting the gospel message to the region's varied Indian tribes. Most of the Indians were illiterate, and each tribe preferred its own unwritten language to Spanish. Seeing this as a problem to be solved by the introduction of the right methods, the organizers began a summer school of linguistics, "Camp Wycliffe," meeting first in Siloam Springs, Arkansas, then at various sites in Oklahoma, Texas, and Saskatchewan, to train frontier missionary translators. Thus was Wycliffe Bible Translators born, by applying the techniques of the social sciences, notably linguistics and anthropology, to the missiological problem of two thousand tribes worldwide not yet reached by the gospel.[88]

The 1940s would bring a proliferation of such specialized and technologically driven missionary agencies. These included Trans World Radio and Far East Gospel Broadcasting Company, both generated out of the exuberant "Youth for Christ" evangelistic rally movement; radio ELWA of Liberia, an improbably

87. Clarence W. Jones, *Radio, The New Missionary* (Chicago: Moody, 1946), 124. For accounts of HCJB's development, see ibid.; and Lois Neely, *Come Up to This Mountain* (Wheaton: Tyndale, 1980).

88. J. Herbert Kane, *Faith, Mighty Faith: A Handbook of the Interdenominational Foreign Mission Association* (New York: IFMA, 1956), 162-63; "Two Score More, 1933–1943," *Translation* 1 (January 1943): 8-9; *Camp Wycliffe Chronicle* (1944), n.p. See also Martha L. Moennich, *That They May Hear: Wycliffe Bible Translators* (Chicago: Chicago Gospel Tabernacle, n.d.); and Wycliffe Bible Translators, *Pass the Word: 50 Years of Wycliffe Bible Translators* (Huntingdon Beach, CA: Wycliffe Bible Translators, 1984).

successful venture hatched out of the technical know-how and missionary idealism of three Wheaton College students; and Mission Aviation Fellowship, started among born-again aviators and mechanics whose military experience overseas prompted visions of converting their skills into "spiritual logistics" for missions. Thus the faith mission itself was being converted into the single-purpose "parachurch agency" that has become the dominant organizational form of late-twentieth-century American evangelicalism.[89]

Conclusion: The Legacy of Fundamentalist Missions

This spurt of innovation played a part, as a subsequent chapter by Richard Pierard will show, in the triumphal ebullience and rapid missionary expansion of the postwar years. Riding a wave of popular evangelical resurgence, a Cold War–inspired renewal of American manifest destiny, and the solid institutional base laid before the Second World War, fundamentalists and their evangelical allies were emerging from oblivion and moving toward numerical parity, if not equal status and intellectual depth, with the Protestant missionary establishment. An important signal of this came with the formation of the Evangelical Foreign Missions Association (EFMA) in 1945, as an affiliate of the recently formed National Association of Evangelicals. Now the scattered mission boards and societies that represented a wide variety of evangelicals were gaining visibility and a sense of significance.[90]

This dynamism owed much to the faith missions' nurturing of the turn-of-the-century vision of world evangelization. At a

89. George Marsden, "Introduction: The Evangelical Denomination," in *Evangelicalism and Modern America*, ed. Marsden (Grand Rapids: Eerdmans, 1984), vii-xvi. See also Richard G. Hutcheson, *Mainline Churches and the Evangelicals: A Challenging Crisis?* (Atlanta: John Knox, 1981), 62-79; and Robert Wuthnow, *The Restructuring of American Religion: Society and Faith Since World War II* (Princeton: Princeton Univ. Press, 1988), chaps. 6 and 8.

90. "The Story of the EFMA," typescript dated 31 October 1950, Records of the Evangelical Foreign Missions Association, Collection #165, box 2, folder 16, BGC Archives.

time when mainline Protestantism was preoccupied with its relations to the "younger churches" in regions already evangelized,
the fundamentalist faith missions (as part of a larger evangelical
missions movement) pressed on to "unevangelized fields." At a
time when mainline Protestant theorists were, for a variety of reasons, entertaining questions about the traditional missionary
mandate's relevance and righteousness, fundamentalists (alongside other evangelicals) were maintaining, more by their actions
than by any sustained theological defense, the universal claims
of Christianity and the right of all of the world's people to hear
what evangelicals believe to be the ultimate in good news.

These patterns became the prelude for the situation of the
1980s, at which time the conservative Protestant agencies would
employ about ten of every eleven career foreign missionaries
from North America.[91] The trend of evangelical and fundamentalist foreign missions in the 1930s and 1940s, then, is much the
same as that of these groups' institutions more generally: a strong
infrastructure was being built that would provide the base for
rapid expansion and increasing salience in the decades to come.[92]

We have seen, however, that the fundamentalist missionary
enterprise left its post-1945 heirs with some other legacies as
well. The movement's separation and isolation from the Protestant mainstream and its avoidance of important issues in missions thought and worldwide Christian relations meant that
when a post-fundamentalist, "neo-evangelical" theological
movement appeared in the 1950s and 1960s, it virtually had to
reinvent evangelical missions theology.[93] Fundamentalists'

91. Robert T. Coote, "The Uneven Growth of Conservative Evangelical Missions," *IBMR* 6 (July 1982): 118-23.

92. I argue this point in "Fundamentalist Institutions and the Rise of Evangelical Protestantism, 1929–1942," *Church History* 49 (March 1980): 62-75.

93. The most thorough discussion of the various trends in recent missions
theology, including evangelicals' role, is Rodger C. Bassham, *Mission Theology,
1948–1975: Years of Worldwide Creative Tension: Ecumenical, Evangelical, Roman
Catholic* (Pasadena: William Carey Library, 1979). See also Hutchison, *Errand to
the World*, chap. 7, "Familiar Debates in an Unfamiliar World," 176-202; Arthur F.
Glasser, "The Evolution of Evangelical Mission Theology since World War II,"
IBMR 9 (January 1985): 9-13; and Efiong Utuk, "From Wheaton to Lausanne: The
Road to Modification of Contemporary Evangelical Mission Theology," *Missi-
ology* 14 (April 1986): 205-19

single-minded emphasis on evangelism in missions also has had lasting and powerful effects. It has fueled the church-growth movement on the one hand and has implanted a strong suspicion of social ethics as a missiological concern on the other.

The result has been an ironic reprise of evangelical missions history. Many of the evangelical leaders representing the more venerable, institutionally mature faith missions and conservative denominational boards have become more theologically reflective, more concerned with questions of Christianity's cultural impact and role, and more responsive to Third World evangelical leaders' calls for social discipleship. At the same time, zealous evangelizers, both young and old, are profoundly uneasy with these developments. They are impatient with theological reflection and have tended to judge any broadening of the church's mission to be a reprehensible distraction from what they see as the church's *one* task, world evangelization. They have been forming new missions and specialized parachurch agencies to complete the task in this generation. Thus the fundamentalist missionary movement's evolution seems to have come full circle. What was once an argument for establishing a separate fundamentalist missionary enterprise now echoes within the confines of the movement itself.

6 Identity, Community, and Status: The Legacy of the Central American Pentecostal Pioneers

Everett A. Wilson

Central America's rapidly growing, grassroots pentecostal churches have made the isthmus, along with Brazil and Chile, a focus of Latin American Protestantism.[1] The republics of Guatemala and El Salvador, according to some estimates, now have evangelical communities that exceed a fifth of the national populations, of which half in Guatemala and two-thirds in El Salvador are pentecostal.[2] The spread of popular Protestantism

1. The term *evangelical*, denoting all non–Roman Catholics except groups like the Latter Day Saints and the Jehovah's Witnesses, is generally preferred to *protestante* in Latin America, where the latter term may have a negative connotation. A discussion of the doctrinal emphases of Central American evangelicals is found in Wilton M. Nelson, *Protestantism in Latin America* (Grand Rapids: Eerdmans, 1984), 49-56. The Congress of Missions of Ibero-America (COMIBAM), held in Sao Paulo in November 1987, released statistics indicating 36.5 million evangelicals in Latin America, of which 80 percent are in Brazil, Chile, and Central America, countries whose populations make up only 45 percent of the total.

2. Although COMIBAM's per capita estimates of evangelicals in Guatemala, El Salvador, and the other three countries are, respectively, 18.4 percent, 12.8 percent, and 12.7 percent, much higher proportions persist in the literature. E.g., Roger Palms, "El Salvador—Alive with the Gospel," *Decision* 28 (April 1988): 23, claims that 26 percent of the population of El Salvador is evangelical. Estimates of the proportion of pentecostals among the evangelical populations of Guatemala and El Salvador were reported in 1981 as, respectively, 52.1 and 67.1 percent (Clifton L. Holland, "El Salvador" and "Guatemala," in *Central America and the Caribbean*, vol. 4 of *World Christianity*, ed. Holland [Monrovia, CA: Missions Advanced Research and Communications Center, 1981], 55, 71).

in this deeply troubled area, beyond its interest for social scientists and missiologists, reveals much about the nature of pentecostalism itself, about the men and women who introduced the often disparaged doctrinal emphases, about the social conditions that existed where these beliefs were embraced, and about the national workers and communities that made the movements flourish.

The beginnings of pentecostalism in Central America indicate that while conventional evangelical missionary work was proceeding there with considerable effectiveness before World War II, a simultaneous yet scarcely visible movement was emerging to fill the spiritual and institutional vacuum that had formed in Central American peasant culture. These local groups of vigorous believers adapted the features and approaches of early pentecostal missionaries to their immediate needs and, in the process, laid the foundations of the mass movements that in recent years have acquired increasing importance.

When the pioneering phase of pentecostal development in Central America was completed soon after World War II, representative groups were firmly established in each of the five republics, and the work was advancing largely at the initiative of national leaders.[3] Writers in the 1950s sometimes characterized these movements as "indigenous" churches whose doctrines and practices, holiness and evangelistic, had Wesleyan tendencies.[4] Observers were aware, however, that even autonomous Latin American denominations had usually been influenced by missionary efforts, sometimes emerging as insurgent movements within a denomination or, like the Otomí church in central Mexico, a movement with a charismatic leader, taking form a generation removed from direct missionary oversight.[5] But even pentecostal churches that originated as denominational missions have resulted less from missionaries' having reproduced their churches overseas than from

3. David J. du Plessis, "Golden Jubilees of Twentieth Century Pentecostal Movements," *International Review of Mission* 47 (April 1958): 193-201.

4. Eugene A. Nida, "The Indigenous Churches of Latin America," *Practical Anthropology* 8 (March/April 1961): 97-103, 110.

5. Ibid., 97-98. See also William A. Wonderly, "Cultural Implications of an Indigenous Church," *Practical Anthropology* (January/February 1958): 51-65.

their having incited Latin Americans to find their own compelling faith.[6]

Nevertheless, a relatively few pioneering missionaries played a strategic role in establishing these rapidly spreading associations through their personal influence and their eminently appropriate beliefs. Their catalytic leadership, emphasizing God's immanence and empowering of believers, no matter how socially marginal and disfavored, was especially suited to peasant peoples, the vast majority of whom were suffering from the region's disruptive economic changes and deteriorating social conditions.[7] Early figures like Albert Hines, the first known pentecostal missionary in Guatemala, and Frederick W. Mebius, the first such worker in El Salvador, represented a gospel that was rugged, authoritative, and persuasive.[8] As a group these early missionaries identified with the common people, adapted to their rustic way of life, and shared their concerns, frustrations, and aspirations. More important, they directed their converts to appropriate biblical teachings for a better life and a higher purpose, to the point of defying social convention and traditional forms of authority.

The effectiveness of these churches in gathering and integrating peoples who had endured the trauma of social dissolution gave ample evidence of their members' buoyant faith. The neatly drawn graphs depicting the rapid rise of pentecostal churches in Latin America, published in church-growth studies beginning in the 1950s, revealed little of the human drama, the fundamental struggle for human dignity, the sacrificial vision

6. The 1961 Taylor/Coggins study, which gave ratios of missionaries to national workers and members for pentecostals in Guatemala and El Salvador as 1:10:1,200, while showing nonpentecostal ratios as 1:1.9:234, suggests as much (Clyde W. Taylor and Wade T. Coggins, *Protestant Missions in Latin America* [Washington, DC: EFMA, 1961], 141, 152).

7. The relationship between social crisis and pentecostalism is treated in Everett A. Wilson, "The Central American Evangelicals: From Protest to Pragmatism," *International Review of Mission* 77 (January 1988): 94-106.

8. Mebius's career is treated in Roberto Domínguez, *Pioneros de Pentecostés*, 2 vols. (San Salvador: Literatura Evangelica, 1975), 2:19-22. Albert Hines is treated briefly in Virgilio Zapata, *Historia de la Iglesia Evangélica en Guatemala* (Guatemala: Caisa Litografía, 1982), 125-27, and in Charles W. Conn, *Where the Saints Have Trod* (Cleveland, TN: Pathway, 1959), 131, 134.

demanded of national workers, and the faithfulness of the rank and file as expressed by their tireless efforts. Yet the network of pentecostal churches, consisting of scores of denominational affiliations and for the most part composed of the most humble social elements, thrived on the basic formulas established by the foreign and national pioneers.

These formulas, providing satisfaction for profound spiritual needs, were developed by men and women who took literally the biblical mandate to make disciples of all nations and who also anticipated that the confirming signs would follow for men and women who believed. Their confidence and willingness to put their faith to the test brought them into contact with populations caught in bewildering social change who, in their distress, were prepared to accept and act on the same mandates.

In general, these movements prompted three kinds of achievements: the reconstitution of a viable way of life and respected values amid a disintegrating society, the formation of communities for people whose extended families and intimate associations were scattered by changing economic circumstances, and the legitimation of these popular associations by legal recognition. Each of these developments has become increasingly important as the social crises have intensified throughout Central America up to the present.

The Guatemalan Pioneers

The introduction of pentecostalism into Central America centers on the careers of several pioneers, notably Charles T. Furman and Thomas A. Pullin in Guatemala and Frederick W. Mebius and Ralph Darby Williams in El Salvador.[9] Furman and Pullin, sponsored by the Full Gospel and Missionary Society (FGMS) of Turtle Creek, Pennsylvania, joined Albert Hines among the

9. Furman's career is treated in Domínguez, *Pioneros*, 193-96; Zapata, *Historia*, 101-3, 125-29; and Conn, *Saints*, 131-38. Brief treatment is given Pullin in the same sources. Williams's contribution has been neglected, largely overshadowed by Melvin L. Hodges, with whom he was associated in Central America and who described the Salvadoran pentecostals in *The Indigenous Church* (Springfield, MO.: Gospel Publishing House, 1953).

Quiché Indians of the Department of Totonicapán in the northern highlands in 1916. Hines, who had been in the country since 1910, shared his colleagues' interest in the pentecostal phenomena that were experienced by their associates at the Christian and Missionary Alliance training school at Nyack, New York, in 1912. In 1920 Furman married Carrie Smith, also of Nyack, who had been directed to Guatemala through a dream.

Having been informed of the mission's inability to continue their support, the Furmans returned from furlough in 1922 under appointment with the Primitive Methodists. Under these auspices the work grew with the acquisition of several independent stations and the arrival of additional personnel. Pullin, who remained with the FGMS but who continued to work closely with Furman, opened churches in the northern limits of Quiché territory in Nebaj, Cunén, and Sacapulas, while Furman, who had inherited Hines's congregations, extended the work eastward to Santa Cruz del Quiché and Santo Tomás Chichicastenango.[10]

The surviving profiles of Charles Furman and strong-willed Doña Carrie portray them as resolute and resourceful persons who readily adapted to Indian customs and the rigors of evangelizing among people who were indifferent or hostile to their objectives. Their effectiveness in attracting resilient, innovative "culture brokers" who like themselves were natural leaders is apparent in the narrative accounts. Among their first converts was Cayetano Aguilar, who became a leading Quiché pastor. A traveling clothing vendor, Aguilar approached the intruders after inner voices prompted him to make an inquiry about the new faith. José María Enríquez, a former soldier, was left in charge of Furman's work in Totonicapán as early as 1921, when J. H. Ingram of the Church of God, Cleveland, visited the field, and Doña Amalia, a notorious proprietress of a tavern, became a convert even though she was not made a full member for some time because of her continuing associations.[11]

Despite a measure of success in extending the work, Furman experienced disappointment and difficulty. He became ill, pos-

10. Domínguez, *Pioneros*, 195.
11. Ibid., 128, 195.

sibly with tuberculosis, and for an extended time retired to Ecuador.[12] On his return to Guatemala, he felt that his efforts had largely failed until a spontaneous revival spread through the entire Quiché country in the spring of 1932. "When we were almost despairing, thinking perhaps our work had been in vain," Pullin later recalled, "a mighty blaze was kindled in Brother Furman's church in Totonicapán. It was the first outpouring of the Holy Ghost in that republic. During this divine show hundreds were wonderfully converted and the sick were healed."[13]

When confronted by his mission with an ultimatum, Furman refused to conform with the Methodist position, claiming that he had always been pentecostal and that he had been given latitude to preach these doctrines from the onset.[14] Within a few weeks Furman accepted an invitation from J. H. Ingram to affiliate with the Church of God, and on his return to Guatemala he devastated the Primitive Methodist work by leading fourteen of their congregations into the pentecostal organization. Pullin, who to that time had remained with the FGMS, joined Furman in the Church of God in 1944 and succeeded him as the denomination's supervisor for Guatemala upon Furman's death in 1947.[15]

Whether or not Furman's disruption of the Primitive Methodist work was prompted by purely spiritual motives, his decisions were determinative for the future of Guatemalan evangelicalism. In the village of Chesuch, near Totonicapán, a gravely afflicted illiterate woman who claimed to have been healed of an evil spell won a large following to the faith. Similarly, some converts' impressive power in confronting sorcery in Chuicacá made the town in later years a center of pentecostalism.[16] An elder, Marcos Lux, later recalled the directive he received in a dream before his conversion, assuring him that he would enjoy riches if he pursued the gospel.[17]

12. Ibid., 195-96.

13. Conn, *Saints*, 135n.

14. Ibid.; Conn states that Furman "had filed with the missions board a full written statement of his belief in the baptism of the Holy Ghost and the evidence of speaking in tongues" in 1929.

15. Ibid., 137-38.

16. Domínguez, *Pioneros*, 176.

17. Zapata, *Historia*, 128.

Church historian Virgilio Zapata assesses Furman's contribution by pointing out that the Church of God became one of the three largest denominations in the country, in large part "as a result of emphasis on giving total responsibility for the churches as well as the work in general to the national pastors and workers."[18] Furman's strategic efforts also may be inferred from the eulogy published at his death, which stated, "Under Furman's fatherly guidance the native workers grew into a capable and fruitful corps of evangelists and pastors. Without the work of the natives, the foreign missionary would do very little boasting about numbers saved."[19] Thus, while most missions in the 1950s were experiencing nationalistic insurgencies, the pentecostal work was essentially in the hands of the Guatemalans from the beginning.

The work of the Church of God in Guatemala in the early stages was not remarkable in comparison with other groups. Throughout the country other evangelical groups had succeeded in establishing an impressive foothold, so observers saw no reason for new missions to enter the field. Kenneth G. Grubb, who surveyed the Central American missions in 1936, exulted that "the relative success of the work has been remarkable. In no republic except perhaps Brazil . . . has similar progress been made. Further, figures fail to show the extent to which the whole life of the nation has been permeated by evangelical influence."[20]

Grubb and other writers have attributed this success to favorable church-state relations instituted by Justo Rufino Barrios in the 1870s, including religious toleration, civil marriage, divorce, secularization of cemeteries, and lay education. In addition, the early missions—the Presbyterian, Central American Mission, Friends, Nazarene, and Primitive Methodist societies—established a constructive reputation for evangelicals, from which other groups undoubtedly benefited. Among the Indians, who comprised more than half of the population, William

18. Ibid.
19. Conn, *Saints*, 135.
20. Kenneth G. Grubb, *Religion in Central America* (New York: World Dominion, 1938), 67.

Cameron Townsend, H. Dudley Peck, and Paul and Dorothy Burgess, among others, carried out extensive translation work while pentecostal churches were still in their infancy.

Grubb's statistical reports in 1936, which scarcely recognized any pentecostal work in Guatemala, ignored the foundations that were being laid. While other groups reached the urban populations or invested in training outstanding individuals for leadership or engaged in educational programs, the early pentecostals encouraged the disintegrating Indian communities to reorganize around evangelical congregations. Guided by assertive missionaries and aggressive local leaders, evangelical converts who represented the social elements that were most subject to dislocation arrogated effective control of their communities to themselves. The Church of God, destined eventually to establish congregations throughout the national territory, remained strong in the Indian departments, perhaps in part because it became a vehicle of ethnic expression.[21]

This explanation of the marginal populations' propensity for pentecostalism makes sense in light of a recent analysis of social and economic conditions in Guatemala when missionaries first entered the country. According to economic historian David McCreery, the time-honored feudalism that had favored retention of Indian communities in order to "train an agricultural work force and sustain these individuals in the off-season or when they became too ill or old for productive use in the export sector" ended about 1920. Thereafter coffee growers turned to "free labor," because many communities of highland Guatemala found themselves increasingly hard-pressed to support their numbers. In the ensuing crisis, private ownership of land, class differentiation within the villages, alienation of resources to outsiders, declining productivity, and overcropping all compounded the problems of Indians whose personal identity and emotional security had been previously guaranteed by their communities and the traditional Christo-pagan religion.[22] If

21. *Directorio de iglesias, organizaciones y ministerios del movimiento protestante: Guatemala* (San José, Costa Rica: PROCADES, 1981).
22. David McCreery, "An Odious Feudalism," *Latin American Perspectives* 13 (1986): 104.

such a sociological explanation is at this stage of investigation merely suggestive, the experience of vigorous pentecostals in the neighboring republic of El Salvador offers a similar portrait of religious assertiveness following social upheaval.

The Salvadoran Pioneers

El Salvador has played a disproportionate part in the emergence of the region's pentecostal churches. Not only does the republic have the largest per capita pentecostal community, but patterns of association developed in El Salvador were directly extended to Honduras and Guatemala and, indirectly, through policy precedents and literature, to much of the rest of Latin America.[23] Yet conditions for evangelical growth were apparently less suitable in El Salvador than in Guatemala in the 1930s. In contrast to the public support given evangelicals in Guatemala, Salvadoran authorities and the nation's elite, whose affluence stood in sharp contrast to the limited means of the wage-earning, subsistence laborers, were generally suspicious of all popular associations. According to Samuel A. Purdie, the first evangelical missionary, employers threatened their plantation workers with economic sanctions if they identified with the evangelicals.[24] And, as McCreery points out, unlike the Guatemalan policy of encouraging Indian communities to survive intact as late as World War I, from the 1880s Salvadoran policy largely destroyed the indigenous communities by prohibiting the corporate ownership of land.[25] Walter LaFeber observes that by 1920 "the rapid expansion of the coffee plantations had torn apart Indian villages and their communal lands which provided the food supply. Peasants and Indians became little more than a hungry, wandering labor force to be used by the oligarchy."[26]

23. The extensive influence of the Salvadoran pentecostals through development of the *Reglamento local* is treated in Everett A. Wilson, "Sanguine Saints: Pentecostalism in El Salvador," *Church History* 52 (June 1983): 186-98.

24. James Purdie Knowles, *Samuel A. Purdie, His Life and Letters* (Plainsfield, IN: Publishing Association of Friends, 1908), 230.

25. McCreery, "Odious Feudalism," 104.

26. Walter LaFeber, *Inevitable Revolutions* (New York: Norton, 1983), 70.

Against this backdrop, Frederick W. Mebius, a Canadian school teacher who reportedly was healed of tuberculosis, appeared in the country during the absence of Robert H. Bender, who for the previous seventeen years had directed the well-organized but still modest work of the Central American Mission (CAM).[27] Mebius's previous association with Bender gave him access to the CAM community, and leaders entrusted him with the oversight of one or more congregations. One may infer from the sketchy accounts of his career that he was impetuous, uncompromising, and indifferent to decorum. Nevertheless, his approaches found immediate acceptance among some evangelical elements. When friction developed from Mebius's insistence on promulgating his own radical religious ideas, he left the capital to work among receptive groups of former CAM and Baptist believers in the western coffee region. There the village of Las Lomas de San Marcelino became the hub of pentecostal activity for the next two decades.

An early witness of the services conducted by the group was told that the emotional meetings were caused by the appearance of a dark animal, the devil, that prompted shouts and cries from the participants.[28] While attending such a meeting out of curiosity, women of the Santo Hurtado family were overcome by a powerful emotion and began to speak in tongues. Other members of the group claimed to see tongues of fire over the women. In the family controversy that ensued, the girls were humiliated, and a reader was called to say a novena. One of the girls reportedly continued to speak in tongues for a week. According to the account, Hurtado's sons, impressed by the girls' sincerity, fell to their knees and prayed to be baptized also.[29]

A year later the family invited a neighbor, Don Sotero Navas, to attend a meeting held in a simple thatched hut. The guest had to stoop to enter the humble structure where the service consisted of Christmas songs and reading of the nativity

27. Mildred W. Spain, *And In Samaria* (Dallas: Central American Mission, 1954), 108-14.
28. Isabel Navas de Paredes, "Origen y desarrollo de las Asambleas de Dios en las repúblicas de El Salvador y Guatemala" (manuscript in the author's possession, 1980), 2.
29. Ibid., 3.

passage from the Gospel of Luke by a scarcely literate preacher. The incident so reminded Don Sotero of his childhood that he immediately offered his home for future meetings and became an ardent pentecostal, receiving the baptism one night when he awakened speaking in tongues.[30] Navas built a chapel for the congregation, and Frederick Mebius, who married a member of the family, took up residence in the vicinity.

Isabel Navas de Paredes, Don Sotero's granddaughter, recalls the early days of the Salvadoran pentecostal movement.

> From the arrival of the first believers, one could hear songs, and as soon as they set foot on the grounds they began to break out in praise and prayer. The ones who had already arrived would come out to greet them, exchanging a holy kiss [osculo santo] and embracing them. No one worried about eating or hospitality. Villagers would improvise food stalls on the long porches of the house where they would sell fish and other foods. From time-to-time some would go to eat, but day and night the church was filled with prayer.[31]

In time the revival seemed to lose its energy, degenerating, according to the reflections of some members, until what was left was "little more than noise."[32] A member of the group, José María Rivera, a tailor, obtained a copy of the hymnal published by Henry C. Ball, director of the Assemblies of God Hispanic churches, headquartered in San Antonio, Texas. Soon the group was making use of literature sent from the United States. In 1927, Francisco Arbizú, proprietor of a leather-working business and a former officer of the Guardia Nacional, the rural police, sold parcels of property and went to San Antonio to meet Ball for himself. Described as a "young enthusiast," Arbizú returned after receiving a few months of schooling at Ball's Bible institute and dedicated himself to itinerating in the churches as an evangelist and teacher.

Unsatisfied with the group's lack of progress, however, Sotero Navas insisted that Arbizú return to the United States to obtain a missionary for El Salvador. After much difficulty

30. Ibid., 3, 4.
31. Ibid., 4.
32. Ibid.

and visits from representatives of the North American Assemblies of God, including Ball, the Salvadorans were informed of the availability of Ralph Williams, who had most recently taught in a school in Mexico City. Williams's coming placed him in the center of a controversy within the pentecostal community, but it was soon clear that the dozen congregations that sponsored him aspired to a more responsible and effective program. For Williams, a Welsh immigrant with an English Methodist background who was well acquainted with the missionary theories of Roland Allen, the opportunity to lay the foundations of a model New Testament church was exhilarating, and he plunged wholeheartedly into making the movement "biblical."

Arriving in El Salvador with only their personal luggage, the Williamses and their young son were greeted by a way of life that was far removed from what Williams had known as a shipwright in his youth. In an unpublished memoir that captures the texture of his pioneering work, Williams recalled that "our style of living during those years was absolutely primitive. Black beans and rice with *tortillas* were staples." The Williamses rented some "almost bare rooms" in town which they abandoned occasionally to scrimp on money. Sharing "the food, the customs and the worship" of the local people, the Williamses met very few "believers" in town, but were assured that throughout the countryside were many who were waiting to meet them. They traveled, largely on foot and carrying their own bundles, with "*hermano* Arbizú" to their first meetings. The roads, Williams recalled, were "dirt gullies with deep ruts cut by oxcarts."

"Our greatest surprise came as we gathered for worship," his account continued. They entered a "grass-roofed building about twenty by forty feet, framed on rustic poles laid out for benches and a few primitive sources of yellow light." Praying aloud, with "real fervor," were "forty or fifty brethren," some prostrate and most kneeling. After that, the singing started, but Williams was astonished to hear each person singing "in his own words." Still, he did not question "the sincerity of their worship or the presence of the Lord" through all the "entirely spontaneous" emanations of "tongues and praises and testimonies." As the night went on, the congregation "seemed untiring, always ready to sing, to pray and to testify."[33]

Williams's efforts for the next months were directed at the errors and excesses that he observed. "We held our opinions of the brethren lightly at first," he explained, but as they visited several congregations, a definite pattern began to emerge. The Williamses discovered that the people believed that "any control or direction of the service was a curtailment of the Spirit." This "mixture of zeal and ignorance" was attributed to a prevalent opinion that "the Lord would teach the Word by the Holy Spirit rather than by reading the Bible." In addition to the "frequent outbursts in tongues and prayer" there were often "physical agitation and prostration," and "some who pantomimed their thoughts or testimonies." Sometimes the "outbursts of worship and blessing with manifestations of the Holy Spirit . . . swept whole groups . . . for two or three days at a time."

"Erroneous doctrine prevailed," continued Williams, "such as believing that once a believer backslides there is no repentance or forgiveness" or that nothing which "enters the mouth defiles, but only that which enters the heart," a verse used to excuse their "making and drinking liquor." Abuses of marriage relations abounded, such as the claim that there was "no need for a marriage license because the magistrate who signs it is a sinner" or that "a man may abandon his companion [if] the woman was not a believer, and . . . [feel] justified in wanting a Christian wife." As Williams encountered or heard about these conditions, as well as "other believers who had higher concepts, read the Bible and yearned for a clearer understanding of the Scriptures," he cast about for a solution, deciding at one point to "separate ourselves . . .[and] build a church of our own," but then he was "forced to recognize the hand of God, struggling to reveal His will to them," and redoubled his efforts to "preach and teach the Word, believing that the Holy Spirit would bring light and understanding." Most of these people, in Williams's judgment, "had been moved by the Holy Spirit and not by the teaching of the Word." Recognizing that these people's "sentiments and emotions always played a large part in their actions and think-

---

33. Ralph D. Williams, unpublished memoirs (n.d.), 11.

ing," Williams learned to appreciate their lack of "inhibitions about praying aloud, praying in tongues, or [giving] spiritual utterance in prophecy. And they were never hesitant about praying for the sick with genuine expectation of being healed."[34]

Convinced of the need for a more biblical orientation of the largely spontaneous work, Williams conferred with Francisco Arbizú. Together they drafted a statement of doctrine and practice and organized a gathering to discuss the issues. Eighty representatives of the dozen cooperating churches met in sessions directed toward the formation of a national conference governed by a constitution. "The kind of decisions we entered upon were new to most of our people," Williams reported. By means of "many questions and arguments" the representatives "tried to understand, but did not always find agreement." Williams and Arbizú urged them to come to "an understanding of doctrine and church order to which all could agree." But the questioners persisted: "'what if the Holy Spirit shows us something different?' and 'Who is to say what is right?' 'What if I want to preach, who is to stop me?' 'What if a man is married?' 'What if a man has another woman?'" Williams recalled "some less spiritual moments" when outbursts erupted because most lacked the patience to hear out others' opinions. "Opposing views were judged carnal or of the devil. Frequently the loudest speaker thought his louder noise was proof of justice. I heard someone shout, 'That man is only a *campesino;* he knows nothing. I'm the one in charge.'" But they finally completed "a constitution . . . which provided for amendments as the work developed." Williams took pride in the outcome; the new constitution "was not a 'hand-me-down,' for these brethren had had a major part in its making, so they understood it and defended it."[35]

Although Williams had conferred with Mebius, who was still considered the pastor of several congregations, the pioneer declined to take part in the conference and soon emerged as the leader of a group that referred to themselves as *libres,* unaffiliated brethren. In 1939, when the Church of God missionary

34. Ibid., 34, 35.
35. Ibid., 38-41.

H. S. Syverson was en route to Panama, he was advised by Charles T. Furman of Mebius's deteriorating health and the need for a successor. Thereupon Syverson met the seventy-year-old Mebius and arranged to have his congregations brought under the supervision of the Church of God. Syverson remained in charge of the work, building a large central church in Cojutepeque and, in 1944, the year of Mebius's death, organizing a Bible institute for the training of Church of God workers throughout Central America.[36]

The pattern of church expansion developed in these formative years was used widely by all pentecostal groups in the region. Typically, promising laymen were placed in charge of a local meeting referred to as a *campo blanco,* making use of latent resources and training new leadership. A Bible institute and a series of training courses provided rudimentary preparation for such workers and guaranteed standards of ministerial conduct and administrative organization appropriate to the initial stages of the movement. A *Standard of Christian Doctrine and Practice (Reglamento local)* established basic doctrines and practices for the members, who were required to demonstate their acquaintance with the document as well as an irreproachable style of life before advancement to full membership. The *Reglamento* was widely adopted throughout Central America, the Andean countries, and as far as Brazil in Assemblies of God churches.

Because of its training schools and the effective organization of its own churches, El Salvador became the staging area for development of the work in both Guatemala and Honduras. Jutiapa became the center of early Assemblies of God work in Guatemala, from which churches were organized in the capital and into the highlands. Similarly, Salvadoran evangelists visited Honduras, opening churches in homes until such time as a national pastor took responsibility for the supervision of a growing cluster of congregations in the western communities. Santos Beltrán, a seriously minded, well-educated son of a priest, and Carlos Flores, a circus performer who had for a number of years itinerated between the small towns of Central America, collaborated in the opening of Honduras, acquiring

36. Conn, *Saints,* 139-42.

wide respect for their organizational effectiveness and personal commitment.[37]

Evangelical Identity, Community, and Status

In regard to the cultural reconstruction achieved by the churches, Eugene Nida has pointed out that Latin American indigenous churches have been largely the creation of the upper-lower and the lower-middle classes, the "creative minority," in Toynbee's phrase, whose aspirations give leadership to the socially inert masses. These social types, consisting of clerical workers, bookkeepers, small businessmen, and teachers, among others, along with independent small farmers, factory workers, tradesmen, domestic workers, and day laborers, have often rallied behind populist political leaders who have promised them improved material conditions and access to the power structure. Many of these people, having rejected revolutionary ideology, have turned to evangelical Christianity as a means of restoring for themselves and their communities the traditional values of integrity, sobriety, and self-respect.[38]

An illustration of this tendency, already reflected in the occupations and social standing of the emergent pentecostal leaders, is the willingness of figures like Sotero Navas and Francisco Arbizú to use their personal resources to fund evangelical efforts, apparently in hope of restoring values to which they themselves subscribed. Ralph Williams described the conversion of another pioneer, Fernando Monroy, a foreman of a coffee plantation and an active member of the *cofradia* (religious fraternity), the group responsible for financing community religious celebrations. Monroy converted after leading a group in harassing evangelical meetings and emerged as a principal pastor and a teacher in the Bible institute. Angela Mañcias, a devout Catholic and a woman respected for her character, converted

37. Williams, memoirs, 66-67, 122-25.
38. Eugene Nida, "The Relationship of Social Structure to the Problems of Evangelism in Latin America," *Practical Anthropology* 5 (March/April 1958): 101-23.

after the bishop of Santa Ana told her that despite being put off the plantations where they worked, the evangelicals persisted in their faith as surely as the water from the mountains flows to the sea. Angela began attending the meetings to determine for herself the secret of the evangelicals' tenacity and concluded that the members did not turn from God but seemed more firmly to turn to him.[39] Still another early leader of the pentecostal movement in El Salvador, José Gustavo Galdámez, returned to the Catholic Church as an adult after having earlier trained for the priesthood. Ashamed of his dissolute life, he was prepared to submit to the moral authority of the local priest. However, at his first mass the homily was a diatribe against the Protestants and an appeal to drive them out of the counrty. Galdámez left in a rage and soon began to associate with the evangelicals.[40]

The pentecostals were adept at restoring the sense of community lost to many of the people recruited to the movement. Dissolution of the extended family and village life through the loss of land and other economic means to sustain social cohesion had created a vacuum. The solidarity of the local congregations provided the support that was needed by large numbers of people. Several community studies recognize this fact. Bryan S. Roberts, in *Organizing Strangers* (1973), reveals the role of evangelical groups in integrating migrants to Guatemala City into urban life. In *God and Production in a Guatemalan Town* (1987), Sheldon Annis treats the role of Protestantism in offering "functional substitutes" to ease the transition from traditional to modern life.[41]

In the 1930s the highly successful pentecostal *confraternidades* (fellowship gatherings) brought together large numbers of believers for a weekend of celebration and reinforcement of their purposes. As Ralph Williams described it,

> The country was accustomed to a whole calendar of religious feasts that combined [with them] civil and industrial interests. A small

39. Williams, memoirs, 32, 33.
40. José Gustavo Galdámez to the author, April 9, 1978.
41. Bryan S. Roberts, *Organizing Strangers* (Austin: Univ. of Texas Press, 1973); and Sheldon Annis, *God and Production in a Guatemalan Town* (Austin: Univ. of Texas Press, 1987).

group of believers, accustomed to criticism and harassment by their neighbors, gained prestige when a crowd of several hundred attended. Local people who had hesitated about identifying with the evangelicals decided that this is what they needed.[42]

The early missionaries also provided the means for social recognition and the groups' juridic legitimacy. If in Guatemala entire communities sometimes became evangelical and thereby instituted new criteria of social recognition, more generally evangelicals sought legal recognition in both of the republics. Invariably churches have petitioned a charter of incorporation (*personería jurídica*) to secure title to real property. A permanent location and a church building that often requires sacrifice of the members is typical of even small congregations, most of whose members own few material possessions themselves.

The rise of the Salvadoran pentecostals during a time of social disruption made these churches suspect and required them to demonstrate that they were not in complicity with radical political organizations. An insurgency among the peasants of the western coffee zone shortly after Ralph Williams began work in the area led to the slaughter of as many as fifteen thousand "Indians" and the proscription of all voluntary associations. Only gradually were pentecostals free to practice their faith with the protection of the authorities and then only by consenting to remain neutral in politics. The *Reglamento local* prohibited members' participation in political movements and reassured the government that churches would not harbor dissidents. In return, the churches were granted assurances of protection of their rights of property and the free exercise of their evangelical faith. Despite local harassment and incidents that illustrated the need for civil protection into the 1950s, evangelicals were identified as political nonparticipants. In Jicalapa, for instance, workers in the 1930s met unusual resistance in their effort to establish a church, including the charge that they were part of a political conspiracy. Several months later, after the jailed believers were released and assurances were given, Williams and students from the Bible institute were aroused late one night by the Guardia

42. Williams, memoirs, 55-57.

demanding to inspect their documents. Still unsatisfied after scrutinizing the students' internal passports *(vialidad)* and Williams's foreign passport and ministerial credentials with their official seals and signatures, the officers insisted on their presenting still another document. Only when they were shown the simple green card issued by the national ministerial fellowship were the members of the Guardia satisfied. "How our students reveled over the respect the authorities had shown it," reported Williams. "They told the story over and over to other preachers and students."[43]

If the evangelical movement has been a sanctuary for several hundreds of thousands of Central Americans during the violence and disruption of the past decade, the foundation of the movement was well established prior to the disturbing events that have been the background of recent church growth in the region. Civil war, natural disasters, economic collapse, migration, and forced relocation have eroded the security and tradition of the popular social groups and facilitated their consideration of religious alternatives. But the characteristic features of the countries' rapidly growing evangelical movement—identity, community, and status—contemporaries owe in large measure to the foundations laid by the pentecostal pioneers.

---

43. Ibid., 146-51.

III AMERICAN GLOBALISM AND EVANGELICAL WORLD VISION, 1945–PRESENT

7 Pax Americana *and the Evangelical Missionary Advance*

Richard V. Pierard

By the end of World War II the United States of America had emerged as the most formidable military and economic power in the history of the world. America's industrial might had sustained its beleaguered allies and enabled the building of a military machine of unprecedented strength. Its armed forces, in cooperation with the Soviet Union and Great Britain, had brought Nazi Germany to its knees and had crushed the far-flung Japanese empire. A United Nations organization was formed that enabled countries to resolve their differences nonviolently and live in peace with one another. The dream of Woodrow Wilson a quarter century earlier that the world could be made safe for democracy and armed conflict be banished from the face of the earth seemed to lie within realization. Writers spoke optimistically of the "American era" or a *Pax Americana*, comparing the situation to that in the early Roman Empire when peace reigned in the Mediterranean basin—the *Pax Romana*—or the British domination of the world in the nineteenth century, the *Pax Britannica*.

This illusion was soon dispelled as the world became polarized through the Cold War while each superpower developed the nuclear capability to destroy the other, as new nation-states appeared in Asia and Africa that would not bow to American wishes, and as the U.S. military machine was thwarted in Korea and Vietnam. Still, the vision of a *Pax Americana* held sway in the early postwar years and was a significant force in the American evangelical missionary endeavor.[1]

How evangelicals perceived the role of their nation in the new era was cogently illustrated by an article in *Moody Monthly* entitled "Christian America's Contribution to World Peace." The author, a Baptist minister in Washington, D.C., pointed out that during the conflict the United States had led in giving voice to the Four Freedoms and had held up the goal of a world in which wars would have no place and, since the end of the war, that it had cooperated with other nations in setting up the machinery for world peace. It was no mere coincidence that "oppressed peoples around the earth have come to look upon America and its ideals as a hope for civilization," because "whatever faith other peoples have in our country must be attributed to the fact that we are a Christian nation and that the ideals for which we strive are those which are consonant with the principles of Christian living." Christian America now occupied the position of a "moral and spiritual leader in world affairs."

America's obligation, the writer argued, was to ensure that all people had the opportunity to worship in accordance with their desires, as was the situation here; but that was not enough. "We must make sure that the message of Christ, with its transforming power, is carried to those who are starving for the Bread of Life." Christian America must give "a spiritual basis" to its good-neighbor policy in its economic and political relations with other countries; it must show that real unity among nations cannot be found on a racial, political, material, or social level, but only through Christ. The writer was forthright: "We are not oversimplifying the problem of world peace when we state that the solution is merely one of elevating the Christian minority to the Christian majority in all nations." Faith in "mere organization" to secure peace was transient and shallow; only Christ was the basis of unity on which the structure of peace could be built.[2]

---

1. An insightful commentary on the relationship between American political and economic power and the missionary advance is provided by veteran Mennonite mission worker David A. Shank in *Mission Focus: Current Issues*, ed. Wilbert R. Shenk (Scottdale, PA: Herald, 1980), 360-65.

2. Luther J. Holcomb, "Christian America's Contribution to World Peace," *Moody Monthly* 47 (October 1946): 98, 126.

The Evangelical Advance

Although one might gain the impression from a perusal of the evangelical literature of the post–World War II decade that an almost boundless future seemed to lie open to missions, in reality, many contemporaries acknowledged the existence of forces that militated against expansion. Already in the 1930s, missionary activity had experienced a sharp decline in volunteers and funding, and some influential voices in the church were questioning whether missions even had a future. Further, the post-1945 world was plagued by a host of problems that had an impact on the missionary enterprise. Among these were the cutting or at least the diminishing of the colonial ties in Asia and Africa; the emergence of new nations whose nationalism viewed Christianity as a vestige of Western imperialism; the existence of communism as a rival faith; the resurgence of non-Christian religions; the unimaginable amount of human suffering resulting from the war, civil and racial strife, and the population explosion; the growth of confidence in science and technology and with it a secularism that ignored God; the dwindling power of Christianity as reflected in the steep decline in church attendance in Europe and theological disarray within the Roman Catholic and mainline Protestant communities; and pessimism about the possibilities of future missionary expansion when the "doors closed" in places like India, Burma, China, North Korea, and the Islamic world. Max Warren, general secretary of the Anglican Church Missionary Society, articulated the doubts that were gripping the Christian community when he declared at the International Missionary Council meeting in 1952:

> We know with complete certainty that the most testing days of the Christian mission in our generation lie just ahead. . . . We have to be ready to see the day of missions, as we have known them, as having already come to an end.[3]

3. Max A. C. Warren, "The Christian Mission and the Cross," in *Missions Under the Cross*, ed. Norman Goodall (London: Edinburgh House, 1953), 40. Representative discussions of the critical situation facing missions in the postwar era are contained in Kenneth Scott Latourette and William Richey Hogg, *Tomorrow Is Here* (New York: Friendship, 1948); T. Stanley Soltau, *Missions at the Crossroads*

Although there was some concern in evangelical circles about the prospects of missions, by and large the postwar years were a time of rapid growth. This was clearly so with respect to North America, where the expansion in the evangelical portion of the total Protestant missionary force was spectacular. While the number of missionaries from all boards more than doubled during the twentieth century, the North American contingent increased sixfold.[4] In the early part of the century North America contributed about one-third of the worldwide force, but by 1969 the proportion was more than 70 percent. An enormous leap in workers occurred especially in the 1950s, but this growth concealed an important shift. The number of people employed by the independent faith missions and parachurch bodies and by the societies operated by conservative denominations (including the Lutheran Church–Missouri Synod, Assemblies of God, and Southern Baptist Convention) grew rapidly and greatly outstripped those from the mainline Protestant denom-

---

(Wheaton: Van Kampen, 1954); Arthur F. Glasser, "The Mission Field Today," in *Changing World—Unchanging Christ: A Missionary Compendium* (Chicago: Inter-Varsity Christian Fellowship, 1955); R. Pierce Beaver, *From Missions to Mission: Protestant World Mission Today and Tomorrow* (New York: Association, 1964); and Ralph D. Winter, *The 25 Unbelievable Years: 1945–1969* (South Pasadena: William Carey Library, 1970).

4. According to published data the number of missionaries increased dramatically over a seventy-year period:

Year	North American Protestant Missionaries	Protestant Missionaries from All Countries
1902	5,000 (est.)	18,164
1911	7,239	21,307
1925	14,043	29,188
1936	11,289	27,677
1952	18,576	35,522
1956	23,058	34,692
1958	25,058	38,606
1960	27,219	42,250
1969	33,290	46,000 (est.)

Occasional Bulletin of the Missionary Research Library, 8 December 1958, 11; ibid., 23 November 1960, 6; *North American Protestant Ministries Overseas* (9th ed., 1970), 2, 15; R. Pierce Beaver, "Missionary Motivation through Three Centuries," in *Reinterpretation in American Church History* (Chicago: Univ. of Chicago Press, 1968), 115-16.

inational agencies, thus ensuring a conservative evangelical preponderance in overseas missions.[5]

The principal ecumenical agency of Protestant missions, the International Missionary Council, received a new lease on life in the postwar period but was finally absorbed into the World Council of Churches in 1961. At its meeting in Whitby, Ontario, in July 1947, the IMC affirmed the necessity for Christian witness in a revolutionary world and the oneness of Christians throughout the world. Although couched in sophisticated terminology, much of what was affirmed about the need for the gospel was acceptable to the conservatives in North America, who were now leading the missionary advance from these shores. However, conservatives would not go along with what they regarded as a weak view of divine revelation in Scripture and the firm emphasis on unity contained in the final statement. The same held true for the IMC conclave five years later at Willingen, Germany, where attention was devoted to the theology of missions.[6] The ecumenically oriented mission bodies and the North American conservative evangelical agencies functioned in almost two separate worlds. The result, as Wilbert Shenk accurately observes, was that

> that part of the missionary movement most closely identified with the Christendom thrust of the Great Century rapidly lost momentum after 1945, while independent and Free Church groups surged forward. The latter often acted as if they were still living in the nineteenth century. They treated sociopolitical issues simplistically and interpreted the missionary call as the simple and unambiguous action of saving souls.[7]

The mission agencies of the mainline denominations as well as some evangelical ones comprised the Foreign Missions Conference of North America, but not all of them followed the FMC

5. Richard G. Hutcheson, Jr., *Mainline Churches and the Evangelicals: A Challenging Crisis?* (Atlanta: John Knox, 1981), 80-81, 92.

6. C. W. Ranson, ed., *Renewal and Advance: Christian Witness in a Revolutionary Age* (London: Edinburgh House, 1948), 206-18; Goodall, ed., *Missions Under the Cross*, 21-23, 238-45.

7. Wilbert R. Shenk, "The 'Great Century' Reconsidered," *Missiology* 12 (April 1984): 142.

when it merged with the National Council of Churches in November 1950. Many of the faith missions belonged to the Interdenominational Foreign Mission Association that had been formed in 1917, but pentecostal societies were excluded. Another conservative ecumenical association, the Evangelical Foreign Missions Association, was created by the National Association of Evangelicals in 1946. The latter included denominational organizations as well as independent groups, and it emphasized united representation before government bodies, cooperative endeavors, and comity arrangements on various mission fields to deter unnecessary duplication of effort and competition. Since the 1960s the two evangelical mission bodies have worked together more closely, but a growing number of mission societies, both small and very large, have operated outside that framework.[8]

Evangelical Missionary Motivation

In some respects, the impetus for missionary service after 1945 was like that found in traditional evangelical piety. Many of the missionary sermons delivered at youth rallies and church conventions or contained in the evangelical press could just as easily have been preached fifty or seventy-five years before with only the geographical and historical references changed. A central theme was, of course, the Great Commission (Matt. 28:19). Kenneth Pike of Wycliffe Bible Translators declared that "our assignment is given, not by government, but by our Lord's Great Commission unto the evangelization of the world." Christ had ordained us "world watchmen" to proclaim the grace of God to all people and alert them to danger. We must not keep redemption to ourselves and fail to warn those nations who have turned

8. Harold Lindsell, "Faith Missions Since 1938," in *Frontiers of the Christian World Mission Since 1938: Essays in Honor of Kenneth Scott Latourette*, ed. Wilber C. Harr (New York: Harper, 1962), 219-30; R. Pierce Beaver, "The Evangelical Foreign Missions Association," in *The Missionary Obligation of the Church: Why Missions?* Report of Commission III on the Role of the Missionary Society (Committee on Research in Foreign Missions, Division of Foreign Mission, NCC, 21 December 1951).

to graven idols and false philosophies and rejected the light of conscience. God called some to go and some to stay and sent out those who were to go. "Stop the gaps in the ranks of watchmen! Take up *your* trumpet!" Pike urged.[9]

Veteran Bible teacher Charles J. Woodbridge insisted that the cessation of hostilities meant the opening of new doors around the world to the preaching of the gospel, and thus the mandate of Christ to go and teach all nations must be reiterated and its precepts put into practice. The only hope of a lost and dying world was the gospel, he believed, and Christians must renew their consecration to the task of world evangelism. We should pray for a mighty outpouring of missionary enthusiasm throughout the body of Christ, he urged fellow fundamentalists; go if the spirit leads us, give with real sacrifice, and "do all that we can to promote and further the cause which has always been, and is today, so close to our Savior's heart."[10]

Possibly the most influential statement of the divine mandate came from the pen of Harold Lindsell, who taught the formal course in missions at Fuller Theological Seminary and made a missionary emphasis integral to the school that was the centerpiece of the postwar "new evangelicalism."[11] Because poor health prevented him from fulfilling his intention to go out to the field after graduation from Wheaton College, he decided to obtain a doctorate in history and devote his scholarly expertise to the theology and history of missions. In 1949 he published *A Christian Philosophy of Missions*, in which he articulated with logic and clarity the evangelical view of the mission enterprise.[12]

Lindsell placed the missions question in the context of the world crisis and argued that Protestant Christianity was

9. Kenneth L. Pike, "World Watchmen," *Moody Monthly* 47 (March 1947): 472.

10. Charles J. Woodbridge, "Go Ye Therefore," *Revelation* 15 (December 1945): 507, 541.

11. George M. Marsden, *Reforming Fundamentalism: Fuller Seminary and the New Evangelicalism* (Grand Rapids: Eerdmans, 1987), chap. 5, calls attention to Lindsell's significance in this context.

12. Harold Lindsell, *A Christian Philosophy of Missions* (Wheaton: Van Kampen, 1949). It was reissued by Zondervan in 1970 under the title *An Evangelical Theology of Missions*. The only changes made were in chapter 1, detailing the situation in the contemporary world.

threatened by three massive forces—secularism-modernism, communism, and Roman Catholicism—as well as by moral decay and economic catastrophe. Modernism was the most serious problem because it questioned the uniqueness of Christianity. Thus, true missions had to be founded on an "either-or" view of the inerrant Bible and the message of salvation through the subsititutionary atonement of Christ. He added to this a firm doctrine of hell, which made missions the supreme effort of compassion.[13]

The consuming urgency of evangelism determined his conception of the church. "The function of the church is the evangelization of the world, and this evangelization is to be completed before the return of the Lord." The task was not to change social structures but to take the gospel to all the world and bring individuals into the church. Doing good, individually or socially, was clearly the "secondary element which is the fruit that comes forth from conversion." This "product of conversion" must not be confused with the task of winning people to Christ, nor "is it to precede that function or be equated with it."[14]

Lindsell perceived churches as centers of missions and evangelism, where the morning worship services should be used for evangelizing the unconverted, not primarily the upbuilding of the saints. Just as the primary function of the church was to evangelize, so it was with the individual believer. Each one must be a missionary. Everyone was called to go, and the world was the field in which the believer would witness. The particular area where one witnessed was not important, since each individual was to do the will of God, regardless of where that might lead. Being a missionary was a universal calling, one given to all, since each generation was summoned to carry out evangelization in its own time. This was not a permeative process working in an evolving fashion. God "calls" enough people to get the job done, and the burden of proof rested on the individual to show that God had not called him or her to go. By implication everyone should be heading toward vocational Christian service unless God directed elsewhere.[15]

13. Lindsell, *Philosophy of Missions,* 54, 77.
14. Ibid., 132-33, 233.
15. Ibid., 159-63.

Another theme in the postwar mission sermons was that of opportunities that must be seized while there was yet time to do so. The venerable Robert Hall Glover of the China Inland Mission stressed that many of the "open doors" in Africa, Asia, and South America were "never entered and made good." When the war came along, they were "closed," but by the mercy of God the doors "are once more opening." The question was, "will the church learn the lesson and seize the opportunity to make up for its past negligence and push forward energetically into 'the regions beyond'?" Glover went on to specify factors that favored a speedy forward movement to complete the missionary task, such as new means of transportation, advances in medicine, and radio broadcasting.[16]

There were numerous variations on this theme. John Smart, a missionary to the West Indies, exulted in the "open door" of opportunity provided by increased literacy for the circulation of the Scriptures, by changed attitudes of non-Christian religionists, and by the accessibility to hitherto unreached peoples through aircraft, roads, and radio. Baptist pastor Walter H. Miekle talked about the opening of a great and effectual door that had provided "the greatest opportunity for Christian witnessing since apostolic days." Revolutionary advances in transportation, language study, and communications and the backlog of manpower and money built up during the war years made rapid missionary advance possible.

The NAE's Clyde Taylor concurred, saying, "The missionary opportunities of our time are far greater than those which any previous generation faced," but he added a note of caution that this might be the last opportunity God will give his church to evangelize the lost. Baptist journalist John Bradbury declared shortly before the end of the war that the churches were "at the crossroads of history." It could be a time of unprecedented activity in ministering the faith to the pagan world, but "should the churches fail God in this hour, they will be preparing for themselves unspeakable suffering through impending judg-

---

16. Robert Hall Glover, "What Should Be Our Post-War Evangelical Missionary Strategy?" *United Evangelical Action* 4 (15 September 1945): 19; idem, "Crisis in World Missions," ibid., 4 (15 February 1946): 6.

ment." A Youth for Christ leader in 1947 warned that "time is running out" and "what we do we must do *now*," because doors that were open to the gospel two years before were closed now.[17]

One theme that cropped up with regularity was that of the unique responsibility of Americans to proclaim the gospel. This reflected the deep sense of national "chosenness" that was part and parcel of American civil religion, which during its postwar revival was being linked in a transcendent fashion to the world Christian mission. No one stated it more eloquently than Glover:

> We are called a Christian nation, however far we fall short of deserving that name. This much is true, at least, that God has signally blessed and prospered America, and has given to her a foremost place of leadership and influence among the nations of the world. Moreover, upon the Christian churches of America there has been providentially bestowed, by reason of the course of world events, predominant share of the manpower and the material resources necessary for carrying forward to completion the work of world evangelization. Surely we should regard this as a gracious favor divinely conferred upon us as a nation. But we must not fail to see in it also a sacred trust, a solemn responsibility to address ourselves wholeheartedly to the task which in the providence of God has thus been committed in such large measure to the Christians of this land.
>
> May our beloved nation rightly discern God's meaning in the special favor He has been pleased to show her! May the United States of America seek and find her highest blessing and success not in getting but in unselfish service for the material and spiritual welfare of the oppressed and suffering peoples of the world![18]

Will Houghton of Moody Bible Institute had been on a similar wavelength when he talked during the war about "America's spiritual responsibility." He defined this as maintaining and proclaiming the gospel in its entirety and simplicity to the

17. John Smart, "The Challenge of the Open Door," *Christian Digest* 11 (June 1946): 51-53; Walter H. Miekle, "A Great Door and Effectual Is Opened," *Moody Monthly* 46 (March 1946): 420; Clyde W. Taylor, "Gates of the Nations Open to Missions," *United Evangelical Action* 4 (1 September 1945): 5; John W. Bradbury, "The Need for a Missionary Revival," *Revelation* 15 (September 1945): 374; Mel Larson, "Youth for Christ World Congress," *Moody Monthly* 48 (October 1947): 86.

18. Glover, "Crisis in World Missions," 6-7.

ends of the earth. Once the war was over, he expected that the young men and women who had been given to war would then be given to the greater conflict for Christ, that of carrying the gospel to the mission fields. He insisted that American Christians would have to think in global terms of a gospel for all the world.[19]

Although missionaries from the United States viewed themselves simply as Americans first and foremost, A. C. Snead of the Christian and Missionary Alliance acknowledged that a larger vision was necessary. To be sure, he agreed that missionaries must be loyal to their own country, but he added that they should realize that they were citizens and ambassadors of a heavenly kingdom and had a deep loyalty to its head, Jesus Christ. Thus,

> We must go to the mission field, not as Americans or Canadians, or those of any other land, but as representing the Lord Jesus Christ. We are to go, not to demand that those of Africa or the East should take our western civilization, but rather that we may present to them the living Christ, who Himself was born in Asia and became the Savior of all men. Remember, when we go to other lands as missionaries, we are the "foreigners," not they.[20]

With such an enlightened view he was surely ahead of his time. Unfortunately, evangelicals from the U.S. had bought heavily into the war-induced revival of civil religion, and most of them engaged in a syncretic confusion of Christianity and Americanism. It was not until the 1970s that prominent evangelical leaders like Mark Hatfield and Billy Graham began to criticize this linkage that contained the potential to undo much of the good work that American missionaries had achieved.[21]

19. Will H. Houghton, "America's Spiritual Responsibility in the War and After," *Moody Monthly* 44 (October 1943): 69-70.

20. A. C. Snead, "The Foreign Missionary in a Changing World," *United Evangelical Action* 7 (1 May 1948): 3-4.

21. At the National Prayer Breakfast in 1973, Senator Hatfield called attention to the "danger of misplaced allegiance" in our failure "to distinguish between the god of an American civil religion and the God who reveals Himself in the Holy Scriptures and in Jesus Christ" (Hatfield, *Between a Rock and a Hard Place* [Waco: Word, 1976], 94). At the Lausanne Congress on World Evangelization the following year, Graham referred to the identification of the gospel with any

RICHARD V. PIERARD

The War Experience and Missions

The most distinctive arguments for missionary service came out of the war experience itself. Although military metaphors and analogies have always been a feature of Christian rhetoric, during the 1940s there was a flowering of terms used to describe some of the ideas expressed during the war. Will Houghton suggested that Christians must begin to think in such terms as *global*, the gospel for all the world; *all out*, everything to be poured into the effort; and *Blitzkrieg*, with its suggestion of intensity, concentration, and immediacy. F. J. Miles, head of the Russian Missionary Society, said that Christians were challenged to carry on warfare characterized by eternal issues and their soldiers were sent by their "Commander-in-Chief" into all the world. The current global war taught Christians "lessons" that would challenge, inspire, and activate them for the "greater campaign." As World War II caught people napping, so the church had been slumbering in its self-contented complacency. Just as war was always characterized by change, so the church must think, pray, and prepare "for an accelerated activity" along its "line of warfare." It must learn to meet the demand of "total war." Although some were looking toward peace, church leaders must be motivating Christians to provide "the men and means now for an acceleration of missionary activities following the armistice."[22]

One of the most striking examples of a war-analogy sermon was one delivered by evangelist Merv Rosell at a conference in Winona Lake, Indiana, in 1945. Its thesis was that American Christians could learn some "constructive truth" from the conflict, namely, that the cause of world evangelism was a warfare that

---

political program or culture as an "error." This was his "own danger," and he insisted that now he went "as an ambassador for the Kingdom of God—not America" (Graham, "Why Lausanne?" in *Let the Earth Hear His Voice*, ed. J. D. Douglas [Minneapolis: World Wide Publications, 1975], 30). The allure that civil religion holds for American evangelicals is discussed in Robert D. Linder and Richard V. Pierard, *Twilight of the Saints: Biblical Christianity and Civil Religion in America* (Downers Grove, IL: InterVarsity, 1978); and idem, *Civil Religion and the Presidency* (Grand Rapids: Zondervan, 1988).

22. Houghton, "America's Spiritual Responsibility," 70, 93; F. J. Miles, "Global and Gospel Warfare," *Sunday School Times*, 19 August 1944, 581.

demanded conquest, advance, and action. It was God's global "Go!" War always connoted change, but the church just droned along in complacency. War challenged thousands to "heart-heroism" while denominational leaders sat around coffee tables drawing up petty peace proposals. War demanded the finest men for the foreign fronts while the church confiscated the Christian commandoes to tend the home fires. War pushed people into the farthest outposts where, as Rosell put it in his colorful style,

> Warriors are carrying guns where men have never met our God. Oil cans are toted by dark-skinned people who have never seen a Bible. Tinsel and baubles outnumber Testaments and Bibles. Jeeps have gone where Jesus' ambassadors have never come. Machine guns bark where missionaries have never proclaimed the Good News, and grenades have preceded the Gospel dynamite in many places. We stand redfaced in the presence of many people who have seen our combs but not our Christ; our trinkets but not our tracts; our generals but not our evangelists; our Red Cross but not the old rugged Cross; our best fighters but not our best preachers. God's army has been resting. Its Leader has not been allowed to lead.

Rosell added that the U.S. Army gets there "fustest with the mostest," while the church could be depended upon to get there "lastest with the leastest." This was not because God planned it so, limited the power, or gave vague orders, but because the liberal "Quislings" had usurped pulpits, the "true army" valued security more than sacrifice, and the "faithful few" looked at human impotence instead of heavenly power. We never reached the ends of the earth with the gospel because the churches sent their best "boys" to become local leaders and future pillars in the self-centered home church instead of pouring them into schools for Christian service to become advancing soldiers of the cross.

The answer was to "see the home base in its true light—an arsenal for world conquest." Young men must be seen as "field generals for God's front lines," and they must be equipped and encouraged for pioneering and Christian conquest. Also, following the example of the enthusiasm in which we purchased war bonds, we should "balance our budget of expenditure with at least half of our investment where it will draw the greatest eternal interest." Just as "men expect to win a great war in one generation" and spare no expense in doing so, so we could make the gospel available to every human being in the world in our generation. "There are days ahead when youth will conquer for Christ, ... even though the triumph may cost blood, ... and taste the sweetness of world-wide victory!" He ended by challenging his listeners to God's global "Go," Christian conquest, and God's "gigantic world plan."[23]

Speaking on the same conference grounds, Robert Hall Glover declared that the present war "furnishes an exact parallel to the missionary enterprise." As we provide munitions and supplies to our soldiers, so must we do in the missionary enterprise that "is another conflict, on a world-wide scale," between the forces of Christ and Satan for possession of human souls. He added that "our brave missionary soldiers are doing their part loyally and effectively," and those in the home base must provide them with reinforcements and support.[24]

Looking to the postwar era, mission supporters continued to use military terminology. R. R. Brown, a Christian and Missionary Alliance district superintendent, emphasized that the work of Christ on foreign mission fields would be more challenging after this war than at any period in church history. He spoke of the "conflict" between liberals who were determined to "Christianize the world" and the evangelical program to preach the gospel, and he looked optimistically for a "new spiritual aggressiveness" in the missionary churches abroad where "heroic men and women" would evangelize and preach. Then, "tried and tested young men and women" would come home from the war and volunteer for world service. They

> would take off their GI shoes and be shod with the preparation of the Gospel of peace, lay aside their machine guns and take the Sword of the Spirit. They will not go out to kill, but to make dead men live.[25]

23. Mervin E. Rosell, "God's Global 'Go,'" *Winona Echoes* 51 (1945): 260-65.
24. Robert Hall Glover, "Strengthening the Stakes of the Missionary Tent," *Winona Echoes* 50 (1944): 93-94.
25. R. R. Brown, "The Challenge of Tomorrow," *Christian Digest* 10 (June 1945): 38-39.

Clarence Jones, the founder of radio station HCJB, Quito, Ecuador, said the future of missions would be "the most glorious victory the world has ever seen if we prepare for it." Thus, the church should consciously plan for missionary advance now and bend every effort to carry out a program of immediate action on the fields after the war. Paul Alderman wrote in *Our Hope* that war had been going on ever since sin entered the race, but Satan would not triumph even through human self-destruction with atomic weapons. God had a program of "reconversion" from war to peace that was the eschatological hope of the final victory of Christ.[26]

Some commentators touted the value of missions in the war effort. For example, *Moody Monthly* editorialized that the work of the missionaries in the South Pacific "is yielding dividends in friendship for our cause and our men on the part of the natives." Christians in the islands "sacrificed to serve our men all because other white men had brought them the gospel of love." Thanks to the missionaries, China had at this hour "the best Christian leadership of any of the Allies" and would play "a great part" in world affairs tomorrow. This was also a factor in challenging people for service. The magazine's editor reported "so many stories have come to us" of the contribution made to our victory by Christian natives in the islands "that it should be easy to convince anyone of the value of missions." Glover mentioned that "the ministry of the missionaries to Chinese war sufferers has newly commended Christianity to the masses." Also, he had talked with American servicemen whose ideas of missions had been "completely revolutionized" by seeing "the amazing contrast" between Christian and non-Christian native groups in the Pacific.[27]

26. Clarence W. Jones, "Missionary Advance—Now!" *Christian Digest* 10 (July 1945): 16-18; Paul Alderman, Jr., "God's Reconversion Program," *Our Hope* 52 (January 1946): 471-80.

27. *Moody Monthly* 45 (September 1944): 5; ibid., (April 1945): 423; Robert Hall Glover, "Missions Go On Despite War," *United Evangelical Action*, 1 August 1945, 12-13; idem, "Crisis in World Missions," 6. To help generate enthusiasm for missions, journalist Dan C. Campien related a melodramatic story of how the martyrdom of a Christian worker on a Pacific island had led to the conversion of the entire tribe responsible for it. During the war three American airmen

Servicemen and Missions

A vital dimension in the postwar surge of missionary activity was the experience of veterans, many of whom had seen combat and experienced life in foreign cultures firsthand. Supported by the GI Bill, evangelical ex-servicemen enrolled in droves in Bible schools and Christian colleges, especially those that emphasized missions, like Wheaton College, Moody Bible Institute, and Columbia Bible College. After graduation many of them entered "full-time Christian service" (the evangelical term for church vocations), often as foreign missionaries. Those who had already finished college, plus a few who had not served in the armed forces, occupied leadership positions. They were mature, dedicated, and intense young men and women who were ready to win the world for Christ.

From this World War II–age cohort (of people born between 1909 and 1925) came the most remarkable group in the history of American evangelical Christianity. This included Torrey Johnson, Billy Graham, Bob Cook, Oral Roberts, Grady Wilson, Cliff Barrows, Bill Bright, Bob Jones, Jr., Jack Wyrtzen, Joseph Bayly, Ted Engstrom, Walden Howard, Jim Rayburn, Carl F. H. Henry, Edward J. Carnell, George Ladd, Francis Schaeffer, Gleason Archer, Harold Lindsell, John Walvoord, Kenneth Kantzer, Vernon Grounds, Bernard Ramm, Timothy Smith, Dennis Kinlaw, and many others who distinguished themselves in evangelism, pastoral ministry, scholarship, and church leadership. Among them must be numbered such outstanding figures in missions as Arthur F. Glasser, Eugene A. Nida, Kenneth L. Pike, Bob Pierce, R. Kenneth Strachan, Ralph D. Winter, Robert P. Evans, H. Wilbert Norton, J. Herbert Kane, Samuel H. Moffett, Paul Freed, Horace L. Fenton, Jr., and Edwin L. "Jack" Frizen.

Several of the veterans became active in existing missionary and evangelistic organizations, in particular, Youth for Christ, which served as a catalyst for the postwar evangelical revival.

---

were downed on this now "Jap-infested" island, but they were rescued by a "kinky-haired black native" who with his comrades were all "hard-working and consecrated Christians" ("Why Send Missionaries?" *Christian Digest* 11 [April 1946]: 51-53).

YFC evolved in the early 1940s out of youth rallies held in various cities. Massive "victory" rallies in Chicago and New York in 1944 catapulted it to national attention, and in 1945 much of the YFC movement was consolidated into an international organization under the leadership of Torrey Johnson.

YFC's aim was to foster world evangelization by young people but not to be a missionary society per se. According to a policy statement adopted on July 25, 1945, Youth for Christ would augment existing bodies by supporting "the missionary cause and spirit" and through "cooperation with existing missionary agencies." In a speech the following year Johnson pledged that the group would give itself "without reservation of any kind, to the evangelization of the whole world, that at the earliest possible moment—even in the lifetime of our generation—the uttermost parts of the earth may hear the gospel." He also said that in the YFC headquarters in Chicago was a world map with the challenge "Go ye into all the world and preach the Gospel to every creature," and in his own office was a map with the motto "Evangelize the world in the present generation." This reminded him every time he sat at his desk that he should pray for the evangelization of the world.[28]

Youth for Christ's executive secretary was Robert P. Evans, a Wheaton graduate and combat-seasoned navy chaplain (wounded in the D-Day invasion of France) who joined YFC upon his release from the service. He was sent back to Europe for evangelistic work and became so burdened for the spiritual condition of the continent that in 1949 he and his wife opened an evening school in Paris to train Europeans in the Bible. Within a year it was transformed into the European Bible Institute, and in 1952 Greater Europe Mission was founded. Evans held a key position in GEM until his retirement in 1986. Also in the YFC leadership elite at this time were Billy Graham, its first full-time worker; Bob Pierce, who founded World Vision in 1950; and several of the Billy Graham Evangelistic Association's principal workers.

28. Billy Graham Center Archives (hereinafter BGC Archives), Collection #48, box 13, folders 36 and 37, passim. For the early history of Youth for Christ see Bruce Shelley, "The Rise of Evangelical Youth Movements," *Fides et Historia* 18 (January 1986): 47-52.

A significant instance of servicemen acquiring a missionary vision was in the Philippines. Soon after the liberation of Manila in February 1945, a group of GIs organized a Christian Service Center with the assistance of a Baptist missionary couple. This blossomed into an extensive program of fellowship and evangelism, and they decided to hold an interdenominational Saturday night meeting. They secured permission to use a mortuary for that purpose, and on May 5, 1945, the GI Gospel Hour began on a regular basis. Run by the servicemen themselves, this was a Youth for Christ–style service with singing, testimonies, an evangelistic sermon by a missionary or chaplain, and an altar call. On Sunday nights the GIs sponsored a full-blown YFC rally for the civilian population in a church. Eventually, the men built a new Christian Service Center and moved all of these activities there.

The servicemen collected money to assist churches, developed a radio ministry, and engaged in some small-scale evangelism among the local people. On September 21, 1945, forty-two missionaries and servicemen met in Manila and founded the Far Eastern Bible Institute and Seminary (FEBIAS) as a faith mission to train Filipinos and other Asians to disseminate the gospel.[29]

By this time, thousands of military personnel had gone to Japan to implement the occupation there, and the pattern of GI Gospel Hours and evangelistic outreach was soon replicated.[30] Ministry by servicemen there also included the creation of gospel medical centers, Bible classes for the local people, hospital visitation, English-language instruction, and a Bible college. Japan offered a peculiar challenge to the GIs because it had been the enemy in the war and now was prostrate, while the indigenous Christian church was weak and demoralized because

29. The early development of the Philippines work is recounted in *The Story of the Far Eastern Bible Institute and Seminary (FEBIAS): Christian GI's in Action* (1946), pamphlet in the Harold Cook Collection, Moody Bible Institute Library; Russell G. Honeywell, *Far Eastern Gospel Crusade and Its Work in the Philippine Islands* (1952), brochure, Harold Cook Collection; Sam Tamashiro, "GI Missionaries to Manila," *Sunday* 7 (February 1946): 26-29, 49-52; Philip E. Armstrong, "GI's Answer the Far Eastern Crisis," *Moody Monthly* 48 (December 1947): 256-67, 260.

30. My firsthand experience with this was my involvement in the leadership of the Tokyo GI Gospel Hour while serving as an enlisted man in the U.S. Army in Japan in 1955-56; I had close relationships with several missionaries there.

of years of oppression and the wartime devastation. Thus, many army and navy chaplains (and enlisted men as well) functioned as *de facto* missionaries and, with the aid of interpreters, engaged in evangelism, charitable endeavors, and Scripture and tract distribution. The chaplains organized the Japan Biblical Seminary in May 1946, and the servicemen formed a missionary body called the GI Gospel Crusade.

These developments took place independently of what had transpired in the Philippines, but the wisdom of coordinating them was readily apparent. Finally, representatives of the two groups met in Denver, Colorado, in January 1947 to form the Far Eastern Gospel Crusade (now SEND, International). This rapidly became one of the major interdenominational evangelical mission agencies working in East Asia. As conditions in Japan normalized, some of the occupation forces took discharges there so they could accept civilian employment and carry on Christian work, while others returned home to study in colleges or Bible schools preparatory to returning under the auspices of FEGC or other evangelical boards.[31]

Unfortunately, the military government was not enthusiastic about this grassroots missionary effort and wished to discourage it. In fact, the activities of the chaplains in assisting Christian institutions and engaging in personal missionary work were so extensive that Dr. William K. Bunce, chief of the Supreme Command's Religious Division, tried in vain during the spring of 1946 to restrict them. In fact, missionaries were allowed into Japan over a year before other foreign civilians could enter, and the zeal of some caused Japanese and occupation authorities "no end of embarrassment," reported William P. Woodard, an official in the Religious Division.[32]

31. For contemporary examples of this see George S. Hixson, "A Chaplain in Japan," *Moody Monthly* 46 (July 1946): 672-73; Carl Blackler, "Japan's Greatest Need—The Gospel of Christ," *United Evangelical Action* 5 (1 October 1946): 4, 8; Cornelius Vanderbreggen, Jr., "Our G.I. Missionaries to Japan," *Revelation* 17 (April 1947): 162-63, 182-84; Margaret McNaughton, "Christian Veterans Face Their Moral Debt," *United Evangelical Action* 8 (1 January 1949): 3-4, 8.

32. Lawrence S. Wittner, "MacArthur and the Missionaries: God and Man in Occupied Japan," *Pacific Historical Review* 40 (February 1971): 91; William P. Woodard, *The Allied Occupation of Japan, 1945–1952, and Japanese Religions* (Leiden: Brill, 1972), 210-11, 222, 225.

Complicating the picture was what biographer Clayton James calls General Douglas MacArthur's "spiritual mission."[33] MacArthur came out in support of Christian missions, even though this ran at cross-purposes to his program to secularize Japan. Although personally he never attended church and counted few chaplains among his friends, he claimed in his memoirs to have been brought up as a Christian and to "adhere entirely to [Christianity's] teachings." At about the same time MacArthur told a reporter, "I am a Christian and an Episcopalian, but I believe in all religions. They may differ in form or ritual but all recognize a divine creator, a superior power that transcends all that is moral." On another occasion he observed that democracy "is the exemplification of Christianity." His views on religion were hardly orthodox, as one can infer from this comment in his *Reminiscences:*

> I have always had a sincere admiration for many of the basic principles underlying the Oriental faiths. Christianity does not differ from them as much as one would think. There is little conflict between the two, and each might well be strengthened by a better understanding of the other.

To achieve this, he asked for "missionaries, and more missionaries" to be sent to Japan.[34]

The various Christian groups were jubilant over this, even if it seemed utterly inconsistent with the religious beliefs of the "Proconsul of the East." They perceived it as a clarion call to send workers at once, and evangelical circles were animated over the prospects. They were further encouraged by several other comments by MacArthur:

> Christianity now has an opportunity without counterpart in the Far East, [which if] fully availed by the leaders of our Christian faith, a revolution of spirit may be expected to ensue which will more favorably alter the course of civilization than has any economic or political revolution accomplished in the history of the

33. D. Clayton James, *Triumph and Disaster 1945–1964,* vol. 3 of *The Years of MacArthur* (Boston: Houghton Mifflin, 1985), 287-95.

34. Douglas MacArthur, *Reminiscences* (New York: McGraw-Hill, 1964), 310; Woodard, *Allied Occupation,* 358-59.

world. (Letter to Louis D. Newton, President of the Southern Baptist Convention, 13 December 1947)

My often repeated conviction remains unchanged that acceptance of the fundamental principles of Christianity would provide the surest foundation for the firm establishment of democracy in Japan. Therefore, distribution of Scriptures and interdenominational evangelistic rallies carried on in cooperation with established religious missions capable of providing continuing follow-up highly welcome. (Cable to Youth for Christ, 24 February 1950)

The Pocket Testament League . . . is promoting in all of Japan a large scale distribution of the Holy Scriptures. This distribution of the Bible in connection with their public meetings for the people of Japan has my hearty endorsement. . . . I have urgently requested the Pocket Testament League to make available to the Japanese people ten million portions of the Scriptures rather than the one million which had been in the original plan.
(Letter, "To Whom It May Concern," 4 April 1949)[35]

Japan was seen as one of the widest open doors, and hundreds of young men and women answered the call to service. Yet from evangelical pulpits and publications across the United States the lament still flowed that so few were responding when the opportunity was so great. General MacArthur's endeavor to remake Japan was probably the most important example of a relationship that was possible between the *Pax Americana* and Protestant missions, but evangelicals did not take full advantage of it.

Anthropology and Linguistics

An important contribution of Americans in the postwar decade was the introduction of scientific methodology into mission practice. This was most evident in the realm of cultural anthropology and the closely related field of linguistics. Long before the war, the Kennedy School of Missions at Hartford Seminary Foundation offered courses in anthropology for missionaries,

35. Quotations taken from Appendix G:4, "General MacArthur's Statements Concerning Christianity in Japan," in Woodard, *Allied Occupation*, 355, 357-59; also 242.

but perhaps more significant for evangelicals was the establishment in the late 1930s of an anthropology program at Wheaton College by Dr. Alexander Grigolia. Many of his majors planned to embark on missionary service, but some, like Billy Graham, entered other fields of ministry.[36] After the war the teaching of anthropology spread to other evangelical schools that also trained workers for overseas service.

One person who did much to foster the study of this discipline by missionaries was Eugene A. Nida, who became secretary of translations for the American Bible Society in 1943 and served until retiring in 1980. His book *Customs and Cultures: Anthropology for Christian Missions* (1954) was a widely used popular introduction to the subject. In 1953 he and several others working in the field founded a scholarly journal, *Practical Anthropology*, which applied its theories and findings to the missionary enterprise.

Linguistics functioned as a subdiscipline of cultural anthropology, and the new breed of missionary scholars readily used it. The Summer Institute of Linguistics, founded by Cameron Townsend and several associates in 1933, and its affiliated organization, Wycliffe Bible Translators, founded in 1942, began a systematic program to reduce spoken languages to writing, translate the Bible into them, and promote literacy. Once the war ended, Wycliffe's endeavors multiplied rapidly, and it utilized aircraft furnished by the newly formed Mission Aviation Fellowship and its own Jungle Aviation and Radio Service to bring translator-missionaries into the most remote regions of the tropics.

Under the able leadership of a professor from the University of Michigan, Kenneth L. Pike, the SIL became the chief center for missionary linguistic training. Nida assisted in the effort with his pioneering textbook *Bible Translating* and his more popular volume *Message and Mission*.[37] The missionary anthropologists and linguists enthusiastically embraced the principles

---

36. William A. Smalley, "Anthropological Study and Missionary Scholarship," in *Readings in Missionary Anthropology*, ed. Smalley (Tarrytown, NY: Practical Anthropology, 1967), 6; Paul M. Bechtel, *Wheaton College: A Heritage Remembered* (Wheaton: Harold Shaw, 1984), 124.

37. Eugene A. Nida, *Bible Translating: An Analysis of Principles and Procedures, with Special Reference to Aboriginal Languages* (New York: American Bible Society, 1947); idem, *Message and Mission* (New York: Harper, 1960).

of their disciplines and applied them in such areas as culture change, cultural relationships, and communication.[38]

Other Elements in the Missionary Thrust

Space does not permit a full telling of all the other dimensions of the postwar evangelical missionary advance, but at least three elements are worthy of mention. One was the creation of the Mission Aviation Fellowship, an agency that brought aeronautical technology into the service of missions. It was a direct product of the war in that its founder, James C. Truxton, was a navy pilot who had the vision of using his talents to further the propagation of the gospel. Like so many of his generation, he talked incessantly about the opportunities for service that must be seized at once before the doors "close in our very faces." He formed MAF in 1944, while still in the service, and his chief coworker in getting the venture off the ground was one of the most remarkable women in the history of twentieth-century missions, Elizabeth "Betty" Greene. She was both a devout Christian and an extraordinarily capable Air Corps pilot, and after her discharge she ran much of the fledgling agency's affairs. Then she became MAF's first missionary pilot on the field.[39]

Another significant element in the advance was student concern. The Student Volunteer Movement, founded in 1886, had all but died out by the 1930s, but Inter-Varsity Fellowship in Canada and the Student Foreign Missions Fellowship in the United States kept the vision alive. The SFMF was formed in 1936 and functioned mainly on Christian college and Bible institute campuses. In 1939 the first Inter-Varsity chapters were established south of the border, and the two groups began cooper-

38. See Smalley, "Anthropological Study," 6-13; and Harvie M. Conn, *Eternal Word and Changing Worlds: Theology, Anthropology, and Mission in Trialogue* (Grand Rapids: Zondervan, 1984), 138-58.

39. BGC Archives, Collection #136, box 1, folders 86, 92; Charles Mellis, Jr., "Wings on the Gospel," *Sunday* 8 (May 1946): 33-35, 60-64. Ruth A. Tucker, *From Jerusalem to Irian Jaya: A Biographical History of Christian Missions* (Grand Rapids: Zondervan, 1983), 395-98, gives Betty Greene the recognition that has long been overdue.

ating to promote the missionary vision. In 1946 they joined forces to sponsor the first missionary convention in Toronto, which drew 575 people. The second convention, two years later on the campus of the University of Illinois at Urbana, attracted 1,294. In that year SFMF merged with IVCF and became its missionary department. The Urbana conventions now are triennial events that challenge students to consider the option of Christian service abroad, and over the years thousands of them have signed cards indicating a willingness to do so.[40]

Also worth mentioning is the manner in which some congregations put extraordinary emphasis upon mission giving. One was the People's Church in Toronto, pastored by the dynamic Oswald J. Smith, which in 1947 raised $134,000 during its annual missionary convention. Another was Park Street Congregational Church in Boston, which that same year pledged $90,000 for missions in its convention.[41] These were large sums for the time and indicative of the missionary vision in the two congregations. But many other churches across the land were giving just as sacrificially to the cause, even if they did not attract media attention.

Conclusion: American Values and the Future of Missions

The record of the North American evangelical advance is only a part of the story of Christian missions after World War II, but it is an important one. The period of the United States' unchallenged preeminence was brief and troubled, and missionary effort did not secure the world peace that its advocates had hoped

40. Charles H. Troutman, "Backgrounds of Evangelical University Witness in the United States," unpublished ms. in BGC Archives, Collection #111, box 20, folder 1; Winter, 25 Unbelievable Years, 56-57; Cindy Smith and Joseph L. Cuming, Rebuilding the Mission Movement (Pasadena: National Student Missions Coalition, 1982); Shelley, "Evangelical Youth Movements," 56-58; H. Wilbert Norton, To Stir the Church: A Brief History of the Student Foreign Missions Fellowships, 1936–1986 (Madison, WI: Student Foreign Missions Fellowship, 1986).

41. Figures reported in United Evangelical Action 6 (1 June 1947): 7, and ibid., 6 (15 July 1947): 3.

for, even though workers from this land availed themselves of the opportunity to carry the gospel to untold millions who had never heard it. Moreover, the overwhelming proportion of North Americans in the force meant that ideas and values from these shores would dominate mission theory and practice. The American impact on the church's world mission would be seen in the emphasis on practical action, boldness, and observable results as well as in the more seamy values of cultural chauvinism and aggression, rugged individualism, divisiveness, and an entrepreneurial spirit among mission workers. On the other hand, such traits as deep piety, self-sacrifice, compassion for souls, and sensitivity to the needs of suffering people also characterized many American laborers in the divine vineyard. One hopes that, in the long run, as these missionaries' heirs come to understand the meaning of the World War II generation's achievements and failures, the latter qualities will prevail over the former.

Indeed, an important force for reform has already appeared, as Charles Van Engen's following essay will show. Evangelical leaders from the so-called Third World have been gaining influence and have been forcing their counterparts in the United States to take a long, hard look at the relationship between word and deed in the realm of social responsibility. Fortified by the national mood during World War II and the Cold War era, many evangelicals uncritically aligned their efforts with civil religion and capitalism. This "unequal yoke" has caused deep concern for Christians in the emerging nations, and Americans eventually will have to come to terms with these matters. Only then will the American messengers of Christ, working together in a global partnership, more nearly become the bearers of the "gospel of peace."

8 American Evangelical Missionaries in France, 1945–1975

Allen V. Koop

Soon after U.S. Navy chaplain Robert P. Evans waded ashore with the Allied invasion of France in 1944, he had an encounter with a French peasant that would shape the rest of his life. Staring wide-eyed at the tanks roaring across the sand, the peasant crossed himself fervently. Evans, mustering up his boyhood French learned in the French Cameroon, where his parents had served as missionaries, asked, "Why do you cross yourself?" The peasant replied, "Wouldn't anybody, to see this?" Evans responded, "Oh, I thought you might be a pious Catholic using the sign of the cross as a prayer." The Frenchman spat contemptuously. "That is what I think of all religion." As an afterthought, he muttered, "What has crossing oneself got to do with religion anyway?"[1] The young chaplain resolved that after the war he would return to these people as a missionary.

Evans was among the first of a growing number of American evangelical missionaries who chose to serve in France.[2] Between 1945 and 1975 the most persistent trend in this story was the steady rise in the number of missionaries. The handful who went to France in the late 1940s grew to over 100 by 1957. The

1. Robert P. Evans, interview with the author, 6 March 1973; idem, *Let Europe Hear* (Chicago: Moody, 1963), 107-8.
2. This chapter is drawn from Allen V. Koop, *American Evangelical Missionaries in France, 1945–1975* (Lanham, MD: Univ. Press of America, 1986). Readers desiring further details, documentation, or discussion of the points presented here should consult this larger work.

1960s saw an even greater increase, so that by 1970 there were more than 250. By 1975 the figure approached 375 (representing nearly forty mission agencies), with plans for continued expansion at an accelerated rate.[3] These missionaries concentrated their efforts on major urban centers: Bordeaux, Grenoble, Marseille, and Paris. Over half worked in the Paris suburbs, but only half a dozen in Paris itself. The rest were scattered unevenly throughout the country.

The establishment of the European Bible Institute and over fifty churches marked the missionaries' most visible and significant achievements. After a decade or more of unsuccessful work in a variety of faltering projects, most missionaries adopted the strategy of establishing new churches. As a result, the late 1960s and early 1970s saw a sharp increase in the size of the French evangelical community. For example, the total weekly attendance at the churches established by the Evangelical Alliance Mission rose from 50 in 1959 to 270 in 1965, 375 in 1970, and 650 in 1975.[4]

It is difficult to evaluate the success of that activity on which the missionaries placed the highest priority: the conversion of the French to evangelical Christianity. Most missionary evangelists thought that they averaged ten or fifteen converts a year, but some of those never joined an evangelical church, and perhaps as many as 50 percent eventually lost interest. The missionaries' own evaluation of their efforts revealed different standards as well. Those attached to large missions with growing churches evaluated their work statistically, while those involved in small groups stressed qualitative factors. All told, most admitted that the results of their evangelistic efforts were slim. While their colleagues in other lands brought back reports of success, American evangelicals in France told of a difficult field.

One might be tempted to choose a more encouraging case study to illumine the character of the postwar surge of evangelical missions, but the very difficulty experienced by American

3. I compiled these figures from a variety of mission rosters, personal notes, and other documents.

4. Robert Vajko, "A History and Analysis of the Church-Planting Ministry of the Evangelical Alliance Mission in France from 1952–1974" (master's thesis, Trinity Evangelical Divinity School, 1974), 252.

evangelicals in France makes their story especially revealing. As a "hard case," it highlights, in ways that success stories may not, the peculiarly American and conservative evangelical incarnation of Christianity that the missionaries were trying to impart. It also shows the sheer difficulty, if not futility, of such an enterprise in a modern, post-Christian nation.

A Post-Christian Society

The Americans who went to postwar France were not the first missionaries to operate in that country. After all, missionaries brought Christianity to southern Gaul nearly two thousand years ago. But the flame of faith barely flickered in the twentieth century. A cruel religious history, the influence of secular philosophies, the stress of industrialization, and the shock of two world wars contributed to the pervasive de-christianization of French society. H. Godin's *La France: Pays de Mission*, published during World War II, demonstrated that the masses were deserting the Roman Catholic Church. The World Council of Churches published case studies that reported the de-christianization of entire regions and social classes, and these studies concluded that urban France was "basically pagan."[5]

When the American evangelical missionaries arrived in France, they concurred readily with these conclusions. But the missionaries claimed that the French churches themselves needed evangelization. The first missionaries regarded all Catholics as lost souls. They made little or no attempt to understand the various factions within French Catholicism. This crippled their efforts. In spite of extensive secularization, the Catholic Church remained a vital force. As many as 85 percent of the French people identified with the church, and for most people, Christianity meant Catholicism.[6] There were variations,

5. H. Godin, *La France: Pays de Mission* (Paris: Ed. Abeille, 1943); World Council of Churches, *Ecumenical Studies: Evangelism in France* (Geneva: Secretariat for Evangelism, 1951), 1 (quoted).

6. International Congress on World Evangelism, *Status of Christianity Country Profile: France* (Lausanne, 1974), 3.

of course. Only some 10-20 percent claimed to be active. Peasants often combined Catholic and pagan traditions, while sophisticated urbanites embraced Vatican II's reforms.[7] Even so, the Catholic Church influenced society and dominated religious life. The missionaries never came to grips with this.

A more natural constituency might have been the French Protestants, who were relatively few in number. Postwar surveys reported varying numbers, but most settled on approximately 800,000, or about 2 percent of the population. Of these, about 450,000 belonged to the Reformed Church, 310,000 were Lutherans (mainly in Alsace), and the remainder was divided among the smaller denominations like the Baptists, Assemblies of God, Mennonites, Free Churches, and the Brethren.[8] But most French Protestant leaders held to liberal theology, which was anathema to evangelicals.

There was a tiny contingent of French evangelicals, and with these the Americans felt some compatibility. One French evangelical leader estimated that there were 20,000 to 30,000 evangelicals outside the Reformed and Lutheran churches with perhaps an equal number within these French denominations.[9] But the French evangelical Christians added some awkwardness to the missionaries' presence in France. The small evangelical churches clung to life but did not exhibit much boldness in their witness. The American missionaries would have preferred to reestablish an evangelical witness from scratch, but the existence of this struggling, indigenous evangelical community complicated matters.

Early Efforts: 1945–1960

The first American missionary efforts in postwar France took the form of itinerant evangelism. Teams went out under the sponsorship of Youth for Christ, the Bible Christian Union, the Navigators, Baptist Mid-Missions, the European Evangelistic Crusade, the Foreign Missionary Society of Brethren Churches,

---

7. Ibid., 3; WCC, *Ecumenical Studies*, 2.
8. ICWE, *Status of Christianity*, 5.
9. Jacques Blocher, interview with the author, 15 June 1973.

the Plymouth Brethren, the Slavic Gospel Mission, and Child Evangelism Fellowship. Although thousands attended some of the youth rallies, these early evangelists produced few lasting results.[10]

Nevertheless, the apparent failure of itinerant evangelism promoted the foremost accomplishment of this early phase, the European Bible Institute. By the summer of 1948, Youth for Christ's Robert Evans was deeply frustrated by his mission's patently American flavor and its inability to retain converts. Evans became convinced that a European country could be evangelized only by Europeans and that Americans could contribute most effectively by providing evangelical instruction. Evans gathered a small group of young adults who were interested in serious Bible study. Beginning with informal classes in his apartment, Evans later opened an evening school in the Latin quarter in 1950.[11]

While the evening school was accepted by the French evangelical leaders, they opposed Evans's plan for a full-time Bible institute, arguing that it would compete with French institutions. They also resented the affluence of the Americans.[12] Ultimately, the European Bible Institute began to overcome French suspicion. Its graduates slowly won the acceptance and recognition of the French leaders as an integral part of their community.

By the end of the 1950s, 150 American evangelical missionaries served in France; but this force was fragmented. Individual missions did little to cooperate with each other or with the French evangelicals. Each group termed its work a "pioneer ministry," a concept borrowed from other missions to label a hitherto unevangelized field. Americans were slow to realize that France was different. Some mission executives contemplated distributing personnel in France according to a plan devised for China. As late as the mid-1970s, several American missions continued to refer to France as a pioneer field. This persistent tendency to disregard the

10. For a detailed account of these early attempts, see Koop, *American Evangelical Missionaries,* 26-33.

11. Evans, interview; idem, newsletter, June 1951, files of the Greater Europe Mission, Wheaton, Illinois.

12. Koop, *American Evangelical Missionaries,* 34-37.

ancient Christian heritage of France did little to ingratiate the Americans to the French evangelicals.[13]

Arriving in France with unbridled optimism, the Americans very quickly became discouraged. The evangelistic methods that had proved successful in the United States usually failed in France. Convinced at first that they could evangelize France in a decade, the success-oriented Americans were confronted with underachievement. Jacques Blocher, a French evangelical leader to whom Americans occasionally turned for assistance, recalled one optimistic American evangelist who came to him just before initiating a summer tent campaign. The missionary wanted to know what to do with all the converts he would win. Blocher advised him to wait and see. In October the missionary wrote to report only one convert. Blocher kindly suggested that it took time to understand France.[14] Discouraged by their slow progress, several Americans concluded that the work and time necessary to produce one convert in France would yield ten to twenty in the United States.

The early 1950s brought the first wave of resident American missionaries to France. At the same time, American technicians, economic advisors, businessmen, and military personnel intervened in France's political and economic life. The American evangelical missionaries were concerned solely with the religious condition of France, but the French people they contacted tended not to see this important difference. They were inclined to view all Americans alike.[15]

Nevertheless, the American missionaries were determined to make their ministries prosper. The most influential missionary in France in the early 1950s was Arthur P. Johnston, the first worker sent by The Evangelical Alliance Mission (TEAM). He and his brother Rodney devoted three years to a youth ministry among Parisian teenagers, only to see it disintegrate during his furlough in the United States.[16] TEAM's youth work suffered

13. Vajko, "History and Analysis," 32.
14. Blocher, interview.
15. See Edward McCreary, *The Americanization of Europe* (Garden City, NY: Doubleday, 1964).
16. Koop, *American Evangelical Missionaries*, 50-54, 76.

from its decision not to cooperate with local French churches. Theological differences and assumptions as well as cultural barriers divided the French and the Americans. Not only were American evangelical missionaries predisposed to reject any cooperation or fellowship with Roman Catholics, but Johnston came to a similar conclusion about the French Reformed Church. He decided that the Americans should build evangelical churches from scratch.[17] In the following two decades most American missions in France would follow TEAM's decision.

The energetic Johnston led TEAM to foster a new French denomination by planting new congregations.[18] Although not a revolutionary concept in the 1950s, church planting was not yet a widely accepted missionary strategy. Many missions took little care to formulate any strategy other than "sowing the seed" or "general mission work." As a major force in European missions, however, TEAM's actions were bound to influence other American missions. In opting for starting a new church rather than cooperating with existing churches, TEAM and other missions were influenced more by the separatist spirit of American evangelicalism and by the customary missionary strategy for the Third World than by careful analysis of the unique situation in France.

TEAM's first attempt to establish a church, at Virty, might be termed at best a marginal success. But the second attempt, at Orly, six miles southeast of Paris, was more promising. Some claimed it to be the American missionaries' highest achievement, as a Bible-study group of three became a church of more than one hundred with a modern edifice. Encouraged by this success, the TEAM church planters went to other southern suburbs of Paris: Orsay, Fresnes, Creteil, and Chilly-Mazarin. The Orsay congregation never grew large enough to build a church, so they remodeled the garage attached to the mission headquarters.[19] It was not uncommon for mission congregations to start in a garage; several remained there.

17. "Guide Plan for France," Evangelical Alliance Mission Annual Report, 1963, in files of The Evangelical Alliance Mission, Wheaton, Illinois (hereinafter cited as "TEAM Files").

18. Ibid.; Koop, *American Evangelical Missionaries*, 76-80.

19. Richard Winchell, associate general director of TEAM, interview with

The Struggle Continues: 1960–1975

As the 1950s gave way to the 1960s, France experienced revolutionary changes. A stagnant society became mobile and affluent, though no less troubled, as the languishing postwar economy shifted into high gear in the 1960s. Swarms of new automobiles choked French cities, clusters of stark concrete apartment buildings sprang up in suburban fields, and television captured domestic life. Preoccupied with planning their leisure time, the French lived for their summer vacations and *le weekend.* France's ancient values were being supplanted by the materialism of a modern consumer society. Already thoroughly secularized, the new France showed even less interest in religion. The American missionaries, who experienced enough difficulty understanding traditional French culture, now faced the additional problem of adapting to a society in rapid transition.

Nevertheless, American evangelicals seemed determined to move forward. The number of missionaries continued to increase between 1960 and 1975, as did the number of boards sending missionaries to France. The strategy discussions of the late 1950s and early 1960s led most missions to conclude that their various activities in France must all relate to the primary task of planting and nurturing churches.[20] Embracing the church-growth movement, however, brought both inspiration and frustration. Missionaries gained confidence when they realized that at last they had a clear strategy, but frustration came when they compared their results with other fields. Reports from places like Bolivia, where forty-one new churches were started in three months, made the progress in France look miniscule.[21] Furthermore, and perhaps more distressing, the church-growth movement called for missions to concentrate their efforts in receptive societies.[22] No one could claim that France was a recep-

the author, 2 February 1973; "1962 Annual Conference Report," TEAM Files; Ivan Peterson, newsletters, July 1963 and May 1969, TEAM Files; Paul Sheetz, *The Sovereign Hand* (Wheaton: The Evangelical Alliance Mission, 1971), 196-98.

20. See Koop, *American Evangelical Missionaries,* 105-22.

21. Report in *Church Growth Bulletin* 9 (July 1973): 334.

22. For a definitive statement of church growth theory, see Donald McGavran, *Understanding Church Growth* (Grand Rapids: Eerdmans, 1971).

tive society for missionaries. So, while the church-growth movement gave the missions in France a plan for action, it implicitly
questioned their continuation.

One of the prominent developments in the 1960s was the
multiplication of Baptist mission agencies working in France.
Most of them had identical goals and beliefs, but they rarely
cooperated with each other. The largest group of new missionaries came from the Conservative Baptist Foreign Mission
Society. Choosing to settle in Parisian suburbs notoriously resistant to religion, they had little to show after a decade of dil-
igent effort. Only one church, moved from a one-car garage in
Arnouville-les-Gonesse to a two-car garage in Villiers-le-Bel,
showed any signs of growth and maturity.[23] The other Baptist
mission boards operating in France were fundamentalist.
Taking aim at neo-orthodoxy, neo-evangelicalism, ecumenism,
liberalism, and pentecostalism, they brought to France the divisive issues peculiar to American fundamentalism. In spite of
the tiny evangelical population, some of these missions taught
their little flocks to separate from Christians of different convictions.[24]

The 1970s brought slow but steady growth to the two most
prominent American missions in France, The Evangelical Alliance Mission (TEAM) and the European Bible Institute (Greater
European Mission). By 1975 TEAM had organized seven
churches and five embryonic congregations with a combined
weekly attendance of over six hundred; five had French leaders.
The number of TEAM missionaries doubled, from sixteen in
1965 to thirty-three in 1975. No other mission had produced
comparable results. TEAM had become a convinced advocate of
church-growth strategies, especially in its work among the receptive Antillian population in the suburbs south of Paris.
Furthermore, TEAM had led in the campaign to convince American evangelicals to consider France as a mission field. Of all the

23. "1969 Annual Report," "1970 Annual Report," files of the Conservative
Baptist Foreign Mission Society, Wheaton, Illinois.

24. For examples of the work and outlook of one of these missions, see John
Mitchell, newsletters, July 1968, October 1968, and May 1970; and Wilbur Barnes,
newsletter, April 1972 all in the files of Evangelical Baptist Missions, Hawthorne,
New Jersey.

missions in France, TEAM appeared to be the most organized, purposeful, and potentially successful.

Yet the mission suffered from at least four weaknesses, each of which was an ironic result of the mission's strengths. The first problem stemmed from the emphasis on church planting. Half of TEAM's twelve churches had fewer than twenty members. Had the Americans demonstrated wisdom by identifying each of its groups as a church, when the stability and viability of each hung by such a slender thread? Could such tiny assemblies attract and sustain interest? What would happen to the mission's credibility if some of these suddenly collapsed? The second problem concerned the predominantly Antillian churches. Would their dramatic growth somehow enable greater penetration of French society? Or would their ethnic character isolate TEAM from the mainstream of French society? Third, the TEAM churches maintained a sectarian stance, belonging to TEAM's *Alliance des Eglises Independantes*. Did this association's clear-cut identity foster growth? Or was TEAM drawing the wagons in a protective circle?

Finally, TEAM's success owed much to its large investment of funds and personnel. TEAM's annual expenditure rose from $14,218 in 1953 to $202,803 in 1975,[25] with a total investment over the period of one million dollars. And the mission's accomplishments depended upon thirty-three missionaries by the mid-1970s. Given this heavy foreign intervention, would the TEAM-founded churches become healthy French congregations, or would they be dependent on American money and missionaries?

The Greater European Mission (GEM) shared with TEAM the preeminence in influence and size. The ultimate goal for each mission was to work itself out of a job by firmly establishing evangelical Christianity in France. However, the two missions differed in strategy: TEAM did church planting, while GEM focused on its European Bible Institute. Yet GEM began a church-planting effort in northern France, while TEAM maintained a close relationship with the French Bible school at Nogent and helped establish the evangelical seminary at Vaux-sur-Seine. GEM, like TEAM, at first projected a heavy (some would say

25. "Annual Report, 1977 Field Conference," p. A-1, TEAM Files.

heavy-handed) American impression. American determination to succeed, coupled with French cultural sensitivity (some would say touchiness), resulted in some hard feelings. But the Americans became more adapted to French culture, and the French evangelicals more appreciative of the Americans' contribution.[26] The European Bible Institute, at first a source of contention, eventually did much to bring the two together.

American Evangelicals and French Culture

By 1975, American evangelical missions in France had entered their second generation, and the ranks now included some grown children of missionaries. Strategists who once planned the whirlwind evangelization of France now thought in terms of generations. The missionaries marched to a slow drummer, and their story held much failure. For every receptive discussion there were hundreds of slammed doors and rude replies. For every letter of inquiry there were thousands of tracts in the waste-basket. Plans were thwarted and strategies fizzled. After much counseling, people professed conversion, only to fall away later. Thousands of "promising contacts" led nowhere.

These persistent failures made the accomplishments seem all the more important. Modest achievements were celebrated as miraculous within a culture that was highly resistant to missionaries. Being more easily discerned, successes received more attention than failures. This pattern poses a problem for the historian, since most histories concern themselves with what happened, rather than with what did not happen. But in this case, much of the story lies in what failed to occur. Yet this pattern is not that uncommon for missionaries. They tend to assume that only a few people will prove receptive to their message, most will be indifferent, and some will be hostile. But few societies in modern times proved more impervious to evangelical missionaries than did France.

26. J. Herbert Kane, *A Global View of Christian Missions* (Grand Rapids: Baker, 1971), 540.

The missionaries did not agree on whether their failure to penetrate French society was due to theological, personal, sociological, or methodological reasons. And yet, as Americans, they felt compelled to find the answer, solve the problem, and become successful. They also felt obliged to explain their failures to their supporters back home. The answer lay somewhere in the relationship between American attitudes, evangelical doctrine, and French society. Some thought the problems might be spiritual: perhaps God had not planned a great awakening for modern France; perhaps France suffered under extraordinary satanic influence; or perhaps a missionary's failure reflected spiritual inadequacies. Yet few were content to attribute their underachievement solely to divine timing. Most missionaries focused on problems that French culture raised.

Some missionaries, and many French evangelicals, believed that the Americans would have been more successful if they had properly adapted themselves to French culture. The failure of the French to respond to the missionaries, these critics believed, was due to the missionaries' distinctive and often offensive American behavior. A larger faction claimed that no matter how much the missionaries attempted to conform to French culture, the response would still be negative. The problem, they said, lay in French culture itself, for it was fundamentally incompatible with evangelical Christianity. Frenchmen could become true Christians only by renouncing certain French values and customs.

Whether the missionary was attempting to change the French or conform to their ways, some adaptation was necessary. Proficiency in the language was an obvious priority, but problems with it put almost all of the missionaries under a handicap. Very few had trained in French before arriving, and very few learned to speak without a heavy accent. This greatly hindered their work among a people who viewed mispronunciation of its language as obnoxious, not quaint. For some missionaries, the language problem was so great that it changed their personalities. Bold effervescence gave way to reserved timidity. Educated minds were limited to shallow conversation. Veteran missionaries bothered by linguistic inadequacies even after fifteen or twenty years in France, claimed that an additional

191

year of language study would have been worth the time.[27] Indeed, the missions usually did not properly stress linguistic proficiency. While some mission leaders dealt with the language problem by tightening the requirements, more often they merely reminded the new missionaries that sincere love for the French people should cover a multitude of grammatical sins.[28]

Another communication problem stemmed from the missionaries' unsure grasp of French thought forms, especially in religious ideas. Audiences accustomed to Cartesian logic and careful arguments were not swayed by canned evangelistic sermons filled with references to obscure fundamentalist American theologians.[29]

American evangelical taboos, especially concerning alcohol, caused further problems. The fundamentalist and separatist missionaries categorically refused wine, even when offered by French hosts. Some missions called for a pledge of total abstinence from both missionaries and their French converts. Many missionaries agreed to this before leaving the United States but then attempted to modify the policy in deference to wine's social importance in France. Permission to change was usually denied, often for economic reasons. Mission executives feared that their American supporters would be deeply offended to learn that their missionaries were drinking wine. Some missions avoided the problem by allowing individual missionaries to follow their consciences, accepting wine in French homes if they felt it would aid their acceptance. Although it seemed tangential to the missionaries' purpose, the issue generated a disproportionate amount of attention. The French could not readily understand this tempest in a wine glass and were even more perplexed by some missionaries' taboos on movies and dancing.

One group of missionaries was convinced that their failure in evangelism was due to their failure to adapt successfully to French culture. These missionaries pointed to the American lifestyle maintained by many of their colleagues and to the American image of some missionary-founded churches with their

27. "1968 Annual Conference Report," 40, TEAM Files.
28. "Chairman's Report," 1955 Annual Report, TEAM Files.
29. Frank Horton, "The Right Kind of Men," His 28 (January 1968): 12.

frothy gospel choruses. Several missionary pastors admitted that their congregation was called "the American church" rather than "the evangelical church." The missionaries who sought more complete assimilation objected strenuously to their colleagues' insistence that French converts follow American fundamentalist standards of behavior. It was difficult enough for a Frenchman to embrace evangelical Christianity without adding the encrustations of American evangelicalism. The evangelization of France was not going to be achieved by turning Frenchmen into Americans.

On the other side stood missionaries who were equally convinced that their task would not be accomplished by turning Americans into Frenchmen. As one unproductive year followed another, an increasing number of missionaries, including several mission leaders, concluded that the problems lay not in the difference between American and French cultures, but in the difference between French culture and evangelical Christianity.[30] If success came with cultural assimilation, this faction argued, why were French evangelicals so unsuccessful? Their conclusion—that French culture was peculiarly resistant to evangelical Christianity—was sobering because it required Frenchmen to estrange themselves from their own culture in order to grasp evangelical Christianity. This reversed the usual sequence, in which missionaries expected individuals to convert and then to renounce those aspects of their culture that were incompatible with their new faith.[31]

Missionaries customarily went to non-Western societies whose values were incompatible with Christianity. But while they sought to achieve enough cultural empathy to earn the right to be heard, they offered something new and essentially beneficial. The invitation to embrace a new religion often brought with it modern medical care, education, and economic development. These ancillary benefits encouraged belief in a religion that seemed true and progressive. Modern, secularized France did not lend itself to this pattern. Missionary identifica-

30. See, e.g., Frank Horton, "What the French Think of Our Missionaries," *Eternity* 28 (August 1958): 23.
31. McGavran, *Understanding Church Growth*, 198.

tion with a secularized culture threatened to undermine their message. Modern France, rather than being ignorant of Christianity, had known it, rejected it, and moved on. Where did the evangelical missionaries plan to lead France? Back into a past Christian era? Forward to another Christian era? There was no clear vision for Christianity's cultural role.

Life in modern France also presented impediments to missionary progress. Urban living seemed to allow no time for religion and reduced missionary schedules to shambles. Commuting, late dinners, and television made evening visitation and meetings inconvenient if not impossible. Since economic pressures often required both husband and wife to work, door-to-door evangelism frequently found no one at home. Fatigue and family gatherings left little time for church activities on Sundays. The weekend exodus to the countryside made for even emptier pews. These logistical problems caused many missionaries to doubt if evangelical Christianity could fit into the schedule.[32]

The social structure of France was another source of confusion and frustration. The vigilantly guarded privacy of the French home and the social insularity of the family impeded evangelism. A rigid class structure limited personal contacts, restricted group dynamics, and denied overtures to the working class as well as to the influential *haute bourgeoisie*. The missionaries in France, like missionaries everywhere, tried to be agents of social change, but they often failed to understand the functional relationships between facets of French culture. Very often the missionaries concentrated upon individuals who had little capacity to shape French society. Their extensive involvement with women and children might have added numbers to evangelical groups, but it did little to advance evangelical Christianity's social influence.

Those who blamed French culture for their evangelistic failures pointed to the success they enjoyed with non-French

32. Roger Mehl, *Traite de Sociologie du Protestantisme* (Neuchatel: Delachaux Niestle, 1965), 275; S. Benetreau, "Obstacles to Evangelism"; and Jacques Blocher, "Basic Aspects of Effective Evangelization of France in Our Generation," addresses given at the annual meeting of the *Alliance des Eglises Evangeliques Independants*, 11 February 1967, both documents in TEAM Files.

people. From the earliest days, the groups formed by missionaries contained Italian, Spanish, Portuguese, African, and Antillian immigrants. In many cases the most active members of missionary churches in France were not Frenchmen. But this concentration of efforts among ethnic groups that were not socially innovative or influential aggravated the problem, for it invited both the indifference and the censure of the socially influential.[33]

The missionaries' status in French society determined the success of their efforts. Their identity was as important as their ideology. People wanted to know who they were before they listened to what they had to say. Although the missionaries could not control how the French perceived them, they made critical choices about the relationships that gave them their identity. This held true in matters of interchurch relations as well as in social relations.

American Evangelicals and the French Churches

Unfortunately for the missionaries, they were most frequently given the labels they hoped to avoid. All too often they were grouped with the secular Americans in France or with the cults. The missionaries thought the growth of the cults pointed to a French desire for religious change, but they were unable to tap it.[34] While their groups resembled cults to most Frenchmen, they looked too much like a church to those drawn to the cults. At first, the Americans saw no need to achieve religious status within French culture. If they thought about the issue at all, they presumed that their American religious identity would be enough. A few missionaries never moved past their own orbit and were puzzled that so few French people knew who they were or what they were doing. By the 1960s most realized that they had to achieve status by identifying with some French Christian com-

---

33. Louis J. Luzbetak, *The Church and Cultures* (South Pasadena: William Carey Library, 1976), 111, 118, 120, 141-43, 295-96.

34. Jacques Seguy, *Les Sectes Protestantes dans la France Contemporaine* (Paris: Beauchesne et ses Fils, 1956), 80-81, 92-95, 162, 174; Mehl, *Traite de Sociologie du Protestantisme*, 209, 223-25, 251-54; Vajko, "History and Analysis," 215-16.

munion, although a few missionaries kept to themselves exclusively and maintained a fundamentalist and separatist stance.

Being identified with the religion that most Frenchmen recognized, Roman Catholicism, was simply out of the question. The missionaries' initial hostility toward Catholicism began to give way, however, when they realized that most French Catholics were only nominally identified with the church. By the early 1960s the doctrines and power of Rome seemed less important than using dissatisfaction with Catholicism as an opportunity for evangelism.[35] By 1970 the changes that followed the Second Vatican Council had brought about change in evangelical attitudes. Wary overtures and limited cooperation replaced the hostility of earlier years. But a rapprochement with Catholicism was still not in sight. The optimism generated by Vatican II could not overcome instinctive suspicion, as the missionaries maintained their distance from the Roman Catholic Church. Nevertheless, some admitted that demanding converts to renounce Catholicism would keep evangelical numbers in France perennially small.[36]

Instead, many missionaries chose to identify, somewhat haphazardly and incompletely, with the tiny evangelical denominations like the Baptists, Brethren, or Free Churches. These French groups shared the missionaries' beliefs, but even so, the American and French evangelicals had their disagreements. The French often termed these differences cultural, while the Americans claimed that they were doctrinal. Initially, economic differences grated upon the French, leading to frosty receptions for Americans' lavish methods, large budgets, and new cars. Differences in education and experience also posed problems. The French felt that the Americans were naive and culturally unsophisticated, while the Americans claimed that the French were parochial and insular.[37]

35. Weldon Clark, "Easter in France," *Missionary Broadcaster* 35 (March 1959): 9; "The Effect of Roman Catholicism on Protestant Missions in France," n.d., files of the Unevangelized Fields Mission, Bala-Cynwyd, Pennsylvania.

36. For a representative response to the "Catholic issue," see "Committee on Roman Catholicism Report," 1970, TEAM Files.

37. Jacques Blocher, "Influence of Foreign Missionaries in France," paper presented to TEAM semiannual conference, November 1960; Arthur Johnston to David Johnson, 2 June 1973, both documents from TEAM Files.

Although American missionaries and French evangelicals continued to annoy each other from time to time, by the 1970s considerable progress had been made. French concerns about American cultural insensitivity became muted as the missionaries deferred to French customs. American criticisms of French reluctance to evangelize were assuaged by new French evangelistic activities. When the Americans understood that differences in attitudes or behavior did not stem from doctrine, cooperation became much easier. The missionaries who made the most progress were those who realized that some secondary doctrines, such as premillennialism, were shaped as much by American evangelical history as by biblical orthodoxy.

The Americans gradually realized that the French evangelicals, after all, had been gracious, cordial, and helpful to uninvited foreign missionaries. After the missionaries had experienced frustration and failure, they appreciated the difficulties faced by their overworked and poorly supported French counterparts. While still pressing the French to move forward, the Americans came to realize how hard it was just to hold even. The French, for their part, recognized that the Americans had made a vital contribution and valued their presence as they grew more culturally sensitive. The pastor of a well-known French evangelical church in Paris termed the missionary work "considerable and eminently useful," while others acknowledged their debt to the Americans in church planting and evangelism.[38]

Indeed, the American missionaries' greatest impact had been made upon French evangelicalism. Their establishment of nearly fifty new churches was a major achievement compared to the French evangelicals' failure to increase the number and size of their congregations. Some of the new churches were large enough to give French evangelicals greater visibility. Equally important were the Americans' contributions to French evangelical education. The European Bible Institute in particular became a focal point for evangelicalism. By 1970 three of the four evangelical schools serving French-speaking Europe (the European Bible Institute, Vaux-sur-Seine, Nogent, and Emmaus) were headed by

---

38. Jacques Dubois, pastor of Tabernacle Church, to Arthur Johnston, 23 May 1966, TEAM Files; Blocher, "Influence of Foreign Missionaries," 12-13.

Americans. This educational influence began to reshape French evangelicals' theology, as the missionaries' doctrines of biblical inspiration, evangelism, and premillennialism made inroads into French evangelical thought. Finally, the missionaries' financial investment had a major impact on the French evangelicals. Sometimes the Americans provided direct grants or loans. But usually the contributions came by way of literature, equipment, buildings, and the missionaries' services. Although it is impossible to ascertain the exact figure, the total invested by the missions amounted to several million dollars.

Although the missionaries were pleased with their influence upon the French evangelicals, this was not the purpose for which they had come to France. They had planned to make an impact upon France itself, not merely upon their co-religionists in that country. But by 1975 their efforts remained unnoticed by most Frenchmen. French evangelical groups wielded almost no influence in France and commanded little visibility or status. The Americans had chosen these associations because of ecclesiastical and doctrinal familiarity, not for strategic missionary advantage.

There was one alternative strategy, however, that held some promise on a local, limited scale. Some creative missionaries sought an approach that avoided any ecclesiastical identity. They presumed that the de-Christianized regions or social segments of France that would not respond to institutionalized Christianity might consider the faith on "neutral" ground. The Grace Brethren operated a chateau at Saint-Albain on this basis, but this ministry still found that it needed to refer its clients to Christian churches.[39] The chateau's staff envisioned it as a bridge between a post-Christian society and institutional Christianity, but they did not intend converts to remain on the bridge. Morever, the entire American missionary force would not pretend to stand between the secular and the religious. The bridge concept could function only if there was a Christian community on the other side. The missionaries and the French evangel-

39. "Chateau de Saint-Albain" (1967); Thomas Julien, "1972 Report"; both in files of the National Fellowship of Brethren Churches, Foreign Missions, Winona Lake, Indiana.

icals formed one such community, but their sectarian image made them rather uninviting.

A more challenging option, though rarely pondered and never attempted, was to cooperate with the most prominent Protestant denomination in France, the Reformed Church. Although not without great problems, this course of action would have addressed the missionaries' lack of status and identity in French society. A cordial relationship with the Reformed Church had much to offer. Although smaller in size than the Catholic Church, the Reformed Church enjoyed historic prestige and a reputation for integrity and patriotism. Moreover, the Reformed ranks included an estimated fifty thousand evangelicals.[40] Identification with this respected French institution would dispel the missionaries' alien image and the sectarian stigma attached to the Mormons and Jehovah's Witnesses. The evangelicals' contention that the Reformed Church had lapsed into theological liberalism and lethargy about evangelization was on the mark.[41] But a minority within the Reformed Church took seriously the imperative to evangelize modern France's mobile population. The Reformed Church's home mission organization, the *Societe Centrale d'Evangelisation,* attracted those who were committed to evangelism. The Protestant communities at Taizé and Chambon-sur-Lignon presented an attractive image of Protestantism, especially to French youth. A relationship with the Reformed Church was more likely to engender the social and religious change the missionaries sought than would an evangelical or American label. Converts could join a venerable French form of Christianity rather than an isolated foreign sect.

But this idea unsettled the American missionaries. Raising their profile did not seem worth the risks in being associated with a liberal denomination. Moreover, the missions insisted on maintaining control over their own destiny in France, no matter how small their impact. Their primary goal had become not the widespread proclamation of the gospel, but control of their own converts and churches. Conservative evangelical missionaries

40. S. Schram, *Protestantism and Politics in France* (Alencon: Coriere and Jugain, 1954), 128; Blocher, interview.
41. "Guide Plan for France"; Kane, *Global View of Christian Missions,* 540.

wanted to protect the clients from liberal or pentecostal ideas, and accountability to the home office and to American supporters also weighed heavily.[42]

The meager chance that the Americans would enter relations with the Reformed Church was swept aside when the church-growth movement prevailed in the 1960s. This did not follow logically, since the movement advocated New Testament models of evangelization and church growth, and the apostles sought interested people at the synagogues, the place of prayer, or even on Mars Hill. The twentieth-century French equivalents were the Catholic and Reformed churches. But the missionaries, hamstrung by their aversion to Catholicism and liberal Protestantism, avoided the places where people interested in Christianity were most likely to be found.

The church-growth movement's global strategy also implied that the missionaries should associate with the older churches, since it mandated concentration of resources in the world's receptive societies. France was obviously an unreceptive society, so according to theory, it should have been awarded a small mission, perhaps in cooperation with the older churches. New churches established under a partnership with the Reformed Church could have been semiautonomous affiliates rather than antagonistic competitors. The Reformed Church's empty sanctuaries could have been provided when missionary churches needed buildings.

Some missionaries did work with the French Reformed Church. But for the most part these were nonevangelical "fraternal workers" from the American mainline denominations. Fraternal workers subordinated their work to a French pastor and did not seek to change French religious belief. They enjoyed identity with the French but did not desire to change the status quo. The evangelicals desired to change the status quo but lacked the necessary identity.

Some missions rejected the concept of fraternal workers because it undermined firm American control. They opposed the idea of affiliation, no matter how compatible the French partner. However, in the 1960s a growing number of evangelical mis-

---

42. See examples of this protective posture on the part of TEAM leaders in Koop, *American Evangelical Missionaries*, 76-79, 123-24.

sions arranged for fraternal workers. The Gospel Missionary Union's bond with the Free Church, the Alpine Mission's collaboration with French Brethren assemblies, the Mennonite alliance with French Mennonites, and the Southern Baptists' projects with the French Baptist Federation were the smoothest and most well-accepted missionary ventures.[43] With the right personalities and considerable tact on both sides, fraternal-worker relationships prospered and brought greater success, as the missionaries were strengthening the French churches rather than competing with them. National differences lessened.

These missionaries did not object to subordinating Americans to Frenchmen, but they did oppose subordinating evangelicals to nonevangelicals. They claimed that confusion among their French contacts as well as among their supporters at home would come from identifying with a liberal denomination. Moreover, American evangelicals would discontinue support for any mission associated with liberal denominations or the ecumenical movement. The home front dictated a separatist strategy.[44]

Pursuing a relationship with the French Reformed Church would have required a significant shift in American mission theory and practice. It also would have required a large amount of courage and faith. In some local instances, the problems would have been minimal. There were a few conservative pastors and many parishioners in the Reformed Church who shared the missionaries' evangelical beliefs. A partnership along these lines might have strengthened these Reformed evangelicals and encouraged them to evangelize France.

Larger problems loomed between an evangelical missionary and a liberal Reformed pastor, but if a Reformed pastor had agreed to cooperate with an American missionary, their col-

---

43. James M. Taylor, "Church Planting in France," *The Gospel Message* 78 (January 1970): 10-11; Annual Reports, 1971–1975, files of the Unevangelized Fields Mission, Bala-Cynwyd, Pennsylvania; "1962 Annual Report," 220, and "1967 Annual Report," 31, both in files of Mennonite Board of Missions, Elkhart, Indiana; Lewis M. Krause, *Scattered Abroad: The Story of English Language Baptist Work in Europe* (Heidelberg: Herstellung-Brausdruck, 1966), 27, 41-42; news bulletins of the European Baptist Press Service (Ruschlikon, Switzerland), no. 66:207 (3 October 1966) and no. 67:45 (8 February 1967).

44. Koop, *American Evangelical Missionaries*, 75-79.

laboration could have profited both. American missionaries would have achieved access to a French audience otherwise denied them, while the overworked Protestant pastors would have acquired help. The missionaries could have focused upon strengthening the spirituality of parishioners and congregations rather than ensuring the longevity of missionary institutions. But American missions were unwilling to sacrifice control for the sake of an expanded impact. The faith missions, as some called themselves, seemed to have more faith that their financial needs would be met than that their converts would be sustained without a tightly controlled religious environment.

Conclusion

So the American evangelical missionaries eschewed relationships with the major Christian denominations in France. Holding out a hand once in a while to minor evangelical groups, they continued to plod along, usually concentrating on their individual projects. Forming a small part of the postwar American involvement in Europe and a small part of the postwar expansion of evangelical missions, they were among the least successful of each. But few could match their personal dedication and resilient confidence. They saw their task as history's highest calling and challenge. They suffered continual disappointment but worked diligently and compassionately among people who considered them anomalous or anachronistic, if they bothered to pay them any attention at all. Their discouragement in French society did not convince them that their endeavor was futile. Instead, they increased their numbers and their efforts, sustained by their professed love for their Lord and the French people. They were content to work against the grain of modern European history. While the French converted empty churches into garages, the American missionaries converted garages into churches.

9 A Broadening Vision: Forty Years of Evangelical Theology of Mission, 1946–1986

Charles E. Van Engen

Introduction

The last forty years have seen the explosive rise of the evangelicals as a religious force in North America, moving, as George Marsden has put it, "from fundamentalism to evangelicalism."[1] This growth has included an expanding evangelical role in North American mission sending, coupled with important developments in the way the evangelicals have articulated their mission theology.[2]

1. George Marsden, "From Fundamentalism to Evangelicalism: A Historical Analysis," in *The Evangelicals*, ed. D. F. Wells and J. D. Woodbridge (Nashville: Abingdon, 1975), 122-42.
2. Some of the more accessible overviews of evangelical mission theology of this period are found in the following: David Bosch, *Witness to the World: The Christian Mission in Theological Perspective* (London: Marshall, Morgan & Scott, 1980); Rodger Bassham, *Mission Theology, 1948–1975: Years of Worldwide Creative Tension—Ecumenical, Evangelical and Roman Catholic* (Pasadena: William Carey Library, 1979); Arthur Glasser and Donald McGavran, *Contemporary Theologies of Mission* (Grand Rapids: Baker, 1983), chap. 7; Arthur Glasser, "The Evolution of Mission Theology Since World War II," *International Bulletin of Missionary Research* 9 (January 1985): 9-13; and Efiong Utuk, "From Wheaton to Lausanne: The Road to Modification of Contemporary Evangelical Mission Theology," *Missiology* 14 (April 1986): 205-19. See also Stephen Knapp, "Mission and Modernization: A Preliminary Critical Analysis of Contemporary Understandings of Mission from a 'Radical Evangelical' Perspective," in *American Missions in Bicentennial Perspective*, ed. R. Pierce Beaver (Pasadena: William Carey Library,

At the risk of oversimplification, I want to present a broad interpretive portrait of the historical development of evangelical mission theology from the birth of the National Association of Evangelicals (NAE) in Chicago in 1943 to the triennial conference of the Interdenominational Foreign Mission Association (IFMA) and the Evangelical Foreign Missions Association (EFMA), which met with the Association of Evangelical Professors of Mission (AEPM) in Pasadena in 1984.[3]

My thesis is that, as North American Evangelicals experienced new sociocultural strength and confidence, changes in ecumenical theology of mission, and developments in evangelical partner churches in the Third World, they responded with a broadening vision of an evangelical theology of mission that be-

---

1977), 146-48; and C. Peter Wagner, *Church Growth and the Whole Gospel* (San Francisco: Harper & Row, 1981).

The relation of evangelical mission theology to conciliar mission theology is highlighted, but also polemicized, in symposia such as Donald McGavran, ed., *Crucial Issues in Missions Tomorrow* (Chicago: Moody, 1972); idem, *The Conciliar-Evangelical Debate: The Crucial Documents, 1964–1976* (Pasadena: William Carey Library, 1977); and Roger E. Hedlund, ed., *Roots of the Great Debate in Mission* (Madras: Evangelical Literature Service, 1981). One of the most helpful treatments of this period and its historical roots, particularly with its twenty-five-page bibliography, is Charles W. Forman, "A History of Foreign Mission Theory in America," in *American Missions in Bicentennial Perspective*, 69-145. See also Orlando Costas, *Christ Outside the Gate: Mission beyond Christendom* (Maryknoll, NY: Orbis, 1982), 135-61.

The relationship of modernity to the revitalization of evangelicalism is one of the major hidden dynamics behind the creation of mission theology during these years. Several analysts have worked on this from the standpoint of the relation of evangelicalism to its surrounding culture. See Martin Marty, "The Revival of Evangelicalism and Southern Religion" in *Varieties of Southern Evangelicalism*, ed. David E. Harrell, Jr. (Macon, GA: Mercer Univ. Press, 1981), 7-9; James D. Hunter, *American Evangelicalism: Conservative Religion and the Quandary of Modernity* (New Brunswick, NJ: Rutgers Univ. Press, 1983), esp. chap. 3; and Marsden, "From Fundamentalism to Evangelicalism," 122-24. Joel Carpenter has given us a very insightful treatment of this matter in "The Fundamentalist Leaven and the Rise of an Evangelical United Front," in *The Evangelical Tradition in America*, ed. Leonard I. Sweet (Macon, GA: Mercer Univ. Press, 1984), 257-59. Carpenter observes, "One of the great and relatively unexplained ironies of American religious history is that many people in immigrant-based denominations found in Fundamentalism an attractive, modern American Christianity" (p. 275).

3. Norman Allison, "A Report on the National Meeting" (Association of Evangelical Professors of Missions meeting in Pasadena, California, September 24-28, 1985), *Evangelical Missions Quarterly* 21 (January 1985): 66-68.

came less reactionary and more holistic without compromising the initial evangelical élan of the "spirit of Edinburgh, 1910."[4]

This broadening took place in four general stages or historical moments, which we might call "Reaction" in the 1940s and 1950s, "Reassessment" in the 1960s, "Reaffirmation" in the 1970s, and "Redefinition" in the 1980s. To show the development more clearly, I will highlight four aspects of mission theology in each historical period: the *context*, the *motivation*, the *goal*, and the *strategy*.

4. We do not have space here to delve into the theological roots of fundamentalism—and, later, evangelicalism—in this century. Just the task of defining the evangelicals is difficult, given the amorphous, untidy nature of the movement. For helpful introductions, see the following: George Marsden, "The Evangelical Denomination," in *Evangelicalism and Modern America*, ed. Marsden (Grand Rapids: Eerdmans, 1984), ix-xvi; and Douglas Frank, *Less Than Conquerors: How Evangelicals Entered the Twentieth Century* (Grand Rapids: Eerdmans, 1986). See also the articles in Wells and Woodbridge, *Evangelicals*, Part I. Martin Marty, David Moberg, and Dean Hoge have used the concepts of "private" and "public" to speak of the differentiation of American Protestantism at the turn of the century. The terms have much to commend them, at least until the post–World War II era. See Martin Marty, *Righteous Empire: The Protestant Experience in America* (New York: Dial, 1970), esp. 177-79; David Moberg, *The Great Reversal: Evangelism and Social Concern* (New York: Lippincott, 1972); and Dean Hoge, *Division in the Protestant House: The Basic Reasons behind Intra-Church Conflicts* (Philadelphia: Westminster, 1976), chap. 3; see also Martin Marty, *Pilgrims in Their Own Land* (Boston: Little, Brown, 1984).

Carl Henry gives a good summary of conservative evangelical theological convictions in *Evangelicals at the Brink of Crisis* (Waco: Word, 1967). Richard Quebedeaux has suggested a typological description in *The Worldly Evangelicals* (New York: Harper & Row, 1978), 18-45, 53-54. Other definitions may be found in Bosch, *Witness to the World*, 30. Bosch mentions John W. deGruchy, "The Great Evangelical Reversal: South African Reflections," *Journal of Theology for Southern Africa* 24 (September 1978): 45-57, as giving a parallel description of five major groupings within evangelicalism. Other interpretations worth consulting are James Deforest Murch, *Cooperation without Compromise* (Grand Rapids: Eerdmans, 1956), 13; Marcellus Kik, *Ecumenism and the Evangelical* (Philadelphia: Presbyterian and Reformed, 1958), v; and Robert E. Webber, *Common Roots: A Call to Evangelical Maturity* (Grand Rapids: Zondervan, 1978), chap. 2.

Martin Marty's excellent definition of the evangelicals is found in "The Revival of Evangelicalism and Southern Religion," in *Righteous Empire*, 9-10. Other definitions are available, but many of them are expressed in negative terms, which I have not found helpful or constructive, because they serve to tell us who the evangelicals are *not*, rather than who they *are*. See, e.g., Harold Ockenga, "Resurgent Evangelical Leadership," *Christianity Today*, 27 May 1966, 11-13, quoted and enlarged upon in Bassham, *Mission Theology*, 173-74.

CHARLES E. VAN ENGEN

Reaction in the 1940s and 1950s

In the 1940s and 1950s the dominant characteristic of evangelical theology of mission seems to have been a reaction to the previous decades.[5] It was "over-against" theology. The war had solidified a certain pessimism concerning humanity, culture, the relevance of the Christian church to society, the condition of the world, and the essential emptiness of the old social-gospel mentality. The threat of communism was always on the horizon during the Cold War era.

Evangelical reaction was expressed in two quite different formulations of mission theology. The contrasting responses to the social gospel[6] can be seen in the titles of two books published within two years of each other. Carl Henry's *The Uneasy Conscience of Modern Fundamentalism*[7] could be taken as an embryonic representative of the revisionary and mutualist "neo-evangelical" position, which eventually departed from the reactionary and separatist fundamentalist point of view.[8] This latter position was more evident in an early work by Harold Lindsell, *A Christian Philosophy of Missions.*[9] What, then,

5. As Carl Henry put it, "The fundamentalist movement became a distinctly 20th-century expression of Christianity, characterized increasingly by its marks of reaction against liberalism" (Henry, *Evangelical Responsibility in Contemporary Theology* [Grand Rapids: Eerdmans, 1957], 33).

6. Harold Lindsell, "Faith Missions Since 1938," in *Frontiers of Christian World Missions Since 1938: Essays in Honor of Kenneth Scott Latourette*, ed. W. C. Harr (New York: Harper and Brothers, 1962), 200, mentions the extent to which modernism pushed the development of fundamentalist mission.

7. Henry, *The Uneasy Conscience of Modern Fundamentalism* (Grand Rapids: Eerdmans, 1947).

8. E.g., a very significant sociological study recently analyzed the differences between these two constituencies of the Ohio Moral Majority in 1986 and found marked differences. See Clyde Wilcox, "Evangelicals and Fundamentalists in the New Christian Right: Religious Differences in the Ohio Moral Majority," *Journal for the Scientific Study of Religion* 25 (1986): 355-63.

9. Lindsell, *A Christian Philosophy of Missions* (Wheaton: Van Kampen, 1949). At the time, Lindsell and Henry were close colleagues at Fuller Theological Seminary. Both were involved in the "neo-evangelical" movement to reform fundamentalism in the late 1940s through the late 1960s. They have differed at a few points through the years, but certainly they have not become the embodiment of opposite tendencies (see George Marsden, *Reforming Fundamentalism: Fuller Seminary and the New Evangelicalism* [Grand Rapids: Eerdmans, 1987]). The point

was the context to which these two groups were reacting in the late 1940s and early 1950s?

The Context of Mission

On the one hand, the terrible world wars had shown that the kingdom of God would not be established immediately on earth. On the other hand, the passive constructionist era of Eisenhower was a high point for renewed church attendance and renewed hopes of creating a brave new world, at least in America. Evangelical churches and missions in North America saw themselves in historic continuity with the Student Volunteer Movement (SVM), Edinburgh 1910, the early days of the International Missionary Council (IMC), and the "watchword" propounded by John R. Mott and others: "the evangelization of the world in this generation."[10] But the dominant theme was one of reaction, of defining the evangelical movement in separatist categories.[11] David Moberg has called this fundamentalist reaction to Protestant liberalism "The Great Reversal."[12] But some fundamental-

here is rather that their early works showed some traits within fundamentalism that would lead the movement to an open split a decade later, even though both Henry and Lindsell were at that time on the progressive side. See Wilbert R. Shenk's response to this chapter in an earlier draft of the paper presented at the conference "A Century of World Evangelization," held at Wheaton College on June 17-19, 1986 (Archives of the Billy Graham Center, Wheaton College).

10. In the late 1940s and 1950s, evangelicals had at their disposal the missiological thoughts of some of the greats like John Nevius, Robert Speer, Samuel Zwemer, and John R. Mott.

11. Joel Carpenter writes,

Fundamentalism, according to George Marsden, has a paradoxical tension in its character. Sometimes it identifies with the "establishment" and sometimes with the "outsiders." At times it presumes to speak for the "mainstream" of American evangelical Christianity seeing itself as the guardian of the "faith once delivered to the saints." ... On the other hand, fundamentalists, like holiness groups, Pentecostal churches, and immigrant-based denominations, often acted like isolated, embattled sectarians.

(Carpenter, "Fundamentalist Leaven," 267-68)

Carpenter is drawing this insight from George Marsden, *Fundamentalism and American Culture: The Shaping of Twentieth-Century Evangelicalism, 1870–1925* (New York: Oxford Univ. Press, 1980).

12. Cited in note 4, above. See also Hunter, *American Evangelicalism,* 30; and Marsden, *Fundamentalism and American Culture,* 92.

ists called the situation "The Great Apostasy" and conceived the challenge as "The Battle of the Century."[13] The fundamentalist reaction produced what Carl Henry termed "The Fundamentalist Reduction"[14] and Charles Forman described as "a new, very conservative type of missiology . . . a defensive reaction to liberalism and the Laymen's Commission."[15]

After the war a host of new missionary recruits coming back from the trenches challenged the fundamentalists to join them in constructing a new conservative evangelicalism that was broader than fundamentalism, as Donald Dayton has pointed out.[16] George Marsden has shown that the result was "the emergence of a self-conscious new evangelicalism out of the original fundamentalist tradition and hence the clear division of that tradition into two major movements—evangelicalism and separatist fundamentalism."[17]

Thus, when the NAE was formed in 1943, Harold Ockenga made a point of the fact that it would not be "a reactionary, negative, or destructive type of organization."[18] Even so, Harold Lindsell has depicted the creation of the NAE as an evangelical reaction to the formation of the World Council of Churches.[19] Two years later, when the EFMA was organized, the emphasis fell on a more constructive note, the "primacy of evangelism in the self-understanding of the NAE."[20]

Meanwhile, the ecumenical Protestants were processing the postwar consequences of the social gospel. Richard Nie-

13. These terms are titles for chapters 2 and 3 in Murch, *Cooperation without Compromise*.

14. Title of chapter 2 in Henry, *Evangelical Responsibility*.

15. Forman, "History of Foreign Mission Theory," 103. Forman is referring here to William Ernest Hocking's work with the Laymen's Foreign Missions Inquiry and its subsequent report, *Re-Thinking Missions: A Laymen's Inquiry after One Hundred Years*, a report that mirrored the more liberal trends in North American "public" Protestantism. Cf. Stephen Neill, *A History of Christian Missions* (New York: Penguin, 1964).

16. Donald Dayton, *Discovering an Evangelical Heritage* (New York: Harper & Row, 1976), 139-40.

17. Marsden, "From Fundamentalism to Evangelicalism," 128.

18. Quoted by Marty in *Pilgrims*, 411. With regard to the formation of the NAE, see Carpenter, " Fundamentalist Leaven."

19. Lindsell, "Faith Missions Since 1938," 192.

20. Bassham, *Mission Theology*, 181.

A Broadening Vision

buhr's *The Kingdom of God in America;* the Hocking report on the "Laymen's Inquiry"; the IMC meetings at Jerusalem (1928), Madras (1938), and Whitby (1947); the organization of the WCC in 1948; and the Willingen conference of the IMC in 1952 failed to convince the evangelicals that the ecumenical movement shared their view of mission.[21] The fundamentalists and evangelicals reacted by shaping and articulating their theology of mission in narrow, clearly definable categories. They carefully set forth their motivation, goals, and strategy for mission in the 1950s.

The Motivation for Missions

The reactionism of this period did not diminish the evangelicals' commitment to preach the gospel to every creature.[22] Obedience to the imperative of the gospel became a major issue for them.[23] Consistent with the evangelical perspective of the day, Harold Lindsell wrote *Missionary Principles and Practice* (1955), suggesting that the motivation for mission should include "the Great Commission, the choice of Israel, the purpose of the Church, realistic eschatology, and the need of the non-Christian world."[24]

In the midst of these imperatives, two overriding motifs stood out: the Great Commission (Matt. 28:18-20) and the com-

21. Ibid., 15-36; Arthur P. Johnston, *World Evangelism and the Word of God* (Minneapolis: Bethany, 1974); Harvey Hoekstra, *The World Council of Churches and the Demise of Evangelism* (Wheaton: Tyndale, 1979); Bosch, *Witness to the World*, 159-78; and Arthur Glasser, "Evangelicals Find Each Other and Join the Debate," 113-19.

22. Marsden, *Fundamentalism and American Culture*, 181-82.

23. See, e.g., David Johnson, "What Does God Expect from Us?" in *Facing the Unfinished Task*, Messages Delivered at the Congress on World Missions, Interdenominational Foreign Mission Association, December 1960, ed. J. D. Percy (Grand Rapids: Eerdmans, 1961), 152-54.

24. Lindsell, *Missionary Principles and Practice* (Westwood, NJ: Revell, 1955), 28-30. See also idem, "Fundamentals for a Philosophy of the Christian Mission," in *The Theology of the Christian Mission*, ed. Gerald H. Anderson (Nashville: Abingdon, 1961), 239-49. Cf. also with the themes presented at the IFMA Chicago conference of 1960, such as John Walvoord, "Foreign Missions in Relation to the Second Coming of Christ," in *Facing the Unfinished Task*, 251-53; and Bassham, *Mission Theology*, 177-79.

ing millennium.[25] Premillennialists interpreted Matthew 24:14 to mean that once the church had preached the gospel of the kingdom to every nation, the millennium would begin. This lent a strong, almost desperate urgency to gospel proclamation because of its link with the Second Coming of Christ and the new kingdom he would establish on earth.

The Goal of Missions

During this time the evangelicals articulated only one major goal of mission: the salvation of individual souls. Harold Lindsell mentions that this emphasis was specifically in response to the social aspects of the National Council of Churches of Christ—Division of Overseas Mission (NCCC-DOM) missiology of the day.[26] "Fundamental to a conservative philosophy of missions," Lindsell said in 1961, "is the assumption that man is a sinner."[27] Whether these individuals lived in Los Angeles, London, or Lusaka, the eternal destiny of their souls was of utmost importance. The social, political, economic, or cultural aspects of the lives of the unsaved were relatively unimportant compared to the question of heaven and hell.

The Strategy of Missions

Interdenominational mission agencies arose with great strength and speed after World War II. When the EFMA was organized in 1945, communications, travel, finances, and organizational structures were sufficiently in place for the evangelicals to begin to play a major role in mission sending. But there was little theoretical reflection. As Arthur Glasser said of the period, "An elaborate theology of mission was not felt necessary."[28] The strategy amounted to one major command of Jesus to his disciples: Go!

---

25. Cf. Ernest R. Sandeen, *The Roots of Fundamentalism: British and American Millenarianism 1800–1930* (Chicago: Univ. of Chicago Press, 1970).

26. Lindsell, "Faith Missions Since 1938," 228.

27. Lindsell, "Fundamentals for a Philosophy of Christian Mission," 245.

28. Glasser, "Evolution of Mission Theology," 9. Cf. Lindsell, "Faith Missions Since 1938."

It is interesting to note, however, that fundamentalist and evangelical missions actually carried out significant educational, medical, agricultural, and social projects in the Third World during this time.[29] Though the major goal was in theory the salvation of souls, the missionaries found that as they fell in love with the people to whom they had been sent, they yearned to help them in any way they could and ended up bringing education, medicine, agriculture, translation, and other things.[30]

Carl Henry was probably on target when he spoke of "the uneasy conscience of modern fundamentalism." On the mission field many interdenominational fundamentalist and evangelical mission agencies found themselves far more socioeconomically and politically active than they would have considered being in North America. Was it because the North American environment had forced them into a "fundamentalist reduction" that could be overcome in other parts of the world? The ever-broadening vision kept calling the evangelicals to further and deeper reflection and eventually drew them to making a careful reassessment of their mission theology.

Reassessment in the 1960s

Arthur Glasser has pointed out that "the year 1966 was truly crucial" for an evangelical theology of mission. "Before it ended," he says, "a tremendous burst of dynamism had been released from within the evangelical wing of the church."[31] But it was

29. Harold Lindsell wrote in 1955 that the "means" of evangelism, education, medicine, literature, and others "must be in harmony with the end" and "must show themselves to be valid ones pragmatically" (Lindsell, *Missionary Principles and Practice*, 189).

30. Christian Weiss of "Back to the Bible Broadcast" made a point of this at the 1960 Chicago Congress of the IFMA (G. Christian Weiss, "An Inquiry into the Obligation of Christians," in *Facing the Unfinished Task*, 259-61).

31. Glasser and McGavran, *Contemporary Theologies of Mission*, 119. Erling Jorstad has called the 1960s "A Fundamental Shift" in the development of North American evangelicalism (Jorstad, *Evangelicals in the White House: The Cultural Maturation of Born Again Christianity 1960–1981* [New York: Edwin Mellen, 1980]).

211

also a time of tremendous challenge for evangelical mission agencies "seeking to engage a revolutionary world."[32]

The Context of Missions

In spite of North American peace, prosperity, and growing love of technology, world events were crying for new analyses and new vision. One of the major factors was the growth of the African nations during the 1960s. In 1960 alone, seventeen new African nations were born.[33] Nationalism was a burning issue around the world.

The Roman Catholic world was in an uproar. The Second Vatican Council met from 1963 to 1965, issuing documents like "Unitatis Redintegratio," "Lumen Gentium," and "Ad Gentes Divinitus." These became indispensable reading for ecumenical and evangelical Protestants, who found some of their own perspectives articulated and stretched by Vatican II.[34]

Evangelical mission theology was also called to respond to the dramatic changes going on in the ecumenical movement. In 1961 at New Delhi the IMC was integrated into the WCC to become the Commission of World Mission and Evangelism.[35] Integration was so controversial that in 1961 Henry Van Dusen

32. Rodger Bassham used this as the title of chapter 5 in *Mission Theology*, dealing with this period.

33. Charles Forman, *The Nation and the Kingdom: Christian Mission in the New Nations* (New York: Friendship, 1964), 17.

34. A. P. Flannery, *Documents of Vatican II* (Grand Rapids: Eerdmans, 1975).

35. Concerning the effects of this very controversial merger, see Emilio Castro, "Editorial," *International Review of Mission* 70 (October 1981): 233-39; Bassham, *Mission Theology*, 40-42, 210-12; Ralph Winter, "Ghana: Preparation for Marriage," *International Review of Mission* 67 (July 1978): 338-53; Max Warren, *Crowded Canvas* (London: Hodder & Stoughton, 1974), 156-58; idem, "The Fusion of the IMC and the WCC at New Delhi: Retrospective Thoughts after a Decade and a Half," in *Zending op Weg Naar de Toekomst*, ed. J. D. Gort (Kampen: Kok, 1978), 190-202; Neill, *History of Christian Missions*, 554-58; and Karsten Nissen, "Mission and Unity," *International Review of Mission* 63 (1974): 539-50. Evangelical assessments of the event may be found in Eric Fife and Arthur Glasser, *Missions in Crisis* (Chicago: InterVarsity, 1961), 126-28; Johnston, *World Evangelism*, 240-42; Hoekstra, *World Council*, 35-48; Costas, *Christ Outside the Gate*, 136; Henry, *Evangelicals at the Brink of Crisis;* and Harold Lindsell, ed., *The Church's Worldwide Mission* (Waco: Word, 1966).

wrote an entire book dedicated to laying its historical and theological foundations.[36] About the same time G. H. Anderson edited *The Theology of the Christian Mission*, which was to provide further foundations for ecumenical mission theory at New Delhi and afterwards.

We cannot underestimate the impact of integration on the evangelicals.[37] In 1966, when the "Congress on the Church's Worldwide Mission" was convened by both the IFMA and the EFMA, the delegates stated, "The birth of the World Council of Churches and the pressures to integrate the International Missionary Council into the framework of that organization brought to the forefront the problem of conservative theological missionary cooperation."[38]

So the fundamentalists and the new evangelicals found that they had to lay aside their differences and gather together to reassess their mission theology and "wake up lest the foundations erode completely," as George Peters expressed it.[39] They held two major conferences in 1966: the Congress on the Church's Worldwide Mission (at Wheaton) and the World Congress on Evangelism (in Berlin). Although these conferences were far from identical, we will treat them here as complementary parts of a larger development of evangelical mission theology. Efiong Utuk calls the Wheaton gathering a "minor miracle,"[40] considering that, just six years before, the IFMA had gathered in Chicago and had excluded the American Council of Churches of Christ (ACCC), the EFMA, the NCCC-DOM, and the pentecostals. As Harold Lindsell put it, "Perhaps who has been left out is as significant as who has been included."[41]

36. Henry Van Dusen, *One Great Ground of Hope: Christian Missions and Christian Unity* (Philadelphia: Westminster, 1961).

37. See Costas, *Christ Outside the Gate*, 136.

38. Lindsell, *Church's Worldwide Mission*, 2. Others have mentioned the link between the New Delhi integration and the move for a united reassessment of evangelical mission theology. See Henry, *Evangelicals at the Brink of Crisis*, 85; Costas, *Christ Outside the Gate*, 136; and Bruce Shelley, *Evangelicalism in America* (Grand Rapids: Eerdmans, 1967), 103.

39. George Peters, *A Biblical Theology of Missions* (Chicago: Moody, 1972), 28.

40. Utuk, "From Wheaton to Lausanne," 209.

41. Lindsell, "Faith Missions Since 1938," 229. It is interesting to note that in this article, published in 1962, Lindsell stated prophetically, "It is regrettable

The Motivation for Missions

Evangelical motivations for missions were also reassessed in 1966. At Berlin, John Stott presented an exegetical study of the Great Commission passages in John, Matthew, and Luke, but the Berlin Congress's message itself mentions the Great Commission only in passing. The "Wheaton Declaration" refers obliquely to "the evangelistic mandate" and also cites the eschatological theme, but no longer with the frantic eschatological instrumentality of a bygone era. What comes to the fore most strongly in 1966 is an intentional continuity with the Edinburgh conference of fifty years before and the SVM watchword. The evangelicals at Berlin said, "Our goal is nothing short of the evangelization of the human race in this generation, by every means God has given to the mind and will of men." At Wheaton it was said, "The gospel must be preached in our generation to the peoples of every tribe, tongue and nation. This is the supreme task of the Church." But evangelicals were wrong in presenting themselves as the only viable descendants of Edinburgh 1910. Both the ecumenical and the evangelical movements were historic children of Edinburgh 1910.

However, at Wheaton and Berlin the evangelicals also began to discover other motivations for missions. Good news for lost humanity (One Gospel), the Lordship of Christ over his church bringing unity and reconciliation to *all* humanity in Christ (One Race), the call to set out God's Word in a broken world (One Task)—these broader, more integrating motivational foundations were quarried from the Scriptures.[42]

---

that fifty years after Edinburgh (1910) there cannot be a world congress for mission which transcends some of the unimportant differences dividing those of similar missionary aims. . . . Perhaps the faith missions may be able to enlarge this vision and provide a creative and dynamic leadership for a new age of missionary advance" (p. 230).

42. Cf. Henry, *Evangelicals at the Brink of Crisis*, 3-6; and Carl Henry and Stanley Mooneyham, *One Race, One Gospel, One Task* (Minneapolis: World Wide Publications, 1967), 1:5-7.

The Goal of Missions

The 1966 documents show a major shift from the strongly individualistic categories of previous decades to an increased emphasis on the church and its encounter with a multiplicity of cultures in the world. Berlin defined evangelism as proclamation for conversion, coupled with "serving the Lord in every calling of life" and having the "fellowship of His Church." These were significant new steps toward broadening the goal of missions, in line with new mission emphases of the era.

Practical Anthropology began publishing in 1953 with people like Jacob Loewen, Eugene Nida, and William Smalley calling the evangelical missionary force to take seriously the church's relation to culture. That same year Melvin Hodges encouraged evangelicals to reassess the importance of the Venn-Anderson "Three-Self" theory and begin wrestling with issues of "the indigenous church" as a legitimate goal of missions.[43] The growing influence of the church-growth movement with regard to people movements,[44] along with issues related to the formation of new, younger national churches, meant a whole new set of goals for evangelical mission. Amid the optimism of a newfound unity of vision and cooperation in mission, there was nevertheless a mood of repentance, humility, and concern for a new impact of the gospel in the world.

The Strategy of Missions

New goals were both the product of and the incentive for developing new mission strategies, and Wheaton and Berlin showed a willingness to experiment with new forms of missionary cooperation, careful partnership with national churches, and a timid openness to new methodology. The new evangel-

43. See, e.g., Melvin Hodges, *The Indigenous Church* (Springfield, MO: Gospel Publishers, 1953).

44. In 1965 Donald McGavran moved the Institute of Church Growth from Eugene, Oregon, to Fuller Theological Seminary (Pasadena, California). Subsequently, the great hopes of the church-growth people at the acceptance of "The Iberville Statement" can be appreciated in McGavran, ed., *Conciliar-Evangelical Debate*, 171-77. See also *International Review of Mission* 57 (July 1968).

icals were experiencing a growing confidence in their role in world mission and were becoming increasingly articulate about their own mission theology, as can be seen in their new publications. *Christianity Today* co-sponsored the Berlin conference in 1966, and both *Evangelical Missions Quarterly* and the *Church Growth Bulletin* first appeared in 1964.

The broadening vision included new concern for unity in cooperative mission endeavors—not only among mission agencies but also with younger national churches. Kenneth Strachan of the Latin American Mission devised the "Evangelism-in-Depth" program, which became very influential in this regard not only in North America but also in Africa and Asia.[45] Beyond this, evangelicals at both conferences made a strong affirmation regarding the use of psychology, anthropology, sociology, business management, statistics, and technological advances for the sake of missions. The Wheaton delegates declared, "The best results come when, under the Holy Spirit, good principles of cultural and social patterns are applied to the proclamation of the Gospel."[46]

And yet in the midst of the new awakening, the vestiges of the old fundamentalist-modernist reactionism were also present. While a strong anti–Roman Catholic sentiment was expressed in spite of Vatican II, the ecumenical movement came in for the sharpest attack. A WCC observer at Wheaton, Eugene Smith, mentioned that nine of the fifteen major papers carried attacks on the ecumenical movement. At Berlin the search for global evangelistic cooperation was clearly divorced from anything that smelled of visible unity *à la* WCC.[47]

This strong negativism colored the evangelical reassessment of mission for the next several years. Evangelical theologians and missiologists reacted especially strongly to the Fourth Assembly of the WCC at Uppsala in 1968 and to a lesser degree against the CWME meeting at Bangkok in 1973.[48] These events

---

45. This program is described in George Peters, *Saturation Evangelism* (Grand Rapids: Zondervan, 1970).

46. Lindsell, *Church's Worldwide Mission*, 232.

47. Bassham, *Mission Theology*, 210-30.

48. Donald McGavran, "Will Uppsala Betray the Two Billion?" *Church Growth Bulletin* 4 (May 1968): 292-97; Peter Beyerhaus, *Missions: Which Way?*:

led up to the most significant evangelical mission conference of these forty years: the International Congress on World Evangelization, convened by Billy Graham in Lausanne in 1974.[49] It was crucial that at Lausanne the new evangelicals succeed in going beyond reaction and reassessment to a reaffirmation of historic evangelical mission theology.

Reaffirmation in the 1970s

When delegates gathered at Lausanne, the world had been turned upside down, and it seemed imperative to evangelicals that they reaffirm their traditional faith. The hippies and the "flower children" had been questioning the most basic American values. The mainline denominations experienced an unprecedented exodus of members.[50] The world that had seemed expansive in 1966 had become a global village in danger of over-population and pollution. The Vietnam war seriously questioned the United States' ability to save the world. The Civil Rights movement ground to a halt after Martin Luther King was assassinated.

The Context of Missions

These and other issues created a whole new context in which evangelicals needed to reaffirm their theology of mission. The

---

Humanization or Redemption (Grand Rapids: Zondervan, 1971); and idem, *Shaken Foundations* (Grand Rapids: Zondervan, 1972). The Frankfurt Declaration, which Beyerhaus spearheaded in 1970 in response to Uppsala, was a significant illustration of evangelical reaction by both the German evangelicals and the North Americans who supported it. See, e.g., John R. W. Stott, "C. Defense and Further Debate: 3. Does Section Two Provide Sufficient Emphasis on World Evangelism?" in McGavran, *Conciliar-Evangelical Debate*, 266-72; and Arthur Glasser, "The Evangelicals: World Outreach" in *The Future of the Christian World Mission*, ed. W. Danker and W. J. Kang (Grand Rapids: Eerdmans, 1971), 98-113.

49. Costas, *Christ Outside the Gate*, 136. Utuk affirms that "Lausanne was to the evangelicals what New Delhi was to the conciliarists—a turning point" (Utuk, "From Wheaton to Lausanne," 212).

50. Dean Kelley, *Why Conservative Churches Are Growing* (New York: Harper & Row, 1972), chaps. 1 and 2.

evangelical world was experiencing what Donald Bloesch called an "Evangelical Renaissance"[51]—a tremendous growth and development at all levels. While Vietnam sapped Americans' zest for overseas crusades, evangelical students were flooding the Urbana missionary conventions and providing a host of new recruits for the burgeoning evangelical mission agencies.[52] Evangelical writers, preachers, and television evangelists were beginning to catch people's attention.

Most significantly for our study, North American evangelicals were suddenly encountering hundreds of able evangelical leaders in the Third World churches. Out of the 2,473 participants present at Lausanne, nearly half were from non-Western countries. Third World theologians who did not own the "Fundamentalist Reduction" would call Lausanne to a more holistic reaffirmation of historic evangelical mission theology.[53]

Lausanne marked the beginning of a new day. As C. Peter Wagner has put it, "The 'Great Reversal' was coming to an end."[54] Although some of the evangelical-ecumenical tensions of previous years were still evident, an atmosphere of greater tolerance and hesitant rapprochement with the evangelicals had been evident at the Bangkok meeting of the CWME in 1973.[55] In relation to the Roman Catholic Church, although "Evangelii

---

51. Donald Bloesch, *The Evangelical Renaissance* (Grand Rapids: Eerdmans, 1973). See also Bernard Ramm, *The Evangelical Heritage* (Waco: Word, 1973).

52. Robert T. Coote, "The Uneven Growth of Conservative Evangelical Missions," *International Bulletin of Missionary Research* 6 (July 1982): 118-23.

53. Billy Graham, "Why Lausanne?" in *Let the Earth Hear His Voice*, ed. J. D. Douglas (Minneapolis: World Wide Publications, 1975), 28-30; and C. René Padilla, "Introduction," in *The New Face of Evangelicalism: An International Symposium on the Lausanne Covenant*, ed. René Padilla (Downers Grove, IL: InterVarsity, 1976), 8-11.

54. Wagner, *Church Growth and the Whole Gospel*, 90. E.g., at Urbana 1970, a growing awareness of the sociocultural and political dimensions of gospel proclamation was quite evident in the main theme and the major addresses. These were published in John Stott et al., *Christ the Liberator* (Downers Grove, IL: InterVarsity, 1971). Richard Pierard, *The Unequal Yoke: Evangelical Christianity and Political Conservatism* (Philadelphia: Lippincott, 1970), was an early and influential critique of evangelicals' sociocultural and political assumptions.

55. Arthur Glasser, "Bangkok: An Evangelical Evaluation," in *Conciliar-Evangelical Debate*, 297-305. Glasser says he was a little encouraged, a little discouraged, but heartened enough to want to work at bridging the gap, listening and learning, bearing witness and serving.

Nuntiandi" did not appear until late 1975,[56] the evangelicals' reaction to the documents of Vatican II had been sufficiently positive so that the old anti–Roman Catholic rhetoric of the past was nearly silent at Lausanne.[57] This new attitude toward Roman Catholics was part of a wider evangelical outlook. René Padilla has commented that

> Evangelicalism on the whole is no longer willing to be identified as a movement characterised by a tendency to isolate evangelism, in both theory and practice, from the wider context represented by the nature of the Gospel and the life and mission of the Church.[58]

John Stott called this broadening perspective "Evangelicalism with a Face-Lift."[59]

Given the fantastic upheaval of the previous decade, it is no surprise that Lausanne was intentionally convened as an act of reaffirmation. In the opening convocation Billy Graham explained,

> This Congress convenes to reemphasize those biblical concepts which are essential to evangelism. There are five concepts that both the evangelical and the nonevangelical world have been studying and debating during the past few years—concepts which we believe to be essential to true evangelism and which I expect we will reaffirm in this congress. . . . First, we are committed to the authority of Scripture. . . . A second concept we expect to reaffirm is the lostness of man apart from Jesus Christ. . . . Thirdly, we expect to reaffirm at this conference that salvation is in Jesus Christ alone. . . . Fourthly, . . . we expect to reaffirm that our witness must be by word and deed. . . . The last concept which we must reaffirm at this congress (is) the necessity of evangelism.[60]

---

56. This major apostolic exhortation on "Evangelization in the Modern World" has appeared in many places. See, e.g., *The Pope Speaks* 21 (Spring 1976): 4-51.

57. Cf. Ramez Attalah, "Some Trends in the Roman Catholic Church Today," in *Let the Earth Hear*, 872-82.

58. Padilla, "Introduction," in *New Face of Evangelicalism*, 10-11.

59. Stott, "Forward," in ibid., 8.

60. Graham, "Why Lausanne?" in *Let the Earth Hear*, 28-30.

The Motivation for Missions

The hesitant broadening of motivational foundations for mission at Wheaton and Berlin became full-blown holistic mission at Lausanne. The main figure in the construction of a broad, biblical motivation for mission at Lausanne was John Stott. While maintaining continuity with the 1940s and 1950s by basing himself on the Great Commission, Stott broadened his own understanding of it. Earlier at Berlin he had argued "that the mission of the Church . . . is exclusively a preaching, converting, and teaching mission." But after Lausanne Stott wrote,

> Today . . . I would express myself differently. . . . I now see more clearly that not only the consequences of the commission but the actual commission itself must be understood to include social as well as evangelistic responsibility.[61]

He was not alone in this. Peter Wagner, for example, began to accept the concept of "holistic mission" as distinguished from "holistic evangelism," due in part, he says, because at Lausanne he "heard such speakers as René Padilla, Samuel Escobar, and Orlando Costas."[62]

A second foundational motivation for mission discovered at Lausanne constituted an evangelical response to the "missio Dei" theology of Willingen and Mexico City.[63] John Stott articulated it this way:

> Mission is an activity of God arising out of the very nature of God. The living God of the Bible is a sending God, which is what "mission" means. He sent the prophets to Israel. He sent His Son into the world. His Son sent out the apostles and the seventy, and the

61. John Stott, *Christian Mission in the Modern World* (Downers Grove, IL: InterVarsity, 1975), 23. See also Carl Henry, "Editorial," *Christianity Today*, 13 September 1974, 67; and Bassham, *Mission Theology*, 231-32.

62. Wagner, *Church Growth and the Whole Gospel*, 91. Costas, Wagner, and Johnston have held an ongoing discussion of this matter, what it means for interpreting the Lausanne Covenant, and the uneasiness of some North American evangelicals with this broadening. Cf. Wagner, ibid., 91-96; Costas, *Christ Outside the Gate*, 158-60; and Johnston, *Battle for World Evangelism*, 301-3. See also Padilla, *New Face of Evangelicalism*, 12; and Henry, "Editorial," 67.

63. See George Vicedom, *The Mission of God: An Introduction to a Theology of Mission* (St. Louis: Concordia, 1965).

Church. He also sent the Spirit to the Church and sends him into our hearts today. So the mission of the Church arises from the mission of God and is to be modeled on it.[64]

So the motivation of the church's mission was understood to lie in the trinitarian nature of God's character itself and, by extension, in the nature of the church.[65] With such broad foundations, Lausanne's vision and goals became wider and more holistic.

The Goal of Missions

Three major goals were reaffirmed at Lausanne: church growth, the kingdom of God, and contextualization. The mark of the church-growth movement on the proceedings at Lausanne is unmistakable.[66] Its effect is evident not only in the strategy papers and global surveys but also in the plenary papers given by Donald McGavran and Ralph Winter. For the church-growth enthusiasts, the goal of mission involved the recognition of homogeneous cultural units and the planting of the church in their midst. This also meant that more attention had to be given to ecclesiology and to the place of the local church both as goal and as instrument of world evangelization.[67]

Second, the goal of missions in relation to the kingdom of God was brought out by Peter Beyerhaus, Andrew Kirk, José Grau, and Billy Graham, among others. This note was then echoed by the Ad Hoc Group on Radical Discipleship, com-

64. Stott, *Let the Earth Hear*, 66. See also Gerald H. Anderson and Thomas F. Stransky, *Mission Trends No. 2* (Grand Rapids: Eerdmans, 1975), 6.

65. Douglas, "Lausanne Covenant," in *Let the Earth Hear*, 327; see the following essays in that book: Howard A. Snyder, "The Church as God's Agent in Evangelism," 327-51; Klaas Runia, "The Trinitarian Nature of God as Creator and Man's Authentic Relationship with Him: The Christian World View," 1008-20; and Hector Espinoza, "The Biblical Mission of the Church in Worship, Witness, and Service," 1093-1100; and Lesslie Newbigin, *The Relevance of the Trinitarian Doctrine for Today's Mission* (London: Edinburgh House, 1963).

66. Graham, "Why Lausanne?" in *Let the Earth Hear*, 32.

67. Howard Snyder, Francis Schaeffer, Henri Blocher, Hector Espinoza Trevino, and Jonathan T'ien-en Chao were among those who emphasized this at Lausanne. See their addresses, published in *Let the Earth Hear*.

posed primarily of persons from the Third World, including René Padilla and Samuel Escobar.[68]

The new evangelical theology of the kingdom of God also lent significance to issues of "contextualization" as a goal of mission. At Lausanne the concept of contextualization as a natural step forward from indigenization was not really questioned. Rather, it was accepted and assumed, then strongly qualified and carefully distinguished from "religious syncretism" and cultural Protestantism.[69]

The Strategy for Missions

Although Lausanne's agenda dealt with missiological reflection and theology, it was dominated by issues of strategy. The mood seemed to be one of pragmatism: "anything goes—if it works." The fact that World Vision's highly technological MARC Center was a major consultant to the congress was a signal that the evangelicals were moving into hi-tech culture. Because of the prominence given to the church-growth movement through Donald McGavran's and Ralph Winter's plenary papers, church-growth strategies for cross-cultural church planting received major attention as well. Third, Lausanne was to be a mobilization congress aimed at achieving unprecedented evangel-

68. See the following, all in *Let the Earth Hear*: Ralph Winter, "The Highest Priority: Cross-Cultural Evangelism," 238-41; J. Andrew Kirk, "The Kingdom of God and the Church in Contemporary Protestantism and Catholicism," 1071-80; José Grau, "The Kingdom of God among the Kingdoms of Earth," 1083-90; and a resolution of the Congress, "Theology and Implications of Radical Discipleship," 1294-96. See also Samuel Escobar, "The Social Responsibility of the Church in Latin America," *Evangelical Missions Quarterly* 6 (Spring 1970): 129-52.

69. See the following essays in *Let the Earth Hear*: Byang Kato, "The Gospel, Cultural Contextualization, and Religious Syncretism," 1216-28; John Mpaayei, "How to Evaluate Cultural Practices by Biblical Standards in Maintaining Cultural Identity in Africa," 1229-37; Petrus Octavianus, "How to Evaluate Cultural Practices by Biblical Standards in Maintaining Cultural Identity in Asia," 1238-50; Pablo Perez, "How to Evaluate Cultural Practices by Biblical Standards in Maintaining Cultural Identity in Latin America," 1251-66; Gunter Wieske, "How to Evaluate Cultural Practices by Biblical Standards in Maintaining Cultural Identity in Europe," 1267-77; Neville Anderson, "How to Evaluate Cultural Practices by Biblical Standards in Maintaining Cultural Identity in the Anglo Saxon World," 1278-93; "Theology and Implications of Radical Discipleship," 1294-96.

ical cooperative organizational unity for world evangelization. Thus strategy was uppermost in the minds of all.[70]

Third World churches expressed their growing restlessness and called for cooperative partnership with North American missions and denominations. This gave emphasis to the way missions relate to national churches. While the ecumenical movement was dealing with issues of "moratorium," evangelicals were seeking new cooperative strategies in education, literacy, interdenominational and inter-mission evangelistic campaigns, leadership-training programs, health, and even dialogue. Thus "visible unity" received a nod but still remained within the arena of "cooperation in evangelism," as it appears in paragraph seven of the Lausanne Covenant.[71]

The new breadth had other limits as well. The relationship of evangelism to social action kept coming up for discussion but was not resolved. Lausanne moved beyond Wheaton and Berlin by relating the two concepts in a positive way and overcoming the dichotomous perspective held before. Lausanne followed John Stott's lead and viewed social action as a *partner* with evangelism. But Lausanne qualified that partnership, stating in paragraph six, "In the church's mission of sacrificial service evangelism is primary."[72] Whether this primacy is related to social action as a *goal*, as a *means*, or as a *product* of mission remained unclear. The Third World theologians in the radical discipleship group decried this hesitation to engage global social problems squarely.[73] More than any other, this issue served to highlight the ambivalence in the fundamentalist perspective of the 1940s and 1950s and the new evangelical viewpoint of the late 1960s. But this weakness does not minimize the importance of Lausanne. Rodger Bassham has stated that

70. Costas, *Christ Outside the Gate*, 137. The official reference volume for Lausanne covers over 500 pages of "strategy papers," and another 150 pages of regional analyses for evangelization.

71. "The Lausanne Covenant," in *Let the Earth Hear*, 5.

72. Ibid.

73. "Theological Implications of Radical Discipleship," in ibid., 1294-96. See also Padilla, ed., *New Face of Evangelicalism;* and Wagner, *Church Growth and the Whole Gospel*, 97-99.

> The meeting itself symbolized the emergence of a worldwide community of evangelicals in which 50% of the participants . . . came from the Third World. Lausanne was one of the most geographically representative gatherings of Christians ever held. . . . The Covenant is the most mature and comprehensive statement produced by evangelicals.[74]

Lausanne as an event and as the birth of a covenant demonstrated to the world the developing unity, growing confidence, increased enthusiasm, and broadened vision of the evangelicals in mission in the world. The ensuing decade would be one of tremendous activity, creativity, and productivity. It would take the next decade just to process the implications of Lausanne with the help of the Continuation Committee. The fourth part of our story, then, deals with a process of redefining the basic issues raised at Lausanne.

Redefinition in the 1980s

As we entered the 1980s, the Vietnam war was not forgotten, but neither was it adequately dealt with. The memory of Richard Nixon's dethronement remained. There was widespread disenchantment with politics. Yet Jimmy Carter opened the way for new evangelical political power[75] as "The Young Evangelicals" began to articulate a new kind of activist word-and-deed synthesis.[76] This brings us to the era of Ronald Reagan, which in domestic affairs brought an ironic outcome to the progressive evangelicals' calls for social action. In evangelical mission theology, however, the progressives' influence grew stronger.

---

74. Bassham, *Mission Theology*, 245.

75. See Robert B. Fowler, *A New Engagement: Evangelical Political Thought, 1966–1976* (Grand Rapids: Eerdmans, 1982), for a discussion of American evangelical political perspectives in the 1960s and 1970s.

76. See Richard Quebedeaux, *The Young Evangelicals: The Story of the Emergence of a New Generation of Evangelicals* (New York: Harper & Row, 1974); and Marsden, ed., *Evangelicalism and Modern America*—an excellent overview in the form of a symposium.

The Context of Missions

A major aspect of the post-Lausanne era was the rapid growth of evangelical strength in all arenas of North American life.[77] Who in the 1940s would have thought they'd see "Evangelicals in the White House," as Erling Jorstad reported in 1981?[78] On the heels of Lausanne the growth of evangelical influence was accompanied by some serious thinking about mission. In March 1976 a "Consultation on Theology and Mission" was held at Trinity Evangelical Divinity School.[79] The next year in Atlanta, Georgia, a "Consultation on Future Evangelical Concerns" was convened to "identify the problems and opportunities facing the evangelical church in the last quarter of this century."[80] Then in 1979 a second "Consultation on Theology and Mission" was held at Trinity Evangelical Divinity School.[81]

But the greatest influence on evangelical theology of mission during this time came from Third World evangelical theologians. By 1975 Third World members comprised the majority of the World Evangelical Fellowship.[82] That influence was clear at major conferences like the one at Pattaya and later at both the "Consultation on the Theology of Development" held in 1980 in Hoddesdon, England, and the "First Conference of Evangelical

---

77. Helpful treatments include Harrell, *Varieties of Southern Evangelicalism;* Marsden, *Evangelicalism and Modern America;* Richard Hutcheson, Jr., *Mainline Churches and the Evangelicals* (Atlanta: John Knox, 1981); and Coote, "Uneven Growth of Conservative Evangelical Missions." See also Richard Hutcheson, "Crisis in Overseas Mission: Shall We Leave It to the Independents?" *Christian Century,* 18 March 1981, 290-92; Carl Henry, "Evangelicals Out of the Closet but Going Nowhere?" *Christianity Today,* 4 January 1980, 16-18. In 1976 Carl Henry wrote a kind of sequel to his *Uneasy Conscience of Modern Fundamentalism* of 1947, titled *Evangelicals in Search of Identity* (Waco: Word, 1976), where he mentions the tremendous rebirth of evangelical influence and its expression in the "Chicago Declaration" of 1974 (pp. 33-38).

78. Jorstad, *Evangelicals in the White House.*

79. See David Hesselgrave, ed., *Theology and Mission* (Grand Rapids: Baker, 1978).

80. Donald Hoke, ed., *Evangelicals Face the Future* (Pasadena: William Carey Library, 1978).

81. David Hesselgrave, ed., *New Horizons in World Mission* (Grand Rapids: Baker, 1979).

82. Waldron Scott, "The Evangelical World Mission and the World Evangelical Fellowship," in ibid., 52-53.

Mission Theologians for the Two Thirds World" held in Bangkok in 1982.[83] This forced evangelicals to deal in a new way with subjects like "Neo-Pentecostalism, Contextualization, Catholicism, Church Growth, Dialogue with the non-Christian Religions, and Mission Strategy and Changing Political Situations."[84]

The hallmark year was 1980, the year of three major conferences. When 850 evangelical mission thinkers gathered in Pattaya, Thailand, in June 1980,[85] the complexities of doing mission in the modern world were highlighted by meeting in a country where hundreds of thousands of Indochinese refugees had sought protection. The theology of liberation was growing in importance and influence in political affairs in Latin America, Africa was following its tortuous track in nation building, and Asian theologians were beginning to ask important and unsettling questions. The Commission on World Mission and Evangelism had just met the month before in Melbourne, Australia,[86] and had reasserted the priority of the gospel's preferential option for the poor. Preparations were also under way for the October World Consultation on Frontier Mission, Edinburgh, 1980, organized by Ralph Winter and others under the rubric "A Church For Every People By The Year 2000."[87]

---

83. See, e.g., Ronald Sider, ed., *Evangelicals and Development: Toward a Theology of Social Change* (Philadelphia: Westminster, 1981); and Vinay Samuel and Chris Sugden, *Sharing Jesus in the Two Thirds World* (Grand Rapids: Eerdmans, 1983).

84. These are some of the subjects covered at the First Consultation on Theology and Mission, Trinity Evangelical Divinity School, March 22-25, 1976.

85. Some general reviews of the Pattaya conference are J. D. Douglas, "Lausanne's Extended Shadow Gauges Evangelism Progress," *Christianity Today*, 8 August 1980, 43-44; Waldron Scott, "The Significance of Pattaya," *Missiology* 9 (January 1981): 57-75 (and responses in subsequent pages); David Stowe, "What Did Melbourne Say?" ibid., 23-25; Wade T. Coggins, "COWE: An Assessment of Progress and Work Left Undone," *Evangelical Missions Quarterly* 16 (October 1980): 225-32; Editorial, "COWE: 200,000 by the Year 2000," *Christianity Today*, 8 August 1980, 10-11; and Ralph Winter, "1980: Year of Three Missions Congresses," *Evangelical Missions Quarterly* 16 (April 1980): 79-85.

86. See *International Review of Mission* 59 (July 1980–January 1981): 275-77.

87. See Allan Starling, ed., *Seeds of Promise* (Pasadena: William Carey Library, 1981).

The Motivation for Missions

Pattaya's motivation for missions represented a curious mixture of the old and the new. In some ways Pattaya was a step backward from Lausanne and a restatement of the SVM "watchword," which had figured so strongly in 1966 at Wheaton and Berlin. Second, obedience to the Great Commission as found in Acts 1:8 was reasserted, stressing the element of "witness." As the writers of the "Thailand Statement" said, "As his witnesses [Christ] has commanded us to proclaim his good news in the power of the Holy Spirit to every culture and nation, and to summon them to repent, to believe and to follow him."[88] This witness was motivated by four major truths: the primacy of evangelism, the urgency of the task, the lostness of man, and the coming of Christ.[89]

The "Thailand Statement" also reaffirmed Lausanne in saying, "We are also the servants of Jesus Christ who is himself both 'the servant' and 'the Lord.' . . . All God's people 'should share his concern for justice and reconciliation throughout human society and for the liberation of men from every kind of oppression.'"

But Pattaya went beyond Lausanne in stressing "love, humility, and integrity" as vital attitudes for the evangelization of the world. Again, it appeared to be the Third World theologians and the North American evangelical social activists who called for a broader outlook on mission. Nearly a quarter of the 875 participants signed "A Statement of Concerns on the Future of the Lausanne Committee for World Evangelization," calling for serious consideration of social, political, and economic issues in relation to world evangelization.[90]

88. The "Thailand Statement" was printed in several places. See, e.g., *International Bulletin of Missionary Research* 5 (January 1981): 29-31.

89. Coggins, "COWE," 225-27.

90. See Philip Teng, "God Is at Work through Men: Ananias and Paul," in *Let the Earth Hear*, 44. Orlando Costas gives an excellent overview and critique of these events from the perspective of a participant in *Christ Outside the Gate*, 135-61.

The Goal of Missions

Waldron Scott has pointed out that the consultation at Pattaya was dominated by one theme: "For ten days it kept before a representative group of Christian leaders a world in which an estimated 16,750 people groups lie beyond the reach (proclamation or service) of any existing church—'hidden' people who will be evangelized only if cross-cultural missionaries are sent from one people to another."[91] The issue of the "unreached peoples" was a natural progression from the talk of "people movements" presented by church-growth folks at Lausanne. But the issue was also a controversial one, with representatives from the Third World arguing strongly against the "homogeneous unit principle." The argument against the HUP was not so much one of strategy as a question of the goal of mission. Was it proper to hold up as the goal of missions a series of separate churches, each within its own ethnocultural people group? What did this say about the unity of the church and the unity of humankind under the lordship of Christ? Four months later at the Edinburgh consultation on frontier mission, the other side of the spectrum would be emphasized.

The second major issue was again the relationship of evangelism and social action as acceptable goals of mission. Pattaya reaffirmed Lausanne's position that, although evangelism and social action are integrally related, evangelism is primary.[92] Pattaya highlighted the social dimensions of the gospel but then redefined them in terms of service. In the last section of the "Thailand Statement" the participants said,

> We pledge ourselves to *serve* the needy and the oppressed and in the name of Christ to seek for them relief and justice. We may say that Pattaya did not go beyond Lausanne in any significant way, leaving the question of "priority" to be solved later.[93]

91. Scott, "Significance of Pattaya," 70.

92. "The Thailand Statement 1980," *International Bulletin of Missionary Research* 5 (January 1981): 30.

93. Ibid., 31. The Grand Rapids Consultation on the Relationship between Evangelism and Social Responsibility questioned the concept of "priority" itself, whether it reflects a truly biblical understanding of the gospel. See Bruce Nicholls, ed., *In Word and Deed: Evangelism and Social Responsibility* (Grand Rapids: Eerdmans, 1985).

The Strategy of Missions

In the area of strategy Pattaya wanted to be at the forefront of mission endeavor. North American evangelicals were anxious to use all the ethnolinguistic, cultural, sociological, statistical, and anthropological tools at their disposal in order to identify the 16,750 separate "unreached peoples" and mobilize the whole church to reach the unreached.

This led to a major stress on cooperative unity that was broader than at Berlin and Lausanne. At Pattaya it was said,

> We joyfully affirm the unity of the Body of Christ and acknowledge that we are bound together with one another and with all true believers. While a true unity of Christ is not necessarily incompatible with organizational diversity, we must nevertheless strive for a visible expression of our oneness.[94]

This emphasis was especially significant given the presence at Pattaya of many specialized parachurch missionary agencies and the increasing strength of Third World mission-sending organizations.[95]

But Pattaya also narrowed the focus, defining the "unreached peoples" in terms of the presence or absence of a church in their midst—with little or no reference to the sociopolitical and economic status of each people group. Was this an overreaction to Melbourne's overemphasis on the socioeconomic? Clearly each conference needed the other, as Thomas Stransky and David Bosch have rightly observed.[96]

Pattaya's focus was narrower than the redefinitions of evangelical mission theology articulated at the time. Major confer-

---

94. "Thailand Statement," 31.

95. See, e.g., James Wong et al., *Missions from the Third World* (Singapore: Church Growth Study Center, 1973); Marlin Nelson, ed., *Readings in Third World Missions* (Pasadena: William Carey Library, 1976); and Lawrence Keyes, *The Last Age of Missions: A Study of Third World Mission Societies* (Pasadena: William Carey Library, 1983).

96. Thomas Stransky, "A Roman Catholic Reflection," *Missiology* 9 (January 1981): 41-51. Cf. P. J. Robinson, "The Belhar Confesson in Missionary Perspective," in *A Moment of Truth*, ed. G. D. Cloete and D. J. Smit (Grand Rapids: Eerdmans, 1984); and John Stott, "Saving Souls and Serving Bread," *Christianity Today*, 7 November 1980, 50-51.

ences had been held covering a wide range of related issues: "Evangelicals and Liberation,"[97] "An Evangelical Commitment to Simple Lifestyle,"[98] "The Church and Peacemaking,"[99] "Evangelicals and the Bishops' Pastoral Letter,"[100] the Glen Eyrie North American Conference on Muslim Evangelization,[101] and the Willowbank Conference on "Studies in Christianity and Culture."[102] Thus one must see Pattaya within the context of an evangelicalism come of age, with progressive and radical evangelicals like Tom Sine, Ronald Sider, Howard Snyder, and Jim Wallis calling for a broader social and political involvement. Meanwhile, Third World theologians were advocating a more holistic approach to mission as, for example, in René Padilla's recent book, subtitled *Essays on the Kingdom*.[103] The increasing strength of the evangelical churches in the Third World demanded better mission-church cooperation and translated into the rise of Third World mission-sending agencies, particularly from Korea and Brazil.

Thus, when the IFMA, EFMA, and AEPM met at the U.S. Center for World Mission in Pasadena in September 1984, they demonstrated both continuity and discontinuity with their heritage. David Hesselgrave and Donald McGavran called for a continuation of the great missionary élan of the "spirit of Edinburgh 1910" and a commitment to proclaiming the gospel of personal faith in Jesus Christ and radical transformation of each person's orientation to God, self, society, and world. At the same time, Ray Badgero, John Gration, and people from MARC highlighted the need for careful cultural

---

97. Carl Armerding, ed., *Evangelicals and Liberation* (Grand Rapids: Baker, 1977).

98. Ronald Sider, ed., *Lifestyle in the Eighties* (Exeter: Paternoster, 1982).

99. Evangelical conference held in Pasadena, California, in May, 1983.

100. Dean Curry, ed., *Evangelicals and the Bishops' Pastoral Letter* (Grand Rapids: Eerdmans, 1984).

101. Arthur Glasser, "Missiological Events," *Missiology* 7 (April 1979): 233-35.

102. John Stott and Robert Coote, eds., *Down to Earth: Studies in Christianity and Culture* (Grand Rapids: Eerdmans, 1980).

103. C. René Padilla, *Mission between the Times: Essays on the Kingdom* (Grand Rapids: Eerdmans, 1985).

analysis, church and parachurch cooperation, and hi-tech sophistication.[104]

Conclusion

North American evangelicals have undergone a significant transformation in these forty years. Reactionary and badly divided in the 1940s, they have begun to gain a unified vision of their mission into the next century. Strongly separatist at the beginning, they have achieved an impressive degree of mutual cooperation. Their increasingly frequent consultations and conferences demonstrate a growing desire to listen to each other. Their broadening vision has enabled them to appreciate other perspectives in dialogue with Roman Catholics, Orthodox, and ecumenical mission theorists.

Where to from here? Evangelicals have the possibility of exciting new developments ahead. They will probably find one of these to involve the theology of the kingdom of God. Arthur Glasser, Howard Snyder, René Padilla, and John Stott[105] are among those who have called for an analysis of the kingdom motif for evangelical theology of mission. This motif could provide a vehicle for greater breadth of vision, including wiser and more careful use of technology, more sensitive understanding of other Christians, and increased cooperation between churches.

Second, evangelicals have yet to understand thoroughly and incorporate the pneumatological developments of the "Third Force in Missions"[106] of the pentecostal and charis-

104. Allison, "A Report on the National Meeting," 66-68. See also John Gration, "Key Issues in Missiology Today," *Evangelical Review of Theology* 9 (July 1985): 244-50.

105. Glasser, "Evolution of Missionary Theology," 12; John Stott, "Salt and Light: The Christian Contribution to Nation-Building," *Evangelical Review of Theology* 9 (July 1985): 267-76; and Howard Snyder, *Liberating the Church* (Downers Grove, IL: InterVarsity, 1983).

106. Paul Pomerville, *The Third Force in Missions* (Peabody: Hendrickson, 1985). See also Gary B. McGee, "Assemblies of God Mission Theology: A Historical Perspective," *International Bulletin of Missionary Research* 10 (October 1986): 166-70.

matic movements, which have been so powerfully demonstrated around the world.

Third, the relationship of evangelism to social action as goals of holistic mission has not yet been resolved. Evangelicals have the possibility of developing a new concept of evangelism for the whole person that combines a deep spirituality with a concern for each individual's total welfare. Third World theologians, less affected by the old fundamentalist-modernist controversies, may be able to construct just such a synthesis. With their help, evangelicals could find the gospel to be a transforming power in society.

Finally, the motif that keeps emerging through all forty years as the principal driving force behind evangelical theology of mission is the "spirit of Edinburgh, 1910." The "watchword" still captures the imagination of the evangelicals.[107] They still consider themselves compelled to proclaim the gospel to the billions of people who have not yet believed in Jesus Christ. So, while some things about evangelicals' mission theology have changed a great deal, this theme endures. Without it, evangelicals wouldn't be evangelical.

---

107. Ben Harder, "The Student Volunteer Movement for Foreign Missions and Its Contribution to 20th Century Missions," *Missiology* 8 (April 1980): 141-54. See also Denton Lotz, "'The Evangelization of the World in This Generation': The Resurgence of a Missionary Idea among the Conservative Evangelicals" (Ph.D. diss., Univ. of Hamburg. 1970).

IV ENDURING THEMES, NEGLECTED ISSUES

10 *Evangelical Theology in the Two-Thirds World*

Orlando E. Costas

The last decades have witnessed a resurgence of evangelical theology and action. Indeed, one could argue that evangelicals have ceased to be a marginal sector of Protestant Christianity and have moved into the mainstream of contemporary society. However, we err if we assume that the "evangelical renaissance," as Donald Bloesch put it,[1] is just a Euro-American phenomenon or that it is theologically, culturally, and socially homogeneous. As Emilio Castro, general secretary of the WCC, has stated in a recent essay on ecumenism and evangelicalism, "In the past . . . evangelical perspectives on spirituality and [theology] came basically from theologians in the North Atlantic region"; today they are coming from all over the world. He also points out that evangelicalism is going through the same process and change which the ecumenical movement has experienced in the last decades, because of the diverse sociocultural settings of its adherents.[2] Castro's comment is verified by the published reports of several world gatherings during the last decades and by a growing body of publications.

It is my contention that while evangelicals around the world share a common heritage, their theological articulation is by no

1. Donald G. Bloesch, *The Evangelical Renaissance* (London: Hodder & Stoughton, 1973), 9.
2. Emilio Castro, "Ecumenism and Evangelicalism: Where Are We?" in *Faith and Faithfulness: Essays on Contemporary Ecumenical Themes*, ed. Pauline Webb (Geneva: World Council of Churches, 1984), 9.

means homogeneous. To be sure, evangelicals in the North Atlantic world have had an enormous impact in what I like to call the "Two-Thirds" World—that planetary space which is the habitat of most of the poor, powerless, and oppressed people on earth, which is to be found in Africa, Asia, the Pacific, the Caribbean, and continental Latin America. One cannot deny the strong presence and pressures exercised by Euro-American evangelicalism on the Two-Thirds World through the missionary movement, literature, electronic media, and theological institutions. Notwithstanding this reality, however, there seems to be developing in the Two-Thirds World a different kind of evangelical theology, which not only addresses questions not usually dealt with by evangelical mainstream theologians in Euro-America but also employs a different methodology and draws out other conclusions.

To argue my case, I propose, first, to outline briefly, as I understand it, the nature of evangelicalism and its leading theological tenets, especially as it has developed in the United States. I shall then proceed to analyze the emerging evangelical theological discourse in the Two-Thirds World, taking as reference representative statements from several theological conferences held within the last five years. I shall conclude with some observations on the mutual challenges of evangelical theology north and south and east and west.

Evangelical Theology in the One-Third World

If there is one single characteristic of evangelical theology, it is its missionary intent. Evangelicalism, as its name suggests, has a burning passion for the communication of the gospel, especially in those areas where it has not been proclaimed. It is not surprising that the Wesleyan Movement, which made such a significant impact on the British Isles during the eighteenth century and in many ways became the basis for Britain's world mission in the nineteenth century, has been described as an evangelical awakening. Nor is it accidental that Joan Jacobs Brumberg's scholarly study of the life, career, and family of Adoniram Judson, the American Baptist pioneer, is used as the key to her analysis of evangelical religion in the United States during the nineteenth century.[3] Wesleyan and Baptist preachers, evangelists, and missionaries founded the evangelical movement with a fervent zeal for world mission and evangelism.

This missiological characteristic is undergirded by four theological distinctives: the authority of Scripture, salvation by faith through grace, conversion as a distinct experience of faith and a landmark of Christian identity, and the demonstration of the "new life" through piety and moral discipline. The first two are derived from the Protestant Reformation; they are the formal and material principles of the Reformation. The others are tied to the so-called Second Reformation—the pietist movement (including the evangelical awakening), which sought to complete the First (or theological) Reformation by advocating the reformation of life. The last two principles are also connected with American revivalism and the holiness movement.

These four theological distinctives have in various ways affected the historical development of the evangelical movement. Thus, European Protestant confessional families, such as Lutherans and the Reformed (including Congregationalists and Presbyterians), define their evangelical terms by two distinctives. But for their "pietist" adherents, it is especially the latter two that really matter (at least in practice, though not necessarily in theory). Likewise, in North America, those churches and Christians who want to stress the orthodox nature of evangelicalism will point to the Lutheran and Calvinist Reformation, and those who stress its practical and experiential side will focus on pietism and revivalism.

Gabriel Fackre has developed a five-fold typology of contemporary North American evangelicalism, using the four distinctives mentioned above as criteria. He classifies evangelicals into the following groups: (1) fundamentalists, (2) old evangelicals, (3) new evangelicals, (4) justice and peace evangelicals, and (5) charismatic evangelicals. In Fackre's view, *fundamentalists* are characterized both by their view of the authority of Scripture

3. Joan Jacobs Brumberg, *Mission for Life: The Story of the Family of Adoniram Judson, the Dramatic Event of the First American Foreign Mission, and the Course of Evangelical Religion in the Nineteenth Century* (New York: Free Press, 1980).

(plenary verbal inspiration of the original autographs), their separate ecclesiology, and their doctrinal militancy against all foes. *Old evangelicals* are those "who stress the conversion experience and holiness of life and seek to nourish these in the revival tradition and in congregations of fervent piety." *New evangelicals* "insist on the ethical and political relevance of faith as articulated by broad guidelines, stress the intellectual viability of born-again faith and of orthodox theology, and seek to work out their point of view within, as well as alongside of, traditional denominations." Fackre identifies as *justice and peace evangelicals* the new generation of Christians who "express their faith in a more radical political and ecclesial idiom," come from Anabaptist, Wesleyan, or high Calvinist stock, and "call into question . . . the accommodation of today's culture and churches to affluence, militarism, and unjust social and economic structures." *Charismatic evangelicals* are identified for their experiential faith, reaching out "for highly visible signs of the Spirit, primarily the gifts of tongues-speaking (glossolalia) and healing, and intensity of prayer, song, and communal life."[4]

All of these groups, and their corresponding theological articulations, have made their way, in one form or another, into the Two-Thirds World. In terms of *theological production*, the most significant group is the new evangelicals, and, in a lesser way, the justice and peace group. The fact that Fackre associates the new evangelicals with *Christianity Today* (and, one might add, with other theologically similar periodicals, publishing houses, and schools) and links the justice and peace evangelicals with journals like *Sojourners* and *The Other Side* is an indication of the theological influence of these two groups.

The new evangelicals, by and large, represent the North American leadership of the Lausanne Movement, the World Evangelical Fellowship (and its North American counterpart, the National Association of Evangelicals), as well as the two large missionary consortia, the Independent Foreign Missions Association (IFMA) and the Evangelical Foreign Missions Association (EFMA). They also have the most visible presence in

4. Gabriel Fackre, *The Religious Right and Christian Faith* (Grand Rapids: Eerdmans, 1982), 5-7.

theological (and missiological) educational institutions. During the last several decades they have been the largest exporters of North American evangelical theology.

On the other hand, the justice and peace evangelicals represent a new generation of scholars and critics with special interests in and ties to the Two-Thirds World. Their criticism of North American religious culture and socioeconomic policies, their commitment to a radical discipleship, and their solidarity with the Two-Thirds World have made them natural allies of some of the most theologically articulate evangelical voices in that part of the globe. Given the leadership and influence of new evangelicals in mainstream North American church and society, however, I shall limit my analysis to them.

New Evangelicals and Biblical Authority

For the new evangelicals, the heart of evangelicalism is its faithfulness to the Reformation's formal principle of biblical authority, as well as its material or content principle of salvation in Christ through faith. But as Kenneth Kantzer (former editor of *Christianity Today*) has stated,

> The formal principle of biblical authority is the watershed between most other movements within the broad spectrum of contemporary Protestantism and the movement (or movements) of twentieth-century Protestantism known as fundamentalism, which is a term often poorly used for the purpose it is intended to serve, or evangelicalism or conservative Protestantism.[5]

Put in other terms, although the new evangelicals have claimed both principles of the Reformation, their primary principle has been that of biblical authority. This formalistic emphasis does not bypass the need to do theology from the text of Scripture. As Kantzer also stated, "The evangelical . . . seeks to construct his theology on the teaching of the Bible, and nothing but the

---

5. Kenneth S. Kantzer, "Unity and Diversity in Evangelical Faith," in *The Evangelicals: What They Believe, Who They Are, Where They Are Changing*, ed. David F. Wells and John D. Woodbridge (Nashville: Abingdon, 1975), 39.

Bible; and the formative principle represents a basic unifying factor throughout the whole of contemporary evangelicalism."[6]

In actual practice, nonetheless, the greater energies of evangelical theological formulations, during the last decade at least, have been focused on the formal question of the authority and inspiration of Scripture rather than on its teachings. It is no surprise that the most widely published representative of this brand of evangelicalism, Carl F. H. Henry (another former editor of *Christianity Today*), entitled his six-volume magnum opus *God, Revelation and Authority*. Nor is it any surprise that Kantzer, in the same essay previously quoted, likens the debate over the authority of Scripture to the debates over the doctrines of the Trinity and Christ's person in earlier periods of Christian history.

Evangelical Theology in the Two-Thirds World

Recognizing that many contemporary evangelical theologians in the Two-Thirds World have been formed and informed (and sometimes deformed!) by new evangelical theologians, they do not appear to be as concerned over the formal authority question as they are over the material principle. To be sure, one can find evangelical theological formulations in the Two-Thirds World that reveal a similar concern over the authority of Scripture. However, such formulations are neither the most authentic expression of evangelical theology in the Two-Thirds World nor the most numerous. To validate this assertion, I will turn to the concluding statements from three major theological conferences on evangelical theology in the Two-Thirds World held in Thailand (March 1982), Korea (August 1982), and Mexico (November 1983).

The Thailand and Mexico meetings had a missiological thrust and a theological content. They were sponsored by a loose fellowship of evangelical mission theologians from the Two-Thirds World. The theme of the Thailand conference was "The Proclamation of Christ in the Two-Thirds World." It produced a final document, "Towards a Missiological Christology in the

6. Ibid., 52.

Two-Thirds World," and a book, published first in India and most recently in the United States.[7] The Mexico meeting focused on the Holy Spirit and evangelical spirituality. It also produced a final statement, "Life in the Holy Spirit," and a book of conference papers.[8] The Korean Third World Theologians' Consultation was sponsored by the Theological Commission of the Association of Evangelicals in Africa and Madagascar, the Asia Theological Association, the Latin American Theological Fraternity, and the Theological Commission of the World Evangelical Fellowship. Working with the theme "Theology and Bible in Context," it produced the Seoul Declaration, "Toward an Evangelical Theology for the Third World."[9]

All three documents express a clear commitment to Scripture as the source and norm of theology. They express an unambiguous commitment to its authority, not only in terms of the content of the faith and the nature of practice but also in the approach to its interpretation. The Scriptures are normative in the understanding of the faith, the lifestyle of God's people, and the way Christians go about their theological reflection. Yet the Scriptures are not to be heard and obeyed unhistorically. Indeed, the normative and formative roles of Scripture are mediated by our respective contexts. These contexts are, generally speaking, characterized in these documents as a reality of poverty, powerlessness, and oppression on the one hand, and on the other, as religiously and ideologically pluralistic spaces. Thus a contextual hermeneutic appears as the sine qua non of evangelical theology in the Two-Thirds World.

Thailand, for example, reported that the participants "worked with a common commitment to Scripture as the norm," but they also insisted that agendas for theology "must be given . . . by [the] respective contexts." Such a contextual reading of the Scripture, the Thailand document declared,

7. Vinay Samuel and Chris Sugden, eds., *Sharing Jesus in the Two-Thirds World* (Bangalore: Partnership in Mission, 1983; Grand Rapids: Eerdmans, 1983).

8. Mark Lau Branson and C. René Padilla, eds., *Conflict and Context: Hermeneutics in the Americas* (Grand Rapids: Eerdmans, 1986).

9. Third World Theologians' Consultation, *The Seoul Declaration: Toward an Evangelical Theology for the Third World* (Taichung, Taiwan: Asia Theological Association, 1983).

should be informed by "the biblical passion for justice, the biblical concern for the 'wholeness' of salvation, and the biblical concept of the universality of Christ."[10] In other words, the Bible has its own contexts and passionate concerns, which must be taken seriously into account in the movement from our socioreligious situation to the Scriptures. The text is equally active in the setting of the theological agenda. One does not simply come to it with any issue that arises out of reality but especially with those that coincide with the concerns of biblical faith. One must also bear in mind those issues that arise out of the text itself and pose questions to one's sociohistorical situation.

Thailand's central concern was Christology and its relevance for the proclamation of the gospel to the Two-Thirds World. It underscored "the historical reality of Jesus . . . in his concrete socio-economic, political, racial and religious context." It also acknowledged that he is "the Incarnate Word of God" and affirmed his "universal lordship." Thus, while expressing "solidarity with the poor, the powerless, the oppressed . . ., with those who are followers of other religions and with all peoples everywhere," it also recognized the universality of sin and the universal significance of Christ's saving work for all people. "We are under the sovereignty of the Lord Jesus Christ, whom we are all committed to proclaim to all, especially our brothers and sisters in the Two Thirds World."[11] Thailand's Christological concern was, therefore, informed by the historic evangelical passion for the communication of the gospel.

Mexico followed the pattern and perspective of Thailand. It assumed what Thailand had said about Scripture, context, and hermeneutics, affirming the Bible as the fundamental source of knowledge concerning the person and work of the Holy Spirit. Beyond this formal statement, the final report was limited to a summary of how the conference understood what the Bible teaches about the Holy Spirit. It demonstrates an overwhelming interest in the *content* of the Scriptures, rather than in its formal authority.

10. "Conference Findings: Towards a Missiological Christology in the Two Thirds World," in *Sharing Jesus*, 409.
11. Ibid., 412.

The purpose of the Mexico conference was "to understand how the person and work of the Holy Spirit relates to the context of other religious traditions and movements for social transformation. . . ." With regard to religious traditions, the final document states:

> No religion is totally devoid of the Spirit's witness. But no religion is totally responsive to the Spirit's promptings. . . . The Gospel . . . provides a measure to evaluate all religious traditions, that measure being Christ himself (and not any form of Christianity). The encounter of Christian revelation with other religions is therefore not that of mutually exclusive systems. Persons of other faiths have been known to discover in Christ the answer to questions raised within their own traditions. We believe that such experiences indicate the sovereign activity of the Holy Spirit with other religions (Acts 14:14-18; 17:22-31; Rom. 1:18-25; 2:7-16).
>
> Thus, when we bear witness to Christ in dialogue with persons of other faiths, we can accept their integrity whilst we affirm the ultimacy of Christ.[12]

This posture reflects a positive attitude toward people of other religions. At the same time, it retains a distinctive Christian character and the evangelistic edge so characteristic of evangelical theology.

The Mexico report points to the category of "justice" as the criterion for evaluating the Spirit's work in movements for social transformation. It states that the Spirit is discerned to be at work in such movements when the transformation they help bring about "results in justice with and on behalf of the poor." The document goes on to assert that "To be faithful bearers of the Spirit who 'comes alongside,' we are called to 'come alongside' such movements not with unqualified acceptance of their agenda, but with the agenda of the Spirit." This agenda is described in terms of "democratization, the socialization of power and the just distribution of wealth." The Spirit calls us as followers of Christ, "to serve as witnesses against the self-interests among those involved in . . . struggles for power, and as chan-

12. "Life in the Holy Spirit," unpublished report of the Second Conference of Evangelical Theologians in the Two-Thirds World, Tlayacapan, Morelos, Mexico, 1984, p. 3.

nels of communication for rival factions having common goals." However, our witness must also "retain its distinctive Christian character and its evangelistic edge."[13]

The Korea Consultation, with a much larger participation and external (Euro-American) influence, did reflect a concern for the formal aspects of biblical authority. Its concluding declaration states emphatically:

> We unequivocally uphold the primacy and authority of the Scriptures. . . . We have concertedly committed ourselves to building our theology on the inspired and infallible Word of God, under the authority of our Lord Jesus Christ, through the illumination of the Holy Spirit. No other sources stand alongside. Despite our varying approaches to doing theology, we wholeheartedly and unanimously subscribe to the primacy of Scriptures.[14]

Yet the Seoul Declaration also states that the commitment to the authority of Scripture "takes seriously the historical and the cultural contexts of the biblical writings." Moreover, it asserts: "For us, to know is to do, to love is to obey. Evangelical theology must root itself in a life of obedience to the Word of God and submission to the lordship of Jesus Christ."[15] Finally, the declaration argues that

> A biblical foundation for theology presupposes the church as a hermeneutical community, the witness of the Holy Spirit as the key to the comprehension of the Word of God, and contextualization as the New Testament pattern for transposing the Gospel into different historical situations. We affirm that theology as a purely academic discipline is something we must neither pursue nor import. To be biblical, evangelical theology must depend on sound exegesis, seek to edify the body of Christ, and motivate it for mission. Biblical theology has to be actualized in the servanthood of a worshipping and witnessing community called to make the Word of God live in our contemporary situations.[16]

Even in those passages where the Seoul Declaration uses formal authority language, it checks it against a contextual and

13. Ibid., 4.
14. Third World Theologians' Consultation, *Seoul Declaration*, 3.
15. Ibid.
16. Ibid.

communal hermeneutic and a Christological and pneumatological underpinning: the Scriptures are under the authority of
Christ and depend on the Holy Spirit for the communication of
its message. Furthermore, the declaration balances its authority
language with its emphasis on Christian obedience, faithfulness
to the biblical message, and the imperative of mission in the life
of the church.

This "material" check and balance helps us to understand
the twofold theological critique of the declaration—against
Western (by which is meant Euro-American) and Third-World
theologies respectively. Western theology, "whether liberal or
evangelical, conservative or progressive," is criticized for being,
by and large, obsessed with problems of "faith and reason."

> All too often, it has reduced the Christian faith to abstract concepts,
> which may have answered the questions of the past, but which fail
> to grapple with the issues of today. It has consciously or uncon-
> sciously been conformed to the secularistic worldview associated
> with the Enlightenment. Sometimes it has been utilized as a means
> to justify colonialism, exploitation, and oppression, or it has done
> little or nothing to change these situations. Furthermore, having
> been wrought within Christendom, it hardly addresses the ques-
> tions of people living in situations characterized by religious plu-
> ralism, secularism, resurgent Islam or Marxist totalitarianism.[17]

This statement may lack precision. However, it does articulate a well-known criticism of Western theologies from both the
Two-Thirds World and minority voices in Europe and North
America. Moreover, it has the merit of including the evangelical critique of Euro-American mainstream theologies. This
makes all the more meaningful the call for liberation "from
[the] captivity to individualism and rationalism of Western theology in order to allow the Word of God to work with full
power."[18]

The Seoul Declaration also criticizes some of the emerging
theologies of the Two-Thirds World, though it does recognize
similarities in their respective sociohistoric struggles. Both have

17. Ibid., 2.
18. Ibid.

suffered under colonialism and oppression, are currently struggling against injustice and poverty in situations of religious pluralism, and acknowledge the need "to articulate the Gospel in words and deeds" in their respective contexts.[19] Yet, the Seoul Declaration is equally uneasy with some of the basic premises of these theologies. It is particularly critical of some liberation theologies. While heartily admitting that liberation theologies have raised vital questions which cannot be ignored by evangelicals, the declaration nevertheless rejects the tendency "to give primacy to a praxis which is not biblically informed. . . ." Likewise, it objects "to the use of a socio-economic analysis as the hermeneutical key to the Scriptures."˙ And finally, it rejects "any ideology which under the guise of science and technology is used as an historical mediation of the Christian faith."[20]

The positive yet critical posture reflected in the final documents of these three meetings demonstrates the authenticity of the evangelical theological reflection which is currently taking place in the Two-Thirds World. Evangelical theologians in these parts of the world are appropriating the best of their spiritual tradition and are putting it to use in a constructive critical dialogue with their interlocutors in and outside of their historical space. For them the term *evangelical* is not locked into the socio-cultural experience of the West. They insist that they have the right to articulate theologically the evangelical tradition in their own terms and in light of their own issues.

Evangelicals North and South, East and West

So far, I have argued that although evangelical theology emerges out of European and North American Protestant Christianity and has been carried to the Two-Thirds World by the missionary movement, theological institutions, and publications, there is an identifiable difference between its most influential and visible contemporary expression (new evangelical theology) and the emerging theological discourse in the Two-Thirds World.

19. Ibid., 3.
20. Ibid.

This difference lies in the latter's concern with the formal principle of Protestant theology. The emphasis on the content of the gospel and the teaching of the biblical text rather than on formal questions of authority and the philosophical presuppositions behind a particular doctrine of inspiration is freeing evangelical theology in the Two-Thirds World to employ a contextual hermeneutics patterned after the transpositional method witnessed throughout the New Testament. This also explains why evangelicals in the Two-Thirds World are more willing to deal with questions of religious pluralism and social, economic, and political oppression than most evangelical theologians in the One-Third World.

Without putting all mainstream evangelicals in the One-Third World in the same bag, I suggest that mainstream evangelical theologians are too obsessed with the Enlightenment and not enough with the explosive social, economic, political, cultural, and religious reality of most people in the world. As Bernard Ramm has stated so candidly,

> The Enlightenment sent shock waves through Christian theology as nothing did before or after. Theology has never been the same since the Enlightenment. And therefore each and every theology, evangelical included, must assess its relationship to the Enlightenment.[21]

It should be pointed out that this obsession with the Enlightenment as an intellectual challenge to the faith pertains basically to its seventeenth- and eighteenth-century phase, which revolved around the issue of freedom from authority through reason. This obsession is shared by practically all Euro-American theologies. Indeed it can be argued that all mainstream theologies in Western Europe and North America, from Immanuel Kant to Carl F. H. Henry, have been, by and large, discourses on the reasonableness of faith. Their primary concern has been the skeptic, atheist, materialist-heathen—the non-religious person. This is why the second phase of the Enlightenment, associated with the nineteenth-century movement from political, cultural,

21. Bernard Ramm, *After Fundamentalism: The Future of Evangelical Theology* (San Francisco: Harper & Row, 1983), 4.

economic, and social oppression, has been in the main a peripheral issue in Euro-American theology. Yet this is one issue of fundamental importance in the theological agenda of the Two-Thirds World. For all its missionary passion and experience, mainstream evangelical theology in North America has yet to learn from its missionary heritage how to ask questions more central to the destiny of humankind and the future of the world, which are the central concerns of the Scriptures.

In airing this criticism I do not mean to belittle the fact that there are always two sides to the problem of unbelief: (1) the absence of faith and (2) the denial (practical or theoretical) of faith. Theology in North America and Western Europe has been generally concerned with the absence of faith and its theoretical denial. But it must be acknowledged that from the evangelical awakening to the present, there have been mainstream Euro-American theologies and theological movements that have sought to address the problem of practical denial of faith in the unjust treatment of the weak and downtrodden. This is the case with the theology of the Wesley brothers, the Oberlin theology of Charles Finney, the theology of the early Reinhold Niebuhr, the political theology of Jürgen Moltmann and J. B. Metz, and the prophetic theologies of mainstream ecumenical theologians (like Robert McAfee Brown) and the peace and justice evangelicals. These theologies have attempted, in varying degrees and in their own peculiar ways, to deal with the problem of social oppression and alienation. In so doing they have built a modest bridge toward a fundamental concern of any theology in the Two-Thirds World, namely, the cry of the oppressed and its disclosure of the practical "unbelief" of professing Christians who oppress their neighbors.

My critique is, furthermore, not intended to obliterate the modest dialogue which has been taking place during the last several years around the question of poverty, powerlessness, oppression, and religious pluralism between some mainstream evangelical theologians and their counterparts in the Two-Thirds World. Indeed, during the Thailand meeting there were two theologians representing European and North American evangelical thought. And while they came to the meeting with questions pertaining to traditional theological issues of the

North Atlantic,[22] they had to cope with other theological agendas (and did so positively and constructively). They realized that their particular agenda was pertinent to a rather small sector of humankind. They also acknowledged that their agenda was even different from that of the two "minority" participants from North America, for whom North American evangelical theology had dealt especially with the truth of God's justice.[23] As one North American minority participant commented,

> The issue that divides me from mainstream white evangelicals is not whether I believe the Bible to be the Word of God, which I do, but . . . that I want to . . . read [it] from my situation . . . of oppression. . . . [While] I stand in a dialectical tension with the system which has kept my people in oppression . . . I coincide . . . with mainstream white evangelicals . . . about belief in Jesus Christ. We . . . are committed to Jesus Christ [as] . . . Lord and . . . Savior. We . . . are judged by the same Word. But when we [ask] what does it mean to believe in Jesus Christ, and . . . "who is this Jesus that we confess as . . . Christ, and . . . Savior and what does [he] command us to do?" at that precise point we start departing from one another.[24]

In November 1983, a consultation was held in Tlayacapan, Mexico, between several types of evangelical theologians from North America and their counterparts in Latin America and the minority communities of the United States This consultation focused on "Context and Hermeneutics in the Americas" and established a methodology that permitted evangelical scholars to wrestle with concrete biblical texts and debate such questions as whether our interlocutor is really the atheist—as evangelical theologians who wrestle with the questions of the first phase of the Enlightenment argue—or the alienated, the nonperson who

22. See Samuel and Sugden, eds., *Sharing Jesus*, for papers by Ronald Sider (USA) on "Miracles, Historical Methodology, and Modern Western Christianity," 351-70; and David Cook (Scotland) on "Significant Trends in Christology in Western Scholarly Debate," 371-408.

23. See, e.g., George Cummings, "Who Do You Say That I Am? A North American Minority Answer to the Christological Question," in *Sharing Jesus*, 319-37.

24. Comment by a minority North American participant in the discussion with George Cummings, in *Sharing Jesus*, 347.

may be religious but has been exploited, marginated, and dehumanized by religious institutions—as many theologians in the Two-Thirds World and North American minority communities would argue. The latter issue was not resolved, but the hermeneutical exercises were very fruitful. Afterwards, Grant Osborne, from Trinity Evangelical Divinity School, observed:

> Everyone present felt that the conference . . . was extremely beneficial. Ways of extending the dialogue were suggested. . . . All in all, it was felt that North Americans need to enter a Latin American setting and do theological reflection in the context of poverty. Those from the North, before passing judgment, should be willing to enter a Nicaragua or an El Salvador and experience those realities from the inside.[25]

One might add that this could apply just as well to the urban ghettoes of North America.

Lest I be misunderstood, let me conclude by saying that it has not been my intention to idealize evangelical theology in the Two-Thirds World nor to endorse the tendency to generalize, avoid precision, and even belittle the significance of Western theological debates. It is readily admitted that evangelical theology in the Two-Thirds World is represented by many voices with divergent views. Indeed, it has a long way to go, and in the process it will have a lot to learn from its counterpart in the One-Third World.

However, I submit that the ultimate test of any theological discourse is not erudite precision but transformative power. It is a question of whether or not theology can articulate the faith in a way that is not only intellectually sound but spiritually energizing and therefore capable of leading the people of God to be transformed in their way of life and to commit themselves to God's mission in the world. As the apostle Paul reminded the Corinthian church many years ago, "The kingdom of God is not talk but power" (1 Cor. 4:20).

---

25. Grant R. Osborne, "Contextual Hermeneutics in the Americas," *TSF Bulletin* 7 (March/April 1984): 22.

11 *Women in Missions: Reaching Sisters in "Heathen Darkness"*

Ruth A. Tucker

I desire to no higher enjoyment in this life, than to be instrumental of leading some poor, ignorant females to the knowledge of the Saviour. To have a female praying society, consisting of those who were once in heathen darkness, is what my heart earnestly pants after, and makes a constant subject of prayer. [I am] resolved to keep this in view as one principal object of my life.[1]

These were the words of Ann Judson after she arrived in Burma. Before she went, she expressed deep feelings of anxiety that were just as real and in no way conflicting with her desire to bring women out of "heathen darkness." "For several weeks past," she wrote, "my mind has been greatly agitated." She knew she would be leaving her family in America, never to see them again, and she realized her very life would be in jeopardy. "I have felt ready to sink . . . and appalled at the prospect of pain and suffering, to which my nature is so averse, and apprehensive, that when assailed by temptation, or exposed to danger and death, I should not be able to endure, as seeing Him who is invisible."[2]

Ann Judson's eagerness to go abroad, despite her deep

1. James D. Knowles, *Memoir of Mrs. Ann H. Judson* (Boston: Lincoln and Edmands, 1829), 58.
2. Ibid., 37-41.

anxiety, reflects the emotional conflict in the minds of countless women who have risked their lives to carry out the Great Commission. Indeed, theirs is an extraordinary saga of fighting against the odds both at home and abroad.

The fact that Christian women have made their greatest ministerial impact in cross-cultural missions is due more to their vision and persistence than to their male counterparts' encouragement. Indeed, for many years, only in the realm of missions were women able to overcome the misguided application of the apostle Paul's admonition for women to be silent. From the early decades of the nineteenth century, American women took up the cause of missions. When they were denied opportunities to serve abroad in their own right, they formed their own "female agencies" and finally were accepted by most mission societies as partners with men. By the early decades of the twentieth century, women outnumbered men on the mission field in some regions by a ratio of more than two to one, and the women's missionary movement itself had become the largest women's movement in the country—larger than the Women's Christian Temperance Movement—with more than three million dues-paying members in America alone.[3] Despite their active involvement in missions, however, women have been largely forgotten by the missions historians. In her research on women in missions Patricia Hill found that what "so frequently happens in the writing of history" had happened again: "the women have simply disappeared."[4]

To ignore the crucial role women played in the American missionary enterprise is to misrepresent the historical data. In similar fashion, to understand the role of women in missions from 1880 to 1980 properly, it is necessary to look back to earlier generations. Except for scattered ventures, primarily in India and in North America, Protestants were not actively engaged in missions until the late eighteenth century. The initial thrust of

3. Patricia R. Hill, *The World Their Household: The American Woman's Foreign Mission Movement and Cultural Transformation, 1870–1920* (Ann Arbor: Univ. of Michigan Press, 1985), 5-8; R. Pierce Beaver, *American Protestant Women in World Mission: A History of the First Feminist Movement in North America* (Grand Rapids: Eerdmans, 1980), 111.

4. Hill, *World Their Household*, 2.

the modern missionary movement came from England, but by the turn of the nineteenth century, Americans—not the least of whom were women—had begun to catch the vision.

A Base of Support

Before women rallied behind the cause, potential missionaries had no support base in America. Indeed, in 1810, Adoniram Judson and his colleagues, aware of the difficulty in raising support among the New England Congregationalists, had contemplated going to England to seek financial support. He realized the potential value of women's fund-raising, and later he "enjoined American women to forsake 'the demon vanity' for the amelioration of their sisters in the East," and he suggested they form "Plain Dress Societies." Church publications supporting missions made similar requests of the women in their denominations; and before long, one historian noted,

> American Christian women were perceived as having a special responsibility to practice 'proper economy' within the home and in terms of their personal attire. The mites they saved by eschewing necklaces, ear ornaments, and the seductions of creative millinery were to be set aside for their heathen sisters.[5]

Even before Judson's appeal, however, women had begun organizing support systems to help meet the need for missionary endeavors. In 1800, Mary Webb organized the Boston Female Society for Missionary Purposes, which was the world's first women's missionary society.[6] Two years later in that same city, the Cent Society was born—a concept that quickly spread down the eastern seaboard. It all began at a dinner party at the home of Mehitable Simpkins and her husband, John, the treasurer of the Massachusetts Missionary Society. As they were eating, the conversation drifted to the subject of missions and the funding that was needed for missionary support. One of the

5. Joan Jacobs Brumberg, *Mission for Life* (New York: Free Press, 1980), 88.
6. Albert L. Vail, *Mary Webb and the Mother Society* (Philadelphia: American Baptist Publication Society, 1914), ii.

guests commented about the cost of a glass of wine—only a penny—and suggested that if that amount were given by families to missions each week, it could go a long way in meeting the pressing financial needs. With that impetus, Mrs. Simpkins took up the challenge and was soon "deluged by pennies." The idea was particularly inviting, claimed historian R. Pierce Beaver, because "one cent a week was about the sum almost any woman might be able to give if she denied herself some little thing. It appealed also to the widow's two mites of Jesus' parable, and the vision of the collective purchasing power of thousands of pennies made each single cent seem significant."[7]

Another very significant effort in support of foreign missions developed in the nineteenth century when Mary Lyon founded Mount Holyoke Female Seminary in 1837. Its purpose was "to cultivate the missionary spirit among its pupils; the feeling that they should live for God, and do something as teachers, or in such other ways as Providence may direct." These teachers were to be home missionaries of sorts, going to cities, rural areas, and even to frontier Indian schools to train children to study Scripture and reverence God.[8]

Women have had a long tradition of involvement in such ministries, particularly in urban missions. During the early decades of the nineteenth century, when women were barred from serving overseas as missionaries in their own right, many initiated mission work close to home. Indeed, many of the inner-city slum missions were founded by middle-class or wealthy women who were seeking to give meaning to their religious faith. Space does not permit adequate coverage of these important "domestic" missions, but one should not neglect the important role women played in this movement nor its significance as genuine missionary work. One influential pioneer in urban missions was Phoebe Palmer, the "Mother of the Holiness Movement." She founded New York City's Five Points Mission, which became a prototype for urban missions. Another important leader was Sarah Doremus, whose missionary experience in New York City eventually led her to go into foreign missions

7. Beaver, *American Protestant Women*, 13-14.
8. Hill, *World Their Household*, 42.

work. She founded the Woman's Union Missionary Society in 1861, the first mission to sponsor single women to carry the gospel overseas.[9]

The Women's Missionary Movement

Without the organizational efforts of women on the home front, it would have been impossible for the women's missionary movement to have become so extensive. Indeed, some of the most noteworthy female guardians of the Great Commission were those who stayed home and carried out organizational, educational, and fund-raising tasks.

The underlying impulse behind the women's missionary movement, however, was single women's vision for missionary service and their rejection by existing mission boards. The need for women to reach their "heathen" sisters was widely acknowledged, but missionary wives were generally too burdened with domestic duties to meet the need. Nevertheless, most mission boards were not prepared to accept women as missionaries in their own right. Many single women felt the call of God, but without a marriage partner who shared that commitment, they were barred from answering their summons.

Following the lead of Sarah Doremus, women began to overcome this obstacle by forming "female agencies" to send their sisters overseas. Doremus had been advised more than two decades earlier of the need for women's work overseas by David Abeel, a missionary to China from her own denomination, the Reformed Church in America. He challenged her with a message from women in China: "O bring us some female men."[10] Doremus was prepared to act immediately, but her vision was

9. Timothy L. Smith, *Revivalism and Social Reform: American Protestantism on the Eve of the Civil War* (Gloucester, MA: Peter Smith, 1976), 169-70; Mary E. A. Chamberlain, *Fifty Years in Foreign Fields: A History of Five Decades of the Woman's Board of Foreign Missions, Reformed Church in America* (New York: Woman's Board of Foreign Missions, Reformed Church in America, 1925), 5-6. See also Charles E. White, *The Beauty of Holiness: Phoebe Palmer as Theologian, Revivalist, Feminist, and Humanitarian* (Grand Rapids: Zondervan, Francis Asbury Press, 1986).

10. Beaver, *American Protestant Women*, 89-91.

dampened by Rufus Anderson, who was then foreign secretary of the American Board of Commissioners for Foreign Missions. He was opposed to sending out single women as missionaries, and she deferred to his wishes. Still, the needs of women in foreign lands continued to weigh on her conscience, and finally, in 1860, she called together women from various denominations to launch the Women's Union Missionary Society. They sent Sarah Marston, a Baptist, to Burma.[11]

Other women's societies were quickly formed along denominational lines, the Congregationalists of New England being the first to take up the mantle. By this time, Rufus Anderson had retired, and the new foreign secretary, N. G. Clark, lent his support to the formation of the Women's Board of Missions, which was incorporated in 1869. Methodist women were next to organize, and the Baptists followed in 1870. In the decades that followed, a new women's mission society was formed on an average of one each year.

The need to maintain growth and solidarity in these women's mission societies spurred their officers to extensive efforts to promote their cause. Mary Clarke Nind, who served as an officer with the Woman's Foreign Missionary Society of the Methodist Episcopal Church, is an example. According to one account,

> Much of her Branch was wilderness. The towns were few and far apart, the churches weak and struggling. . . . Her courage never faltered as by faith she laid the foundations of this great organization in Minnesota, the Dakotas, Montana, Idaho, Washington, and Oregon, traveling . . . in wagon, or cart, or sleigh, in summer and winter, by day and by night, by freight train or day coach . . . compassing as many as 5,000 miles in a single year.[12]

Educating women through the printed word was another important aspect of the work on the home front. Books written by women and published by their missionary societies sold widely. Magazines in particular kept women abreast of what

---

11. Ibid., 90.
12. C. S. Winchell, "Mary Clarke Nind," *Woman's Missionary Friend* 37 (November 1905): 382-83.

was happening overseas in a more intimate and personal way than many of the magazines published and edited by male leaders of the denominational mission societies.

In addition to the women's missionary movement's accomplishments in the work of missions were its advances in mission theory and strategy. The late nineteenth century was the high point for women in missiology as they developed programs and new approaches to world evangelization.

While some women worked actively with interdenominational mission efforts, others campaigned within their own denominations. Annie Armstrong, for example, held the powerful position of corresponding secretary for the Women's Missionary Union of the Southern Baptist Convention for seventeen years at the turn of the century. She had initially worked in the Maryland women's mission organization and then became a strong advocate for a national organization. By 1888, she had gained enough national visibility and influence to bring the Women's Missionary Union into being.[13]

Soon after Annie assumed the office of corresponding secretary, she was confronted with the powerful male domination of the Southern Baptist Convention. She had fully concurred in the limited authority that the Women's Missionary Union wielded as an auxiliary organization (and a very restricted one at that), but when the limitations affected her work personally, she began to respond. For example, when her efforts to support a chapel in Rio de Janeiro met with disappointment, she charged that "the rug had been pulled out from under the WMU" by church officials. To the president of the board, she wrote: "Pardon me if I seem to be calling in question [a male official's] judgement in this matter, but . . . if our work is to amount to anything, we must not be placed in a position where it would [seem] that we do not know what we are about." Yet, in 1890, one of the male officials of the Foreign Mission Board wrote to her that the best thing the women could do for missions was to "raise money for the Board and let the Board appropriate it."[14]

13. Bobbie Sorrill, *Annie Armstrong: Dreamer in Action* (Nashville: Broadman, 1984), 19, 32, 39, 57, 59, 68, 77, 81.
14. Ibid., 267, 93-95.

Other women leaders enjoyed far more influence, though. The most noted of these were Helen Barrett Montgomery, an officer in several Baptist women's organizations, and Lucy Waterbury Peabody, a widowed Baptist missionary to India. They made a powerful team; R. Pierce Beaver described them as the "dynamic officers" of the Woman's American Baptist Foreign Mission Society and important leaders in the interdenominational missions fellowship.[15]

Montgomery and Peabody's organizational work on the national level began in 1900, the year of the Ecumenical Missionary Conference held in New York City. At that time the Central Committee for the United Study of Foreign Missions was formed. Peabody headed up this organization while Montgomery helped to organize summer-school programs for women and taught some of the courses.[16] Montgomery and Peabody encouraged ecumenical unity among the mission societies and made the movement a force to be reckoned with. The major purpose of their organization was to educate lay women so they would be more intelligently involved in missions. Montgomery challenged female missions leaders: "We have done very little original work. We have made very few demands upon the brains of the women in our missionary circles. And as a result, we have been given over to smallness of vision in our missionary life."[17] In response to such prodding, the women's missionary movement made more demands on the brains of its adherents than any other missionary movement before or since.

In addition to her organizational work, Montgomery became a prolific writer and a thought-provoking missiologist. Her first book, *Christus Redemptor: An Outline Study of the Island World of the Pacific* (1906), was unlike so many written by missionary enthusiasts because it gave a straightforward account of the problems wrought by Western imperialism. After producing an English translation of the New Testament, Montgomery became deeply concerned that the Bible be translated for the many

15. Beaver, *American Protestant Women*, 152.

16. Louise A. Cattan, *Lamps Are for Lighting: The Story of Helen Barrett Montgomery and Lucy Waterbury Peabody* (Grand Rapids: Eerdmans, 1972), 36-43.

17. Hill, *World Their Household*, 143.

peoples of the world and used effectively in promoting missions.[18] Although most of her writing was to a Western audience, she recognized the work and often superior methods of Third World Christians. For example, she pointed to the ministries of Kagawa, Oneoto, and Kobayashi in Japan as examples of effective urban strategy.[19]

Both Montgomery and Peabody had worked tirelessly to promote the jubilee celebration in 1910 which recognized the five decades of women's missionary work. Forty-eight two-day celebrations were held in major cities, and many one-day meetings elsewhere. As many as four thousand attended the larger meetings, and more than a million dollars was collected in offerings. One of the more lasting contributions of the jubilee celebration was Montgomery's book *Western Women in Eastern Lands* (1910). She summed up the past fifty years of women's missions as "a wonderful story. . . . We began in weakness, we stand in power. In 1861 there was a single mission in the field . . . in 1909, there were 4,710 unmarried women." She enumerated other increases: in numbers of women involved, from a few hundred to two million; and in financial giving, from two thousand dollars to four million. But the greatest accomplishments occurred overseas, she insisted. The gospel had reached many regions where women had never before heard it, and there were now nearly 6,000 Bible women and native helpers, some 800 teachers, 140 physicians, 79 nurses, and 380 evangelists.[20]

In the decades following the 1910 jubilee, the women's missionary movement declined. Successful fund-raising campaigns continued, but the movement as a whole weakened. Denominational boards now readily accepted single women missionaries, and women's societies were being pressured to merge with their "parent" boards. Many women fought these mergers, fear-

18. See esp. Montgomery, *The Bible and Missions* (West Medford, MA: Central Committee on the United Study of Foreign Missions, 1920); and idem, *The Preaching Value of Missions* (Philadelphia: Judson, 1931).

19. Helen Barrett Montgomery, *The King's Highway: A Study of Present Conditions on the Foreign Field* (West Medford, MA: Central Committee on the United Study of Foreign Missions, 1915), 244-48.

20. Helen Barrett Montgomery, *Western Women in Eastern Lands* (New York: Macmillan, 1910), 243-44.

ing the loss of female leadership and participation once their work was taken over by male-dominated boards. The denominational boards prevailed, however, and the women did lose their influence. The once vibrant educational and publishing ventures of the women's missionary movement were also absorbed and eventually abandoned. Women continued to have a lively interest in missions, but their focus was dissipated and divided, and many turned to the new faith missions. Lucy Peabody, for example, in 1927 became the first president of an independent fundamentalist society, the Association of Baptists for the Evangelization of the Orient.[21]

Innovations in Field Strategy

As important as mission strategy was on the home front, it was in the field where the innovations of women were most deeply felt. From the early days, new concepts were born out of the needs of the unreached women in foreign lands. Eliza Bridgman, wife of the first American missionary to China, made an appeal in her book, *Daughters of China,* for women to come and teach Chinese women so that they could in turn teach each other, for "the missionary—the ordained minister of the gospel who goes forth to preach, cannot gain access to the Daughters of the land. . . . Shall woman then be there neglected?"[22] Adele Fielde was one of the many women who answered this call.

Fielde was a spirited, independent woman who defied any stereotype of a female missionary. She was born in East Rodman, New York, in 1839, and grew up as a Universalist. After graduating from college, she taught school, but she yearned, according to her biographer, "to be a wife and mother."[23]

That compelling desire for marriage and the fact that she

21. Hill, *World Their Household;* Robert T. Coote, *Six Decades of Renewal for Mission: A History of the Overseas Ministries Study Center* (Ventnor, NJ: Overseas Ministries Study Center, 1982), 11-12.

22. Eliza Gillett Bridgman, *Daughters of China; or, Sketches of Domestic Life in the Celestial Empire* (New York: Robert Carter & Brothers, 1853), viii.

23. Helen N. Stevens, *Memorial Biography of Adele M. Fielde: Humanitarian* (New York: Fielde Memorial Committee, 1918), 80.

was approaching her late twenties prompted her to take a doubly drastic step. After a whirlwind courtship with Cyrus Chilcot, a Baptist missionary candidate, she converted to the Baptist faith and agreed to serve as a missionary wife halfway around the world. Cyrus sailed off to Siam, where she was to join him some months later. When she arrived in 1865, she learned that Cyrus had died. It was a devastating blow that would have caused most women to return home to the comfort of family and friends. But Adele Fielde was an extraordinary woman. She stayed on—determined to make her fiancé's work her own. In a letter she wrote soon after she arrived, she reported that "several of the Chinese members of the church have been to see me. . . . They feel their loss deeply. There is no doubt that I have something to do here."[24]

Fielde's hard work and commitment to ministry were not enough to endear her to other Baptist missionaries in Siam. She was outspoken, and she strongly protested that her salary was only half the amount of that of her single male colleague. An additional complication was that she was the only single woman missionary among them and was new to the straitlaced Baptists. She soon began socializing with the business and diplomatic community and engaged in conduct unbecoming to the Baptists—dancing, card playing, and even experiments with opium smoking. When confronted by her peers, she complained that giving up dancing would be "a living death," but she agreed to curtail her activities for the sake of the mission. Her opponents still insisted that she was a hindrance to the work, and the Baptist mission board dismissed her.[25]

On her return trip to America, Fielde's commitment to missions became a more deeply spiritual force in her life. She caught the vision for women's work while spending a short time in a Chinese port city and then pleaded with her directors to be reinstated. In 1872, she was back in China training native women. According to her biographer,

24. Ibid., 86.
25. Frederick B. Hoyt, "'When a Field Was Found Too Difficult for a Man, A Woman Should Be Sent': Adele M. Fielde in Asia, 1865–1890," *The Historian* 44 (May 1982): 318-22.

Here she conceived a plan which, in a measure, revolutionized the missionary service in the Far East. This innovation is comprehensively described as the "Biblewomen" plan and consisted in organizing, instructing and sending out native women to do the pioneer work of evangelism.[26]

Fielde founded a school, wrote texts, taught classes, and conducted field training. During her twenty-year term of service, she instructed some five hundred women to evangelize and teach their own people.[27] Unlike so many missionaries who bemoaned the difficulties of working with Chinese people, Adele praised their work and apparently had excellent rapport with them: "The superintendence of the Biblewomen has become much less wearing to me than formerly," she once reported, "because the women have grown in grace and in knowledge of the truth, and I now rely much upon their helpful wisdom and patience in the management of all trying cases that arise. They are a perpetual joy to me."[28]

After Fielde retired from active missionary service, she began a career of scientific research that resulted in the publication of several articles. But her ministry to China did not end. Some forty years after she had first written gospel tracts in Chinese, "a great many of them" were still being used by missionaries in China. Such lasting usefulness, she confessed, was "among the durable satisfactions" of her life.[29] When Fielde died in 1916, her former mission did not even publish her obituary. Ten years later, however, the Baptist Foreign Mission Society eulogized her as the "mother of our Bible women and also the mother of our Bible schools."[30]

Fielde's work with Bible women inspired many other missionary women—especially in Asia—to carry out similar ventures. Indeed, during the last decades of the nineteenth century, the number of training schools for Bible women dramatically increased. By 1900 there were forty female training schools in

26. Stevens, *Memorial Biography*, 111.
27. Ibid., 115.
28. Ibid., 119.
29. Ibid., 125.
30. Hoyt, "'When a Field Was Found Too Difficult,'" 334.

China alone, and two of those, the Wesleyan Training School for Women at Canton and the Charlotte Duryee Training School at Amoy, enrolled nearly fifty students each. In India there were more than thirty such schools, and in Japan and elsewhere in the Far East there were yet more female seminaries.[31]

Sex Discrimination and Feminism

For all their contributions to foreign missionary endeavors, women have rarely been treated as equals of their male counterparts. This has been largely due to the restrictions placed on women in Christian ministry in general, based on perceived biblical admonitions and church traditions. In many instances constraints on women in missions were tighter than any biblical passage might have warranted, and this sometimes created dissension between the sexes. But were missionaries feminists, as R. Pierce Beaver would have us believe from the subtitle of his book, *American Protestant Women in World Mission: A History of the First Feminist Movement in North America*? This issue has been debated in recent years. Some feminist historians have implied that because women missionaries accepted such daring roles and because other women at home supported them in these ventures, they must have been reflecting a feminist position. On the other side are those who would strongly deny *any* correlation between missionary women and feminism. Elisabeth Elliot is an example of the latter; she once complained that

> strident female voices are raised, shrilly and *ad nauseam*, to remind us that women are equal with men. But such a question has never even arisen in connection with the history of Christian missions. In fact, for many years, far from being excluded, women constituted the majority of foreign missionaries.[32]

31. Ruth A. Tucker, "The Role of Bible Women in World Evangelism," *Missiology* 13 (April 1985): 135.
32. Elisabeth Elliot Leitch, "The Place of Women in World Missions," in *Jesus Christ: Lord of the Universe, Hope of the World*, ed by David M. Howard (Downers Grove, IL: InterVarsity, 1974), 124-25.

Elliot assumes that, because women were in the majority, they never raised their voices for equality. Not only is her logic faulty, but so is her conclusion. Women did raise their voices for equality. But were they motivated by feminism? Feminism is difficult to define, especially when it involves historical interpretation. Jane Hunter, who has studied American women missionaries in China, argues that feminism was not a conscious factor in motivating women missionaries. In her study of their correspondence and published articles she found that the vast majority of women missionaries were motivated by commitment to God more than by a desire for recognition or power. "For feminism to have gained a foothold among the women's missionary community," Hunter argues, "it would have been forced to replace the underlying premise of women's mission work, self-denial, with its opposite, self-advocacy."[33]

While it is hard to contend that feminist instincts prompted women to enter missionary service, these women did show a strong proclivity for independence. Nancy Cott astutely observed that if the popularity of female missionaries' memoirs is any indication, then the missionary ideal, "which proposed a submission of self that was simultaneously a pronounced form of self-assertion, had wide appeal."[34]

Despite their independence, missionary women generally acknowledged the leadership of the male sex with little complaint. In some cases they protested any suggestion that they might be feminists. Sue McBeth, who planted churches and preached among the Nez Perce Indians in the late nineteenth and early twentieth centuries, objected to being categorized as a feminist. She wrote that she had "no affinity" for the women's rights movement, that she enjoyed "more 'rights' now" than she could use, and that her only aim was "to try to be with God's help a true woman."[35]

---

33. Jane Hunter, *The Gospel of Gentility: American Women Missionaries in Turn-of-the-Century China* (New Haven: Yale Univ. Press, 1984), 88.

34. Nancy F. Cott, *The Bonds of Womanhood: "Woman's Sphere" in New England, 1780–1835* (New Haven: Yale Univ. Press, 1977), 140-41.

35. Leecy A. Barnett, "Hundreds of Pious Women: Presbyterian Women Missionaries to the American Indians, 1833–1893" (M.A. thesis, Trinity Evangelical Divinity School, 1985), 127.

Women in missions generally accepted the restrictions placed against them and sometimes went beyond the call of duty to accommodate critics. Isabella Thoburn agreed to speak at a Sunday service while home on furlough only if she could answer questions from the front pew instead of "preaching" from the pulpit.[36]

Some women missionaries objected to the role that was thrust upon them, protesting the conditions that required them to do what was typically regarded as men's work. Jeannie Dickson, who worked with the Dakota Mission, resented having "to take a man's position in everything" but being granted none of the advantages. She complained that if "it is my Father's will concerning me that I preach the Gospel or wash the dishes, I want to do it for His glory, but if I have a man's responsibility, why can I not also have a man's privilege in knowing something of the many matters in connection with this mission."[37] Typical of the female response to male leadership was that of Mrs. Ethan Curtis, who assured her audience at the 1891 Women's Board of Missions conference in Brooklyn, "Nowhere do we oppose man. Our first object is to be his ready and willing assistant."[38]

If there is serious doubt about women missionaries as feminists, there is no question that they face frequent opposition. In many cases it is subtle, as was true when Isabella Thoburn, at her brother Bishop James Thoburn's request, went to India to begin educational work for girls. During the early months after her arrival, he kept her so busy with his personal secretarial duties that she had no time to devote to teaching. She finally insisted that he allow her to conduct her own work, and he acknowledged the injustice of his actions. Speaking of himself, he wrote: "He understood for the first time that 'a Christian woman sent out to the field was a Christian missionary, and that her time was as precious, her work as important, and her rights as sacred as those of the more conventional missionaries of the other sex.'"[39]

36. Robert Speer, *Servants of the King* (New York: Interchurch, 1909), 144.

37. Barnett, "Hundreds of Pious Women," 129.

38. Mrs. Ethan Curtis, "The Reflex Influence of Missions," *Missionary Review of the World* 15 (March 1892): 183.

39. James Thoburn, *Life of Isabella Thoburn* (Cincinnati: Jennings and Pye, 1903), 120.

In other instances the prejudice against women was much more blatant. This was particularly true in the mid and late nineteenth century, when women missionaries were a novelty. Although married women often worked as hard as their husbands in the ministry and in some instances accomplished as much as their single sisters, in many cases they received no salary at all. Helen Holcomb, a Presbyterian missionary in India, complained of this to the board, telling of the difficult financial circumstances that compelled her to write in order to augment her husband's meager salary. Single women often fared little better; Adele Fielde's experience of receiving only half the salary of her single male colleague was not uncommon.[40]

A more common complaint concerning sex discrimination related to women's lack of representation in board meetings and field-council conferences. In 1899, Bertha Caldwell wrote an indignant letter to the secretary of the Presbyterian Board of Foreign Missions, explaining why she boycotted the annual meeting: "This year it was given out that the gentlemen did not wish the ladies at all in their sessions, and so the latter sat stupidly about, and gossiped or slept and wished Annual Meeting would be over." She then listed several women and their significant ministries and protested that despite this active involvement in the mission the women "get no voice at all in the matter unless specially asked, and absolutely no vote. . . . I fear this Mission is much behind the times."[41] When missionary women challenged such restrictions, they seemed most concerned about the immediate implications for their ministry. Women's rights per se was simply not the issue that tugged at their heartstrings. They had made extraordinary sacrifices for the cause of world evangelism, and it was a cause worth fighting for. It was on this basis, then, that women such as Lottie Moon fought for equal rights.

Charlotte Diggs "Lottie" Moon (1840–1912) has become the "patron saint" of Southern Baptist missions because of the influ-

40. Mrs. James F. Holcomb, Correspondence, *Woman's Work for Woman* 12 (1882): 300; Hoyt, "'When a Field Was Found Too Difficult,'" 317.

41. Quoted in Leslie A. Flemming, "Women and Witness: American Presbyterian Women Missionaries in North India, 1870–1910," paper delivered at conference, "A Century of World Evangelization," at Wheaton College, 17 June 1986.

ence she had on missionary outreach and giving. She was raised on a Virginia plantation and following the Civil War pursued a teaching career in Georgia, but her heart was in foreign missions. She was motivated not only by her faith in Christ but also by her desire to move beyond the restrictive routine of a woman's life in the post–Civil War south. Other family members had "marched out to fight for the Stars and Bars" and had performed "splendid service" while she had remained home on the plantation. Now it was her opportunity to become involved in an exciting venture.[42]

Lottie Moon pleaded her sex's case often, but always in the context of her ministry. She was not pleading for women's rights as much as for the right to fully employ women's gifts in ministry. "What women want who come to China," she argued, "is free opportunity to do the largest possible work. . . . What women have a right to demand is perfect equality." It is interesting that one of her bitterest enemies on this issue was a woman (a not uncommon scenario in women's history). A Congregational missionary wife, Mrs. Arthur Smith, questioned Lottie's mental stability and denounced her "lawless prancing all over the mission lot." In Mrs. Smith's view the appropriate role of a woman missionary was to attend "with quivering lip" her own children.[43]

Moon's insistence on doing evangelism and church planting was not readily endorsed by her field director. Indeed, she feared that he might seek to rescind some of the ministry opportunities and rights for women already allowed in the Southern Baptist mission, such as their vote in mission meetings—a liberty not granted to some other women missionaries. So Moon made her position clear: "Simple justice demands that women should have equal rights with men [both] in mission meetings and in the conduct of their work." And in reference to her field director's high-handed tactics regarding her ministry, she wrote, "If that be freedom, give me slavery."[44]

42. Irwin Hyatt, *Our Ordered Lives Confess: Three Nineteenth-Century American Missionaries in East Shantung* (Cambridge: Harvard Univ. Press, 1976), 95.
43. Ibid., 104-5.
44. Ibid., 106.

Despite her field director's initial opposition, Moon success-fully conducted evangelistic work at her post in P'ing-tu. By 1889 her achievement was described as the greatest among the Southern Baptists in China. Her remarkable accomplishments were in part due to her own personality and gifts; she found great joy, she said, in "saving souls." But her sex and its per-ceived limitations no doubt had much to do with her success. As an unordained woman, she was not allowed to lead the churches she planted. Thus it was more critical for her than for her male counterparts to train an indigenous ministry as soon as possible. This worked in favor of a strong local church. Indeed, within two decades, the Chinese pastor at P'ing-tu had baptized more than a thousand converts.[45]

Fortified by her own successful ministry, Moon aggressively appealed for women at home to raise funds for China missions and to sponsor single women as missionaries. "What I hope to see," she wrote, "is a band of ardent, enthusiastic, and experi-enced Christian women occupying a line of stations extending from P'ing-tu on the north and from Chinkiang on the south." For that to happen, she asserted, a "mighty wave of enthusiasm for Women's Work for Women must be stirred." Her emphasis on recruiting women was based not only on her confidence in them but also on Southern Baptist men's virtual default on the work of China missions. She found it

> odd that a million Baptists of the South can furnish only three men for all China. Odd that with five hundred preachers in the state of Virginia, we must rely on a Presbyterian to fill a Baptist pulpit [here]. I wonder how these things look in heaven. They certainly look very queer in China.[46]

Moon identified closely with the Chinese people, and when a famine afflicted her Chinese friends, she gave them her own food. She was simply unable to eat when starving children came to her door begging for food. As a result, she died on Christmas Eve, 1912, at the age of seventy-two, from complications relat-ing to malnutrition. Ironically, she had initiated a Christmas

45. Ibid., 115, 117.
46. Ibid., 113.

offering for the China work, and her death served as a symbolic offering that stirred the consciences of Southern Baptists. The Lottie Moon Christmas offering became a widely celebrated fund-raising tradition for missions among Southern Baptist women that in recent years has netted tens of millions of dollars annually.[47]

For all that she did to promote women's involvement at home and in China—showing that women indeed could function equally with men—Lottie Moon could not change the perception of women that some men would always have. The highest tribute that the *Foreign Missions Journal* could offer her was to call her "the best man among our missionaries."[48]

Indeed, by the time of her death, the apogee of women's missionary leadership had been reached, and fresh opposition to the movement would soon emerge. In the tainted atmosphere created by the fundamentalist-modernist eruptions in the 1920s, perceptions of women's contributions and capabilities soured considerably. It was as if the male leaders, particularly those on the conservative side of Protestantism, felt that women were somehow at fault for Christianity's declension.[49] The opposition of fundamentalist John R. Rice is an extreme yet revealing example of the discrimination women encountered in missions. "The deputation work of great missionary societies has suffered greatly at the hands of women missionaries," Rice complained.

> If godly, Spirit-filled men, manly men, should go to the churches with the appeal that those whom God has called for His work should come prepared for toil and sweat and blood and tears, it would do infinitely more for the mission cause than the prattle about dress and customs and food, with stereopticon slide pictures of quaint heathen groups presented so often by women missionaries, largely to groups of women and children.... It certainly vio-

47. Ruth A. Tucker, *From Jerusalem to Irian Jaya: A Biographical History of Christian Missions* (Grand Rapids: Zondervan, 1983), 238.

48. Catherine Allen, *The New Lottie Moon Story* (Nashville: Broadman, 1980), 288.

49. Margaret L. Bendroth, "Fundamentalism and Femininity: The Reorientation of Women's Role in the 1920s," *Evangelical Studies Bulletin* 5 (March 1988): 1-4. This article is a condensed version of a yet-to-be-published essay which is available from its author at the Department of History at Northeastern University.

lates the command of God for women to speak before mixed audiences of men and women and to take the pulpit in the churches. And we may be sure that the work of the gospel of Christ among the heathen is not prospered by this sin.[50]

Not all fundamentalists shared Rice's opinions (even if most still opposed women's ordination), for their faith missions had come to depend heavily upon women volunteers. Yet the devaluation of women's talents persisted. An example of this ambivalent posture comes from the China Inland Mission's call in 1929 for 200 new missionaries in two years. Of the 91 North Americans who were accepted by the mission, 61 were single women. The mission took them on, even though its stated intention was to commission a majority of males.[51]

During these years, some women, particularly in the older denominational missions, raised their voices against such discrimination and called for greater sexual equality in ministry. Perhaps the most vocal was Pearl S. Buck, the well-known author, who was raised in China by her missionary parents. She was no friend of missions in later life, and she vehemently attacked the sexism that was so tied to the missionary life-style. Her reflections on her mother bear this out: "Since these days when I saw all her nature dimmed I have hated Saint Paul with all my heart and so must all true women hate him, I think, because of what he has done in the past to women like Carie, proud free-born women, yet damned by their very womanhood."[52]

Where were the more positive, affirming perspectives of women Christian leaders in the 1920s and 1930s? After the decline of women's missionary societies, the leaders of prior decades lost their influence. As Patricia Hill notes, Helen Barrett Montgomery's progressive evangelicalism lost its audience as Protestantism and its missionary enterprise polarized between

---

50. John R. Rice, *Bobbed Hair, Bossy Wives, and Women Preachers* (Wheaton, IL: Sword of the Lord, 1941), 64-65.

51. D. E. Hoste, "For the Evangelization of Unreached Areas," *China's Millions* 37 (May 1929): 67-68; "Editorial Notes: A Call for New Workers," *China's Millions* 37 (July 1929): 111. For a list of North American candidates, see "North America's Contribution to the Two Hundred," *China's Millions* 40 (February 1932): 30.

52. Pearl S. Buck, *The Exile* (New York: Reynal & Hitchcock, 1936), 283.

militant conservative and extreme liberal positions. And Lucy W. Peabody, who had become the president of a fundamentalist mission, eventually gave in to the prevailing prejudice in that movement. She resigned her post in 1935, acting, as she put it, out of deference to the principle of "masculine leadership in the Church."[53]

Specialized Ministries

As the twentieth century progressed, women continued to play a major role on the mission fields, even if their leadership had diminished. Indeed, they expanded their roles far beyond ministries of women's educational work and evangelism, though very often the new lines of service they took up were closely linked with those traditional roles. Two of the specialties most influenced by women in the twentieth century have been medicine and Bible translation.

Medical missionaries often had opportunities to reach certain individuals that might have been out of the range of an ordinary evangelist or church planter. The healing of a young child or a wounded warrior could turn the heart of a tribal chieftain from hostility to gratitude and pave the way for the acceptance of the Christian faith among the people. In more sophisticated societies, perhaps a high-ranking government official would plead with the missionary doctor to bring medicine to his dying wife. Medical work was very closely tied to evangelism, and medical missionaries were well aware of the status conferred on them when they performed their services well.

The pioneer among American women missionary physicians, Clara Swain, began her work in India in 1870 under the sponsorship of the newly formed Woman's Missionary Society of the Methodist Episcopal Church. During her first year she treated some fifteen hundred patients—not a high number for a missionary doctor. Indian women were hesitant at first to seek

53. Hill, *World Their Household*, 180-91; William J. Hopewell, *The Missionary Emphasis of the General Association of Regular Baptist Churches* (Chicago: Regular Baptist, 1963), 55.

her out. Within a decade, however, she was treating some seven thousand patients a year. Yet she considered herself primarily an evangelist and focused her attention on sharing the gospel with the women she treated.[54]

Perhaps the most notable and emulated American woman medical missionary of the twentieth century was Ida Scudder (1870–1960). She was one of a long line of Scudders who had served as medical missionaries to India under the Reformed Church in America. The forty-three members of the Scudder missionary family eventually logged over eleven hundred years of missionary service. It was an illustrious family, but Ida had determined not to follow family tradition. She had known the deprivation of living and serving in India, and her dream was to have a better life—one that included luxuries and pleasure and one that allowed families to stay together without the agony of long separations.[55]

As a youth, Ida returned to America for her education, but she was called home to India to be with her ailing mother. During that visit, she helped with the ministry but still was repelled by the idea of sacrificing her life for the work. Yet that attitude changed when the need for women's medical work was forcefully brought home to her during a night of anguish in which three young Indian girls died for lack of a female to give them medical care. After a profound spiritual struggle, Ida "went to my father and mother and told them that I must go home and study medicine, and come back to India to help such women."[56]

Ida returned to America in 1895, where she earned her medical degree at Cornell Medical College. She then rejoined her family in India. She had publicized her anticipated ministry, and as a result she brought ten thousand dollars to begin a program of medical work for women. This work became the Vellore medical complex, which offered Indian women the comprehensive

54. Dorothy Clarke Wilson, *Palace of Healing: The Story of Dr. Clara Swain, First Woman Missionary Doctor, and the Hospital She Founded* (New York: McGraw-Hill, 1968), passim.

55. Dorothy Clarke Wilson, "The Legacy of Ida S. Scudder," *International Bulletin of Missionary Research* 9 (January 1985): 26.

56. Mary Pauline Jeffrey, *Dr. Ida: India* (New York: Revell, 1938), 49-51.

medical services they so desperately needed. Medicine was never seen in isolation from evangelism, however; Annie Hancock, an evangelist, worked closely with Ida and led many patients to faith in Christ.[57]

Scudder was still active in the work in 1950, when she helped plan the fifty-year golden jubilee celebration at Vellore. She had retired four years earlier and turned the work over to Dr. Hilda Lazarus, one of her students, but she remained actively involved for many more years. She had become a celebrity of sorts among supporters back home and throughout India. That fact was demonstrated when a letter addressed "Dr. Ida, India" was delivered to her, one woman in a nation of some three hundred million.[58]

In addition to those women missionaries involved strictly in medical work (as doctors or, more commonly, as nurses), many provided other humanitarian services. Some women were not missionaries per se, but they functioned as missionaries. For example, many women served abroad under the auspices of the Young Women's Christian Association (YWCA). Over eight hundred American YWCA teachers, administrators, and social workers served overseas between 1895 and 1970.[59]

These women formed an army of humanitarian workers who were prepared to serve in virtually any situation. According to their historian, they were "posted in refugee camps in Poland, in the slums of Buenos Aires and Istanbul, and in villages in rural China." Although many of them insisted "we are not missionaries," most of these young women considered themselves "emissaries of Christ." One of them, Ada Grabill, asserted that her "sole motive in China is to show Christ," and that outlook was common among YWCA women who went abroad. Their work was humanitarian, but always with the motive of demonstrating the compassion of Christ.[60]

Like medical and social ministries, Bible translation has historically been regarded a male profession. In the nineteenth and early twentieth centuries, it was no more appropriate for a

57. Tucker, *From Jerusalem to Irian Jaya*, 334.
58. Ibid., 337.
59. Nancy Boyd, *Emissaries: The Overseas Work of the American YWCA, 1895–1970* (New York: Woman's Press, 1986), 3-5.
60. Ibid.

woman to be a Bible translator than to be an ordained minister or a seminary professor. That restriction began to weaken, however, by the 1930s, as conservative evangelicals in the faith missions network began to organize new translation efforts. With the founding of Wycliffe Bible Translators in 1933 by missions promoter L. L. Legters and William Cameron Townsend, a missionary to Guatemala, women as well as men caught the vision for translating the Bible for people in remote tribes. Still there was strong opposition. Not only was it thought to be inappropriate for women to be translating and interpreting the Word of God; many considered it unthinkable to send women to work in dangerous remote regions.

Townsend, however, was quicker to accept women than most of his colleagues were. For some it took years to become convinced that women were as equal to the task as men—and that in some cases were far superior. Leaders' fears of women being killed by "savage" tribesmen proved to be generally unfounded. Indeed, women were typically exposed to less danger than were men. For example, Loretta Anderson and Doris Cox went to Peru to work among the head-hunting Shapras in 1950. Their translation work was successful, and within a few years many of the people had become Christians. Years later, Tariri, the tribal chief, confided to Townsend, "If you had sent men, we would have killed them on sight. Or if a couple, I'd have killed the man and taken the woman for myself. But what could a great chief do with two harmless girls who insisted on calling him brother?"[61]

Women's involvement in modern Bible translation work began, however, with Eunice Pike and Florence Hansen in the earliest years of the Wycliffe translators. These two women enrolled at the mission's Summer Institute of Linguistics in 1936 to prepare for a ministry of Bible translation. They were given less than an enthusiastic welcome. According to one source, they "did not impress Legters as appropriate pioneer material. This he felt was a job for rugged men. He had not encouraged women to join the crusade—but these two had turned up."[62]

61. Clarence W. Hall, *Adventurers for God* (New York: Harper & Row, 1959), 119.

62. Ethel Wallis and Mary Bennett, *Two Thousand Tongues to Go* (New York: Harper & Row, 1959), 98.

They received some grim warnings, Pike later related:

> Some people had reminded Mr. Townsend that Latin American women never traveled alone, never lived alone, and were always well chaperoned. With genuine concern for Florrie and me, they had said that any attempt on our part to live in an Indian village would be misunderstood by the people and could only end in disaster.[63]

Despite the objections, they were assigned to do linguistic and translation work among the sixty-five thousand Mazatec Indians, 90 percent of whom spoke no Spanish. They lived in the remote town of Chalco, a ten-hour horseback ride across the mountains from "civilization." Though many viewed their work inappropriate for women, without them, the language might have gone untranslated for many years. As Pike recalled,

> When we first arrived in Mexico, almost nothing was known about the Mazatec language. Three and a half years later we were talking it—with lots of errors—had figured out something of the grammar, and had our opinions about the alphabet with which it should be written.[64]

Women found that they had some advantages over men in tribal translation work. For reasons of propriety, a language informant had to be chosen very carefully. Men and women alone together were presumed to be involved sexually. Women informants who knew Spanish were difficult to find, but they often proved to be the most reliable, because an informant had to endure hours of tedious conversation. Tribal men were particularly vulnerable to boredom and restlessness because language work was sedentary and it took them away from their customary activities. Women, on the other hand, could do tasks like sewing while working as informants.[65]

In 1941, after less than five years among the Mazatec Indians, Pike and Hansen completed the first draft of the New Testa-

63. Eunice V. Pike, *Not Alone* (Chicago: Moody, 1964), 10.
64. Eunice V. Pike, *Words Wanted* (Huntington Beach, CA: Wycliffe Bible Translators, 1958), 8-9.
65. Pike, *Not Alone*, 78.

ment. After many more drafts and continued work with the people, they were ready to move on. In the years that followed, Pike worked with other partners and in village visitation, using her nurse's training to the advantage of the gospel and selling Scripture portions and Christian books that had been translated into the Mazatec tongue. She demonstrated repeatedly that single women can be effective Bible translators in remote tribal areas, and the example she set encouraged hundreds more women to follow in her footsteps.

Telling Her Story

One special missions task for which women have not taken a backseat is missionary writing. Many of the most insightful and honest books about the realities of missionary work have been written by women. Without the woman's perspective, missionary literature would be sorely deficient. Women often deal with the trials of family life and the inner spiritual struggles in greater depth than men do, and they are often more open in admitting their own personal conflicts than are men.

This tradition of perceptive missionary writing continued in the twentieth century, thanks to such gifted conservative evangelical women as Elisabeth Elliot and Isobel Kuhn. In her books, Elliot confesses weaknesses and temptations that are rarely dealt with in missionary literature, as does Kuhn, who shares her struggle with doubts and pride and tells how she was initially denied full candidacy with the China Inland Mission. Elliot addresses problems and concerns that relate especially to single women; Kuhn does the same for married women— though their writings speak to everyone who has a heart for missions. They possess a timeless quality that guarantees them a place among the great Christian classics.

The most widely publicized tragic drama of modern missionary history might be virtually forgotten today were it not for the writings of one of the surviving widows. Operation Auca, which claimed the lives of five American missionaries, was related in detail in three publications authored or edited by Elisabeth Elliot, including the classic *Through Gates of Splendor*.

Through this ministry of writing, she inspired and challenged tens of thousands of Christians to deepen their commitment to overseas missions. In addition to her creative and masterful style, Elliot had a strong message to convey—a message that did not always depict a pretty picture of missions. This was true especially of her novel, *No Graven Image,* and her autobiographical account of her early years as a single missionary, *These Strange Ashes.*

These Strange Ashes is more than an autobiography. It is a handbook for missionaries—single women in particular—who are considering ministry in remote tribal regions. The excitement and adventure of such work quickly dissipates in the pages of this volume, while loneliness and deprivation become a stark, tangible reality. The missionaries, including Elliot herself, are real people struggling with the irritations of everyday life as well as the inner conflicts that arise when human success seems so illusive.

The main characters in the book—Elliot and her partners, Dorothy, Doreen, and Barbara—are all single women who, except for Barbara, "badly wished to be married." They were committed to reaching the Colorado Indians for Christ, but they struggled with the pain of loneliness and their desire for marriage and family.[66]

Other problems and issues plagued these women, who were isolated by miles of rugged jungle roads from the nearest reminders of modern civilization. Things they had taken for granted suddenly became what they missed the most. "One of my recurring dreams was of going into a dimestore," wrote Elliot. "That became to me almost a dream of paradise—to be able to wander freely among the displays of vegetable parers and shining pots, dishcloths, notebooks, Scotch tape, nail files, the little ordinary things that made the difference between a civilized life and the life around us." She often found her work and life to be very frustrating, confessing in a letter that "the days drag by" and that she was "fed up with life" in the jungle. "I find that because nothing actually presses me to activity, I

66. Elisabeth Elliot, *These Strange Ashes* (San Francisco: Harper & Row, 1979), 72-73.

dawdle in quiet time, let my mind wander in prayer, and day-dream when trying to study."[67]

The struggle with self-discipline often created doubts in her mind as to what the will of God actually was for her. But even darker doubts clouded her consciousness—especially when tragedies occurred that were beyond her control. After one dis-heartening setback, she found herself blaming God: "In my heart I could not escape the thought that it was God who had failed. Surely He knew how much was at stake. . . . To my inner cries and questionings no answer came. . . . There was nothing but darkness and silence."[68] Elliot began to question her call to missions, at one point "asking for assurance that the call was God's voice and not a figment of my own mind." She struggled with her lack of accomplishment and the obstacles that con-fronted her and asked, "Had I come here, leaving so much be-hind, on a fool's errand?"[69]

Like Elisabeth Elliot's books, Isobel Kuhn's books have had a wide influence on Christian missions. She served many years in Asia with the China Inland Mission, and, as with Elisabeth Elliot, her writing was prompted by misfortune. In 1954 she underwent surgery in Thailand for breast cancer, a disease she fought for more than two years before it took her life in the spring of 1957 at the age of fifty-five. Those years of fighting, however, were produc-tive years. In 1956 alone, she completed three books and began writing another. Her writing of missionary books had begun years earlier when she served in China and later was isolated in a shanty high in the mountains of northern Thailand, while her husband, a mission superintendent, was away sometimes for months at a time overseeing his regional work.[70]

Even as Elliot identified with the problems of single women, so Isobel Kuhn identified with those of married women. One of the first collisions that occurred between her and her husband involved their household help. John had brought into the marriage Yin-chang, a Chinese cook, who was himself mar-

67. Ibid., 75, 85.
68. Ibid., 82-83.
69. Ibid., 108-9.
70. Carolyn L. Canfield, *One Vision Only* (Chicago: Moody, 1959), 10, 177, 186.

ried—making two sets of newlyweds in one household. Though she had vowed she would be a good mistress, Isobel immediately clashed with them. The situation exploded when Isobel criticized Yin-chang's work to John in front of him. To her surprise, she later wrote in her *Vistas*, "John turned on me, siding with Yin-chang." That was too much for her. "Hot with temper, I said nothing but put on my hat and coat and walked out. . . . I wasn't going to live in a house where a lazy servant was condoned and given preference over the wife!"[71]

Another area that created conflict in their marriage was that of writing prayer letters. For Isobel, a letter to supporters back home was a creative work of art, and her friends enjoyed forthright honesty and humor. But she and John had their differences. Letter-writing day became what Isobel called "an exasperating trial." John questioned the accuracy of her details and argued with her recollections. Yet Isobel later expressed her gratitude for John's criticism of her writing. "God was preparing to use my pen in relating stories of His work in human hearts. I couldn't afford to let that pen grow careless as to facts. The blue pencil showed me that a Christian writer can't be too particular that every point be according to reality."[72]

Isobel's honest "stories of His work in human hearts" told of joys and grim realites in cross-cultural missionary work. Unlike the project orientation of many missionary narratives written by men, Kuhn's stories, like those of other women missionary writers, focus on the people she and her husband had come to serve, on intimate family experiences, and on genuine spiritual struggles.

Most important of all, these women authors give glimpses of the role of women in world evangelization that would otherwise be lost. Women have comprised the vast majority of the missionaries, both on the old-line Protestant denominational boards and in the twentieth-century evangelical missionary enterprise. Throughout the history of modern missions, women have been more strongly attracted than men to the challenge of sharing the gospel worldwide, especially with other women.

71. Ibid., 69.
72. Ibid., 138-39.

Ruth A. Tucker

Even though the churches' male leaders have narrowed women
missionaries' opportunities to serve and have overlooked their
achievements, these female guardians of the Great Commission
have persistently pursued their vision.

12 *Second Thoughts on the Great Commission: Liberal Protestants and Foreign Missions, 1890–1940*

Grant Wacker

In his portrait of the mythical village of Lake Wobegon, Minnesota, Garrison Keillor noted that "Clarence [Bunsen] is a Lutheran but he sometimes drops in at the rectory for a second opinion." Keillor does not tell us exactly what brand of Lutheran Bunsen was, but we know that whatever theological stripes he may have worn on the outside, on the inside, in his heart of hearts, Bunsen probably was a liberal. The reason is simple. For the better part of a century—from the 1880s through the 1940s— liberals were in the business of seeking and offering second opinions on almost every aspect of evangelical Protestant thought. And nowhere was that more true than in regard to the evangelical view of foreign missions.[1]

It is possible, of course, to overplay the differences between liberal and evangelical missionary ideologies. For one thing, partisans at home tended to be more self-conscious about theological refinements than their counterparts overseas ever dreamed of being. Even as the modernist-fundamentalist conflict was beginning to heat up in the 1910s, one missionary quipped that "one of the reasons why sectarianism has not been more emphasized in the mission field is [that] natives of no mission country are able

---

1. Garrison Keillor, *Lake Wobegon Days* (New York: Viking, 1985), 222, quoted in Martin E. Marty, "Second Opinion . . . in Health, Faith, and Ethics," *Second Opinion* 1 (1986): 8-9.

to pronounce correctly the names of the leading denominations of the West." Whatever the truth of that remark, there can be little doubt that the missionaries themselves—with some notable exceptions—were prone to overlook theological differences in the interest of working together in an alien and frequently hostile environment. But liberal and evangelical missionaries also shared a deeper and more disturbing trait. Bluntly stated, they displayed remarkably similar assumptions about the superiority of Western culture in general and of Western forms of Christianity in particular. Historian William R. Hutchison has described that outlook as a common inclination to "define and conquer"; a common propensity to believe that Westerners possessed the right "not only to conquer the world, but [also] to define reality for the peoples of the world."[2]

A representative example taken from each side of the theological fence suffices to illustrate the point. George A. Gordon, pastor of Old South Congregational Church in Boston, may well have been the most influential liberal thinker at the turn of the century. He often stressed the universality of God's self-disclosure and occasionally uttered grave doubts about the likelihood of eternal punishment for anyone. Even so, Gordon never questioned the "absolute incomparableness of Christianity." "Take the Hindu race," he sniffed in an 1895 sermon.

> Their gift lies in the direction of metaphysics. [Yet] even here there is a certain cheapness about the product. . . . Talk by the mile . . . worn out with immeasurable imbecilities, exhausted by an immemorial divorce of the intellect and the will, and corrupted by illimitable clouds of spurious sentiment.

Evangelicals rarely did better. Even thoughtful and generally broad-minded ones like William Cleaver Wilkinson, professor of religion and literature at the University of Chicago, found it difficult to imagine that other faiths, other cultures, might possess their own inner integrity. While individual Buddhists or

---

2. The missionary quip was from James L. Barton, "The Modern Missionary," *Harvard Theological Review* 8 (1915): 5. William R. Hutchison, "A Moral Equivalent for Imperialism: Americans and the Promotion of 'Christian Civilization': 1880–1910," *Indian Journal of American Studies* 13 (1983): 59.

Hindus may have risen to "great ethical heights," Wilkinson acknowledged in an 1893 address, the Bible condemned other religions with "no hesitation, no reservation, no qualification, no exception, no complaisance, no quarter shown of any kind." Consequently the proper attitude of Christians toward other religions should be one of "universal, absolute, eternal, unappeasable hostility."[3]

Keeping such qualifications about the commonalities between liberals and evangelicals in mind, it is clear, nonetheless, that by the turn of the century the gap between them had become very real and by World War I it had become virtually unbridgeable. The way that each faction reacted to the 1893 World's Parliament of Religions in Chicago shows how great the distance really was. Just before the parliament opened, David Swing, a liberal Presbyterian pastor in Chicago widely hailed for his pulpit oratory, confidently predicted that the event would "make millions feel that man is indeed . . . traveling toward eternity upon the great stream of faith." Fifteen years later, the social gospel pioneer Washington Gladden concluded that the parliament may have been the "most important religious gathering" ever assembled. When the World Fellowship of Faiths met in Chicago in 1933, Jabez T. Sunderland, a Unitarian patriarch who had spoken at the parliament forty years before, judged that ever since that event it had been "impossible for intelligent men to take [a] narrow and bigoted view of the non-Christian religions." But that was the rub. Many prominent evangelicals asserted that the parliament had been a disgrace to Christianity precisely because it had made the other religions seem so attractive. Professor Herrick Johnson of McCormick Seminary dismissed the parliament as a "monstrous absurdity," while Morgan Dix, rector of Trinity Church in New York City, scored it as a "masterpiece of Satan." A. T. Pierson, editor of the

3. George A. Gordon, *The Gospel for Humanity: Annual Sermon before the American Board of Commissioners for Foreign Missions* (1895), reprinted in *American Protestant Thought: The Liberal Era*, ed. William R. Hutchison (New York: Harper & Row, Harper Torchbooks, 1968), 101-2. W. C. Wilkinson, "Attitude of Christianity to Other Religions," in *Neely's History of the Parliament of Religions and Religious Congresses at the World's Columbian Exposition*, ed. Walter R. Houghton (Chicago: Neely, 1893), 761-64.

Missionary Review of the World, judged that the parliament had done "measureless harm." It had served as a forum for the "usual cheap tirade against Christianity," he charged, a place where "God's elect flirted with the daughters of Moab." With that, Pierson vowed to banish the parliament from his mind, praying that "such a gathering may never again give occasion to the enemies of the Lord to blaspheme!"[4]

The parliament may not have been, as one reporter exclaimed, "the supreme moment of the nineteenth century,"[5] but it did prompt Protestants of all persuasions squarely to confront the warrant for missions. Was the theological difference between Christianity and other religions absolute? Or was it one of degree? If the difference was absolute, did that then mean that the missionary was to uproot indigenous faiths regardless of the consequences? Or if the difference was one of degree, did that then mean that the missionary was to present the Christian message as a better, but not necessarily as the exclusive, solution to humankind's spiritual needs? Indeed, given the growing understanding of the integral if not indissoluble relationship between religions and the cultures in which they were born, was it possible that men and women of other faiths simply should be left alone to work out their own salvation in their own culturally unique ways?

Through the mid twentieth century the evangelical answer to those questions remained unequivocal: other religions possessed no redeeming value, and souls who died without a

4. David Swing, "Building a Great Religion," in *Neely's History,* 977. Washington Gladden, *The Church and Modern Life* (1908), 37-38, quoted in Carl T. Jackson, *The Oriental Religions and American Thought: Nineteenth-Century Explorations* (Westport, CT: Greenwood, 1981), 253. Jabez T. Sunderland, "The Two World Parliaments of Religion—1893 and 1933," in *World Fellowship: Addresses and Messages,* ed. Charles Fredrick Weller (New York: Liveright, 1935), 514. Herrick Johnson, "The Proposed Parliament of Religions at the World's Fair," *Independent,* 24 March 1892, 401, quoted in Jackson, *Oriental Religions,* 245. Morgan Dix, letter to John Henry Barrows, in *The World's Parliament of Religions,* ed. John Henry Barrows (1893), 2:1557, quoted in Paul A. Carter, *The Spiritual Crisis of the Gilded Age* (DeKalb, IL: Northern Illinois Univ. Press, 1971), 213. Arthur T. Pierson, "The Parliament of Religions: A Review," *Missionary Review of the World* 17 (1894): 889, 882, 893-94.

5. The reporter was John W. Postgate, an official stenographer; see *Neely's History,* 35.

saving knowledge of Jesus Christ faced eternal damnation. Hudson Taylor's admonition to the Student Volunteer Movement in Detroit in 1894 memorably captured that point of view: "There is a great Niagara of souls passing into the dark in China," he declared. "Every day, every week, every month they are passing away! A million a month in China they are dying without God." Taylor's views persisted without modification. A half century later his China Inland Mission continued to affirm "the eternal punishment of the lost." This position remained almost universal among American evangelicals. Sociologists' surveys taken in 1940 and in 1964 showed that virtually all evangelicals believed that the heathen would suffer eternal torment in hell, whether they had heard the gospel or not. For the great majority of evangelical Protestants, in short, religious pluralism almost always presented itself as a spiritual challenge to be met rather than as a theological problem to be solved.[6]

Liberals, on the other hand, started seriously to question the conventional wisdom about the fate of the heathen and about Christians' responsibility to save them, as early as the 1880s. Their inclination to see greater salvific possibilities in God's general revelation to humanity accompanied deepening worry about the disruptive effects of Christian missions upon other peoples. Their sensitivity to those questions does not necessarily mean that they were more intelligent or more humane than their evangelical counterparts. Rather, such tendencies grew quite directly from the assumptions and affirmations of liberal theology itself.

We can summarize the underlying features of the liberal outlook which molded the liberal philosophy of missions as follows:

6. Hudson Taylor, quoted in Paul A. Varg, "Motives in Protestant Missions, 1890–1917," *Church History* 23 (1954): 71. China Inland Mission, *Statement of Policy* (1928 [reaffirmed in 1950]), reproduced in M. Searle Bates, "The Theology of the American Missionaries in China, 1900–1950," in *The Missionary Enterprise in China and America*, ed. John K. Fairbank (Cambridge: Harvard Univ. Press, 1974), 153. Surveys taken as recently as the mid-1980s reveal that nearly all evangelicals continue to believe in the existence of hell as a place of eternal torment and that at least two-thirds believe that the heathen will suffer in hell whether or not they have fairly heard the gospel. For quantitative data on evangelical beliefs about the fate of the heathen, see James Davison Hunter, *Evangelicalism: The Coming Generation* (Chicago: Univ. of Chicago Press, 1987), 35-40.

(1) an inclination, which was temperamental as much as anything else, to esteem open-mindedness and tolerance for diversity as admirable character traits; (2) a distaste for traditional sources of authority, especially for sources that would arbitrarily or automatically define Christian religious experience as authentic and non-Christian experience as inauthentic; (3) a tendency to value intellectual integrity, whatever the cost, over confessional regularity; (4) a conviction that God's self-revelation was rendered wholly within the ordinary processes of history, which meant that all of history—Christian and non-Christian, Western and non-Western alike—bore revelatory significance; (5) a respect for the methods and "assured conclusions" of modern science, especially for emerging social sciences such as sociology and cultural anthropology, which tended to relativize all absolutist value systems; (6) a preference for ethics over metaphysics, which put a greater premium upon the cash-value benefits of religious faith in the present life than hoped-for benefits in the hereafter; (7) a belief that the world was an evolving, ideal whole, which meant that it was difficult, if not impossible, to draw hard-and-fast distinctions between the saved and the lost, the converted and the unconverted; (8) an inclination to affirm the essential goodness of humankind, which fostered appreciation for all forms of achievement, wherever found; (9) a conviction that common religious experiences undergirded all of the world's major or "high" religions and thus provided common standards by which all religions were to be judged; and (10) an assumption that most religious language, certainly all supernaturalistic terminology, is symbolic rather than realistic, connotative rather than denotative. That meant, among other things, that liberals increasingly shifted their intellectual energies from apologetics to hermeneutics, from the seemingly futile attempt to assess the objective truth or falsity of religious claims to the more fruitful attempt to interpret properly the meaning of religious claims for the men and women who made them.[7]

7. This summation of liberal assumptions is based upon a variety of primary and secondary sources. For the former see, e.g., Lewis French Stearns, *Present Day Theology: A Popular Discussion of the Leading Doctrines of the Christian Faith* (New York: Charles Scribner's Sons, 1893), esp. the Appendix, "The Present

By 1890 or so, that cluster of dispositions, assumptions, and affirmations, along with certain social factors, such as the financial means for graduate education and extended travel in Europe, had led liberals to a distinctive philosophy of foreign missions. The latter entailed, at the outset, an acknowledgment that all religions—or at least the "high" ones of Hinduism, Buddhism, Confucianism, and Islam—offered a genuinely saving knowledge of God. In numerous places (esp. Acts 14:15-17; 17:22-31; and the prologue to the Gospel of John), Scripture itself had stated that God had not left himself without a witness in the non-Christian world. Not surprisingly, the liberals' inclination to highlight the New Testament passages that seemed to affirm the universality of God's loving self-revelation soon led to a modification of and, by 1910 or so, outright rejection of the venerable idea of hell as the fate of the morally upright heathen.[8] Nonetheless—and this was a second distinct tenet in the liberal philosophy of missions—Scripture also stated that God had most *fully* revealed himself in Jesus Christ. This meant that Christ alone could fulfill the spiritual aspirations of the other religions. Christianity's claim to be the "final" or "absolute" religion was valid not because Christianity constituted the exclusive avenue to salvation, but because it offered a system of spiritual and ethical ideals that stood qualitatively superior to all others.[9]

Direction of Theological Thought . . . in the United States," 531-45. Among secondary sources I am chiefly indebted to Hutchison, *American Protestant Thought,* 2-3; Claude Welch, "Theology," in *Religion,* ed. Paul Ramsey (Englewood Cliffs, NJ: Prentice-Hall, 1965), 227-40; and George Hunston Williams, "The Attitude of Liberals in New England Toward Non-Christian Religions, 1784–1885," *Crane Review* 9 (1967): 60-89.

8. For the demise of hell in liberal thought see Stearns, *Present Day Theology,* 543-45; William Jewett Tucker, *My Generation: An Autobiographical Interpretation* (Boston: Houghton Mifflin, 1919), 125-26; and R. Pierce Beaver, "Missionary Motivation through Three Centuries," in *Reinterpretation in American Church History,* ed. Jerald C. Brauer (Chicago: Univ. of Chicago Press, 1968), 130.

9. My description of the tenets in the liberal philosophy of missions at the end of the nineteenth century is influenced by but not identical to the descriptions in William R. Hutchison, "Modernism and Missions: The Liberal Search for an Exportable Christianity, 1875–1935," in *Missionary Enterprise,* esp. p. 116; and William R. Hutchison, *Errand to the World: American Protestant Thought and Foreign Missions* (Chicago: Univ. of Chicago Press, 1987), 102-11. For primary sources that make similar points see Barton, "Modern Missionary," esp. p. 304;

The first two tenets led to a third: if Christian faith was to be successfully exported, its Western and sectarian barnacles would have to be stripped away, leaving only the Pauline message of "Christ and him crucified." Liberals, like most Christians, often found that it was easier to affirm the ideal of a purely supracultural Christianity than to apply it in the real world—as the example of George Gordon makes clear. Even so, the formula was simple enough: preach the religious faith *of* Jesus rather than a set of doctrines *about* him. Exactly what that meant was open to a spectrum of interpretations, but for most liberals it entailed a shift from a Bible-centered, doctrine-oriented message to a Christ-centered, example-oriented message. Thus missionaries' achievements were to be measured not so much by the number of conversions they effected as by the Christ-likeness of their lives. The sole question, as the acclaimed China missionary Pearl Buck wrote in 1932, was whether one's life "conveyed anything to the people about Christ. . . . What people ever understood what the word meant until it was made flesh and dwelt among them?" That redefinition of the missionary's aims proved enormously significant. As James I. Barton, a missionary to Syria, pointed out in 1915, the issue was not conversion versus a Christ-like life. Rather, conversion itself was now defined—or more precisely, redefined—as the ability to live and to foster within others a Christ-like life.[10]

At the eve of the twentieth century the liberal philosophy of missions could be described, then, in terms of three closely related convictions: first, that God had disclosed saving knowledge of himself among all the major religions of the world; second, that Christianity nonetheless stood qualitatively superior

---

Archibald G. Baker, "Thought Concerning Protestant Foreign Missions," in *Religious Thought in the Last Quarter-Century,* ed. Gerald Birney Smith (Chicago: Univ. of Chicago Press, 1927), 207-27; proceedings of the 1910 World Missionary Conference in Edinburgh, published as the Report of Commission IV, *The Missionary Message in Relation to Non-Christian Religions* (Edinburgh: Oliphant, Anderson & Ferrier, 1910), esp. pp. 267-68; proceedings of the 1928 International Missionary Council in Jerusalem, published as *The Christian Life and Message in Relation to Non-Christian Systems of Thought and Life* (New York: International Missionary Council, 1928), esp. pp. 402-5.

10. Pearl S. Buck, "The Laymen's Mission Report," *Christian Century,* 23 November 1932, 1435, 1437. Barton, "Modern Missionary," 6-7.

to all other religions; and third, that Christ-likeness—rather than doctrines about Christ—constituted the living heart of the Christian message. It could be said that all three of those convictions continued to characterize liberal thinking about missions through the 1930s, but it would be more accurate to recognize that over the course of the half century liberals initially emphasized the second tenet, then the first, then came to rest their case almost entirely upon the cogency of the third. Indeed, as the years passed they gradually downscaled even the third, so that by World War II something like a fourth distinct emphasis had emerged. For analytical purposes I shall label those four more or less successive stages as the (1) conquest, (2) fulfillment, (3) collaboration, and (4) pluralist models of Christian missions.

The conquest approach was well represented by John Henry Barrows, a Presbyterian pastor and college president who is best remembered as the general chairman and organizing genius of the World's Parliament of Religions. Speaking in Bombay three years later, Barrows explained to Indian religious leaders why Christianity was rightly destined to become the only "world-religion." He readily acknowledged that the "ethnic Faiths" were not "mere curiosities or moral monstrosities." Indeed, he allowed, the more the leading religions are studied, the "more beauty, truth and good are discovered in them." But sooner or later Christianity would overwhelm the ethnic religions by the "very law of its being."[11]

Barrows offered several reasons for Christianity's inevitable triumph. For one thing, "all the truths of other religions are found in Christ's Gospel," but in Christianity they are found in "completer and purer form." Further, Christianity met universal spiritual needs. "We can hardly think of a Western Buddha," he judged, yet we discover nothing "local or provincial" in Jesus Christ. But most importantly, Christianity constitutes the very

11. John Henry Barrows, *Christianity, the World-Religion* (Madras: Christian Literature Society for India, 1897), 157, 12, 14. For my general understanding of Barrows I am indebted to Richard Seager, "John Henry Barrows, 1847–1902: The Genteel Worldview of an American Evangelical," seminar paper, Harvard Univ., 1985. Despite Seager's title, I would argue that Barrows was very much a mainstream liberal.

soul of Western civilization: "The power which belongs to Christendom . . . is chiefly due to Christianity. . . . A wise man must look at the trend of events, must watch the gulf stream of history, and note that to-day it is Christianity only which is cosmopolitan." And why? Because non-Christian civilizations were culturally impotent. "Oriental speculation," Barrows crowed, has "scarcely made a ripple on the deep surface of our Western life. . . . The best which the non-Christian faiths [can muster] appear pitifully meagre." A thousand pages of liberal (and, for that matter, evangelical) perceptions of the non-Western world came together in Barrows's timeless one-liner: "Civilization [is] the secular name for Christianity."[12]

Cheerleaders like Barrows were soon eclipsed by more thoughtful spokesmen. William Newton Clarke, a Baptist theologian at Colgate Seminary, ably represented the second stage of liberal thinking. As noted, that phase, which emphasized the breadth of God's saving revelation, might be called the fulfillment model of missions. Clarke's principal contribution to the discussion was *A Study of Christian Missions*, first published in 1900. Clarke, like Barrows, admitted that other religions led their adherents to a genuine albeit partial knowledge of God. And Clarke, also like Barrows, admitted that Christianity was rightfully destined to displace other faiths. But there the similarity ended, for the tone of Clarke's work revealed deeper appreciation for God's general revelation in history and nature, a richer sense of the saving (versus the "civilizing") power of the gospel, and a more sober awareness of the difficulties ahead.

Drawing upon Paul's address to the Athenians, Clarke argued that God had not left himself without a witness among any people, that God had "appointed the seasons and bounds of their habitation," and that God therefore was "not far from any one, since 'in him we live, and move, and have our being.'" Moreover, John's Gospel made clear that Christ was the "'true light that lighteth every man.'" Thus "God has never forsaken any part of his providence." Even so, Clarke declared, "the religion of Jesus Christ is a missionary religion." Only Christianity offers personal knowledge of a holy and loving God, and

12. Barrows, *Christianity*, 110, 97, 21-23, 151, 171, 25.

only Christianity offers a deliverance from sin that is grounded in the very "heart and character of God."[13]

In the present context Clarke is significant primarily because he was acutely aware that all major religions had entwined themselves in the root systems of their respective cultures. Missionaries, he warned, must first understand the "spirit of the religion" they hoped to displace. "How shall we defend ourselves from the charge of impertinence and trifling with sacred things," he demanded, if we "try to win men away from an ancient religion, without an honest endeavor to understand that religion as it really is?" When we recognize that the "established condition of life in China is the result . . . of twenty thousand years of continuous resident life in that country," he admitted, we shall see that "it is a far greater undertaking than our fathers thought to overthrow so ancient an order."[14]

As noted, the difference between Barrows and Clarke was principally one of tone and coloration. The difference between both of them and the third stage in the development of liberal thinking was substantive as well. That third position, which one might call the collaborative model, was best expressed by Daniel Johnson Fleming, professor of missions at Union Seminary in New York from 1918 until 1944. Author of more than thirty books and scores of articles, Fleming was the most prolific, influential, and creative liberal theorist of missions between the world wars.[15]

Fleming took it for granted that missions were intrinsic to Christianity. "More clearly now than at any previous time," he wrote in 1925 in a volume portentously titled *Whither Bound in Missions?*, is it realized that "the world's welfare demands that Jesus Christ and His way be made known to every people." The Great Commission, taken by itself, was not the problem. The problem, rather, was that Christians had treated other cultures as if their only reason for existing was to receive Christian mis-

13. William Newton Clarke, *A Study of Christian Missions* (New York: Charles Scribner's Sons, 1910), 99-101, 1, 11, 13.

14. Ibid., 110-11, 183-86.

15. Fleming's work is ably assessed in Lydia Huffman Hoyle, "Making Missions Ethical: Daniel Johnson Fleming and the Re-thinking of the Missionary Enterprise" (M.A. thesis, Univ. of North Carolina at Chapel Hill, 1987).

sions. A more profound theology would start by recognizing the essential equality of all peoples. "No part of mankind has a monopoly of His gifts"; everywhere there are "lovers of truth and goodness." A more profound theology also would start by recognizing that the old Christian/heathen dichotomy was indefensible, for no society was wholly Christianized, and none was wholly devoid of Christ's transforming love.[16]

How then should Christians treat the religions of other lands? Fleming offered two basic principles. The first was sharing and listening: Christians sharing what they knew of God's love in Christ and, in turn, listening to what others knew of God's redeeming work. Fleming never doubted that Christianity, among all the religions of the world, best met the "deepest needs of the spirit," but he also believed that missions should serve as contact points through which Christians should seek not only to change others but also to be criticized and transformed by the spiritual insights of non-Christians. That did not mean that all religions were equally valuable or equally true. Each had to prove its worth empirically, just as any scientific theory or social system worth its salt had to prove itself in the modern world. But Fleming thought that it was the height of effrontery that Christians presumed always to teach, yet never to be taught; presumed always to give, yet never to acknowledge that other religions also had something to bring to the "common store."[17]

Fleming's first principle led directly to the second: taking the Golden Rule with radical seriousness. He insisted that the latter obliged Christians to ask how they would respond if the tables were turned. How would American Christians react "If Buddhists Came to Our Town"—as one of his most influential articles was called—and sought to become public school teachers in order to convert our children? How would we regard such missionaries if they failed to acknowledge that there was a big difference between Buddhism in theory and Buddhism in practice? What would we say if they exaggerated the depravity of their hearers and inflated the results of their work when they re-

16. Daniel Johnson Fleming, *Whither Bound in Missions?* (New York: Association, 1925), vii, 86.
17. Ibid., 42, 116.

turned home? Or tried to keep pupils from thinking for themselves? Or prohibited them from reading the Bible or other classics of Christian culture? Assuredly "God intends us to share in
His great purpose of developing a world-wide society of Christ-
like personalities," Fleming concluded (in another work). Nonetheless, we must squarely face the fact that others "have the
same right to their opinion as we have to ours, and that one must
not forcibly overrule another's habit of thought, principle of
living, or ways of doing things."[18]

If professional missiologists could ask such searching questions, it is not surprising that other thoughtful Protestants, who
were not vocationally committed to foreign missions, would press
toward the logical conclusion. That brings us to the fourth and
final stage of liberal thinking about missions, the pluralist. William Ernest Hocking, professor of philosophy at Harvard and an
earnest Congregational layman, stands out as the most notable
representative of that outlook. Hocking's views were expressed
in numerous works, but the best known was *Re-Thinking Missions:
A Laymen's Inquiry after One Hundred Years*, a collaborative study
published in 1932. The ferocity of the debate that that volume provoked has obscured the fact that Hocking did not (at that time)
question the fundamental legitimacy of foreign missions. "At the
center," he wrote, "is an always valid impulse of love to men: one
offers one's own faith simply because that is the best one has to
offer. . . . Mission in some form is a matter not of choice but of obligation. . . ." Nor did he doubt that Christianity must, in the final
analysis, refer "its conception of God, of man, and of religion to
the teachings and life of Jesus." What Hocking did doubt was that
Christianity was either destined or entitled to displace the other
highly developed religions of the world.[19]

To begin with, Hocking pointed out, the missionaries' view
of other religions was filtered through their vocational self-in-
terest. "Since the value of one's work is proportionate to the
need of the people, the missionary [tends] to exaggerate the need

18. Daniel Johnson Fleming, "If Buddhists Came to Our Town," *Christian
Century*, 28 February 1929, 293-94; Fleming, *Whither Bound*, 196-97.
19. William Ernest Hocking et al., *Re-Thinking Missions: A Laymen's Inquiry
after One Hundred Years* (New York: Harper and Brothers, 1932), 4, 6, 55.

... by minimizing the worth of the religions there prevalent." The typical missionary, moreover, failed to see that modern communications and technology were rapidly creating a unitary world civilization in which the real enemies were not rival faiths, but the absence of any faith. Increasingly, he wrote, the Christian argument is "less with Islam or Hinduism or Buddhism than with materialism, secularism, naturalism.... What becomes of the ... merits of one sacred text and another when the sacredness of all texts is being denied?"[20]

Since the real threat was not so much false religion as no religion at all, Hocking urged the modern mission "first of all to know and understand the religions around it, then to recognize and associate itself with whatever kindred elements there are in them," for the "life that begins with an amputation can seldom reach full vigor." That meant, for one thing, that the missionary's task was to help men and women of all religions to come to a "truer interpretation" of their own faith, seeking always to preserve the "deep-running spiritual life" of other cultures. But Hocking insisted that the missionary's next task was "something far more difficult": namely, to seek, through dialogue with non-Christians, a deepened "grasp of what Christianity actually means." Sharing becomes real, he insisted, "only as it becomes mutual, running in both directions, each teaching, each learning ... each stimulating the other in growth toward the ultimate goal, unity in the completest religious truth." In *Living Religions and a World Faith* (1940) and *The Coming World Civilization* (1958), Hocking moved further, advocating a "reconceptualization" of Christianity that would lead to a new universal religion more suitable to the needs of the dawning era. But in 1932 he was still content to say that "ministry to the secular needs of men in the spirit of Christ *is evangelism*."[21]

Looking back in 1962, Sydney Ahlstrom judged that Hocking's *Re-Thinking Missions* marked the culmination of the liberal attempt to forge a distinctive philosophy of world missions. There was an obvious sense in which Ahlstrom was correct, for

20. Ibid., 16, 29, 32.
21. Ibid., 33 (emphasis in original), 30, 37, 38, 45 (second part emphasized in original), 46, 44, 68.

it is difficult to imagine how anyone could have expressed more admiration for the integrity of other religions or more solicitude for their survival without giving up one's own identity as a Christian. But Ahlstrom was correct in another respect as well. The 1930s marked a watershed in the history of liberal influence upon foreign missions boards in the mainstream denominations. Only a handful of theologically radical missions theorists, such as Archibald G. Baker at the University of Chicago Divinity School, and disillusioned missionaries themselves, such as Pearl Buck, endorsed Hocking's ideas.[22]

Through the 1930s, in short, the majority of liberal Protestants who wrote about missions seem to have conceived them largely in terms of the conquest, fulfillment, or collaboration models described above. The conquest model flourished in the sunlit years of the 1890s within the major denominational missions boards, as well as among actual missionaries on the field, but soon gave way to the fulfillment model, which predominated until after World War I. In the inter-war years, the collaborative model moved to the forefront. By World War II the pluralist position may well have been garnering the most publicity, especially in the secular press, but its impact upon the boards and upon real-life missionaries seems to have been minimal.

Having said all that, a number of qualifications are needed. For one thing, some otherwise conservative Protestant theorists, such as William O. Carver, professor of missions at Southern Baptist Seminary, and J. P. Widney, the one-time Nazarene president of the University of Southern California, articulated views about missions that sounded more like William Newton Clarke or even Daniel Johnson Fleming than like Hudson Taylor. At the other end of the spectrum were radical thinkers who felt little or no discomfort with the prospect of wholesale religious syncretism. Methodist Bishop Francis McConnell fell into that cate-

22. Sydney E. Ahlstrom, *The American Protestant Encounter with World Religions* (Beloit, WI: Beloit College, 1962), no pagination. Buck, "Mission Report," 1434-37. Archibald Baker, "Reaction to the Laymen's Report," *Journal of Religion* 13 (October 1933): 379-98, esp. p. 380. Hocking's later, more radical works apparently exerted little or no influence at all. See, e.g., Henry P. Van Dusen, *World Christianity: Yesterday, Today, Tomorrow* (New York: Abingdon-Cokesbury, 1947), 197.

gory, as did many Friends and the Unitarian and the Universalist denominations as a whole.[23]

Another qualification that is needed is that many writers either changed their views after exposure to another culture (usually evangelicals becoming more liberal)[24] or found themselves hopelessly ambivalent about the whole issue. The latter tendency was exemplified in the work of Charles Augustus Briggs, a leading Old Testament scholar at Union Seminary in New York at the turn of the century. A strong advocate of what was then called a comparative-religions approach to the Bible, Briggs insisted that one could not properly understand Scripture unless it was placed in the context of other Near Eastern religions. Even so, he seems never to have doubted that when compared, the Judeo-Christian tradition would prove incomparable. "Comparative religion," he boasted, "eliminates one religion after another as we rise in the scale of religions until at last Christianity is seen grandly towering above all in its heavenly uniqueness." Briggs seems to have been uncertain about the proper aim of missions as well. On one hand he insisted that non-Christians ultimately would be judged not by their knowledge of the gospel, much less by the adequacy of their grasp of Christian doctrine, but by the quality of their lives. In virtually the same breath, however, he excoriated the church for "wasting her energies . . . in interdenominational strife, when it should economize them . . . for the conversion of the world," which he clearly understood largely in doctrinal terms.[25]

After World War II, in any event, liberals who wrote about missions largely moved in one of two directions. Either they

23. William Owen Carver, *Out of His Treasure: Unfinished Memoirs* (Nashville: Broadman, 1956), 75-76, 80. Joseph Widney, *Race Life and Race Religions: Modern Light on Their Growth, Their Shaping and Their Future* (Los Angeles: Pacific, 1936), chap. 11. Francis McConnell in *World Fellowship,* 9, 535. For Friends see Hutchison, "Modernism and Missions," 130; for Unitarians and Universalists see Williams, "Liberals in New England," esp. p. 88.

24. Majorie Jane Harris, "Educating Missionaries to China: The Effects of the SVM's Missions Education Program upon Missionaries' Perceptions of Chinese Religions" (M.A. thesis, Univ. of North Carolina at Chapel Hill, 1988), chap. 3.

25. Charles Augustus Briggs, "The Scope of Theology and Its Place in the University," *American Journal of Theology* 1 (1897): 59, 65, 70.

abandoned the idea entirely, or they adopted an ameliorative social-service outlook similar to Hocking's. Thoughtful progressives like Edmund Davison Soper at Garrett Seminary and
Charles Forman at Yale Divinity School moved to the forefront.
Striking a moderate posture—which might be described as a
mixture of evangelical fervor, neo-orthodox biblicism, and social
science realism—they effectively captured the leadership of the
mainline mission boards. But on the surface, at least, it was all for
nought. By the 1980s the missionary enterprise had become so
dominated by ultraconservative evangelical groups like the Assemblies of God and the Seventh-Day Adventists that the very
idea of moderate, not to mention old-fashioned liberal, foreign
missions seemed a bit anachronistic, almost like a musty sepia
photograph of someone's Victorian grandmother. Even so, one
could argue that broad public support for humanitarian programs such as the Marshall Plan, the Peace Corps, and world
famine relief marked not the demise but the consummation of
the liberal search for a mandate that would respond to the deepest impulses of Christian faith while respecting the integrity of
other cultures. There is considerable truth, in other words, in the
bromide that old soldiers— or in this case, old theologies—never
die. Sometimes they do not even fade away, at least for long.[26]

Let us return finally to our paradigmatic liberal, Clarence
Bunsen. Given that foreign missions have become virtually the
exclusive preserve of evangelicals in the latter part of the twentieth century, it is good for evangelicals to ask what they might
learn from the Clarence Bunsens of the world who once dominated the missionary boards of the mainstream denominations
and produced a learned as well as extensive missiological literature. Why should evangelicals care? My answer is that liberals,

26. I have briefly surveyed the shifting configuration of liberal, moderate,
and conservative Protestant missions thought after World War II in "A Plural
World: The Protestant Awakening to World Religions," in *The Protestant Establishment in the Earlier Twentieth Century,* ed. William R. Hutchison (New York:
Cambridge Univ. Press, 1989 [forthcoming]). For the all-but-complete demise
and at least partial eclipse of moderate, American Protestant foreign missions
endeavors in recent years see Hutchison, *Errand to the World,* 176-77, 193; Richard N. Ostling, "The New Missionary," *Time,* 27 December 1982, 50-56; and
idem, *"Protestantism's Foreign Legion," Time,* 16 February 1987, 62.

whatever their shortcomings, squarely faced the two most searching challenges that modern secular culture persistently raises against the missionary movement.

The first challenge is essentially theological. Given the endless variety of ways that human beings have experienced the holy, how, or on what grounds, can anyone—including any evangelical—assert that his or her experience of the holy is normative for other people? Or, to turn the question slightly, given the endless variety of ways that human beings have understood and symbolically rendered their conceptions of the divine, how can anyone assert that his or her understanding is solely veracious while the understandings of others, rooted in different cultures and worldviews, are not? I am not suggesting, as many in the modern university would, that the only credible answer to those questions is a radically relativist one. But I am urging that liberals manfully (and sometimes womanfully) wrestled with the problem long before most evangelicals even recognized that it exists.

The second fundamental challenge modern secular culture raises against the missionary movement is essentially moral. Simply put, is missions a euphemism for imperialism? More critically, is missions a particularly insidious form of imperialism precisely because it is not military or economic but cultural and spiritual? Differently stated, is it possible to uproot the religious foundations of one culture and replace them with the religious foundations of another culture without inflicting irreparable damage? Again, more than a century ago liberals started to struggle seriously with those questions. Many came to the conclusion that in fact it was not possible to proclaim the superiority of one's faith without harming or even destroying the very people one sought to save. That position can be challenged, but evangelicals have not yet come close to persuading thoughtful and sympathetic—much less hostile—secular critics that liberals were altogether wrong.[27]

27. For an early yet thoughtful attack upon foreign missions as arrogant and destructive of other cultures, see Wilson D. Wallis, "Missionary Enterprise from the Point of View of an Anthropologist," *American Journal of Theology* 19 (1915): 268-74. For a recent critique by one of the most distinguished of living scholars, see John K. Fairbank, "Assignment for the '70s," *American Historical Review* 74 (1969): 861-79, esp. p. 879. But evangelicals, or at least some of them, are rapidly changing. In re-

To my mind, evangelicals also must come to terms with the third and ultimately more critical challenge, posed not so much by secular culture as by liberal Protestants themselves, implicitly if not explicitly. Until 1960 or so liberal Protestants virtually spearheaded the scholarly study of world religions in the West, and even today a good many of the leaders in that field publicly identify themselves with liberal or mainstream Protestant bodies. Evangelicals, on the other hand, have conspicuously avoided the scholarly study of world religions. To be sure, individual evangelicals have written knowledgeably about one or another non-Christian religion, but none has come close to achieving the international stature of scholars like Mircea Eliade or Wilfrid Cantwell Smith.[28]

Why is this? Some have said that evangelicals have been too activistic, too pragmatic, to undertake years of advanced study in highly selective doctoral programs that specialize in the history of religions. That explanation seems unlikely, given that evangelicals have long since proved that they could rub shoulders with the best in historical and biblical studies, publishing with the foremost university presses and holding positions of leadership in the professional organizations of those fields. Others have suggested that the problem has been more akin to the dilemma of a creationist trying to work in a university anthropology department—namely, that the very rules of the game have been such that one has been precluded from play-

---

cent years the parochialism and insensitivity of evangelical missions theory and practice have come under sharp review by evangelicals themselves. For a few of the many items that reflect the ferment see Charles J. Kraft, "Cultural Anthropology: Its Meaning for Theology," *Theology Today* 41 (1985): 390-400; Max L. Stackhouse, "Christ and Culture in the South Seas," *Christian Century*, 20 October 1982, 1052-56; and Ralph P. Covell, *Confucius, The Buddha, and Christ: A History of the Gospel in Chinese* (Maryknoll, NY: Orbis, 1986).

28. Whatever the exact connections, it is indisputable that classical Protestant liberalism provided the institutional and cultural matrix within which world religion scholarship was born and grew to maturity, both in North America and in Europe. See George F. Thomas, "The History of Religion in the Universities," *Journal of Bible and Religion* 17 (1949): 102; Joseph M. Kitagawa, "The History of Religions in America," in *The History of Religions: Essays in Methodology*, ed. Mircea Eliade and Joseph M. Kitagawa (Chicago: Univ. of Chicago Press, 1959), 1-7; and Eric J. Sharpe, *Comparative Religion: A History* (New York: Charles Scribner's Sons, 1975), 146-48, 252.

ing in the first place. Again, that seems unlikely, given that evangelicals have long since learned to compartmentalize their intellectual lives so that they are able to work within the publicly defined rules and protocols of all sorts of fields and professions in which overtly Christian premises are not admissible. My own guess is that the problem has been more personal, more "existential." Evangelicals have in fact ventured into the academic study of world religions, but they soon found that the more they learned about the functionally similar roles that all religions play in their respective settings, the less they were able to support the eradication of those religions through conversionist missionary programs. Thus they have felt impelled to distance themselves, publicly at least, from evangelical Christianity in general. Whatever the reason, it is indisputable that evangelicals have not yet proved that they are able to hold their hand against the hot flame of sustained, disciplined study of world religions—and keep their evangelical convictions.

Solomon Schecter, president of the Conservative Jewish Theological Seminary of America, implored his colleagues not to leave the scholarly study of Scripture to liberal Protestants. "This intellectual [battle] can only be fought by intellectual weapons," he warned. "A mere protest in the pulpit or a vigorous editorial in a paper . . . will not help us. We have to create a really living, great literature [ourselves]."[29] Schecter's admonition is equally applicable to the contemporary missionary establishment. When evangelicals do the kind of work in world religions that earns recognition in professional academic societies like the Association for Asian Studies, or publish articles in journals such as *Numen* or *History of Religions,* or hold endowed chairs in Islamic or Buddhist studies in the nation's leading universities, they will have earned their missiology spurs as well. Until then, and perhaps even after then, liberals like Clarke and Fleming and Hocking deserve to be heard, not simply as men who possessed a measure of wisdom for their own time, but perhaps a considerable measure for all times.

---

29. Solomon Schecter, *Seminary Addresses and Other Papers* (1915), reprinted in *A Documentary History of Religion in America: Since 1865,* ed. Edwin S. Gaustad (Grand Rapids: Eerdmans, 1983), 408.

13 *Mission and the Modern Imperative— Retrospect and Prospect: Charting a Course*

Lamin Sanneh

In a stimulating essay, Patsy Palmer, a doctoral student at the Harvard Divinity School, remarked on how religious leaders in the late nineteenth century exploited millenarian expectations for the purposes of mission and evangelization and in doing so attempted to set about their task in what veteran missionaries in China and elsewhere characterized as an "around-the-world-in-eighty-days spirit."[1] A similar stir appears to be in the air today, although we seem less excitable than our nineteenth-century predecessors, for whom two major wars and the Holocaust in one century were scarcely imaginable.

One of the most urgent tasks, therefore, that confronts us as scholars is the rehabilitation of the study of mission. Much of our past endeavors has consigned mission to a subcategory of colonial history. Mission acquired the status of Western religious mischief in the wider context of European and American imperialism. Students of these subjects have tended to criticize or defend mission, but in either case to expand it as an extension of white domination abroad. The historical convergence of mission and colonialism, for example, is assumed to express an ideological connection, particularly since both mission and colonialism had a common European origin. Furthermore,

---

1. Patsy J. Palmer, "'Under the Illumined Dome': Arthur T. Pierson and Late 19th Century Missionary Imagery of the 20th Century," unpublished paper, New World Colloquium, the Divinity School, Harvard Univ., 17 October 1984.

given the fact that nationalist rhetoric articulated fully the short-comings of missionaries as linked in the chain of oppression that needs to be broken, students of missiology conceded the ground before they had properly explored it. Much atoning ink was spilled to assuage the alleged wrongs of mission, with schemes of restitutionary donation suggested as suitable settlement.

All these actions played straight into the hands of those committed to the view that one cannot take religion seriously. Positing it as always a camouflage for gain and power, they set about to unmask missionaries as the historical relics of an out-moded worldview. Thus missionaries were pinioned like rare specimens in a reductionist frame of reference, where they be-came easy targets for nationalist criticism.

One result of this approach was to emphasize the Western, ideological dimension of the missionary movement and to suppress evidence drawn from field experience, or at any rate to make it of secondary interest. In the atmosphere of post–World War II reconstruction, scholars were determined not to miss the chance to join in the secular celebration of the passing of the religious age. What people saw as the discrediting of Christian missions was seized as proof that the forces of post-modernity were spreading throughout the world. Third World reaction against Christianity, it was felt, was the pre-industrial version of the rationalism that had at long last attained its final stage in the West. In the effort to dismiss every type of Western Christian mission, scholars overlooked the possibility that in-digenous criticism of mission might have occurred for reasons that accord well with the religious claims of missionaries. It be-came popular to put down mission, although, like the prickly pear, it was impossible to escape its negative stigma. Thus the academic study of missions suffered a triple setback, with criti-cal scholars and aggrieved patriots combining to point to the al-leged Western source of missionary wrongheadedness rather than to bring the debate to the ground in Africa and elsewhere.

Many serious scholars—C. P. Groves, Kenneth Scott La-tourette, and Stephen Neill, to name only a few—have, I think, embarked on their enterprise without a rigorous assessment of the operative assumptions of Western scholarship. By failing to examine these assumptions in the fresh setting of missions' field experience, these eminent scholars have implicitly or explicitly conceded the force of the attack on mission either by choosing to analyze the missionary effort and its organization and direction from the West or by assessing missionary impact on the field in terms of statistical gains. Either way, we gain little understanding of the world the missionaries explored in such rich and meticulous detail.

Students of anthropology, political science, and history, for their part, were able to exploit from the center what missionary chroniclers left exposed on the flanks. Mission was depicted as the local scale of the worldwide imperialist agenda, penetrating indigenous cultures to prepare a class of collaborators necessary for cutting through local resistance. Conversion, in this view, was in fact merely a shorthand for collaboration. That is one of the reasons why Christianity outside the West has been treated on the distaff side as the illegitimate offspring of a forced union.

A corollary to this adverse view of mission is the directing of attention to the motives of mission, a subject that is highly amenable to ideological manipulation or at least to making mission an epiphenomenon of prevailing ideas and currents of fashion. Modern historiography, deeply influenced by Darwinian or Marxist categories of analysis, has become extremely wary of using motives as a driving force of historical movements. In much of the sophisticated work on Christian missions, however, we have what amounts to variations on the theme of motives.

Seldom do these studies address the fact that the acts accomplished by missions left an indelible mark on the societies affected. Western jurisprudence, of course, has made motives a crucial part of our heritage. Whether, for example, unlawfully taking another human life is considered first-degree murder, and thus without much hope of parole, or the much less serious crime of manslaughter, depends on whether or not motives or premeditation can be established. Yet in either case it does not really affect the fundamental point that a killing has occurred and that the lives of the victim's relatives and others have been unalterably affected. By analogy, whatever their intentions or motives, when missionaries executed their projects, they let loose forces that set the relevant societies on a new, unalterable course. Despite this growing rejection of motives as a category of historical analysis and interpretation, we have continued to use them as a vestigial hangover in the historical exposition of Christian missions. On such religious terrain, historians have been much less inhibited in assessing motivation than when they are dealing with political, economic, or military history.

Now I should be the last to deny the importance of motivation in the religious life and would, indeed, argue for a place for it in all of intellectual and cultural history. Yet we need not take account of motives only as a pernicious historical fifth column but also as a criterion of accountability. Missionaries who took their religious mandate seriously, for example, felt compelled to declare their hand and to be faithful recorders of what they saw and heard. They felt duty-bound to admit where the evidence warranted it that they had misunderstood or failed to appreciate the significance of what they saw and heard or thought they saw and heard. Understanding the rites of baptism, ordination, and commissioning that marked them out for service in the field, many missionaries felt compelled, under oath and before God, to note down as faithfully as they could certain customs and usages in the field and who participated in them, even when they were opposed to such customs. Consequently, they left records of many customs and practices that would otherwise have been without evidence or with only incomplete documentation. When we combine this scrupulous honesty, which is such a critical factor in rules of historical evidence, with the willingness of missionaries to admit failure and confess their shortcomings, then we have a unique example of motives as self-scrutiny and a force to generate action. The advantage of proceeding in this fashion is that it allows us to keep theory and practice together and to appraise rhetoric in light of field investigations. It should become an accepted part of the methodology that scholarly works on mission should make fieldwork indispensable.

Even with present limitations, many scholars feel peculiarly unsatisfied with the continued deprecation of the missionary enterprise, for, when they look closely at the facts, there seem to be glaring discrepancies between interpretation and evidence. On the most superficial level such scholars find instances of genuine missionary alignment with local people, or at any rate evidence of serious rift and conflict with the colonial authorities who should have been their natural allies. Further, it is an incontestable fact that most of the nationalist leaders were educated in mission schools, and, although we may understand their attitudes if a small proportion of such leaders was mission-educated but non-Christian, in fact a much larger proportion was affected in this way. It is scarcely adequate to contend that mission had failed with these leaders in order to explain why they rejected the religion of their educators. Scholars groping for answers looked to such obvious exceptions as inconsistencies in the framework within which they were accustomed to viewing the subject.

Yet such exceptions never really added to a real methodological breakthrough, for they still leave mission as a languished subject in the occasional lapses from colonial oppression. It is my contention that, when viewed correctly, the practice of mission was based on a fundamentally divergent notion in relation to the assumptions of colonialism, and until we bite that bullet, we shall not see truly the magnitude of the promise that awaits us.

It is a general fact that mission at its most authentic was distinguished by the development and promotion of the vernacular languages. Behind the efforts to produce the Scriptures in the vernacular lie the enormous tasks of ethnographic survey and field investigation; linguistic development and documentation; the gathering of resources calculated to enhance the exalted goal of translation; the establishment of grammars, primers, and dictionaries; and investment in vernacular literacy in areas where no such thing had ever existed. Rather than look to the spread of the universal values of the colonial empire, mission instead committed itself to the development of vernacular cultures, a commitment that had far-reaching effects throughout the indigenous world.

The vernacular role of mission remains an enduring legacy of the whole enterprise. But in this area, too, our academic habits of analysis and interpretation have lagged far behind missionary accomplishment. For example, we have on the one hand continued to charge that, since missionaries went out to make converts, they did so by alienating converts from their roots and thus are guilty of cultural imperialism. Yet, on the other hand, we have castigated missionaries for encouraging the vernacular and thus preventing converts from acquiring fluency in the language of the colonial administration. Such a contradictory indictment cannot totally carry the case we wish to bring against missions, and the only reasonable course is to abandon it. Many scholars are reluctant to take that step since it removes from their hands the standard weapons they have learned to deploy with much effect. All of which goes to suggest that in the writing of the history of missions, scholars are also writing about themselves, and their interests have become bound up with the effective discrediting of the subject.

It is either that kind of intertwining of interests or a similar bifocal predisposition that has enabled scholars to walk through, for instance, the vernacular gains of mission without an effect on their approach. When the vernacular issue has been identified, it has been denigrated, with critics alleging that in actual fact missionaries despised mother tongues as inferior "dialects." Yet if we as scholars had not dismissed the religious foundations of mission, we might have seen that its denigration would not be consistent with its adoption as the vehicle of the divine revelation. After all, the enterprise of mission depended on creating in local communities a sense of participation in God's salvific work, and to despise the vernacular as the unique bearer of the language of that work is like cutting off your nose to spite your face.

Indeed, the evidence suggests that once missionaries successfully engaged the vernacular, they became correspondingly dubious about the value of "civilization" in the economy of God. There is a subsidiary point, namely, that missionary doubts about "civilization" left them increasingly critical of the effects of Western contact on indigenous populations. Let me, however, return to the issue of mission and "civilization." Whatever their initial confidence, there is little doubt that missionaries became disenchanted with the gathering speed of colonial conquest. Writing to those European Christians who might be tempted to perceive colonialism as serving a providential purpose, J. Lewis Krapf penned what may be considered a manifesto against the doctrine that mission would succeed as indigenous societies lapsed under colonial control:

Expect nothing, or very little from political changes in Eastern Africa. Do not think that because East Africans are "profitable in nothing to God and the world" they ought to be brought under the domination of some European power, in the hope that they may bestir themselves more actively and eagerly for what is worldly and, in consequence, become eventually more awake to what is spiritual and eternal. On the contrary, banish the thought that Europe must spread her protecting wings over Eastern Africa, if missionary work is to prosper in that land. . . . Europe would, no doubt, remove much that is mischievous and obstructive out of the way of missionary work, but she would probably set in its way as many and, perhaps, still greater checks.[2]

Such suspicion of the value of any possible collaboration between mission and colonialism stems in large measure from the vernacular destiny of mission, a point that a missionary statesman like Henry Venn (d. 1873) erected into the principle of the missionary enterprise as such.[3] It led numerous missionaries to become unrelentingly critical of colonial rule, and none was more forthright in this matter than Dr. Walter Miller, the pioneer CMS missionary in North Nigeria. Miller started out as a fervent believer in the virtues of British civilization and no doubt would have remained a child of his age had he not also ventured out into missionary work. He arrived in North Nigeria slightly ahead of the advancing British forces who eventually defeated the local armies and took control. Miller at first encouraged this process but later changed his tune radically as his mastery of the Hausa language and his knowledge and love for the people increased. He became a perpetual thorn in the flesh of the British authorities, playing an active role in moves to establish the first political organization in North Nigeria to press for claims against the British and then helping to mobilize popular opinion against the continued presence of the British. A leading Nigerian historian says that as

2. J. Lewis Krapf, *Travels, Researches and Missionary Labors* (London: Trubner, 1860), 512.
3. See Wilbert R. Shenk, *Henry Venn, Missionary Statesman* (New York: Orbis, 1983); and Max Warren, ed., *To Apply the Gospel: A Selection of the Writings of Henry Venn* (Grand Rapids: Eerdmans, 1971).

an uncompromising, highly opinionated believer in the virtues of British civilization, including the equality of men and women and compulsory universal education for Northern Nigerians in the first decade of British occupation of Northern Nigeria, Miller became so identified with the Hausa that by 1910 he had decided that whenever he died it must be in Hausaland. He had great love and sympathy for the Hausa. . . . Miller should be remembered as the first man, European or Nigerian, to conceive the idea of independence for the Hausa. . . .[4]

In the prelude to political independence, Miller wrote a highly incendiary political tract, giving it the explosive title *Have We Failed in Nigeria?* It was an unflattering inventory of British misrule and was appropriately seized on by Muslim political leaders, who saw in Miller an ally of unusual credentials and insight. He gave the Muslim leaders credibility, a sense of pride in themselves, a logic for repudiating colonialism, and the psychological advantage of doing so with the work of a missionary who was also an Englishman.[5]

One last example on this colonial theme must suffice. A missionary contemporary of Miller was the German Adam Mischlisch, who had served with the Basel Mission in Togoland and adjoining areas. When the Germans took over Togo in 1894, Mischlisch was invited to serve as colonial administrator. Just at that time his mission station had been attacked and burned down by liquor merchants in retaliation for the missionary's public strictures against alcohol. Mischlisch quickly established a working relationship with a leading Muslim scholar, and in his new capacity as the German administrator he prevailed upon the scholar to write down the history, culture, and handicrafts of Hausa society before all of that was unalterably changed by European rule. Mischlisch made this a matter of urgent importance, and my theory is that his habits as a missionary made him reserve a special place for the vernacular in the dramatic setting of colonial overlordship. He

4. Emmanuel A. Ayandele, "The Missionary Factor in Northern Nigeria: 1870–1918," *Journal of the Historical Society of Nigeria* 3 (December 1966): 503-22, 512.

5. See John Paden, *Religion and Political Culture in Kano* (Berkeley and Los Angeles: Univ. of California Press, 1973), 285-87.

was knowledgeable in several African languages, including Hausa and Twi.[6]

While we may see Mischlisch as confirmation of the close ties between mission and colonialism, we should notice the manner in which he set about his role. He appealed to indigenous sources and ethnographic materials as the basis on which Europeans should learn to encounter their subject races rather than assuming that the colonial agenda was either necessary or sufficient in itself. At the least this indicates a profound tension between the methods of mission and the goals of colonialism. Several other examples can be cited, but we must leave the subject there.

A subsidiary question that is worth examination is where mission stood in relation to "civilization." Dr. David Livingstone, the foremost missionary of his era, is credited with formulating "civilization" as a component of the modern missionary agenda. Livingstone had written that civilization, commerce, and Christianity, the three Cs, must go hand in hand if any one of them was to succeed. Others voiced colorful variations on this theme, such as Thomas Fowell Buxton's idea that "the Bible and the plough" were destined to make a successful combination, or the notion developed by African Christian leaders in Nigeria that Christian evangelists must take with them the gospel of cocoa, coffee, and cotton. Historians have used such pronouncements as conclusive proof that the religious strand was secondary to the secular motive. In fact, they have viewed the missionary formulation as nothing more than a trick of the trade. Even if we were to assume that missionaries came out with a firm belief in the inevitability of social Darwinism, it would still be the case that on the field, and in light of vernacular forces released by missionary translation, a completely different scenario overtook them. Those who, in spite of field experience, remained wedded to imported theories found themselves rapidly pushed to the peripheries as local populations

---

6. I owe these points to a short essay by D. J. E. Maier, "The Changing Political Views of al-Hajj 'Umar of Kete-Krachi," unpublished paper, Department of History, Univ. of Northern Iowa. See also idem, *Priests and Power: The Case of the Dente Shrine in Nineteenth-Century Ghana* (Bloomington: Indiana Univ. Press, 1983); and Edward Hulmes, "Walter Miller and the *Isawa*: An Experiment in Christian-Muslim Relationship," *Scottish Journal of Theology* 41 (1988): 233-46.

embarked on the creative adaptation of Christianity to local conditions, seeking ways in which their faith could be in tune with ideas and attitudes that the vernacular Scriptures already legitimated. A surprisingly large number of missionaries saw this vernacular logic in the system, became distrustful of Europe's "civilizing" mandate, and cast their lot with the indigenous people.

Livingstone, for example, became quickly aware that "civilization," however defined, was a problematic issue for the gospel, the Western representation of it being particularly worrisome for mission. His field labors led him to develop a highly critical stance toward not only the West but the very roots of the Western church itself. He urged us to see that

> The popular notion, however, of the primitive church is perhaps not very accurate. Those societies especially which consisted of Gentiles . . . were certainly anything but pure. In spite of their conversion, some of them carried the stains and vestiges of their former state with them when they passed from the temple to the church. If the instructed and civilized Greek did not all at once rise out of his former self, and understand and realize the high ideal of his new faith, we should be careful, in judging of the work of missionaries among savage tribes, not to apply to their converts tests and standards of too great severity. If the scoffing Lucian's account of the imposter Peregrinus may be believed, we find a church probably planted by the Apostles manifesting less intelligence even than modern missionary churches.[7]

It is clear from this passage that Livingstone considered Greek achievements of no greater, or worse, advantage in the scales of the kingdom than the fortunes of simple societies. Indeed, he appears to be less complacent about the effects of Western contact on the transmission and reception of the message, looking with concern on what mission schools might do in infiltrating native originality with foreign elements. Livingstone develops his position most cogently when considering the matter of vernacular translation. In one place he writes frankly about this. "It is fortunate," he pleads,

7. David Livingstone, *Missionary Travels and Researches in South Africa* (London: J. Murray, 1857), note 107.

that the translation of the Bible has been effected before the language became adulterated with half-uttered foreign words, and while those who have heard the eloquence of the native assemblies are still living; for the young, who are brought up in our schools, know less of the language than the missionaries; and Europeans born in the country, while possessed of the idiom perfectly, if not otherwise educated, cannot be referred to for explanation of any uncommon word.[8]

In another passage Livingstone reflected seriously on the nature of language as an attribute of humanity, convinced that no one language is inherently superior or inferior to another even when we are comparing the language of a complex civilization with that of a simple people. Commenting on the Sichuana language that he studied, he said,

The language is however so simple in its construction, that its copiousness by no means requires the explanation that the people may have fallen from a former state of civilization and culture. Language seems to be an attribute of the human mind and thought, and the inflections, various as they are in the most barbarious tongues, as that of the Bushmen, are probably only proofs of the race being human, and endowed with the power of thinking; the fuller development of language taking place as the improvement of our other faculties goes on.[9]

Livingstone was, of course, a very complex figure, playing many roles at once. Yet his perceptive and lucid account of the significance of the vernacular Bible remains one of the most enduring tributes to his achievement. He saw in strikingly vivid terms how the vernacular Bible would act as the engine of the Christian movement, driving the momentum of Christian transmission from the West toward an inevitable indigenous destiny. He identified this vernacular factor as the common feature of the missionary enterprise, one that characterized all the major missions in spite of their different theological differences. He observed that

8. Ibid., 114.
9. Ibid.

> Protestant missionaries of every denomination in South Africa all
> agree on one point, that no mere profession of Christianity is suffi-
> cient to entitle the converts to the Christian name. They are all
> anxious to place the Bible in the hands of the natives, and with abil-
> ity to read that, there can be little doubt as to the nature.[10]

We could argue that Protestant missions on the whole were
unrealistically optimistic about the virtues of the vernacular
Bible, that this led them to embark on hastily conceived and
poorly executed translations, that they rejected the indigenous
implications of the vernacular Bible, and that local converts
often ignored the import of vernacularization by wishing to
emulate the Western church. However, all these points do not
affect the issue of the translatability of Christianity and missionary agency in that process. After all, the Western church itself is
the embodiment of Christianity's translatability, and mission is
the application of it in other cultures.

I have so far dealt with two issues: the question of the relationship between mission and colonialism and that of the
cultural presuppositions of the missionary enterprise. I now
wish to move the discussion forward to the impact of mission
on contemporary academic disciplines. We are all familiar
with the critical position modern anthropology has taken
toward mission. Yet anthropology itself would have been in-
conceivable without the missionary enterprise. The seminal
work of Sir Edward Evans-Pritchard, for example, on Nuer religion and his succinct classic *Theories of Primitive Religion*
draw profoundly on missionary materials and insight. Godfrey Lienhardt, another Oxford anthropologist, says in the introduction to his groundbreaking study, *Divinity and Experience*, that his work would have been impossible without
the field achievements of mission:

> I owe a great deal to the Verona Fathers, and especially to the mis-
> sionaries in Wau and Kwajok. Without Fr. Nebel's work on Dinka
> language and thought, my own would have been made immensely
> more difficult. I hope that the numerous references to him in this

10. Ibid., 117-18.

book will be accepted as a tribute to his authority, and to the work of the Congregation of Verona.[11]

It is equally hard to imagine anthropological gains in parts of West Africa without missionary contribution: Johannes Christaller's brilliant translation work that supplied the foundation for the work of anthropologists like Rattray; or the American missionary T. J. Bowen, who furnished solid documentary foundations for a similar enterprise in Nigeria; and so on. Furthermore, missionary interest helped to protect many ethnic societies from total extinction, or at least helped to preserve a record of such societies before they disappeared altogether. John Batchelor's work among the ancient Ainu of Hokkaido, Japan, is one example.[12] Joseph Kitagawa, the Japanese historian of religion, says, "Batchelor, who lived for over fifty years among the Hokkaido Ainus, has contributed perhaps the most factual account (even though somewhat colored by his views) and the one with the most comprehensive type of information on the subject."[13] Batchelor also provided the first detailed scientific documentation of the Ainu language. And while on Japan, it is interesting to remember that it was the Italian Jesuit Valignano who introduced movable type into Japan in 1590, employing it for religious translation work, which had an impact on the study of Japanese culture and linguistics. "The literature eventually produced by the mission press," argues historian George Elison, "included not only devotional tracts and the rather quaint intrusion of Aesop into Japan but also works of monumental importance for the study of contemporary Japanese linguistics. . . ."[14]

Furthermore, what we know today as the history of religion owes no small part of its origin to the effects of Christian mission. We only have to think of Max Muller, that extraordinary

11. Godfrey Lienhardt, *Divinity and Experience: The Religion of the Dinka* (Oxford: Clarendon, 1961), vii.

12. See John Batchelor, *The Ainu and Their Folk-Lore* (London: Religious Tract Society, 1901).

13. Joseph M. Kitagawa, "Ainu Bear Festival (Iyomante)," *History of Religions: An International Journal for Comparative Historical Studies* 1 (Summer 1961): 95-151, 140-41.

14. George Elison, *Deus Destroyed: The Image of Christianity in Early Modern Japan* (Cambridge: Harvard Univ. Press, 1973), 20.

genius and an architect of the history of religion, to recognize that there was a close historical connection.[15] And before Max Muller came the brilliant pioneering work of William Carey and his colleagues at Serampore. The serious scholarly study of the *Vedas,* including the *Rig Veda,* can be traced directly to the linguistic efforts of such early missionary pioneers. And what a harvest such efforts have yielded in India and beyond, one that deserves the scriptural recognition of "good measure, pressed down, shaken together, and running over" (Luke 6:38).

I could also mention the academic study of Islam, which is my own specialty, and mention, *inter alia,* a modern scholar like the magisterial Duncan Black MacDonald, and others such as L. Bevan Jones, Samuel Zwemer, Calverley, J. W. Sweetman, Louis Gardet, George Anawati, Kenneth Cragg, W. Montgomery Watt, J. Spencer Trimingham, Wilfred Cantwell Smith, Willem Bijlefeld, and Antonie Wessels to show the enormous contribution committed Christians have made to the exploration of the subject. The establishment of Islamic studies in the modern Western academy owes an incalculable debt to Christian missionary enterprise and interest.

Let me return to Livingstone for the last time and observe that his efforts were crucial for historical understanding of contemporary society in South Africa and that his scientific investigations were eagerly followed by the scientific community in Europe and North America. In an address before the Royal Geographical Society, for example, Lord Curzon, its president, paid tribute to Livingstone's triple contribution to mission, science, and the humanitarian cause.[16]

Equally importantly, national historiography in much of the Third World depended very much on the work of missions, including the meticulous record keeping that enabled the research enterprise to proceed on firm foundations. Scholars, of course, are inured against taking the missionary at his word, for suspicion of missionary bias has been a familiar intellectual gadfly. But at least missionaries were not biased enough to conceal their

15. See Muller's address at Westminster Abbey, published as *On Christian Missions* (New York: Scribner, Armstrong & Co., 1874).
16. *Geographical Journal* 41 (1913): 422-23.

bias, and consequently scholars can engage in critical analysis and independent evaluation based on missionary records without necessarily surrendering to missionary judgments. The research facilities that are supplied by missionary archives have provided some excellent conditions for sound scholarship, providing a standard for emulation in other branches of study.

The connection between mission and colonialism and between mission and Western culture, whatever it may be, is clearly not beyond analysis and exposure by the most rigorous standards of modern scholarship. We ought at least to welcome this open-mindedness that the study of mission has helped to foster, encouraged by the diverse and at times conflicting views of missionaries themselves. There is a certain Talmudic virtue to allowing for a lively variety of opinion on matters of concern, and mission certainly has its share of liveliness on this point.

All the considerations we have so far taken up are in the final analysis peripheral to the central task of mission and to its exposition. If we agree that mission was first and last occupied with vernacular translation and its inevitable wider repercussions, then we are forced to ask what effects that had on indigenous societies, with or without missionary encouragement. This makes indigenous societies the primary focus for the missionary enterprise, suggesting that we judge missions by field performance rather than exclusively by the statistical and ideological rules of mission boards.

That is a slightly different subject and is perhaps best taken up elsewhere. Allow me briefly to indicate the scope and nature of that different task. First, the encouragement of vernacular translation actually laid the basis for cultural and linguistic pluralism, a factor of enormous consequence for the uniform and centralizing values of the empire. The missionary view of the salvific value of indigenous languages conflicted at a deep level with the assumptions of colonialism about the intrinsic inadequacy of local cultures. Second, the attention to the vernacular excited the spirit of cultural nationalism, enabling hitherto illiterate populations to develop esteem for themselves and to acquire the skills necessary to do that. Third, vernacular translation work helped to expose adjacent tribes to each other in an atmosphere of peaceful exchange outside the constraints of tribal warfare and interethnic

strife. I realize, of course, that denominational rivalry was a factor in interethnic hostility, but the force of the vernacular Scripture
was to weaken it with the call for a higher and nonmilitant accountability. Fourth, the adoption of indigenous terms for the central categories of the gospel shifted the ground from a Western
conceptualization of Christianity to a non-Western one. Notice the
paradox here of Western missionary agents becoming the instruments themselves for this radical de-Westernization of Christianity. This has implications, by the way, for how we read someone
like Ernst Troeltsch or even Arnold Toynbee.[17]

Finally, indigenous cultural vitality became a precondition
for the assimilation and renewal of Christianity, which is one of
the reasons why the modern religious map of Africa, for example, shows a striking overlap between areas of deepest
Christian impact and those of strong indigenous cultural roots.
Conversely, the spread of Christianity appears to suffer in proportion to the reduced significance of vernacular languages. To
throw in a comparative angle at this stage, precisely the opposite
seems to be the case with Islam; that is, the areas of strongest
Islamic influence are also the areas of the weakest vernacular
languages. Islam succeeds in proportion to its success in staging
a return to the *hijrah* (migration) of the Prophet, whereas Christianity triumphs by the relinquishing of Jerusalem or any fixed
universal center, be it geographical, linguistic, or cultural, with
the result that we have a proliferation of centers, languages, and
cultures within the church. Christian ecumenism is a pluralism
of the periphery, with only God as the center.

Thus it turns out that, by changing our perspective on the
history of Christian mission, we come into possession of a rich
field of inquiry. Whatever the present situation concerning the
rights and wrongs of overseas mission, I am confident that in
the study of the subject we are on the threshold of a tremendous
opportunity, and I think it is right that we should now place the
study of mission on a firm curricular basis rather than continue
to look to existing disciplines to show us where we ought to go.

17. I say "even" because on the face of it Toynbee's thinking was developing along the lines of a de-Westernized Christianity though he misidentified the
nature of Christian mission in that process.

14 *North American Evangelical Missions since 1945: A Bibliographic Survey*

Wilbert R. Shenk

"Except for histories of women in American religion," observed Leonard I. Sweet, "the history of evangelical missions has been one of the least favorite inquiries in American religious history during the last 20 years" (Leonard I. Sweet, ed., *The Evangelical Tradition in America* [Macon, GA: Mercer Univ. Press, 1984], 51). This neglect is regrettable for two reasons. First, to a degree not true of other Christian traditions, evangelical identity has been shaped by its commitment to evangelism and world mission. Second, during the period since 1945 evangelicals have come into a commanding position as a percentage of the total Protestant missionary force.

This survey covers books published since 1945 because writings by evangelicals on missions prior to that time were popularly written for promotional purposes. (The important survey by Charles W. Forman, "A History of Foreign Mission Theory in America," in *American Missions in Bicentennial Perspective*, ed. R. Pierce Beaver [South Pasadena: William Carey Library, 1977], 69-140, demonstrates that the term *evangelical* did not function as a partisan label until well into the twentieth century. The Forman study also shows that those identified with the emerging fundamentalist-evangelical movement did little theorizing about mission before 1945.) One sign of the growing maturity of the evangelical movement is the scope and growth in quality of the literature on missions produced since 1945. In this essay we will conduct a reconnaissance of the literature of the period. Within this brief compass, the goal is to be representative rather than comprehensive.

Theological

In comparison with other categories of missions literature, evangelicals have produced relatively few scholarly works on the theology of mission. In 1945 books on mission did not draw sharp distinctions between theology, missiology, and methodology. The best-known and most widely used evangelical work on missions of that period was *The Progress of Worldwide Missions* by Robert Hall Glover (Chicago: Doran, 1924; rev. ed. 1939). A revised and enlarged edition by J. Herbert Kane was published in 1960 (New York: Harper & Row). In 1946 Glover published a second book, *The Bible Basis of Missions* (Los Angeles: Bible House of Los Angeles). An important step toward differentiation was taken with the appearance in 1949 of Harold Lindsell's *A Christian Philosophy of Missions* (Wheaton: Van Kampen). Significantly, when Lindsell's book was reissued in 1970, the title was changed to *An Evangelical Theology of Missions* (Grand Rapids: Zondervan). Following in the Glover tradition, Harold R. Cook's *Introduction to the Study of Christian Missions* (Chicago: Moody, 1954) quickly became a standard text in Bible schools and colleges. J. Herbert Kane wrote *A Global View of Christian Missions: From Pentecost to the Present* (Grand Rapids: Baker, 1971). Subsequently, Kane produced *Christian Missions in Biblical Perspective* (Grand Rapids: Baker, 1976), which was widely used.

George W. Peter's *A Biblical Theology of Missions* (Chicago: Moody, 1972) was the first comprehensive presentation by an evangelical of the Christian mission following a more precise biblical-theological approach. An influential interpretation of the theological basis of the Christian mission by the British evangelical John R. W. Stott appeared in 1975: *Christian Mission and the Modern World* (Downers Grove, IL: InterVarsity). Another valuable biblical study was Richard R. DeRidder's *Discipling the Nations* (Grand Rapids: Baker, 1975). Arthur F. Glasser furnishes an overview of the period in "The Evolution of Evangelical Mission Theology since World War II," *International Bulletin of Missionary Research* 9:1 (January 1985): 9-13.

Missiological

Missiology, the scholarly study of the Christian mission, has had an uncertain status in academia since its introduction in the nineteenth century. Missiology as a discipline was not supported by a professional association until the formation of the Association of Professors of Missions in 1952. Evangelicals did not become active in professional missiology until the 1950s.

In 1955 John Caldwell Thiessen wrote a comprehensive survey of missions highlighting evangelical initiatives: *A Study of World Missions* (Chicago: InterVarsity). Harold Lindsell's *Missionary Principles and Practice* (New York: Revell, 1955) and Harold R. Cook's popular *Missionary Life and Work* (Chicago: Moody, 1959) dealt with missionary life, methods, and strategy. J. Herbert Kane added to this genre of literature with *Understanding Christian Missions* (1974) and *Life and Work on the Mission Field* (1980, both published in Grand Rapids by Baker).

Evangelicals were challenged to come to terms with the changing world in the post–World War II era. T. Stanley Soltau's *Missions at the Crossroads* (Wheaton: Van Kampen, 1954) offered an early assessment and urged a recovery of emphasis on the indigenous church. Eric S. Fife and Arthur F. Glasser, *Missions in Crisis—Rethinking Mission Strategy* (Chicago: InterVarsity, 1961) grappled with the far-reaching changes worldwide that would impinge on the Christian mission. In *Frontiers in Missionary Strategy* (Chicago: Moody, 1971), C. Peter Wagner delineated frontier issues facing evangelicals.

The Evangelical Foreign Missions Association and Interdenominational Foreign Mission Association held a major meeting in 1971 to study the tensions that had developed between missions and churches. Some Third World church leaders had proposed that a moratorium be placed on the sending of Western missionaries to other continents. Evangelicals recognized that such tensions could not be ignored and that mission agencies had to take positive steps. Vergil Gerber edited the proceed-

WILBERT R. SHENK

ings: *Missions in Creative Tension—The Greenlake '71 Compendium* (South Pasadena: William Carey Library, 1977). A Third World contribution to the discussion was the book by Pius Wakatama, *Independence for the Third World Church: An African's Perspective on Missionary Work* (Downers Grove, IL: InterVarsity, 1976).

Alan R. Tippett grappled with key theological themes of mission in *Verdict Theology in Missionary Theory*, 2d ed. (South Pasadena: William Carey Library, 1973). Four members of the faculty of the Fuller School of World Mission, Arthur F. Glasser, Paul G. Hiebert, C. Peter Wagner, and Ralph D. Winter, teamed up to write *Crucial Dimension in World Evangelization* (South Pasadena: William Cary Library, 1976). In the late 1970s, Trinity Evangelical Divinity School, Deerfield, Illinois, sponsored two consultations and published the papers in volumes edited by David J. Hesselgrave: *Theology and Mission—Papers Given at Trinity Consultation No. 1* (1978) and *New Horizons in World Missions: Consultation on Theology and Mission* (1979). Baker Book House, Grand Rapids, Michigan, published both.

A major *Festschrift* was presented to George W. Peters, longtime professor of missions at Dallas Theological Seminary, on his eightieth birthday in 1988. Edited by Hans Kasdorf and Klaus W. Muller, it was entitled *Reflection and Projection: Missiology at the Threshold of 2001* (Bad Liebenzell: Verlag der Liebenseller Mission). Each essay appears in German and English. David J. Hesselgrave emphasizes the issues on which the future course of mission will hinge in *Today's Choices for Tomorrow's Mission* (Grand Rapids: Zondervan, 1988).

Missionary Anthropology and Linguistics

The pioneering work of Eugene A. Nida, Kenneth L. Pike, and others from the early 1940s onward demonstrated the importance of the disciplines of anthropology and linguistics to missionary work. Although this development touched all Christian traditions engaged in mission, evangelicals in particular were stimulated by the fresh insights coming from this source. Evangelical missiology would be shaped by the impact of the social sciences, more than theology, during the next two decades. An early textbook was Gordon H. Smith's *The Mission-*

320

ary and Anthropology (Chicago: Moody, 1945). In 1952 Nida published *God's Word in Man's Language* (New York: Harper & Row), followed by *Customs and Cultures* (1954), *Message and Mission: Communication of the Christian Faith* (1960), and *Religion Across Cultures* (1968). Howard W. Law's *Winning a Hearing: An Introduction to Missionary Anthropology and Linguistics* was published in 1968 (Grand Rapids: Eerdmans). A primary vehicle for developing and disseminating missionary anthropology was the journal *Practical Anthropology,* which Nida and others founded in 1953 under the editorship of William A. Smalley. Selections of the articles from the nineteen volumes of *Practical Anthropology* have been reprinted in William A. Smalley, ed., *Readings in Missionary Anthropology* (New York: Practical Anthropology, 1967); *Readings in Missionary Anthropology II*, rev. and expanded (South Pasadena: William Carey Library, 1978); and Jacob A. Loewen, *Culture and Human Values* (South Pasadena: William Carey Library, 1975). The writings of Paul G. Hiebert, especially his *Anthropological Insights for Missionaries* (Grand Rapids: Baker, 1985), have continued to provide help from the social sciences for missiology.

Indigenization and Contextualization

The period since 1945 has seen a major conceptual shift in mission thought, i.e., from "indigenization" to "contextualization." In classical mission thinking the goal of mission was the establishment of the indigenous church. A widely read restatement of this time-honored ideal was by the Assemblies of God missions administrator Melvin L. Hodges: *The Indigenous Church* (Springfield, MO: Gospel Publishing House, 1953). In the early seventies the term *contextualization* was introduced. Proponents argued that the new term preserved all that was implied by *indigenous* but took it further. After some initial hesitation, evangelicals embraced *contextualization.* This shift was made easier by the groundwork laid by the anthropologists and linguists. A new journal, *Gospel and Culture,* edited by Charles R. Taber, was founded as a forum for exploring the many facets of contextualization. Only two volumes of the journal were published, 1976 and 1977. A symposium, *Evangelicals and Liberation*, ed. Carl

Armerding (Grand Rapids: Baker, 1977) included an important essay by Harvie Conn on contextualization. A collection of essays that built a bridge between the earlier concepts and the proposed new formulation was edited by Charles H. Kraft and Tom N. Wisely, *Readings in Dynamic Indigeneity* (South Pasadena: William Carey Library, 1977). Under the auspices of the Lausanne Continuation Committee's Theological Commission, a special consultation was held at Willowbank, Bermuda, and the proceedings published as *Down to Earth: Studies in Christianity and Culture*, ed. John R. W. Stott and Robert T. Coote (Grand Rapids: Eerdmans, 1978). A useful, brief theological study of contextualization is Bruce J. Nicholls, *Contextualization: A Theology of Gospel and Culture* (Downers Grove, IL: InterVarsity, 1979). The major work on the contextualization of the gospel is Charles H. Kraft's *Christianity and Culture* (Maryknoll, NY: Orbis, 1979). Kraft's book met with some criticism among evangelicals. A thoughtful, balanced response to it was made by Harvie M. Conn, *Eternal Word and Changing Worlds* (Grand Rapids: Zondervan, 1984). David J. Hesselgrave has applied insights from anthropology, communications theory, and theology in *Communicating Christ Cross-Culturally* (Grand Rapids: Zondervan, 1978) and *Planting the Church Cross-Culturally* (Grand Rapids: Baker, 1980).

Church Growth and Applied Missiology

The genius of evangelicalism is perhaps best understood through the innovations it has made in missions and methods and its commitment to a pragmatic—in contrast to a theoretical—view of missiology. Two new movements were germinating in the 1950s: Evangelism-in-Depth and church growth. Evangelism-in-Depth was the brainchild of R. Kenneth Strachan of the Latin American Mission. W. Dayton Roberts described the concept and first years of the movement in *Revolution in Evangelism* (Chicago: Moody, 1967). A critical evaluation of EID is found in George W. Peters, *Saturation Evangelism* (Grand Rapids: Zondervan, 1970).

In 1955 Donald McGavran published his path-breaking *The Bridges of God*, followed in 1959 by *How Churches Grow* (both published in New York by Friendship Press). In 1961 McGavran founded the Institute for the Study of Church Growth, which in 1965 was relocated and integrated into the new School of World Mission of Fuller Theological Seminary. McGavran's most comprehensive treatment of church growth is to be found in *Understanding Church Growth* (Grand Rapids: Eerdmans, 1970; 3d ed. 1990). McGavran's first colleague in the institute was the Australian missionary anthropologist Alan R. Tippett. Together they pioneered a new interdisciplinary approach to the study of the processes of church growth, drawing particularly on insights from the social sciences. "Church growth" has emphasized the importance of "applied missiology." An early sampler of the range of issues addressed by church growth and the methodological concerns is found in Alan R. Tippett, ed., *God, Man, and Church Growth* (Grand Rapids: Eerdmans, 1973). Dozens of published and unpublished case studies of church growth from all parts of the world have been carried out. Some of the early studies were published in the church-growth series by the William B. Eerdmans Publishing Company. See, e.g., Roy Shearer, *Wildfire— Church Growth in Korea* (1966) and William Read, *Latin American Church Growth* (1969). In addition to McGavran's work on church-growth theory, Tippett contributed from his anthropological studies. Some of his contributions have been brought together in Alan R. Tippett, *Introduction to Missiology* (South Pasadena: William Carey Library, 1987). C. Peter Wagner has promoted and popularized McGavran's "homogeneous unit principle," treating it extensively in *Our Kind of People* (Atlanta: John Knox, 1979). A sympathetic theological examination of church-growth thought was made by J. Robertson McQuilkin, *How Biblical Is the Church Growth Movement?* (Chicago: Moody, 1973).

While there has been widespread appreciation for the practical concerns expressed through the church-growth movement, its use of the HUP has created uneasiness. Several symposia have focused on these concerns: Wilbert R. Shenk, ed., *The Challenge of Church Growth* (Scottdale, PA: Herald, 1973); Harvie M. Conn, ed., *Theological Perspectives on Church Growth* (Nutley, NJ: Presbyterian and Reformed, 1976); and Wilbert R. Shenk, ed., *Exploring Church Growth* (Grand Rapids: Eerdmans, 1983). Charles E. Van Engen studied the ecclesiological dimensions of church growth in *The Growth of the True Church* (Amsterdam: Rodopi, 1981).

Pentecostal Contribution

The pentecostal movement began in the first years of the twentieth century as a humble and scorned movement. But it has proved to be one of the most dynamic developments of the twentieth century. Between 1970 and 1985 professing pentecostal/charismatic Christians grew from 6.4 percent to 18.9 percent of all Christians. Donald W. Dayton has investigated the background of the pentecostal movement in *The Theological Roots of Pentecostalism* (Grand Rapids: Zondervan, 1987). A comprehensive study of the movement was made by Walter J. Hollenweger in *The Pentecostals: The Charismatic Movement in the Churches* (Minneapolis: Augsburg, 1972). Other histories include Gary B. McGee, *This Gospel Shall Be Preached: A History and Theology of the Assemblies of God Foreign Missions to 1959* (Springfield, MO: Gospel Publishing House, 1986); L. Grant McClung, Jr., ed., *Azuza Street and Beyond: Pentecostal Missions and Church Growth in the Twentieth Century* (South Plainfield, NJ: Bridge, 1986); Paul A. Pomerville, *The Third Force in Missions* (Peabody, MA: Hendrickson, 1985). Earlier, Melvin L. Hodges wrote *A Theology of the Church and Its Mission* (Springfield, MO: Gospel Publishing House, 1977) as a theology of mission from a pentecostal perspective. A major reference work on the movement that appeared in 1988 is *Dictionary of Pentecostal and Charismatic Movements*, ed. Stanley M. Burgess and Gary B. McGee, Patrick H. Alexander, assoc. ed. (Grand Rapids: Zondervan).

Consultations and Congresses

Since 1960 evangelicals have staged significant consultations and congresses at national, regional, and international levels to forge new strategies and reinforce the priority of commitment to world mission. The Interdenominational Foreign Mission Association (IFMA) sponsored a Congress on World Missions in Chicago in 1960 that sought to reclaim the Student Volunteer Movement's turn-of-the-century slogan, "The evangelization of the world in this generation" (J. D. Percy, comp., *Facing the Unfinished Task: Messages Delivered at the Congress on World Missions, IFMA, December 1960* [Grand Rapids: Zondervan, 1961]). Under the sponsorship of the Evangelical Foreign Missions Association (EFMA) of the National Association of Evangelicals, a book with contributions from some of the best-known evangelical mission leaders was published in 1963: *Facing Facts in Modern Missions— A Symposium* (Chicago: Moody). It covered (1) the motives and goals of world missions, (2) missionary relationships, (3) international cooperation, and (4) the divine affirmation. The challenge and threat evangelicals felt coming from the wider missiological currents is clearly reflected in this volume. During this time the two associations began to collaborate more closely. The proceedings from some of these joint meetings were published, including *Evangelical Missions Tomorrow*, ed. Wade Coggins and E. L. Frizen, Jr. (South Pasadena: William Carey Library, 1977).

In 1966 the IFMA and EFMA cosponsored the Congress on the Church's Worldwide Mission at Wheaton, Illinois, April 4-16. The proceedings were edited by Harold Lindsell and published as *The Church's Worldwide Mission* (Waco: Word, 1966). The Wheaton meeting sought to define evangelical positions on a variety of missiological and theological issues as over against those of conciliar Protestants. Later that year the World Congress on Evangelism convened in Berlin. The proceedings were edited by Carl F. H. Henry and W. Stanley Mooneyham, *One Race, One Gospel, One Task: World Congress on Evangelism, Berlin, 1966*, 2 vols. (Minneapolis: World Wide Publications, 1967). One direct result of the Berlin meeting was several regional gatherings. The Asia-Pacific Congress on Evangelism was held in Singapore, November 5-13, 1968, and a conference volume was published afterward: W. Stanley Mooneyham, ed., *Christ Seeks Asia* (Minneapolis: World Wide Publications, 1969).

Third World evangelicals' concerns for an identity that included social justice and cultural integrity converged with a similar disquietude arising from within North American evangelicalism. Already at Wheaton and Berlin in 1966 signs could be detected of uneasiness over the dichotomy that had come to mark evangelical thought in the twentieth century, namely, the separation of word from deed and social concern from evangelism. The sixties were a time of widespread social unrest in the United States over the race question and U.S. involvement in the war in Vietnam. When evangelicals gathered for the International Congress on World Evangelization held at Lausanne, Switzerland, July 16-25, 1974, an influential minority, including many non-Western leaders, threw down the gauntlet. The conference compendium was edited by J. D. Douglas: *Let the Earth Hear His Voice* (Minneapolis: World Wide Publications, 1975). C. René Padilla edited a symposium on the Lausanne covenant, allowing this new viewpoint to be expressed, entitled *The New Face of Evangelicalism* (Downers Grove, IL: InterVarsity, 1976). Lausanne gave impetus in at least three areas: (1) strategy of missions, (2) the role of the Third World churches, and (3) the relationship between ethics and evangelism. A continuation committee was created to ensure that follow-up work would be done.

At the congress, Donald McGavran and Ralph Winter introduced the concept of the "hidden" or "unreached" people and estimated that there were some seventeen thousand groups of people in the world where there was still no established church capable of carrying out the evangelization of that group. Six reference volumes have been published clarifying this concept and providing information on many such groups: C. Peter Wagner and Edward R. Dayton, eds., *Unreached Peoples '79* (Elgin, IL: David C. Cook, 1978); idem, *Unreached Peoples '80—The Challenge of the Church's Unfinished Business* (Cook, 1980); and idem, *Unreached Peoples '81—Focus on Asia* (Cook, 1981); and Edward R. Dayton and Samuel Wilson, eds., *Unreached Peoples '82—Focus on Urban Peoples* (Cook, 1982); idem, *Unreached Peoples '83—The Refugees Among Us* (Monrovia, CA: MARC, 1983); and idem, *Unreached Peoples '84—The Future of World Evangelization* (MARC, 1984).

Another tool produced to assist mission agencies in carrying out the task of world evangelization was the manual by Edward R. Dayton and David A. Fraser, *Planning Strategies for World Evangelization* (Grand Rapids: Eerdmans, 1980; rev. ed. 1990). This is a sophisticated approach to planning and management applied to Christian mission. A consultation on the "unreached peoples" theme resulted in another volume: Harvie M. Conn, ed., *Reaching the Unreached: The Old-New Challenge* (Phillipsburg, NJ: Presbyterian and Reformed, 1984).

A further emphasis to come out of the Lausanne movement was that of the urban challenge. Ray Bakke and others held a series of consultations with Christian leaders from around the world. Fresh material on the urban challenge to mission began to appear. Of Francis M. DuBose's *How Churches Grow in an Urban World* (Nashville: Broadman, 1978) one reviewer said, "This book comes closer than any other to being a single comprehensive textbook on urban church growth and evangelization." Roger S. Greenway edited *Discipling the City: Theological Reflections on Urban Mission* (Grand Rapids: Baker, 1979) as a contribution to a more adequate theological foundation for urban witness. Harvie M. Conn's writings have underscored the importance of the city to Christian witness, including *A Clarified Vision for Urban Mission* (Grand Rapids: Zondervan, 1987).

Evangelicals have traditionally been concerned with revival and renewal of the church. In the 1970s, partly as a result of the stimulation of the Lausanne Congress, some attention was given to the renewal and adaptation of structures—both congregational and mission agency. Howard A. Snyder exerted particular influence through books such as *The Problem of Wineskins* (1975) and *The Community of the King* (1977), both published by InterVarsity Press, Downers Grove, Illinois.

In 1978 evangelicals convened a consultation on witness to Muslim peoples. The proceedings were published as *The Gospel and Islam: A 1978 Compendium* (Monrovia, CA: MARC, 1979). Richard R. DeRidder has written two books on the theme of evangelism in relation to Jewish people: *My Heart's Desire for Israel—Reflections on Jewish-Christian Relationships and Evangelism Today* (Nutley, NJ: Presbyterian and Reformed, 1974) and *God Has Not Yet Rejected His People* (Grand Rapids: Baker, 1977).

A formative new force in world evangelicalism was just emerging as the decade of the seventies began. Publication in 1973 of *Missions from the Third World* (South Pasadena: William Carey Library) by James Wong et al. put the spotlight on this important new trend. This was followed by a volume edited by Marlin Nelson, *Readings in Third World Missions* (South Pasadena: William Carey Library, 1976). The most recent study of this development is Lawrence E. Keyes, *The Last Age of Missions: A Study of Third World Mission Societies* (South Pasadena: William Carey Library, 1983).

In 1980 a sequel to the Lausanne Congress was held at Pattaya, Thailand, with the goal of formulating more precise and comprehensive plans for reaching the people groups. In preparation for Pattaya, work groups organized around "unreached peoples" were convened, and their reports were published as part of a new pamphlet series, Lausanne Occasional Papers. Twenty-four titles have appeared in this series. Drawing on history as well as futurology, David B. Barrett has produced several studies on world evangelization, including *Cosmos, Chaos, and Gospel: A Chronology of World Evangelization from Creation to New Creation* (Birmingham, AL: New Hope, 1987) and, together with James W. Reapsome, *Seven Hundred Plans to Evangelize the World: The Rise of a Global Evangelization Movement* (1988).

Through the Lausanne movement and parallel developments, Christian leaders from the non-Western churches have played an increasingly prominent role internationally. A notable early contribution was by Orlando E. Costas, *The Church and Its Mission: A Shattering Critique from the Third World* (Wheaton: Tyndale, 1974). Later Costas wrote *Christ Outside the Gate: Mission Beyond Christendom* (Maryknoll, NY: Orbis, 1982). C. René Padilla produced a number of important essays that were published as *Mission Between the Times* (Grand Rapids: Eerdmans, 1985). Samuel Escobar, in collaboration with John Driver, wrote *Christian Mission and Social Justice* (Scottdale, PA: Herald, 1978). Under sponsorship of the World Evangelical Fellowship, a group of evangelical theologians met in Thailand to discuss the theme of Christology. These papers were edited by Vinay Samuel and Chris Sugden under the title *Sharing Jesus in the Two-Thirds World* (Grand Rapids: Eerdmans, 1983).

In 1947, a rising evangelical theologian, Carl F. H. Henry, wrote *The Uneasy Conscience of Modern Fundamentalism* (Grand Rapids: Eerdmans), in which he challenged evangelicals to take up their responsibility to society by meeting the intellectual and social challenges of the day. Henry would reiterate this concern often over the years in such books as *A Plea for Evangelical Demonstration* (Grand Rapids: Baker, 1971). The historian Timothy L. Smith, in *Revivalism and Social Reform in Mid-Nineteenth Century America* (Nashville: Abingdon, 1957), presented a picture of evangelicalism quite different from that of the twentieth century.

David O. Moberg, *The Great Reversal: Evangelism and Social Concern* (Philadelphia: Lippincott, 1972), urged that evangelicals reclaim their rightful heritage. This impulse was fanned into a movement, in part through the prodding of non-Western evangelicals and in part through the influence of younger leaders like Waldron Scott, John Perkins, and Ronald J. Sider. Scott wrote a major study: *Bring Forth Justice—A Contemporary Perspective on Mission* (Grand Rapids: Eerdmans, 1980). Perkins issued a challenge: *Let Justice Roll Down* (Glendale, CA: Regal, 1976). Among Sider's many writings, the most influential has been *Rich Christians in a Hungry World* (Downers Grove, IL: InterVarsity, 1977). Robert L. Ramseyer edited a collection of essays addressing the theme of *Mission and the Peace Witness: The Gospel and Christian Discipleship* (Scottdale, PA: Herald, 1979). Harvie M. Conn made a compelling statement for a whole gospel in *Evangelism: Doing Justice, Preaching Grace* (Grand Rapids: Zondervan, 1984). A study that focuses on a geographical region in light of Christian responsibility is *Let My People Live—Faith and Struggle in Central America*, ed. Gordon Spykman, project coordinator (Grand Rapids: Eerdmans, 1988). Although evangelicals have been reluctant to use the vocabulary of liberation theology, several works have addressed this topic. Emilio Nunez in *Liberation Theology* (Chicago: Moody, 1985) offers an evangelical approach. Raymond C. Hundley, *Radical Liberation Theology: An Evangelical Response* (Wilmore, KY: Bristol Books, 1987), gives an evangelical critique of liberation theology.

Theological ferment among evangelicals has been most evident in the area of ethics in relation to Christian witness. Tensions among those who wished to maintain the traditional dichotomous formulation—whereby proclamation of the gospel is always the priority obligation for Christians while concern for social and physical needs must be viewed as secondary—and those who felt such a dichotomy to run counter to the gospel continued to manifest themselves. Two important consultations were held in which protagonists for the various positions, representing Christian churches throughout the world, sought to reach a *modus vivendi*. The first of these meetings was held in Grand Rapids, Michigan, in 1982. The papers, which Bruce J. Nicholls edited, *In Word and Deed—Evangelism and Social Responsibility* (Grand Rapids: Eerdmans, 1985), reveal the dimen-

329

sions of the debate. Wheaton '83 proposed the concept of "transformation" as a way to express the wholeness of the gospel witness. Its proceedings have appeared as *The Church in Response to Human Need,* ed. Vinay Samuel and Chris Sugden (Grand Rapids: Eerdmans, 1987).

Identity and Mission

The period since 1945 has been one of rapid change in all areas of life. Evangelical identity has been subjected to a variety of stresses. Evangelicals have continued to react to and to define themselves over against mainline Protestants. Donald McGavran has been particularly vocal in his criticism of the mainline church leadership, especially as reflected in mission strategies and vision. He compiled a volume of essays by both evangelicals and conciliar Protestants under the rubric *The Eye of the Storm: The Great Debate in Missions* (Waco: Word, 1972; expanded ed. titled *The Conciliar-Evangelical Debate: The Crucial Documents, 1964–1976* [South Pasadena: William Carey Library, 1977]). English translations of several books by the German missiologist Peter Beyerhaus have been published in the United States: *Missions: Which Way? Humanization or Redemption* (1971); *Shaken Foundations* (1972); and *Bangkok '73: The Beginning or End of World Mission* (1974), all published by Zondervan, Grand Rapids, Michigan. Evangelicals were especially exercised by the World Council of Churches' Uppsala Assembly in 1968 and the Bangkok '73 meeting of the Commission on World Mission and Evangelism (CWME). Ralph D. Winter edited *The Evangelical Response to Bangkok* (South Pasadena: William Carey Library, 1973), responses that expressed considerable dissatisfaction with conciliar understandings of mission. Arthur P. Johnston wrote an extensive critique of conciliar Protestants in *World Evangelism and the Word of God* (Minneapolis: Bethany, 1974), followed by *The Battle for World Evangelism* (Wheaton: Tyndale, 1978). Harvey Hoekstra also criticized the WCC for what he perceived to be a loss of commitment to evangelism in *The World Council of Churches and the Demise of Evangelism* (Wheaton: Tyndale, 1979). In *Contemporary Theologies of Mission* (Grand Rapids: Baker,

1983), Arthur F. Glasser and Donald McGavran offer a critical appraisal of current theological emphases in missions, especially as found among conciliar Protestants.

Comparative Studies

Concerned to move beyond stereotypes that each side holds of the other and in the hope of discovering the considerable common ground on which all Christians stand with regard to the mission task, a number of missiologists have prepared studies that aim at clarifying the positions taken by evangelicals and conciliar Protestants on fundamental missiological questions. *Protestant Crosscurrents in Mission: The Ecumenical-Conservative Encounter,* ed. Norman A. Horner (Nashville: Abingdon, 1968), was a noteworthy first attempt. A broader synthetic study is that of Rodger C. Bassham: *Mission Theology, 1948–1975: Years of Creative Tension—Ecumenical, Evangelical, and Roman Catholic* (South Pasadena: William Carey Library, 1979). A major effort in forging a constructive theology of mission that holds the three major Christian traditions together is that of David J. Bosch, *Witness to the World: The Christian Mission in Theological Perspective* (Atlanta: John Knox, 1980). A more recent survey is James A. Scherer's *Gospel, Church and Kingdom: Comparative Studies in World Mission Theology* (Minneapolis: Augsburg, 1987). The results of years of dialogue between evangelicals and Roman Catholics are summarized in John Stott and Basil Meeking, eds., *The Evangelical–Roman Catholic Dialogue on Mission 1977–1984* (Grand Rapids: Eerdmans, 1986).

Student Movement

No understanding of the evangelical movement is complete without taking into account the dynamic part played by students in Bible colleges, colleges, and universities. Since 1945 evangelical students have demonstrated a sustained interest in the cause of missions. The focal point for cultivating and sustaining this interest has been the InterVarsity Christian Fellowship missionary conventions (popularly known as the "Urbana Conventions") held every two or three years since 1946. Reports have appeared for 1946, 1948, 1951, 1954, 1957, 1961, 1964, 1967, 1970, 1973, 1976, 1979, 1981, 1984, and 1987 (Downers Grove, IL: InterVarsity Press). A popular history of the student mission movement is David M. Howard's *Student Power in World Missions,* rev. ed. (Downers Grove, IL: InterVarsity, 1979). A short study is H. Wilbert Norton, *To Stir the Church: A Brief History of the Student Foreign Missions Fellowships, 1936–1986* (Madison, WI: Student Foreign Missions Fellowship, 1986).

History, Biography, and Reference

Given the scale of evangelical mission work since 1945, it is surprising how modest the scope of historical writing has been. J. Herbert Kane's *A Concise History of the Christian World Mission* (Grand Rapids: Baker, 1978) has become the standard history of missions by an evangelical. A valuable perspective on developments among evangelicals in this century is given in Denton Lotz, "'The Evangelization of the World in This Generation': The Resurgence of the Missionary Idea among the Conservative Evangelicals" (Ph.D. diss., Hamburg Univ., 1970). Several denominational histories have appeared in recent years. Baker J. Cauthen et al. produced *Advance: A History of Southern Baptist Foreign Missions* (Nashville: Broadman, 1970). Winston Crawley's *Global Mission—A Story to Tell* (Nashville: Broadman, 1985) is a well-written presentation of the full sweep of Southern Baptist world missions. For the centennial of the Christian and Missionary Alliance, a denomination that grew out of a missionary society, a history was prepared by Robert L. Niklaus, John S. Sawin, and Samuel J. Stoesz: *All for Jesus: God at Work in the Christian and Missionary Alliance Over One Hundred Years* (Camp Hill, PA: Christian Publications, 1986). Although Alvyn J. Austin's *Saving China: Canadian Missionaries in the Middle Kingdom, 1888–1959* (Toronto: Univ. of Toronto Press, 1986) seeks to encompass the total Canadian missionary effort in China, it is strongest on the Protestant part of the story. Allen V. Koop has made a valuable study of *American Evangelical Missionaries in France, 1945–*

1975 (Lanham, MD: Univ. Press of America, 1986). The China Inland Mission has served as the prototype of the "faith" or nondenominational mission agency, which has been an important
feature of evangelical mission history. Many North Americans
have served with the CIM—renamed Overseas Missionary Fellowship after the closing of China to Western missions in 1949.
Five volumes of a planned six-volume history on the China Inland Mission have been published under the general title *Hudson Taylor and China's Open Century;* all volumes are by A. J.
Broomhall. Individual volume titles are *Barbarians at the Gate*
(1981); *Over the Treaty Wall* (1982); *If I Had a Thousand Lives* (1982);
Survivors' Pact (1984); *Refiner's Fire* (1985); and *Assault on the Nine*
(1988), all published by OMF Books / Hodder & Stoughton (London). J. Herbert Kane wrote a history of the Interdenominational
Foreign Mission Association: *Faith Mighty Faith: A Handbook of
the IFMA* (Wheaton: IFMA, 1956).

Missionary biographies have always run the risk of slipping
into hagiography. Perhaps because of this questionable image,
missionary biography has not flourished over the past four decades. Elisabeth Elliot has written several widely read biographies, including an account of the martyrdom of the five missionaries to the Auca Indians, *Through Gates of Splendor* (New
York: Harper & Row, 1957); *Shadow of the Almighty: The Life and
Testament of Jim Elliot* (New York: Harper & Row, 1958); and *Who
Shall Ascend: The Life of R. Kenneth Strachan* (New York: Harper
& Row, 1968). James Hefley has written various popular ac-
counts of missionary life and work, including *Uncle Cam: The
Story of William Cameron Townsend, Founder of Wycliffe Bible Trans-
lators and Summer Institute of Linguistics* (Waco: Word, 1974).
Ruth A. Tucker used biography as a vehicle for recounting the
history of missions in her book *From Jerusalem to Irian Jaya: A Biographical History of Missions* (Grand Rapids: Zondervan, 1983).
Leroy Fitts has preserved an important story in his biography of
Lott Carey: First Black Missionary to Africa (Valley Forge, PA: Judson, 1978). In *A History of Black Baptists* (Nashville: Broadman,
1985), Fitts includes a chapter on the missionary work done by
black Baptists.

The standard reference work on the Christian movement
worldwide is David B. Barrett, ed., *World Christian Encyclopedia*

(Nairobi: Oxford Univ. Press, 1982), a massive compendium of statistics and analytical pieces indispensable to anyone wishing to study the history and present situation of the church throughout the world. Another valuable reference tool is *Mission Handbook: North American Protestant Ministries Overseas,* 13th ed. (Monrovia, CA: MARC, 1986). This includes individual entries on all Protestant missionary agencies that send people and other resources abroad.

Missiological Periodicals

Evangelical writings on all aspects of missions can be found in a wide range of scholarly professional journals such as the *International Review of Mission, Missiology, International Bulletin of Missionary Research,* and *Missionalia.* The *Evangelical Missions Quarterly* is the official publication of the EFMA and IFMA. In addition, many mission societies have their house organs, through which they interpret their policies, strategies, and goals to their supporting constituencies.

Conclusion

Evangelicals have written prolifically on missions since 1945. In the process they have produced a notable body of scholarship to undergird their missionary endeavors. This in itself marks a shift in self-understanding from the time when it was assumed that the blueprint for missions was well-defined—and all that remained was to follow it—to the realization that revolutionary times demand flexibility and adaptability in missionary response. This bibliographical survey points up the areas of greatest concentration of effort by evangelicals: applied missiology, strategy and methods, and interaction with churches from other parts of the world, especially as this involves the ethical dimension and content of Christian witness. It also discloses areas that have received relatively less attention: theology of mission, history, and the Christian witness in relation to other world religions.

Appendix: The Evangelical Missionary Force in the 1930s

Joel A. Carpenter

In the preface and in chapter 5, I have asserted that roughly 40 percent of the North American Protestant missionary force during the mid-1930s was sent by denominational boards or independent societies supported by conservative evangelicals. This statement is based on my location of an estimated 4,784 conservative evangelicals out of a total of 11,899 North American Protestant missionaries. These figures were calculated from the tables found in Joseph I. Parker, ed., *Interpretative Statistical Survey of the World Mission of the Christian Church* (New York: International Missionary Council, 1938), 40-45. This book reports the results of a survey conducted in 1935-36.

My first step in locating conservative evangelicals was to divide Parker's list of North American Protestant agencies (pp. 43-45) into "conservative evangelical" and "mainline" categories (see Tables 3 and 4 below). I based this largely on my knowledge of the various North American Protestant traditions and movements and of how each regarded itself in the 1930s. This bipolar division will not fully satisfy many who are knowledgeable of American religious history, because the distinctions and shadings therein are not nearly so simple or bipolar. To cite one example, I grouped all of the Lutheran boards except the Missouri Synod with the "mainline," although most of the Lutheran synods were at that time rather ethnocentric and theologically conservative.

On the other hand, some evangelical denominations that

would have either consultative or full affiliation with the Department of Foreign Missions of the National Council of Churches by the early 1950s, such as the Assemblies of God, the Evangelical Covenant Church, and the Seventh-Day Adventists, did not properly belong under a "mainline" rubric, I decided. Furthermore, any divination of the number of conservative evangelical missionaries serving with mainline denominational boards would be virtually impossible to verify, so it was ruled out. So it goes with generalizations. Once having been made, they must be qualified. At any rate, this division is narrow rather than overly generous in its estimate of the conservative evangelical missionary force.

These were the totals for each group: mainline, 7,115; evangelical, 4,015.

My research has persuaded me, however, that Parker's list of North American agencies and their missionaries was not sufficient, because hundreds of North Americans served with independent faith missions that were not on this list. So I added an estimated 769 North Americans who were serving with eight of the largest of these missions, which Parker had grouped under "British" or "international" categories. Each of these eight societies was affiliated at the time with the fundamentalistic Interdenominational Foreign Mission Association, and each maintained offices in North America. The societies and their estimated North American contingents are listed in Table 1.

Table 1 North Americans Serving with International Faith Missions, 1935-36

Africa Inland Mission	(119)
Ceylon and India General Mission	(18)
China Inland Mission	305
Evangelical Union of South America	(40)
Latin America Evangelization Crusade	(23)
Regions Beyond Missionary Union	(17)
South Africa General Mission	(67)
Sudan Interior Mission	(180)
TOTAL:	769

These estimates (with the exception of the exact figure of 305 for CIM, drawn from Alvyn Austin's chapter in this volume) were calculated by multiplying the total number of missionaries for each as listed in Parker by the percentage of North American missionaries reported for each agency in the 1953 document "Interdenominational Foreign Mission Association: Missionary Personnel under Member Societies" (files of the Missionary Research Library, Union Theological Seminary, New York City). While it may not be safe to assume that these percentages all remained unchanged between 1935 and 1953, that assumption seems very safe for the Africa Inland Mission, Latin America Evangelization Crusade, and Sudan Interior Mission; each of these three was founded in North America, and their missionary staffs were always dominated by North Americans.

The "fundamentalist" mission force, at an estimated size of 1,721 in 1935-36, amounted to a significant proportion (35.9 percent) of the larger "conservative evangelical" grouping. Fundamentalist totals, calculated from Parker, *Interpretative Statistics*, are shown in Table 2.

Table 2 Fundamentalist Missionaries from North America, 1935-36

Denominationally Related

Independent Presbyterian BFM	11
Christian & Miss'y Alliance	447
Evangelical Free Church	32
SUBTOTAL:	490

Independent

Algerian Missionary Band	23
Bolivian Indian Mission	53
Central American Mission	64
Congo Inland Mission	26
Gospel Missionary Union	42
Inland S. Am. Miss'y Union	41
Orinoco River Mission	21
Scandinavian Alliance Miss.	95
South China Boat Mission	12
Unevang'd Africa Mission	13

Unevang'd Tribes Mission	48
Woman's Union Miss'y Society	24
China Inland Mission	305
Africa Inland Mission	(119)
Sudan Interior Mission	(180)
Evang. Union of S. America	(40)
Ceylon & India Gen. Mission	(18)
Regions Beyond Miss'y Union	(17)
Latin America Mission	(23)
South Africa General Mission	(67)
SUBTOTAL:	1,231
TOTAL FUNDAMENTALIST MISSIONARIES:	1,721

Fundamentalist and other evangelical missionaries probably have been significantly under-reported, since they are difficult to locate. Untold numbers went overseas under obscure circumstances: with newly founded agencies that eluded the statistician's gaze for a while, such as the Association of Baptists for the Evangelization of the Orient, founded in 1927 but not listed in Parker; or, as above, with agencies not based in North America; or as wholly independent "free-lance" missionaries. For example, some American evangelical groups, such as the Plymouth Brethren and the Churches of Christ, did not approve of forming mission boards but still sent out hundreds of independent missionaries.

In sum, this exercise shows that while William Hutchison has claimed that the "mainline boards retained a ten-to-one dominance" over the conservative boards and societies "throughout the Depression decade" (Hutchison, *Errand to the World: American Protestant Thought and Foreign Missions* [Chicago: Univ. of Chicago Press, 1987], 175), conservative Protestant agencies accounted for four times as many North American missionaries as that claim implies; and fundamentalist missions alone accounted for over 14 percent of the total force. The moral of the story is that conservative evangelicals' marginalized status and lack of intellectual acuity in the wake of the fundamentalist-modernist controversies should not lead us to assume that their missionary activity was diminished also.

Table 3 North American Mainline Protestant Missionary Societies, 1935-36 and 1952

	1935-36	1952
AME Ch.	14	108
AME Zion Ch.	17	???
ABFMS & Wom. ABFMS	587	488
ABCFM	495	354
Am. College, Sofia	22	—
Am. Friends BFM	34	38
Am. Hosp. of Istanbul	2	—
Am. Luth. Ch. BFM	79	112
Am. Univ. of Beirut	146	—
Am. Univ. of Cairo	22	17
Anatolia College	15	—
Assoc. Ref. Pres. Ch.	22	—
Aug. Syn. BFM	47	166
Bd. Chr. Wk—San Domingo	3	—
Canadian Bapt. FMB	98	—
Can. Bapt. Miss-Manchuria	3	—
Ch. of Breth., Gen. MB	91	110
Ch. of Engl. in Canada	58	—
Evangelical Church, MS	46	—
United Breth. in Christ, Df&FMS	9	E.U.B.140
Un. Breth. in Christ, FMS	55	—
Ev. and Ref. Ch. BFM	116	96
Friends of Phila., MB	9	—
Kwato Extension Association	14	—
Lingnan University	3	—
Lott Carey Bapt. FMC	17	75
Luth. Bd. of Missions	9	28
Lutheran Orient Mission	4	2
Meth. Epis. Ch. BFM & WFMS	978	
M. E. Ch., South, BOM	355	Meth. BFM 1,527
Meth. Prot. Ch., BOM	19	—
National Bapt. Conv. FMB	21	500
Norw. Luth. Ch. of A., BFM	136	
Presby. Ch. of Canada, GBM	60	—
Presby. Ch. in U.S., CFM	402	379

Presby. Ch. in U.S.A., BFM	1,356	1,116
Prot. Epis. Ch. in USA	427	206
Ref. Ch. in Am., BFM	140	178
Santiago College	12	—
Soc. Un. Breth. Prop. Gospel	19	—
United Christian Miss. Soc.	173	213
Un. Ch. of Canada BFM & WMS	452	—
United Luth., Ch. Am. BFM	163	227
United Presby. Ch. BFM	342	310
Univer. Ch. MA	5	—
Yale-in-China Ass'n	18	—
TOTAL MAINLINE FOR. MISSIONARIES:	7,115	6,390

Sources: Parker, *Interpretative Statistical Survey,* 43-45; R. Pierce Beaver, "The Protestant Missionary Enterprise of the United States," *Occasional Bulletin of the Missionary Research Library,* 8 May 1953, 1-15. This second source is obviously not as complete as is Parker, but it does allow some comparisons to be made of the more prominent boards from the U.S.A.

Table 4 North American Conservative Evangelical Protestant Missionary Societies, 1935-36 and 1952

	1935-36	Affiliation[1]	1952
Advent Chr. Ch.	6	EFMA, DFM#	8
Algerian Mission Band	23		
Am. Advent Miss. Soc'y	3		
AOG For. Miss. Dept.	230	EFMA, DFM#	626
Bapt. China Direct Miss.	5		
Bolivian Indian Mission	53	IFMA	70
Breth. in Christ FMB	42	DFM	63
Breth. Ch. FMS	29	DU	—
Brdcst Tr. Prs & Faith Orphs	2		
Central Am. Mission	64	IFMA	142
Central Yearly Mtg. Friends	12	DU	15
China Menn. Miss. Soc.	16		
Chr. & Miss. Alliance	447	DU	667
Chr. Ref. BOM	10		
Ch. of God, MB	37	DFM	72
Ch. of Naz., DFM	88	EFMA	200
Chs. of God, N. Am. BOM	7		

Congo Inland Mission	26	DFM	65
Cumb. Pres. Wom. Bd. FM	6	DFM	14
Evangel Mission	3		
Ev. Free Ch. Mis. Bd.	32	EFMA	101
Ev. Luth. Ch. of Mo., BFM	141	DFM#	102
Evang. Soc. of Pitt. B.I.	16	IU	15
Free Meth. Ch., GMB	81	EFMA, DFM#	128
Friends of Arabia Mission	6		
Friends Ch. CA Yearly Mtg.	14	DFM#	
Friends FMS, OH Yearly Mtg.	13	EFMA	15
Friends, KS, Afr. Gosp. Mis.	5	DFM	19
Friends, OR Yearly Mtg.	4	EFMA	10
Gen. Conf. Menn. FMB	34		
Gospel Miss'y Society	10		
Gospel Miss'y Union	42	IFMA	120
Heart of India Miss'y Band	1		
Hebron Mission	4		
Hepzibah Faith Miss. Ass'n	11		
Holiness Mvt. Ch.	11		
Inland S. Am. Miss. Union	41	IFMA	88
Int. Ch of Foursq. Gosp. FMD	48	DU	53
Krimmer Menn. Breth. Mission	1	EFMA	18
Mennonite Bd. of M. & Char.	52	DFM#	109
Menn. Breth. in Christ, UMS	23	DFM	—
Menn. Breth. Ch., BFM	22		
Metropolitan Ch. Ass'n	27	DFM	21
Mid-Yunnan Bethel Mission	5		
Mission to Araucanian Inds.	3		
Miss'y Bands of the World	24	EFMA	12
Nat'l Hol. Ass'n Miss. Soc.	30	EFMA	149
North East India Gen. Miss.	2		
Oriental Miss. Society	36	EFMA	89
Orinoco River Mission	21	IFMA	52
Peniel Mission, Congo	2		
Peniel Missionary Society	10	IU	2
Pent. Assemblies of Canada	38		
Pent. Assemblies of World, FMD	10	DU	3
Pent Holiness Mission	41	EFMA	64
Philipp-Borneo Faith Miss.	4		

Pilgrim Hol. Ch., FM	35	EFMA	93
Indep. Presby. BFM	11	ICCC	79
Ref. Episc. Ch. BFM	3		
Ref. Presby. Ch. BFM	31	EFMA	3
Ref. Presby. Ch. Gen. Syn. BFM	27		
Scandinavian Alliance Mission	95	IFMA	636
Seventh-Day Adv. Gen. Conf.	1,240	DFM#	1,107
Seventh Day Bapt. MS	11		
South China Boat Mission	12	EFMA	21
S. Bapt. Conv. FMB	405	DU	855
Standard Ch. of Am., MDpt	6		
(Swed.) Evangel. Cove. Ch.	38	DFM	123
Unevangelized Africa Mission	13		
Unevang. Tribes Mission	48	IU	23
United Free Gosp. & MS	21		
Wesleyan Meth. Conn. MS	21	EFMA	71
Woman's Union Miss'y Soc.	24	IFMA	23
TOTAL EVANGELICAL FOREIGN MISSIONARIES:	4,015		6,146

Sources: Parker, *Interpretative Statistical Survey*, 43-45; Beaver, "Protestant Missionary Enterprise."

1. Beaver, "The Protestant Missionary Enterprise in the United States," listed agencies by their affiliation (or lack of it) with missions fellowships and consortia. He used the following categories: Department of Foreign Missions of the National Council of Churches (DFM or DFM# for consulting status), Evangelical Foreign Missions Association (EFMA), Interdenominational Foreign Mission Association (IFMA), International Council of Christian Churches (ICCC), unaffiliated denominational boards (DU), and unaffiliated independent boards (IU). These categories proved helpful in classifying certain boards as "conservative evangelical" or "mainline," although, as one can see from the table, some agencies had overlapping affiliation.

Contributors

Alvyn J. Austin, a doctoral candidate in history at York University, is a writer living in Toronto. He has produced programs for Canadian radio, has done research for the Canadian Missionaries to East Asia Project, and has written *Saving China: Canadian Missionaries in the Middle Kingdom, 1888–1959* (1986).

Joel A. Carpenter now directs The Pew Charitable Trusts' program in religion. Prior to that he taught history at Wheaton College and directed the Institute for the Study of American Evangelicals. His latest publication is *Fundamentalism in American Religion 1880–1950* (1988), an edited facsimile series in forty-five volumes.

Orlando E. Costas was dean and Judson Professor of Missiology at Andover Newton Theological School. His latest work, which was published posthumously, is *Liberating News: A Theology of Contextual Evangelization* (1989).

Allen V. Koop is a professor of history at Colby-Sawyer College and the author of *American Evangelical Missionaries in France, 1945–1975* (1986).

James Alan Patterson is associate professor of church history at the Mid-America Baptist Theological Seminary. Among his publications is "Robert E. Speer, J. Gresham Machen, and the Presbyterian Board of Foreign Missions," *American Presbyterians: Journal of Presbyterian History* 64 (Spring 1986).

Richard V. Pierard, professor of history at Indiana State University and secretary-treasurer of the Conference on Faith and History, has published six books and over forty articles on religion and politics, evangelicalism, and Christian missions. His latest work is *Civil Religion and the Presidency* (1988).

Dana L. Robert, assistant professor of missions at Boston University School of Theology, is the author of several articles on premillennialism and missions. Her current project is a book on women in mission, to be published by Mercer University Press.

Lamin Sanneh, a Gambian, is professor of missions and world Christianity at Yale Divinity School. He is the author of *West African Christianity: The Religious Impact* (1983) and *Translating the Message: The Missionary Impact on Culture* (1989).

Wilbert R. Shenk became director of the Mission Training Center, Associated Mennonite Biblical Seminaries, in 1990 after twenty-five years on the staff of the Mennonite Board of Missions. He served as secretary-treasurer of the American Society of Missiology, 1979-1988, and is the author of *Henry Venn: Missionary Statesman* (1983).

Ruth A. Tucker is a visiting professor of mission at Trinity Evangelical Divinity School. She is the co-author of *Daughters of the Church: Women and Ministry from the New Testament Times to the Present* (1987) and the author of *Guardians of the Great Commission: The Story of Women in Modern Missions* (1988).

Charles E. Van Engen, assistant professor of missiology at Fuller Theological Seminary, was born in Mexico and served there for twelve years as a theological educator. He is the author of *The Growth of the True Church* (1981).

Grant Wacker, associate professor of religious studies at the University of North Carolina, is the author of several works on the history of American religion, including *Augustus H. Strong and the Dilemma of Historical Consciousness* (1985) and a forthcoming study of the origins of American pentecostalism.

Andrew F. Walls directs the Centre for the Study of Christianity in the Non-Western World at the University of Edinburgh. He has held academic appointments in Africa, Europe, and North America, has authored many works on African Christianity, and has also served in editing roles for the *Journal of Religion in Africa* and the *International Review of Mission*.

Everett A. Wilson is professor of Latin American studies and Christian missions and is academic dean of Bethany Bible College in California. He is the author of several essays and articles on the expansion of pentecostalism in Central and South America.

Index